SCRIBBLE, SCRIBBLE, SCRIBBLE

Simon Schama is University Professor of Art History and History at Columbia University in New York, and was awarded a CBE in 2001. His art columns for the *New Yorker* won the National Magazine Award for criticism and his journalism has appeared regularly in the *Guardian* and the *Financial Times* where he is Contributing Editor. His award-winning books include *Citizens: A Chronicle of the French Revolution*, *The Power of Art*, *Rough Crossings*, *Rembrandt's Eyes*, *A History of Britain* and most recently, *The American Future: A History*.

SIMON SCHAMA

Scribble, Scribble, Scribble

WRITINGS ON ICE CREAM, OBAMA, CHURCHILL AND MY MOTHER

VINTAGE BOOKS
London

Published by Vintage 2011

2 4 6 8 10 9 7 5 3 1

First published in Great Britain in 2010 by
The Bodley Head

Vintage
Random House, 20 Vauxhall Bridge Road,
London SW1V 2SA

www.vintage-books.co.uk

Addresses for companies within The Random House Group Limited can be found
at: www.randomhouse.co.uk/offices.htm

The Random House Group Limited Reg. No. 954009

A CIP catalogue record for this book
is available from the British Library

ISBN 9780099546658

The Random House Group Limited supports The Forest Stewardship
Council (FSC), the leading international forest certification organisation.
All our titles that are printed on Greenpeace approved FSC certified
paper carry the FSC logo. Our paper procurement policy can be
found at www.randomhouse.co.uk/environment

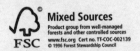

Mixed Sources

Product group from well-managed
forests and other controlled sources
www.fsc.org Cert no. TT-COC-002139
© 1996 Forest Stewardship Council

FSC

Typeset in Sabon by
Palimpsest Book Production Limited, Falkirk, Stirlingshire
Printed and bound in Great Britain by
CPI Bookmarque, Croydon CR0 4TD

To my editors, with gratitude

Another damned, thick, square book! Always scribble, scribble, scribble! Eh! Mr Gibbon?

The Duke of Gloucester to Edward Gibbon

Contents

List of Illustrations xiii
Introduction xvii

1.   *Travelling*

Sail Away 3
The Unloved American 14
Amsterdam 26
Washington DC 34
Brazil 42
Comedy Meets Catastrophe 46

2.   *Testing Democracy*

9/11 55
The Dead and the Guilty 59
The Civil War in the USA 67
Katrina and George Bush 73
Obama Rising 77
Bye-Bye, Dubya 81
The British Election, 2005 86
Virtual Annihilation 95

3. *Talking and Listening*

TBM and John 107

Isaiah Berlin 122

J. H. Plumb 140

Rescuing Churchill 146

Churchill as Orator 158

The Fate of Eloquence in the Age of The Osbournes 163

Barack Obama 172

4. *Performing*

Richard II 189

Henry IV, Part II 193

Martin Scorsese 195

Charlotte Rampling 200

Clio at the Multiplex 206

True Confessions of a History Boy 217

5. *Picturing*

The Matter of the Unripe Nectarine 223

Dutch Courage 240

Rubens 248

Turner and the Drama of History 254

James Ensor at MoMA 264

Rembrandt's Ghost 268

Anselm Kiefer (1) 278

In Mesopotamia: Anselm Kiefer (2) 284

John Virtue 293

Avedon: Power 305

6.   *Cooking and Eating*

Cool as Ice 311
Sauce of Controversy 320
Cheese Soufflé 325
Simmer of Love 331
My Mother's Kitchen 339
Mouthing Off 343

7.   *Remembering*

Omaha Beach 357
Gothic Language: Carlyle, Ruskin and the Morality
of Exuberance 361
A History of Britain: A Response 379
The Monte Lupo Story 391
No Walnuts, No Enlightenment 396
Abolishing the Slave Trade in Britain and America 405

8.   *A League of Its Own*

Red October 421

Acknowledgements 425

List of Illustrations

1. Frans Hals, *c.*1580–1666, *The Marriage Portrait of Isaac Massa and Beatrix van der Laen*, *c.* 1622. (Isaac Massa, merchant in Haarlem, 1586–1643; Oil on canvas; 140 x 166.5cm; Rijksmuseum, Amsterdam; © photo: akg-images)

2. Peter Paul Rubens, 1577–1640, *The Four Philosophers*, *c.*1608. (From left: self-portrait of the artist, his brother Philip Rubens, Justus Lipsius, Jan van der Wouwere; Oil on wood; 164 x 139cm; Inv.no. 86; Palazzo Pitti, Palatine Gallery, Florence; © photo: akg-images/Rabatti–Domingie)

3. J.M.W. Turner, 1775–1851, *A Disaster at Sea*, *c.* 1835. (This canvas was never exhibited and is probably not quite finished, but it seems to be well on the way to becoming one of Turner's most powerful statements on the Romantic theme of maritime disaster; Oil on canvas; 171.4 x 220.3 cm; Tate Gallery, London; © photo: akg-images / Erich Lessing)

4. J.M.W. Turner, 1775–1851, *The Burning of the Houses of Lords and Commons*, 1835. (Oil on canvas; 92 x 123cm; John Howard Mc Fadden Collection, Philadelphia Museum of Art, Philadelphia; © photo: akg-images)

5. James Ensor, 1860–1949, *Scandalised Masks*, 1883. (Oil on canvas; 135 x 112cm; Inv. 4190; Royal Museums of Fine Arts of Belgium, Brussels; © DACS 2010; © photo: J. Geleyns/www.roscan.be)

6. Pablo Picasso, 1881–1973, *'Ecce Homo', After Rembrandt* from *Suite 156*, 1970. (Etching and aquatint; plate: 49.5 x 41 cm, sheet: 68.1 x 56.7 cm; Tate Gallery, London; © Succession Picasso/DACS 2010)

7. *Picasso At Work*, c. 1970. (Hulton Archive; © photo by Keystone/Getty Images)

8. Anselm Kiefer, b.1945, *Karfunkelfee*, 2009. (Gold paint, cloak, brambles, acrylic, oil, emulsion, ash and shellac on canvas in steel and glass frame; 382 x 576 x 35 cm; © Anselm Kiefer; © photo: Charles Duprat; Courtesy White Cube)

9. Anselm Kiefer, b.1945, *Shevirath Ha Kelim*, 2009. (Terracotta, acrylic, oil and shellac on canvas; 330 x 760 x 1300 cm; © Anselm Kiefer; © photo: Charles Duprat; Courtesy White Cube)

10. John Virtue, *Landscape No. 711*, 2003-4. (Acrylic, black ink and shellac on canvas; 350 x 732 cm; © John Virtue)

11. Donald Rumsfeld, Secretary of Defense, Washington, D.C., May 7, 1976. From *The Family*, a portfolio of 69 portraits. Photograph by Richard Avedon © The Richard Avedon Foundation

Scribble,
Scribble,
Scribble

Introduction

I have two styles of writing, anal and loopy, both adopted in slavish but futile imitation of models who used a fountain pen as though they had been born with one in their hands. I had not. My primary-school exercise books, an Abstract Expressionist field of blots and stains, looked as though the nib had wet itself on to the page rather than been purposefully guided over the paper to form actual words. And yet I loved – and still do – the purchase the metal makes on paper, and can't begin a chapter or a script or a newspaper piece without first reaching for a fountain pen and notebook. I scribble, therefore I am.

At university I thought my bizarre handwriting – more or less the calligraphic equivalent of Tourette's Syndrome, disfigured by ejaculatory whiplashes above the line – ought to submit itself to a sterner form that might attest to my arrival at an Age of Reason. So I strove for a version of the professor's hand when he corrected my essays. This was a backward-leaning row of indentations and projections: a Cambridge minuscule. The letters rose, as if they were unsure about the worthwhileness of the effort involved, a bare millimetre from flat-line horizontal and had a tightness that I thought conveyed densely packed critical power. In the professorial hand the little ts and ds were barbs on a high-voltage wire and they snagged you with small, piercing lunges of pain. 'This paragraph five times as long as it needs to be,' the hand said, or 'Do you *ever* tire of adjectives?' My chastening superego, such as it was, reached for mastery of an economic style, but the unmannerly slob of id lurked to foul its plans. So my version of the professor's writing resembled the secretion of a crippled ant, one leg dragging behind the body as it crept from left to right across the page.

But this is still the hand I use, involuntarily, when correcting the work of my own students, or printed drafts of my own. Sometimes, the students beg me to decode a completely illegible set of comments, but I reckon that decipherment is part of their educational challenge. Hell, it did *me* no harm.

'Do you know,' chuckled the girlfriend from the 1970s, a queen of the nib, waving a page of my fractured minuscule – written, I blush to recall, in green ink – 'I had *no* idea until you wrote me that note, that I was going out with a serial killer! Of course I could be wrong,' she added, flashing me one of her fine-boned sardonic smiles, 'you might just be a paranoid schizophrenic.' It wasn't her forensic diagnosis of my hand-writing that stung, it was the merry way she laughed whenever she saw it, as if no one in their right mind could be expected to bother, except clinically. For our relationship to prosper, I realised I would have to make my hand lean in the opposite direction, with a degree of forwardness that testified to my ardour. On the other hand, it could not be a servile imitation of her own elegantly oblique manner, penned with long white fingers, for that would seem offputtingly craven, a bit like calligraphic cross-dressing. But wasn't I the yid with the id?

So I just let it out of the kennel to see what it could do, and thus was born that wowser of a hand: loopy, big, brash, vauntingly cursive, and often entirely out of control. Loopy is to my writing what fox is to hedgehog, Tigger is to Eeyore, Bugs is to Elmer, Rabelais to Montaigne, Björk to Coldplay. Loopy bounds and leaps and lurches and can't *wait* to get to the end of the line because – gee, gosh, boy oh boy – there's *another* line to fill, and omigod, a whole half-*page* waiting just for me to do my thing all over it. Loopy will not be confined. Loopy's hs snake skywards like a fly-fisher's line, the tails of Loopy's fs and gs and ys drop deep into the pond, Loopy frisks and gambols, Loopy jives, Loopy got da mojo, Loopy LIVES! And people – well, some people – tell me they can actually read it. Or so the nice ladies in the Burlington Arcade pretend when they watch me try out another antique Swan or Parker 51. Of course it could be in their interest to keep their smile of disbelief to themselves as Loopy goes for a test run on their scratch-pads, but they're usually called Heather so, what the hell, I trust them. And the queen of the nib? Oh, she was tickled.

And so it has been – well before my encounter with, let's call her Italica – that the call of Loopy moved me instinctively towards a kind of writing that was driven by the pleasure principle, or at least danced to a different drummer than Carefully Considered Academic Analysis. That beat is called journalism and I have always, unapologetically, enjoyed committing it. Most of the pieces collected in this book were written for the many newspapers and magazines generous enough to indulge my habit and actually pay me for the exercise. (My first book review was for the venerable *Saturday Evening Post* and I got paid $25.) A few of the lengthier, more spaciously considered pieces – catalogue essays, the occasional lecture, book reviews – made the cut if they retained something of the nervous tingle of the moment, even if the high-wire act was performed in front of an audience rather than exacting editors and their readers. In some ways the title of this collection could not be less apt, for the joke of the Duke of Gloucester's breezy enquiry at what Gibbon might be up to is comical only when one registers the pains and time it took the historian to produce every baroquely rolling sentence of his masterpiece. In that sense the pieces here are most unGibbonish, written on the fly (though after much thought): capers and flourishes that try to share the passion – whether enthusiasm or grief – for their subjects. If they were not always hot off the press, they were often hot from my head.

But then I got the hot-metal romance early. I wasn't even out of grey flannel short trousers and snake belt when our class got taken to Fleet Street some time in the mid-1950s. The *Daily Mirror* had it all, I thought: shrivelled trolls with the right kind of fungal pallor, chained to machines that chattered out type; trays of set pages; even the occasional green eyeshade; the whole wizard's den culminating in sheets of raw newsprint cascading into bins. Was there ever a headier bouquet – cheap cigarettes and printers' ink? They had to drag me back to the school coach.

Paradise got postponed. I signed up as soon as I could for the secondary-school magazine, but it was a prim production called *The Skylark*, bound in air-force-blue paper and featuring deadly reports on the doings of the school hockey team interspersed with juvenile odes to the Grampians. The paper signified the sky part, I supposed, but I was more interested in the lark. I got it when the school librarian, the son of a Labour MP, got busy with a subversive publication, printed clandestinely in the art rooms after school. Called *Perspective*, like all lefty broadsides which didn't really have any, it railed gloriously against British policy in Cyprus and defended EOKA bombs and ambushes as legitimate self-defence. I was but a baby gofer to the sixth-form comrade editor whose extreme unfriendliness I took as a sign of iron political discipline, but I loved every minute of the transgression, stacking copies in the inner sanctum of the library office, unbeknownst to the kindly Latin teacher whom we were getting in the hottest of water. It was a tribute to our modest powers of circulation, I suppose, that at some point, men in pork-pie hats and raincoats (I swear) paid a visit to the headmaster and invoked, so we heard, the Official Secrets Act. While we were happy not to be expelled along with our mastermind, our reverence for his steely wickedness only intensified with the glamour of his indictment.

The first pieces I got published in a newspaper appeared in *The Jewish Chronicle*, where I was working to keep myself in winkle-pickers, as a cutter and paster in the library. But the real bonus was getting dates with the editor's curvy daughter, who in turn procured for me the occasional classical music review. From the beginning, then, journalism was a pleasure, the only snag being that I knew absolutely nothing about classical music, save the occasional well-intentioned lunchbreak tutorial from a schoolfriend who would lecture me about Bruckner and Shostakovich, which would have been instructive had I not been distracted by the fragments of amateurishly assembled egg-salad sandwich that clung gothically to his front teeth. But for this girl I was willing to learn and through careful study noticed, in the reviews of those who did actually know something about the subject, the recurrence of certain key terms: 'lyrical', 'stirring', 'sensitive', 'brilliant' and so on. Off I went with the date to Annie Fischer, David Oistrakh or the Amadeus Quartet and, back home, more or less randomly assembled the adjectives in plausible order. You would be amazed how often they coincided with the professional notices.

At Cambridge my precocious knack for hackery found the perfect outlet, not in the classic *Varsity*, which seemed to me dominated by public-school oligarchs who said '*yaar*' indicating 'yes', while actually meaning 'not on your fucking life, sunshine'. 'Hey, could I have a job at *Varsity*?' 'Well, *yaar*.' So my friends and I peeled off to found a rival paper, called with unoriginal optimism: *New Cambridge*. I wrote, I edited a bit, I loved the picador thrusts at the opposition rag and chewed lustily on a pipe like Charles Foster Kane. On the side, my mate Martin Sorrell – the financial brains of our publishing duo – overran a glossy magazine that high-mindedly devoted itself to a single issue per issue: the state of British prisons in Michaelmas term, the state of British art in Lent. With authentically undergraduate lack of irony, it called itself *Cambridge Opinion*, and unsold towers of it were stashed in a mysterious cavity in the rooms of the amiable anthropologist Edmund Leach, who was even more chaotic than the editor (yours truly) and treated its unique combination of unsellability and pretentiousness as a tremendous hoot. Martin and I would get a sudden order for five copies of *British Art: The Future* from the Whitechapel Gallery, would scoot over to Leach's lair and attempt to extract them from his cupboard. One or other of us would disappear within its shadowy depths, sometimes torch in hand, but inevitably fail to find the missing numbers. Meanwhile, Leach's fireplace burned with suspicious brilliance. 'You wouldn't know where they might be, Dr Leach, would you?' we would ask. 'Oh no,' he would chortle, 'behind *Africa Today* possibly? Have another glass.'

Towards the end of our last year, another prolifically literary pal, Robert Lacey, won an essay competition orchestrated by the *Sunday Times* as an exercise in talent-scouting. Robert's prize was a job on the paper, then edited by Harold Evans in his sensational (but not sensationalist) prime. It was the moment when the paper took the daring step of inventing what was then called a 'colour supplement' that could include nifty advice on the best years for St-Emilion along with harrowing Don McCullin pictures of the war in Vietnam. The cheerful and, at that time, almost spherical Godfrey Smith presided over this mini-colony of the paper where Robert had his desk. From one of their shrewd brains came the notion that a drop in summer sales might be countered by an ongoing series of Educational Value that readers might be induced to collect, week by week, and then assemble in their very own black plastic binder. It was to be called *A Thousand Makers of the Twentieth Century*, each micro-biography running to a few hundred words, whether the subject was Rasputin or Rommel, Pétain or Picasso. (Space allowances were made for the outsize monsters of history. Hitler must have got 800.) Organised alphabetically, it began naturally with Alvar Aalto and ended (I think) with Zog of Albania. Lacey was a hotshot editor and, being the good egg he was and is, sublet some of the work to his mates languishing in tutorial chores back in the Fens.

So I did Nazis and Dutch persons (though not Dutch Nazis) and would make trips down to the Gray's Inn Road, lurking ecstatically amidst the journalists' desks until they noticed me and even gave me the occasional reporter's chore. I was in hack heaven.

Thousand Makers was just crazy enough to succeed. Punters bought their black plastic binders by the crateload. We were a big hit and I learned something about conciseness, with which the Schama style had not hitherto been much associated. Communiqués of delight came down from On High, the office of Roy, the First Baron Thomson of Fleet. What also came down one day was an enquiry about who was going to be penning the item on the Queen. Somehow the royal name had gone unaccountably missing from our lengthy list of twentieth-century Makers. What, I thought, had she made? People happy? On the whole, tick, but what could be said about that? The TV monarchy? There was an idea. I wrote round the Usual Suspects, but no takers, so it fell to muggins, being the lowest on the totem pole. Off went something about the televised coronation, but with the faintest, merest hint that the royal round of Commonwealth ceremonies were not invariably a day at the beach (or gymkhana). Harrumphing sounds were heard from Above to the effect that something more entirely reverential was called for. The writers of *Makers*, including the doughty Godfrey, stood by my piece, but at the last minute an editorial courtier broke ranks and produced a piece of unexceptional flattery. Someone, though, leaked the story to *Private Eye*, which ran the pieces — Establishment and Not — side by side. I was, inadvertently, the custodian of integrity. But as Isaiah Berlin used to say, just because the honours that come one's way may be richly undeserved doesn't mean to say we won't take them.

I'd had my tiny taste of trouble and I wanted much more, especially since for most of the working week I was having to behave myself as a history don, dishing out anything from Abelard to Adlai Stevenson to my student victims. It wasn't the pay — £800 a year and all the Amontillado I could drink — that kept me down on the farm. I was hooked on history and would stay that way. But I needed my journalism jag too, so in between moonlighting in London and supervising in College I took on the editing of the weekly academic magazine, *The Cambridge Review*. This had been the closest a journal could get to sherry and still be made of paper. But it had been going for nearly eighty years, and now and then its pages would make room for the likes of Bertrand Russell or Sylvia Plath. It was, as everyone pointed out, An Institution. Which of course made it a prime target for the Furies who were very much at large in 1968. I had two colleagues in the editorial hot seat, both American, one Marxist, one an economist who would later make serious money. I was the wet liberal centrist in between, but most of all I wanted the *Review* to mix things up a bit. There was tear gas on the boulevards (I got a whiff of it one day in Montparnasse). Imagination had been declared by Jean-Louis Barrault to be *en pouvoir*, and in Cambridge Situationists were making silly buggers of themselves in the Senate House, along with more serious sitters-in who had the fantastic notion that some sort of academic democracy might be *en pouvoir* on King's Parade. It was absurd, but it made for fabulous copy and we dished it up, the covers of the magazine being black modernist designs on dark red and blue. Moody! Not exactly what the dons were expecting, but never mind, I hired pals like Clive James to do reviews and attempted to hold the sententiousness of my American co-editors somewhat at bay. Every week saw a panicky rendezvous with the composing printer round the corner and some heavy imbibing after we put it to bed.

A year or so later, the Revolution in the Fens but a heady memory, we dreamed up the idea of an anthology of some of the best writing over the life of the *Review* and, to our amazement, Jonathan Cape agreed to publish it. Out it came in 1972, bejacketed in a peculiar shade of pink (more or less my politics), grandly entitled *The Cambridge Mind*. Though we had pieces by examples of the most rarefied regions of the Cantabrigian medulla – G. E. Moore, J. J. Thompson, William Empson – I knew this was asking for trouble of the chucklesome kind, but I was outvoted by my more serious colleagues and collaborated in an introduction of numbing loftiness. The anthology was reviewed, rather kindly, by Hugh Trevor-Roper, who pointed out that *The Oxford Magazine* had published a similar anthology some time before called *The Oxford Sausage*. The difference in titles, he implied, with that thin literary smirk he assumed at moments of intense self-amusement, was all you needed to know. In private I knew he was right.

There followed the years of Rain in The Hague: gallons of it streaming down the windows of the old National Archive where I endured a lonely research vigil, thinking – a lot – about one of my best friends who had decided to do his research in Venice. Whenever I could I hightailed it to Amsterdam, then in the throes of stupendous cultural uproar, a non-stop porno-dope-anarcho-rock-and-roll madness. Major publications were called things like *Suck* and knew, it is fair to say, even by the standards of the time, no bounds. In a disused church a coagulated jam of bodies swayed (dancing was physically impossible) to violent music, while lava-lamp blobs oiled their way over a huge screen where once an altar had stood. Limbs became confused, and then the rest of us. Back in Cambridge, Lawrence Stone was contrasting the slow historical evolution of sex and marriage with the outbreak of what he called, smiling merrily (and quoting *that* line of Philip Larkin's), 'polymorphous sexuality'. In Amsterdam I knew what he meant.

As I slowly and painfully assembled the source materials for my first book, Carlyle's phantasmagoric vision of the archive as an interminable coral reef stretching away as far as could be imagined often appeared before me. The danger of drowning was real. So, more than ever, I needed to surface and get a hit of oxygenated journalism. Kindly, clever John Gross came to my aid with assignments to write about art for the *TLS*, and lots of hospitable editors followed – at *New Society*, Tony Elliott at the young *Time Out* (which was decent of him since I'd been part of the gang that tried to compete with him with a Richard Neville publication, *Ink*, a gloriously stoned and thus inevitably short-lived affair). After my first book appeared in 1977, to mostly positive reviews, editors on both sides of the Atlantic began commissioning pieces, which I turned in always on time and always overwritten, both length-wise and adjective-wise.

I have been lucky ever since; more than most, I think, in the generosity with which editors of all styles and philosophies have let me run around, not just in history, art and politics – the fields in which I graze in my book-length scholarly life – but in other departments of enthusiasm: music, film, theatre and, the writing which is simultaneously most challenging and most rewarding, words about food. Cooks – at least those who don't have to sweat it for a living – will tell you that the whole business is about the delivery of pleasure; the sampling of that lovely moment when, if one has done fairly well, even the most garrulous company will fall silent after a bite or two and get lost in delight. This salmagundi – a thing of various tastes and textures – is likewise offered to my readers in a similar hope that some of it, at least, might go down a treat.

Travelling

Sail Away: Six Days to New York on the *Queen Mary 2*

New Yorker, 31 May 2004

Overlooked – literally – by the seventeen-deck *Queen Mary 2*, as she slid into her berth at Pier 92 on 22 April 2004, was the dead white bird. Laid out on its funeral barge beside the USS *Intrepid*, as flightless and obsolete as the dodo, Concorde wasn't going anywhere. The sleek dream of supersonic speed, the princess of whoosh, which got you there before you'd started, was now, officially, a museum piece. The future – as the mayoral bloviations greeting the ship's midtown docking affirmed – belonged to 150,000 tons of steel capable of grinding through the ocean at all of thirty knots (that's around thirty-five m.p.h. to you landlubbers). The latest and most massive of the transatlantic liners takes twenty times as long to carry you from New York to England as a Boeing or an Airbus. And that's the good news – the reason, in fact, for Commodore Ronald Warwick, the master of the *Queen Mary 2*, to brag, at the quayside ceremonies, that Cunard was poised to compete with the airlines for a serious share of the transatlantic business.

Like those of us who had sailed with him through Force 10 gales and thirty-foot swells, the Commodore may have been pardonably giddy at coming through the worst that the feisty ocean could throw his way on a maiden North Atlantic voyage and still getting to the Statue of Liberty on schedule. But could this be the start of something really big and really slow? We take for granted the appeal of velocity, that there is money to be made and pleasure to be had from the gratification of the instantaneous: the three-gulp Happy Meal, the lightning download, the vital mobile phone message that I am here and are you there? And where has this culture of haste got us? Baghdad, apparently, where the delusions of the get-it-over-with war are being compounded by the unseemly rush to exit, leaving the whole gory mess for some other loser to sort out.

It has been thus, as Stephen Kern, in *The Culture of Time and Space 1880–1918*, points out, ever since the orgiasts of speed at the turn of the twentieth century made acceleration the necessary modern ecstasy. In 1909, the Italian writer and artist Filippo Marinetti declared, in his *Futurist Manifesto*, that 'the world's magnificence has been enriched by a new beauty: the beauty of speed'. On an afternoon two years later, a sixteen-frames-a-second movie of the investiture of the Prince of Wales was developed in a darkroom on a British express train and taken to London, where it was shown the same night. Translated into military strategy by the overarmed Great Powers, as the historian A. J. P. Taylor liked to note, the imperatives of railway timetables drove the logistics of pre-emptive mobilisation. A pause to ponder was already a defeat. So modernity bolted out of the starting gate in 1914: Archduke shot, millions of men in grey and khaki precipitately herded into railway carriages, carnage begun right on cue – before the Flemish mire slowed everything down and millions plodded to their doom.

For much of its history, Cunard has been part of this feverish hurry-up. In 1907 its flagship, the *Mauretania*, captured the Blue Riband for fastest transatlantic crossing, and kept it for twenty-two years, spurring jealous – and fatal – competition. A novel by Morgan Robertson, *The Wreck of the Titan; or, Futility*, appearing in 1898, had featured a liner named *Titan* that cuts another ship in two simply 'for the sake of speed'. And the captain of the *Titanic* was blamed for sailing full steam, even in an area notorious for ice floes, in deference to the White Star Line's determination to wrest the Blue Riband from Cunard.

Abraham Cunard, a Philadelphia shipwright, had settled in Nova Scotia, in the loyalist diaspora, after the American Revolution. The loyalists, severed from not only their homes but the mother country, had good reason to want their mail delivery to take less than six weeks, the time often needed for sailing ships to cross from Britain to Canada or the West Indies. Abraham and his son Samuel prospered with a small mail fleet, and in the 1830s Samuel, watching George Stephenson's locomotive the *Rocket* hurtle along the tracks at thirty m.p.h., became convinced that on the oceans, too, steam propulsion was about to replace sail.

Paddle-driven steamers had been in common use in both American and British coastal waters and rivers since the early nineteenth century, and steam-assisted masted ships had crossed the Atlantic since 1819. But it was only in 1838 that the first full steam crossing was made, by the St George Steam Packet Company's ship *Sirius*. Immediately the journey was cut to two weeks (twelve days to Halifax, fourteen to Boston). The *Sirius* was followed by Isambard Kingdom Brunel's *Great Western*, which added style to speed. It boasted 128 staterooms, bell ropes to summon stewards, a ladies' stewardess and a seventy-five-foot saloon, decorated with panels celebrating 'the arts and sciences'.

Disdaining both opulence and reckless speed, Samuel Cunard offered something else when, in 1839, he made a tender to the Admiralty for the conveyance of Her Majesty's Mail: dependability, guaranteed by the novel presence of an on-board engineer. In July 1840 the *Britannia*, the first of Cunard's packets, docked at Boston after a two-week crossing. A wooden-hulled ship with two masts and a central funnel, it was a footling 1,150 tons and about 200 feet long (compared with the *QM 2*'s 150,000 tons and quarter-mile length). In the port where the American Revolution began, *Britannia* was greeted with gun salutes, a performance of 'God Save the Queen' and the declaration of Cunard Festival Day.

The word 'historic' was much repeated over the public-address system last 16 April, as the *Queen Mary 2* moved out into the Solent from its Southampton berth under a classically grey English spring sky. The maiden North Atlantic crossing was hugely subscribed, and, despite the famous superstitiousness of sailors, no one aboard seemed to have been deterred by, or even to have spoken of, the tragedy that cast a shadow over the ship's prospects even before she had been formally launched. On 15 November 2003, while the *QM 2* was still in the shipyard at Saint-Nazaire, in Brittany, where it was being built, a gangway, bearing fifty people, collapsed, throwing some of them fifty feet to the concrete bed of the dry dock. Fifteen were killed and twenty-eight injured. Many of the dead and injured were shipyard workers and family members and friends, who were visiting the liner before its sail to Southampton.

In defiance of ill omens, the transatlantic send-off was exuberant; for those braving the raw breezes there was sparkling wine on the upper-deck terrace. But anxieties about the target of opportunity presented by a mass of slowly moving Anglo-American steel precluded all but a vigilantly screened handful from the dockside 'sailaway'. A spirited band did what it could with 'Rule Britannia' and 'Life on the Ocean Wave', but neither was able to compete with a phantom soprano hooting from the loudspeakers. Then the ship's whistle drowned out everything else, and streamers were tossed from the decks, landing beside flocks of indifferently bobbing seagulls. Waving hankies were to be seen only in blown-up photographs of Cunard's past glory days mounted on walls in the ship's interior.

And where were the cows? Samuel Cunard had made sure that each of his packets was equipped with at least one ship's cow, to provide a steady supply of fresh milk, which, to anyone faced with trays of small plastic miniatures of 'dairy-taste' creamer, seems like an idea whose time should come again. There would be risks, of course. During the fourth crossing of Brunel's immense *Great Eastern*, in 1861, the seas were so high that, according to one report, they not only tore off the paddles, but knocked over the deck-mounted cowshed, sending one of the animals through the skylight of the saloon, where it landed on an understandably surprised barfly. This might have happened early in the morning, for in the halcyon days of the packets saloons opened for business at 6 a.m. and closed at eleven at night. A decent breakfast on the *Britannia* in the 1840s was steak and Hock, which Cunard might think of adding to room service, as a more cheering way to start a day on the tossing waves than weak tea, overstewed coffee and dried-out croissants. And anyone who has waited all his life for the moment when, from a blanket-wrapped steamer chair, he could interrupt his reading of Anita Loos or Evelyn Waugh to summon a steward for a cup of piping-hot bouillon will have to wait a bit longer, for on the *QM 2*, I regret to report, bouillon was there none.

What there is on the *QM 2* is grandeur: lashings of it, Bel-Air baroque, heavy on the upholstery. The dominant style is officially described as 'Art Deco', but it is more *le grand style Ginger et Fred*: sweeping staircases (especially in the triple-decker main restaurant); long, curved bars (very handsome in the Chart Room); leopard-patterned carpets; and, in one theatre, bronze bas-reliefs that feature disporting deities, as in the pre-multiplex yesteryear, though the athletic statuary posted at the doors summons up Albert Speer and

'Honour the Komsomol', rather than Garbo and Groucho. Over the shipboard 'art' a tactful veil should be drawn, but there *is* great art on the *Queen Mary 2*: namely, the exterior of the ship itself – a thrilling scarlet-and-black tower of a funnel and four heroically scaled brushed-steel propeller screws mounted on deck seven, as mightily torqued as anything from the hand of Richard Serra.

Even though the ship is a small floating town – 2,600 passengers and 1,300 crew – it seldom feels crowded. It helps if you have a cool $27,000 to spare, for then you get a share of the Balmoral Suite: 2,249 square feet of what the brochure describes as 'sheer extravagance', including a dining area for eight; two interactive plasma-screen TVs; your own exercise equipment; and (the least they could do, really) 'a fully stocked bar'. For $18,000 less, you rate a not so fully stocked bar and about 250 square feet of elegant, if rather narrow, cabin and balcony. This would still be nearly 200 square feet bigger than Charles Dickens's stateroom aboard the *Britannia* in 1842. For his thirty-five guineas Dickens got a claustrophobic twelve by six: two stacked curtained bunks (no room to stow his trunk); two washstands, with jugs of water brought by stewards; a niggardly porthole, rather apt to leak; and a single oil lamp. But even this austerity was princely compared with steerage on such ships, where passengers slept communally in rows of swinging bunks 'tween decks' and cooked in their own utensils without much help in the way of lighting or ventilation.

For the cabin-class passengers, the centre of the *Britannia*, both socially and physically, was the grand, coal-heated saloon, which Dickens described, in *American Notes*, as

> a long narrow apartment, not unlike a gigantic hearse with windows in the sides; having at the upper end a melancholy stove, at which three or four chilly stewards were warming their hands; while on either side, extending down its whole dreary length, was a long, long table, over each of which a rack, fixed to the low roof and stuck full of drinking-glasses and cruet-stands, hinted dismally at rolling seas and heavy weather.

Dinner, taken on oilcloth-covered tables – which, predictably, aggravated the roll of crockery in heavy weather – was at one: roasted potatoes, baked apples and much pork, in the form of pig's head or cold ham (for some reason, pig was thought to lie easiest on ocean-going stomachs). At five, a cheerless supper was served, usually of boiled potatoes and mouldering fruit, washed down with brandy-and-water or wine, but then there was always the saloon to repair to. Those among the crew who could play a tune or two sometimes did, and there were a few books in the saloon. Only in the second half of the nineteenth century, when wooden hulls were replaced by steel and paddles by screw propellers, did a comprehensively stocked and magnificently panelled and furnished library become a crucial fixture. The heavily used library on the *QM 2* runs the gamut from Danielle Steel to Tom Clancy; there is a wall of less intensively visited Everyman classics, and I found, improbably lurking amid the bodice-rippers and spy thrillers, Albert Camus's *The Plague*.

Though the best thing about a week's Atlantic crossing is an eyeful and a day full of nothing other than the rhythm of the sea and the silvery curving rim of the world, and although Old Cunarder hands insisted that was the way that crossings, rather than mere vulgar cruises, should be, Cunard is now owned by the mother of all cruise companies, Carnival Corporation. And the job description of its toiling entertainment directors begins with the abhorrence of a vacuum. So the gym rumbles with massed treadmilling; the Canyon Ranch spa is packed with heavy massaging; the herbal sauna is crammed with oversized marine mammals (bipedal). In front of the two huge theatres, passengers line up by the statuary to hear a glamorous string trio of Ukrainian musicians dressed in miles of retro-ballgown satin taffeta give their all to 'Jealousy'; or watch spirited young British actors throw themselves into greatest hits from *Romeo and Juliet* and *A Midsummer Night's Dream*; or listen to lecturers like me pontificating about Atlantic history.

In the Queen's Room, a frighteningly accurate bust of the actual Queen Mary, the present Queen's grandmother – a human galleon who seemed to sail fully rigged through state ceremonies as lesser craft chugged contemptibly about her – surveys Gavin Skinner and Lydia Lim, the dance teachers, as they steer giggly novices through the samba, cha-cha or foxtrot, the 'walk-walk, side-together-side' contending with the unhelpful motion of the waves. On the parquet, middle-aged 'gentlemen hosts' hired to squire single ladies through the dances glide their partners around with courtly grace. After being screened for ballroom-dancing prowess and other credentials of respectability, the gentlemen hosts sign on for at least two voyages, and pay a token sum for the privilege. But if Gordon Russell Cave, an impeccably turned-out widower, is any guide, the hosts see their work more as vocation than as vacation: the purveying of shipboard happiness. The moments Gordon recalled with most pleasure were those befitting a *preux chevalier*. One widow told him, after he had walked her back to her seat, that it was the first time she had danced since her husband's death, four years before. 'I think it helped, that little moment,' he said.

Nothing aboard the ship, though, gets as much exercise as the jaws. Indeed, devoted chowhounds could spend the waking hours of the entire six-day voyage doing little more than grazing the vessel, bow to stern, since, as the ship proudly boasts, there is somewhere to eat something twenty-three hours out of twenty-four. Not surprisingly, things British are done best. If fish and chips with mushy peas is your idea of spa food (and why not?), you'll not be disappointed at the ship's pub. Come four o'clock, the Winter Garden is packed with tea parties gobbling cucumber sandwiches made of regulation-issue white-bread triangles, while a tristful harpist completes recollections of rainy afternoons trapped in British seaside palm courts, even though the trees here are fake.

Upmarket on the eighth deck, the Todd English restaurant pretty much lives up to the starry reputation of the chef of Boston's Olives by offering potato-and-truffle love letters, succulent braised short ribs and the inevitable fallen chocolate cake. But the best food on board is probably to be had at the Chef's Galley, where, in the style of a celebrity-chef TV programme, Sean Watier, an exuberantly wise-cracking chef, talks a dozen or so diners through the preparation of the meal. As he was about halfway through a mango-and-crab salad, things started to get exciting in a Quentin Tarantino kind of way. Sean capped his demo about the importance of really sharp knives by gashing his thumb. Later, while he was blowtorching the crème brûlée, he was asked about problems of cooking in heavy weather and was about to offer a breezy reply when the answer came from a phantom guest who had been there all along – the Atlantic Ocean, which lifted us all up in its big cat's paw and unceremoniously set us down again. It was exactly the 'heave and shudder . . . as of the breast of a man in

deep sleep' that Evelyn Waugh has Charles Ryder sense in the midst
of his transatlantic crossing in *Brideshead Revisited.* 'Either I am a
little drunk,' Charles's wife, Celia, says as the cutlery starts to slide,
'or it's getting rough.' For me, back in the cabin, on deck twelve, with
the floor at a tilt, and the bed the only safe place to be, the two conditions seemed mutually and unhappily self-reinforcing.

Though huge 'resort' ships like the *QM 2* come with acres of deck,
big picture windows and balconies, they go to great lengths to allow
passengers who may have mixed feelings about the ocean to ignore
it. The planetarium, the casino, the umpteen watering holes, the
golf simulator, the spa, the disco, the ballrooms, the unceasing frenzy
of entertainment in big, dark spaces are all designed to keep the
seawater well out of the way and even out of sight. But on this night
old man Poseidon, evidently assisted by Tritons with serious attitude, was crashing the scene. On the Beaufort wind scale of 1 to 12,
this one, howling around the ship like a marine banshee, was a 10,
eventually getting up to seventy miles an hour, which is not far short
of hurricane force. Likewise, the motion of the sea is measured by
a range going from Moderate through Rough to High, the last being
well beyond Very Rough. That night and much of the following day,
our piece of the Atlantic was Very High, beyond which the only
available term is Phenomenal, and by then your cabin is probably
filling with water and men in tuxedos are ushering women and children to the boats.

As the mango-and-crab salad and I became unhappily reacquainted,
the gale certainly seemed to be turning phenomenal. Everything that
could fall in the cabin did so, including me. The *Queen Mary* seemed
to be locked in a frenzied dance with the elements, the ship reaching
and rising and then, on the crest of the churned water, going into a
wicked shimmy, its sides shaking and jangling like a belly dancer on
spliff, before sinking back voluptuously into the trough. Eventually a
message came over the PA system from the Officer of the Watch, whose
voice, resembling that of a firm but fair English schoolmaster, had
already established itself as authoritative. It was not reassuring: 'Code
Bravo, Code Bravo, Code Bravo.' And then it added, 'Control group to
muster.' True, it spoke without much inflection, as if reporting a cricket
score from a sticky wicket. But since the same announcement had been
made earlier that day, followed by the information that this was a prac-

tice, repeat practice, fire drill, a real Code Bravo was not what anyone wanted to hear in this situation. An hour later the announcement 'Stand down' was heard, and another announcement, a bit later on, referred to a 'minor incident, now completely under control'.

The thing about a crew of 1,300 — which includes, after all, masseurs, cabaret singers and wine waiters — is that not all of them are trained, in the British merchant-marine tradition, to keep mum about trifling things like a fire at sea on a maiden voyage in the midst of a Force 10 gale. It was, I was assured, a teeny-weeny fire, just a razor socket burning up in a crew cabin. At the time, however, it certainly made an impression.

The next morning, the sea was still Very High, but Professor Schama, due to deliver a lecture at eleven-fifteen, was Very Low (and, for that matter, Very Rough). But I was billed to talk about the man who had given the very first lecture aboard a Cunarder, the *Cambria*, in August 1845: the African-American author and orator Frederick Douglass. Douglass was en route to what turned into a triumphal lecture tour of Britain and Ireland and had been befriended by the Hutchinson Family Singers (Asa, Jesse, Abby, John and Judson), from New Hampshire. Staunch abolitionists, the Hutchinsons had the inspired idea that Douglass might give a lecture on the iniquities of slavery, notwithstanding the fact that among the passengers were several slave owners from Georgia and Cuba. Douglass — with mixed feelings, one suspects — agreed, subject to permission of the captain, the famously capable Charles Judkins. Judkins, as it happened, was a former slave owner (perhaps a slave trader) who had seen the light, and was happy to oblige. Standing on the saloon deck, Douglass began to read from the brutal slave laws of the south, when, predictably, he was drowned out by heckling and threats of physical assault from the outraged slave owners. The Hutchinsons weighed in with inspirational songs but, until Captain Judkins called for the bosun and vowed to put the rioters in irons unless they desisted, the situation looked ugly. The captain's gesture amazed Douglass, who began his tour of Britain (as he would end it) with an unrealistically awestruck view of British racial tolerance. About Cunard, however, he felt less charitable on the return journey, also on the *Cambria*, in 1847, since it accepted his forty guineas and assured him that he would be accommodated in cabin class, only to demote him to steerage when he boarded, a scandal that made the correspondence columns of *The Times* and drew from Samuel Cunard himself a public guarantee that this sort of thing would not happen again.

Duty required that, unsteady or not, I offer this history to any hardy souls who managed to lurch and stagger their way to the theatre. But was there enough left of the lecturer to get the job done? A sympathetic programme assistant, Penny Folliott, had the answer: 'Try the injection.' I did, and whatever was in the nurse's potent syringe not only banished the queasiness but effected a startling transformation, whimpering academic translated into approximation of Russell Crowe in *Master and Commander*. The talk got delivered, seated, and diagonally. I slid a bit. But the audience slid with me.

The Atlantic had definitely got our attention; its illimitable breadth, the great kick of its kinetic energy registered in our groggy bodies. We offered it our sincere respects. All the seats in front of the big windows were now filled with people mesmerised by the immense opera of the deep-grey swell, the rolling waves as bulky and meaty as elephants in a temper. Every so often, beside ladies doing watercolours, a particularly angry, torn-up wall of seawater would slap and hammer against the window.

After a day of respite, the Atlantic returned – another gale, less brutal, but serious enough for deck joggers to be ushered inside by the crew. Shuffleboard was postponed again. Quoits were out of the question. But by this time most of us had got our sea legs and had learned to respect the motion of the ocean, moving with it. Foxtrot was recommenced in the Queen's Room, and disco caught a new beat. For that matter, the towering ship itself seemed to be having a ball, breezing ahead to the rough music of the wind and the swell. And as the *QM 2* forged along, so it became, for most of the passengers, no longer a floating resort hotel drifting innocuously into Caribbean harbours under postcard skies. This one, we told ourselves, appropriating some of the credit for its performance, was a liner, made for crossing, not cruising. 'Oh, the passengers would like it,' Commodore Warwick said, smiling, 'if I told them that was the worst weather I'd ever sailed in, but . . .' The smile continued; the sentence didn't. He wasn't about to wreck our newfound talent for salty yarns. At the dockside celebrations in New York, he conceded that the crossing had been 'turbulent'.

When the Verrazano Bridge came looming through the gentle fog and the first tugs and pilots began to spout red-white-and-blue jets of water in dwarfish greeting, many of us were caught off guard by a sense of proprietorial affection. Emotions doubled. There was the catch in the throat as, right on cue, the morning sun picked out the Statue of Liberty and then travelled from plinth to torch with telegenic precision; there was the flood of memory, the empathy – even among the Queen's Grill high-rollers – with the destitute millions who had come this way through their own storms and stresses; and the jolt of recognition, as we made the turn up the Hudson, that this, too, had been, and was still, America, perhaps the one that really mattered.

All that, I suppose, could have been predicted. What took us by surprise, as we were ushered by Lydia and Gavin, kitted up in smart grey disembarkation suits, to the immigration desks set up in the ball-room, was a valedictory urge to wish the ship well, and to try and find the words to tell others who might normally opt for Newark Airport and the seven-hour air tube to Heathrow that they might want to give the *QM 2* a go; that, *mirabile dictu*, there are worse things than being made to sit down and fill the eyes with nothing but sky and rain and wind-whipped water as 150,000 tons of big ship does what it can to ride it at thirty-five miles an hour. In fact, there are few things better.

The Unloved American:
Two Centuries of Alienating Europe

New Yorker, 10 March 2003

On the Fourth of July in 1889, Rudyard Kipling found himself near Mammoth Hot Springs in Yellowstone with a party of tourists from New England. He winced as a 'clergyman rose up and told them they were the greatest, freest, sublimest, most chivalrous, and richest people on the face of the earth, and they all said Amen'. Kipling – who had travelled from India to California, and then across the North American continent – was bewildered by the patriotic hyperbole that seemed to come so naturally to the citizens of the United States. There were many things about America that he loved – battling with a twelve-pound Chinook salmon in Oregon; American girls ('They are clever; they can talk . . . They are original and look you between the brows with unabashed eyes') – and he did go and live in Vermont for a while. But he was irritated by the relentless assurances that Americans seemed to require about their country's incomparable virtue. When a 'perfectly unknown man attacked me and asked me what I thought of American Patriotism,' Kipling wrote in *American Notes,* his account of the journey, 'I said there was nothing like it in the Old Country,' adding, 'always tell an American this. It soothes him.'

The Norwegian writer Knut Hamsun, who spent two miserable periods in the American Midwest in the 1880s – working as, among other things, farmhand, store clerk, railroad labourer, itinerant lecturer and (more congenially) church secretary – treated the street parades of veterans 'with tiny flags in their hats and brass medals on their chests marching in step to the hundreds of penny whistles they are blowing' as if the events were curiously remote tribal rituals. The fact that streetcars were forbidden to interrupt the parades and that no one could absent himself without incurring civic disgrace both interested and unsettled Hamsun. Something ominous seemed to be hatching in America: a strapping child-monster whose runaway physical growth would never be matched by moral or cultural maturity. Hamsun gave lectures about his stays in the United States at the University of Copenhagen, and then made them into a book, *The Cultural Life of Modern America*, that was largely devoted to asserting its non-existence.

Emerson? A dealer in glib generalisations. Whitman? A hot gush of misdirected fervour. For Hamsun, America was, above all, bluster wrapped up in dollar bills. 'It is incredible how naively cocksure Americans are in their belief that they can whip any enemy whatsoever,' he wrote. 'There is no end to their patriotism; it is a patriotism that never flinches, and it is just as loudmouthed as it is vehement.' It took a future Quisling to know this.

By the end of the nineteenth century the stereotype of the ugly American — voracious, preachy, mercenary and bombastically chauvinist — was firmly in place in Europe. Even the claim that the United States was built on a foundation stone of liberty was seen as a fraud. America had grown rich on slavery. In 1776, the English radical Thomas Day had written, 'If there be an object truly ridiculous in nature, it is an American patriot, signing resolutions of independency with the one hand, and with the other brandishing a whip over his affrighted slaves.' After the Civil War, European critics pointed to the unprotected labourers in mines and factories as industrial helots. Just as obnoxious as the fraud of liberty was the fraud of Christian piety, a finger-jabbing rectitude incapable of asserting a policy without invoking the Deity as a co-sponsor. This hallelujah Republic was a bedlam of hymns and hosannas, but the only true church was the church of the Dollar Almighty. And how could the cult of individualism be taken seriously when it had produced a society that set such great store by conformity?

The face of the unloved American did not, of course, come into focus all at once. Different generations of European critics added features to the sketch, depending on their own aversions and fears. In the early nineteenth century, with Enlightenment optimism soured by years of war and revolution, critics were sceptical of America's naive faith that it had reinvented politics. Later in the century American economic power was the enemy, Yankee industrialism the behemoth against which the champions of social justice needed to take up arms. A third generation, itself imperialist, grumbled about the unfairness of a nation's rising to both continental and maritime ascendancy. And in the twentieth century, though the United States came to the rescue of Britain and France in two world wars, many Europeans were suspicious of its motives. A constant refrain throughout this long literature of complaint – and what European intellectuals even now find most repugnant – is American sanctimoniousness, the habit of dressing the business of power in the garb of piety.

Too often, the moral rhetoric of American diplomacy has seemed to Europe a cover for self-interest. The French saw the Jay Treaty, of 1794, which regularised relations with Britain (with which republican France was then at war), as a cynical violation of the 1778 Treaty of Alliance with France, without which, they reasonably believed, there would have been no United States. In 1811, it was the British who felt betrayed by the Americans, when Madison gave in to Napoleon's demands for a trade embargo while the 'mother country' was fighting for survival. But the gap between principles and practices in American foreign policy was as nothing compared with the discrepancy between the ideal and the reality of a working democracy. Although nineteenth-century writers paid lip service to the benevolent intelligence of the Founding Fathers, contemporary American politics suggested that there had been a shocking fall from grace. At one end was a cult of republican simplicity, so dogmatic that John Quincy Adams's installation of a billiard table in the White House was taken as evidence of his patrician leanings; at the other was a parade of the lowest vices, featuring, according to Charles Dickens, 'despicable trickery at elections, under-handed tampering with public officers . . . shameless truckling to mercenary knaves'.

A few transatlantic pilgrims, of course, saw American democracy haloed with republican grandeur. When, in 1818, the twenty-three-year-old Scot Fanny Wright, along with her younger sister Camilla, visited the Capitol, the congressional morning prayer – 'may the rod of tyranny be broken in every nation of the earth!' – caused her to tremble with admiration. Only later did she concede that she might have mistaken the commercial bustle of the country for democratic zeal. And, indeed, for most European travellers extravagant idealism was followed by an equally unbalanced disenchantment. Nikolaus

Lenau, a German poet who told a friend he meant to stay in the United States for five years, managed only a brief period, from 1832 to 1833. He could not tolerate a country where, he claimed, there were no songbirds. (In the eighteenth century, the Dutch naturalist Cornelius de Pauw, lecturing on America to the court of Frederick the Great, had solemnly insisted that dogs in the New World never barked.)

Other characteristics of American life alienated the Romantics: the distaste for tragedy (a moral corrective to illusions of invincibility); the strong preference for practicality; the severance from history; and, above all, what the Germans called *bodenlosigkeit*, a willed rootlessness, embodied in the flimsy-frame construction of American houses. Europeans watched, pop-eyed, while whole houses were moved down the street. This confirmed their view that Americans had no real loyalty to the local, and explained why they preferred utilitarian 'yards' to flower gardens. No delphiniums, no civility.

The British who arrived in the United States in the 1830s and '40s had imagined the young republic as a wide-eyed adolescent, socially ungainly and politically gauche, but with some hint of promise. What they found was a country experiencing an unprecedented growth spurt, both territorial and demographic, and characterised by an unnerving rudeness, in both senses of the word. Ladies and gentlemen dodged quids of tobacco juice and averted their gaze from the brimming cuspidors that greeted visitors to steamboat saloons and hotel and theatre lobbies. The hallmark of Jacksonian America seemed to be a beastly indifference to manners, the symptom of a society where considerateness to others was a poor second to the immediate satisfaction of personal wants.

The conduct of Americans at dinner said it all. They wolfed down their food, cramming corn bread into their sloppy maws during meals that were devoured in silence, punctuated only by slurps, grunts, scraping knives and hacking coughs. (All those cigars.) At the Plate House, in the business district of New York, the naval captain and travel writer Basil Hall was astonished by the speed at which the corned beef arrived and then by the even greater speed at which it was demolished: 'We were not in the house above twenty minutes, but we sat out two sets of company at least.' Only the boy waiters yelling orders at the kitchen broke the quiet. The lack of polite conversation suggested the melancholy and dispiriting monotony of American life, on which almost all the early reporters commented. Tocqueville explained the apparent paradox of anxiety amid prosperity as the result of the relentless obligation to be forever Up and Doing.

The European commentators' dismay at the tyranny of American materialism was disingenuous, since many of them had come to the United States to repair their tattered fortunes or make new ones. Frances Trollope decided to sojourn in America when a rich uncle did the Trollopes the disservice of marrying late in life and, still worse, begetting an heir. Fanny Wright, whose ardour for America had been relit by the Marquis de Lafayette's triumphal tour in 1824 and 1825, visited Mrs Trollope at her expensive rented house at Harrow Weald, outside London, in 1827 and persuaded her to join her. Wright had bought 2,000 acres of land on the Wolf River at Nashoba, Tennessee, with the aim of establishing a communal settlement where slaves would receive the education and practical skills that would fit them for freedom. Mrs Trollope planned to visit the Nashoba utopia, with three of her five children, and then proceed from Memphis, fifteen miles away, up the Mississippi and Ohio Rivers to the thriving new city of Cincinnati, where she intended to make a smart little bundle.

But Fanny Wright's settlement turned out to be a cluster of woebegone huts. Plank floors were set only a few feet above sodden mud. The chimney in the hut Mrs Trollope shared with Wright caught fire several times a day. Instead of a model farm, there were a few slaves who were barely subsisting. Of the all-important school there was no sight and no prospect. Mrs Trollope, aghast at the filth and the fever-bearing mosquitoes, fled with her children to Cincinnati, which was, alas, an 'uninteresting mass of buildings', where hogs rooted in the streets. Together with the French painter Auguste Hervieu (who had intended to teach at Nashoba), she flung herself into show business, remodelling a 'Western Museum', which had hitherto been a collection of natural curiosities and patriotic waxworks. Her son Henry became the Invisible Girl, booming prophecies in creepy darkness, and, with the help of glass transparencies, she created a vision of the Infernal Regions, featuring frozen lakes with erupting fountains of flame, and electric shocks should the customers, peering through grates, try and touch the exhibits.

Mrs Trollope's next venture, a galleried, gaslit emporium of consumer wonders, stocked with fancy goods supplied from Harrow by her husband, ended in debt practically before it began. Mrs Trollope was not quite prepared to admit defeat, but one of her children was seriously ill, and she decided that they had to return to England. She stopped in Washington, then spent five months with a hospitable friend in Stonington, Maryland. There, filling notebooks with a tart, vivid account of her experiences, Frances Trollope took a genteel revenge on the land that had betrayed her. 'As I declare the country to be fair to the eye and most richly teeming with the gifts of plenty, I am led to ask myself why it is that I do not like it,' she wrote. She was struck by the fact that servants called themselves 'help', and bewildered that so many thousands of young women would rather toil 'half-naked' in factories than seek to enter domestic service. When a Cincinnati neighbour, 'whose appearance more resembled a Covent Garden market-woman than any thing else', made the mistake of taking her arm and walking her about, 'questioning me without ceasing', Mrs Trollope noted that, while democracy was very fine in principle, 'it will be found less palatable when it presents itself in the shape of a hard greasy paw and is claimed in accents that breathe less of freedom than onions and whiskey'.

Domestic Manners of the Americans made Frances Trollope, at the age of fifty-two, a sudden literary reputation and £250 from the first edition. Her book was popular in Britain because it documented the stereotypes of cultural inferiority and boorish materialism that the Old World was avid to have confirmed about the New. Stendhal annotated a copy and concluded that there was indeed a 'smell of the shop' about the country. Baudelaire remarked that it was the Belgium of the West. But the book sold equally well in Boston and Baltimore, albeit to scandalised and infuriated readers. 'Trollope' soon became a popular shout of abuse in American theatres, and on display in New York was a waxwork of the author in the shape of a goblin.

The wounds inflicted on American self-love by Mrs Trollope were superficial compared with the deep punctures made by Charles Dickens. In 1842, when Dickens published *American Notes*, an account of a visit to the United States, he had a huge American readership. His novels were instant best-sellers there, and many of them – most notably *Nicholas Nickleby* and *Oliver Twist* – had been dramatised on the popular stage. Despite, or perhaps because of, the unhappiness *American Notes* engendered, 50,000 copies were sold in a week in the US.

Dickens's America is all Yankee repression and southern stupor. He saw Boston, New York and Philadelphia through the keyhole of the prison cell and the madhouse. The Tombs, in New York, served as a metaphor for the dark, unforgiving world in which it was situated. And the geographical heart of the country, though not a jail or an asylum, or a reeking warren like the Five Points, was a river of death. Decades before Joseph Conrad steamed his way upstream into the heart of imperial darkness, Dickens, travelling from Cincinnati downstream to Cairo, Illinois (reversing Mrs Trollope's route), experienced the Mississippi as a septic ooze, a turbid soup of animal and vegetable muck. Cairo lay in the stinking belly of the beast: 'The hateful Mississippi circling and eddying before it, and turning off upon its southern course a slimy monster hideous to behold; a hotbed of disease, an ugly sepulchre, a grave uncheered by any gleam of promise: a place without one single quality, in earth or air or water, to commend it: such is this dismal Cairo.'

The sense of America as a sink of contamination extended to its society and its institutions. In the Capitol, where Fanny Wright had been flooded with tremulous rapture, Dickens saw 'the meanest perversion of virtuous Political Machinery that the worst tools ever wrought' – a clamorous gang of fakes, fools and tricksters. His habitual outrage extended to the unrepentant practice of slavery in the South, but he never took the North's support for emancipation as evidence of moral uprightness. The North, he wrote in a letter to a friend, hates the Negro quite as heartily as the South, but uses slavery as a pretext for domination.

Many people in the governing circles of both Britain and France were sympathetic to the South, not only because of the threatened interruption of raw-cotton supplies, but also because a Confederate victory would pre-empt the emergence of a gigantic and powerful nation. In November 1861, when an American warship stopped the British steamer *Trent* to remove two Confederate agents bound for London and Paris, the ailing Prince Albert had to intervene to restrain British calls for war. According to Philippe Roger, whose *L'Ennemi Américain* (2002) is a brilliant and exhaustive guide to the history of

French Ameriphobia, the fate of the South became a sentimental fashion in Napoleon III's Paris.

When the American republic failed to break up, the European angst about its economic transformation and territorial expansion became a neurosis. For some time the British government, worried about the growing imperial rivalry of the new Germany and the French Republic, had complacently assumed that American expansionism could be manipulated to keep its rivals at bay. If the American fleet would, for its own purposes, prevent European undesirables from straying into the Pacific at no cost to the British taxpayer, jolly good for the Stars and Stripes. The Spanish-American War of 1898, which the French treated as the unmasking of Yankee imperialism, was looked at in London with relaxed tolerance. Rudyard Kipling's lines on 'the White Man's burden' were written not in praise of some triumph of the Union Jack beneath far-flung palm and pine, but to celebrate the fall of Manila.

Much as he loved the energy of America, Kipling became progressively unhappy the farther east he went. Soot-black, fog-fouled Chicago, its scummy river speckled with rust and grease, was, he thought, an apparition of the American future. He stood on a narrow beam at the Chicago stockyards, looking down on the 'railway of death' that carried squealing hogs to an appointment with two lines of butchers. The fact that the stockyards were also a tourist attraction only heightened his stupefaction. Unforgettably, he saw 'a young woman of large mould, with brilliantly scarlet lips, and heavy eyebrows . . . dressed in flaming red and black, and her feet . . . were cased in red leather shoes. She stood in a patch of sunlight, the red blood under her shoes, the vivid carcasses tacked round her, a bullock bleeding its life away not six feet away from her, and the death factory roaring all round her.'

It is hard to know where fact ends and fiction begins in Kipling's *American Notes*, but the book's bravura passages established the *idées fixes* of Europeans about the muscular republic on the verge of its imperial awakening: awesomely carnivorous, racially mongrel and socially polarised, both ethically primitive and technologically advanced. At the turn of the century, that stereotype, along with America's cultural poverty (exceptions were always made for Mark Twain), imprinted itself in the literature of reporters from the Old World. In an age absorbed by the physiology of national types, *Homo americanus* seemed to have evolved for the maximisation of physical force. While chewing gum was preferable to chewing tobacco, its ubiquitousness mystified French observers like Jules Huret, until he decided that it was a workout for the over-evolved Yankee jaws and teeth, which needed all the power they could get to tear their way through the slabs of steak consumed at dinner.

Likewise, the appeal of American football – the Harvard–Yale game became almost as much a fixture of foreign itineraries as the stockyards – was explicable only as quasi-Spartan military training. What really startled Europeans was the blood-lust the sport seemed to provoke in spectators. At one Harvard–Yale game, Huret listened in appalled fascination as a nineteen-year-old yelled 'Kill him!' and 'Break his neck!' from the bleachers.

Modern anti-Americanism was born of the multiple insecurities of the first decade of the twentieth century. Just as the European empires were reaching their apogee, they were beset by reminders of their own mortality. At Adowa in 1896, the Ethiopians inflicted a crushing defeat on the Italians; in 1905, the Russian Empire was humiliated in war by the Japanese. Britain may have ruled a quarter of the world's population and geographical space, but it failed to impose its will decisively on the South African Boers. And Wilhelm II's Germany, though it was beginning to brandish its own imperial sword, remained fretful about 'encirclement'. The unstoppability of America's economy and its immigrant-fuelled demographic explosion worried the rulers of these empires, even as they staggered into the fratricidal slaughter that would ensure exactly that future.

It was self-evident that France and Britain should have been grateful for the mobilisation of American manpower in 1917, which tipped the balance against the Germans and Austrians. Colonel Charles E. Stanton's declaration 'Lafayette, we are here', and the subsequent sacrifice of American lives for a European cause, seemed to herald a restoration of transatlantic good feelings. But, as Philippe Roger (and others, like the historians David Strauss and Jean-Philippe Mathy) explains, if the war created a brief solidarity, the peace more decisively destroyed it. When Woodrow Wilson failed to persuade Congress to ratify the Treaty of Versailles and America withdrew into isolationist self-interest, all the old insecurities and animosities returned.

Wilson was perhaps the most detested of all American presidents by the French, for whom his self-righteousness was compounded by his failure to deliver results.

American generosity (in the French view) towards German reparation schedules fed into the conspiracy theories that seethed and bubbled in the anti-American press in the 1920s and early '30s. In *The American Cancer*, Robert Aron and Arnaud Dandieu went so far as to argue that the First World War had been a plot of American high finance to enslave Europe in a web of permanent debt, a view that was echoed in J.-L. Chastanet's *Uncle Shylock* and in Charles Pomaret's *America's Conquest of Europe*. The newspaper *France-Soir* calculated the weight of debt to the United States at 7,200 francs for every French man and woman. Nor was there much in the way of sentimental gratitude for General Pershing's doughboys. Why, it was asked, had the engagement of American troops on the western front been delayed until 1918? The answer was that the United States had waited until it could mobilise a force large enough not just to win the war, but to dominate the peace.

For French writers like Kadmi-Cohen, the author of *The American Abomination*, the threat from the United States was not just economic or military. America now posed a social and cultural danger to the civilisation of Europe. The greatest 'American peril' (a phrase that became commonplace in the literature) was the standardisation of social life (the ancestor of today's complaints against globalisation), the thinning of the richness of human habits to the point where they could be marketable not only inside America but, because of the global reach of American capitalism, to the entire world. Hollywood movies, which, according to Georges Duhamel, were 'an amusement for slaves' and 'a pastime for the illiterate, for poor creatures stupefied by work and anxiety', were the Trojan horse for the Americanisation of the world. Jean Baudrillard's belief that the defining characteristic of America is its fabrication of reality was anticipated by Duhamel's polemics against the 'shadow world' of the movies, with their reduction of audiences to somnolent zombies sitting in the dark.

The charge that the United States was imposing its cultural habits on the prostrate body of war-torn Europe returned with even more force after 1945. Americans thought of the Marshall Plan (together with the forgiveness of French debts) as an exercise in wise altruism; European leaders like de Gaulle bristled with suspicion at the patronising weight of the programme. Complaints against Coca-Colonisation, the mantra of the anti-globalisers, were already in full cry in the 1950s. But as Arthur Koestler, who bowed to no one in his loathing of 'cellophane-wrapped bread, processed towns of cement and glass ... the Organisation Man and the Reader's Digest', put it in 1951, 'Who coerced us into buying all this? The United States do not rule Europe as the British ruled India; they waged no Opium War to force their revolting "Coke" down our throats. Europe bought the whole package because Europe wanted it.'

Yet somehow, in the present crisis American democracy has let itself be represented as American despotism. Some in the European anti-war movement see the whole bundle of American values – consumer capitalism, a free market for information, an open electoral system – as having been imposed rather than chosen. Harold Pinter told peace marchers in London two weeks ago that the United States was a 'monster out of control'. And while representatives of the Iraqi exile community in Britain narrated stories of the atrocities their families had endured at the hands of Saddam Hussein, banners in Hyde Park equated the Stars and Stripes with the swastika.

These cavils are not necessarily false, just because they've been uttered by Ameriphobes. Fast-food nation was invented in the 1830s, and Captain Hall's puzzled observation that in America the word 'improvement' seemed to mean 'an augmentation in the number of houses and people and above all in the amount of cleared land' has not lost any of its validity with the passing of 170-odd years.

Early on, Europeans identified appetite and impatience as the cardinal American sins. Among the many anxieties of European friends, as well as enemies, of the United States is that Americans are not being told that what lies ahead may be much more testing than a fly-by war and a drive-through peace.

But of all the character flaws that Europeans have ascribed to Americans, nothing has contributed more to widening the Atlantic than national egocentricity (a bit rich, admittedly, coming from the French). Knut Hamsun put the emphatic celebration of separateness down to a lack of education about other places and cultures and commented, perhaps waspishly, 'It is almost incredible how hard America works at being a world of its own in the world.' Virtuous isolation, of course, wasn't a problem so long as the United States saw the exercise of its power primarily in terms of the defensive policing of its own continental space. But now that policing has gone irreversibly global, the imperious insistence on the American way, or else, has only a limited usefulness in a long-term pacification strategy. Like it or not, help will be needed, given America's notoriously short attention span, intolerance of casualties and grievously wounded prosperity. Serving the United Nations with notice of redundancy should its policies not replicate those of the United States and the United Kingdom might turn out to be shortsighted, since in Europe, even in countries whose governments have aligned themselves with America, there is almost no support for a war without UN sanction.

Perhaps Mrs Trollope put it best after all: 'If the citizens of the United States were indeed the devoted patriots they call themselves, they would surely not thus encrust themselves in the hard, dry, stubborn persuasion, that they are the first and best of the human race, that nothing is to be learnt, but what they are able to teach, and that nothing is worth having, which they do not possess.'

Amsterdam

An abridged version of this essay was published in John Julius Norwich's, *The Great Cities in History*, 2009

The clever thing to do is to fly in at night. Down you go into the Schiphol, where not so long ago, a mere handful of centuries, there was the inland sea, the Haarlemmermeer, and tubby buses and cogs, their holds laden with herring or grain, bobbing on the grey water. Your plane takes for ever to taxi, skimming along beside and over motorways, keeping pace, cheek by jowl with the traffic, on and on until you wouldn't be surprised if it were to flop into a canal and sail serenely all the rest of the way to the haven city. You come into Amsterdam from the south-west, through a loosely threaded knot of freeway lanes and down into a broad open *plein*, engirdled with dimly corporate modernisms, the usual pallid incandescence, doing no one any harm and no one much good. But that's the last you'll see of bland uni-Europe; the interchangeable parts of a couldbeBaselcouldbeMalmöcouldbeBirmingham kind of place. Into Amsterdam Zuid you go, welcomed by the soft screams of the trams as they bend round the tracks. The peculiar brew of Amsterdam aromas comes at you through the cab window: cooking grease; tobacco smoke – *half zware shag* – the smoke that refuses to die even when the smokers do; and hanging over everything the greenish-briny-scummy smell of the black-water canals themselves, where palings gently rot and swans tuck their wings for the night. It's not much of a night walkers' city; no, not even those night walkers who prefer, still, to sit in their windows bathed in lurid magenta; and the throngs who sit outside on the Leidseplein street, sipping coffees as if it was Paris or Rome, are mostly tourists. Amsterdam hubbubs are indoors; inside the brown cafés from which people holding their *pils* spill on to the street, tugging at their cigarettes.

On you go, past the walls of the darkened city broken by the pale glimmer from the Showarma joints and the porno-shops and the fuming *frites* stalls, before you rise over the humps of the canal bridges and hang a right over the cobbles. Bike riders, imperiously reckless, because also lovers – the boy pedalling hard, the girl sidesaddling behind – swoop right and left like maddened swallows of the night, daring you to get in their way, you in your squat taxi, and you'll get a laugh or a shout, one of those big thick-diphthonged Amsterdam laughs, the deep-lunged teeth-baring indecorous chuckle Rembrandt makes in the double portrait where he poses as the carousing Prodigal Son, Saskia his big-hipped whore on his lap. And the girl will dismount from the bike and stand, impossibly leggy, six feet in her thigh-high boots, bob-cut, leather-jacketed, kohl-eyed, tattooed, an alternation of black and scarlet, and it's all a bit much and never ever enough, not here, not in the city of laughing money and dangerous design. *Welkom in Amsterdam!*

And why was this the clever thing to do? Because after all the night action you go to your high bed in the little hotel by the *gracht*, and after a bit there are no more sounds of smashed bottles or drunken glee or screaming trams bearing the last waiters off home to Muiderpoort, only and always the lap of the water, and you sink into sleep as if barge-born and wake to a Miracle. There it is. Beyond the lace curtains and the table set with freshly boiled egg and brown bread and ham and cheese, *echte ontbijtstuk*. A place from another century; from 1640 to be somewhat more exact, caught in the time-net like a thrashing codfish, only much, much prettier. Nowhere else in the world that I know of – except of course the Other Canal Empire on the Adriatic lagoon – has this uncanny sense of graceful admission to its built memory. And the waters, history, have been kinder (or its magistrates wiser) to Amsterdam than to Venice. The *impoldering*, draining large tracts of the Zuider Zee, creating cultivable, habitable East Flevoland, took away the threat of deluge – only to bring a whole new set of problems, social and ecological, for although the city is not dying or descending into the sea, the balance of marine life has been badly damaged. But you're not going to worry yourself about all that, not this morning when you step outside and face a length of elegant canal houses: vertical, like the girl on the bike but not as broad-beamed, their gables sporting stucco dolphins that ride the roofline billows, the older brick step-gables or the sinuous curved ones shaped like an inverted bell, the *klokgevels*. Directly below them is the iron hook used to pulley up whatever couldn't be taken through the narrow street doors, and beneath the hook the shuttered doors to a loft space to store whatever that might have been: a tall mirror, ebony-framed; a heavy chest, from where it could descend to the room that awaited it. And below the shutters the rectangular, leaded windows, two or three abreast and then another storey of them before the main door, painted in gloss black that when opened would lead you into the front *voorhuis*, its floor chequered black and white, its walls lined at their skirting with tiles; a single low oak buffet, maps and paintings hanging, a many-armed brass chandelier, burnished to an almost golden glow, this hall opening through low doors (*such* low doors for such an elongated people), left and right into smaller *zijkamers*, a few chairs covered in watered damask or plush velvet, and at its far end into a grander receiving *saal* boasting its gold-stamped leather wall coverings, a tall armoire atop which sit Kung Hsi pots. And before you turn round to go down the flight of low stone steps to the street you could swear you caught a swish of petticoats on the tiled floor and the eager padding of a sleek hound.

It will do that to you, the city, pull you up alleys of time. Because the thing about Amstelredam is that no other city in the world rose to fortune *so* quickly and, once arrived, as if glutted with history's benevolence, decided not to push its luck and stayed put. There were 30,000 Amsterdammers around 1600; 200,000 a century later, but also 200,000 or even slightly fewer in 1900. There have been surges of fresh building beyond the late seventeenth century, each with its own architectural imprint. South Amsterdam (through which your car rushed) – *Amsterdam Zuid* – is itself a place of peculiar magic, touched by the genius of Berlage who built the most beautiful Bourse in the world, an encaustic theatre of investment. Inside his building, but also along the façades of the houses and apartments Berlage designed, bricks flow and glide, walls gently swell and dip. So, then, in the heart of the city, here are no skyscrapers, no International Style boxes; and where modernism was given space in the gaps blasted by war, say in the university buildings close to the Waterlooplein, the glass, plaster and brick and steel wear the aspect of intimate merriment, which is – in case you hadn't figured it by now – the style of the *stad*.

Amsterdam has an undeserved reputation for modest understatement. It's no Las Vegas, but it's always blown its own trumpet whenever it could, as if not quite believing its luck. The first full-on eulogy to its glories of untold wealth, fame, freedom was Johannes Pontanus's *Rerum et Urbis Amsteldodamensium*, published in 1614, when the city was, compared to what it would become, relatively small beer. Twenty-four years later the city officially received Marie de Medici, the Queen Mother of France, estranged from her son Louis XIII and his government dominated by Cardinal Richelieu. She had been the subject of the most spectacular cycle of allegorical paintings ever made by a Netherlandish artist, albeit a Catholic Fleming, Peter Paul Rubens, in which she features as omnipotent, omniscient, all-benevolent quasi-deity. But in 1638, although greeted with triumphal arches, firework displays, swaggering parades of the militia companies, masques staged on floating islands, processions and banquets, and though celebrated by the city orator, Caspar van Baerle, for the 'quality of her blood and that of her ancestors', that distinction was evidently equalled if not surpassed by 'the greatness of this city in trade . . . the good fortune and happiness of her citizens'. Since the gravamen of the accusations against the Queen Mother in her own country was that, in spite of Rubens's best efforts, she had brought none of those blessings to her own realm, the back-handed compliment could not have gone unnoticed.

But soon, Marie, like most of those who came to Amsterdam in the golden seventeenth century, was too busy shopping to care, haggling like an old hand with the merchants. And because Amsterdam had indeed become the *emporium mundi*, there was nowhere else she needed to go to buy anything her queenly heart desired: spices and ceramics from the Orient; perfumed tobacco from America; steel and leather from Iberia (for being at war with Spain was no bar to doing business with its traders); Turkey rugs, Persian silks; Russian sable; or perhaps even an exotic animal for a princely menagerie, one of the lions or elephants Rembrandt sketched.

But Amsterdam's spectacular fortunes were built on provisioning the bulky commonplace needs, not just the luxuries, of seventeenth-century Europe. Before it could become the place you went to buy Malacca cloves or Brazilian emeralds, it was the place that supplied wheat, rye, iron, cured fish, linens, salt, tar, hemp and timber for markets near and far. Why would you go there if you were, say, from

Norwich or Augsburg, rather than just have the things shipped directly from source? Because you knew they would be available and cheaper. And why was that? Because Amsterdam's merchants had understood that the key to market domination was the transformation of shipping. So they had used their accumulation of capital (the Amsterdam Exchange Bank was established in 1609, the first year of a twelve-year truce with Spain) to finance an extraordinary interlocking system of shipbuilding and bulk carrying. Whole Norwegian forests were bought in advance; harvests of Polish rye likewise, many years in advance, in return for making money immediately available to hard-pressed landowners. Timber, hemp – the wherewithal needed to build a fleet – were consigned to the satellite towns and villages in the countryside north of the city, where each specialised in a particular stage of shipbuilding; some in the yards on the Zaan, as carpenters; others as anchorsmiths, others still as canvas- and sail-makers. The makings of ships, designed to be sailed with smaller crew, and to maximise cargo space, were then brought by barges down to the shipyards on the IJ and the Amstel. Whether a venture was off to the Baltic, to the White Sea or to the Mediterranean, the voyage could be accomplished at a freight cost that made it impossible for merchant fleets to compete. And so the world came to Amsterdam to do its shopping and to take in the outrageousness of a city built to sate the appetites.

But it might also come for freedom. More than anywhere else in the world, Amsterdam and the Dutch saw that becoming a world city – providing living space for those who were confined to ghettos elsewhere, or who were allowed only a clandestine life – Jews, Mennonites, Muslims – was also good for business. Sefardi Jews in particular brought with them from their half-life as Marranos in the Spanish world a great chain of personal and commercial connections from the tobacco and sugar colonies of the Atlantic, to the great bazaars of the Maghreb. In Amsterdam they became (as they could not in Venice) merchant princes of the city, allowed to build spectacular synagogues and handsome dwellings in the heart of the Christian metropolis. Amsterdam became the hub of liberty in other ways, too – the centre of a free printing press and international book trade.

By the time that Jacob van Campen's great Town Hall, with its Maid of Peace holding her olive branch over the Dam, was completed in the 1660s, and the rotunda topped off, did the 'regents' of the great families who dominated Amsterdam politics – the Huydecopers, de Graaffs, Backers and Corvers – believe all this would last for ever, that somehow a great mercantile empire would be immune from the laws of hubris that had laid low others of that ilk to whom they constantly compared themselves – Carthage and Tyre and, more recently, Venice? If endurance as the unrivalled world city were just a matter of business, they could be confident of their staying power. But that was never the case. Immense riches generated envy, fear and hatred from neighbours. Even within the United Provinces and the state of Holland, there were plenty who despised Amsterdam's habit of throwing its weight around; wanted the republic to be as strong in land power as Amsterdam insisted it should be at sea; and who thought the great city's pragmatism a drag-weight on building a secure state. In 1650 the Stadholder William II had actually marched on Amsterdam to impose his will on the imperial city. But providence had, at least temporarily, smiled on Amsterdam. The Prince of Orange's soldiers got lost in a fog; the siege was barely begun and the Stadholder died shortly thereafter, precipitating an anti-dynastic coup in which the decentralised nature of 'Holland's Freedom' was institutionalised.

There was no sudden Carthaginian destruction (although the incursion of Louis XIV's armies into the republic in 1672, combined with an English naval attack, came close to it). If you went to Amsterdam in the middle of the eighteenth century, you might have noticed more beggars and street whores; the houses of correction full, and as the poor got poorer, the rich swaggered in a more international way, with stone facings, pedimented and pilastered, Frenchified double-doored buildings on the canal houses; more in the way of perruques and Italian singing masters catering to the plutocrats. But in most essentials, the lives of Amsterdammers, copiously fed, riotously entertained, went on in much the same way. Voltaire may have been churlish to the place where he could get published, calling Holland the land of '*canaux, canailles et canards*'. But there was still true grandeur, bravery and business in the printing of freedom.

It was only the long, grim wars of the French Revolution and Napoleonic periods that sent the city, for a while, into smoky obscurity and hardship. Amsterdam became something the regents of the golden age could never have imagined: a poor city, a church-mouse commonwealth; cheese and beggary. The *klokkenspel* carillons still sounded from the graceful church spires, but the clamour of the place had — temporarily — faded. For a while, during the decade of the Batavian Republic from 1795 to 1805, there was an upsurge of patriotic euphoria, a sense of the city taken back from the regents by its citizens. But as the brutal reality of Amsterdam's subjection to French military needs became apparent, that optimism disappeared in the mundane desperation of survival. The 'wonder of the world' — the Town Hall — was converted to become a palace for the younger brother of Napoleon, King Louis, who surprised the Emperor by taking to his people so enthusiastically that he became Koning Lodewijk.

Amsterdam had bent history to its purposes, but an age of mass mobilisation and munitions was rolling over Holland. The city suffered the most humiliating of all fates: quaintness. It became, in the nineteenth century, a cosy nook of Europe: tulips, clogs, skaters, pot-bellied stoves, pancakes and street organs; old boys in flat caps puffing at their pipes while barges filled with nothing anyone cared about drifted along from one more important place to another. For a long while its luck lay in not unduly inconveniencing the Big Boys; not getting in their way; doing them the occasional favour in regard to banks, diamonds, cigars, Indonesian rubber. Live and let live. But then there were some Big Boys who took offence at this very principle and who wanted, for example, Holland's Jews not to live. But what is so thrilling amidst the tragic horror of the great war memoirs — and if you've read Anne Frank then you must also read another masterpiece of resolution, Etty Hillesum's *Interrupted Life* — is the unquenchable sense of breeze-driven vitality, standing against the guns and the gas; something sweet waiting for its moment of rebirth.

That sweetness did burst forth again after the war, and how it exploded! Long delayed to shelter the pearly old city, a technological revolution happened and Holland and Amsterdam went from sleepy cuteness to explosive modernism in the wink of an eye. Quaintness disappeared and sharpness rushed in. Suddenly, Amsterdam was at the cutting edge of design, architecture, painting, writing. In the Sixties only London could rival the Dutch city for no-holds-barred creative mayhem, the old and the new hooked up on a dope-happy blind date. The club where you went to hear hard rock amidst swaying, sweating bodies was just off the Leidseplein and since it was housed in a disused church was called, naturally, the Paradiso.

Amsterdam once more revelled in a cosmopolitanism that looked out towards the world without ever forfeiting its intricate, domestic peculiarity. How was it — and the rest of the Netherlands — to know what was coming? That was: anger, hatred, murder; the unforeseen blow-back of precisely the liberal pluralism that, as a matter of principle, had kept its hands off the Muslim culture that moved into the city along with mass immigration. All of Amsterdam's traditions predisposed the city to believe that Turks and Moroccans would subscribe to the mutual toleration, the easy-going heterogeneity that had been at the centre of the city's culture since the seventeenth century. And that the habit of Amsterdammers to take ferocious satire, pungent polemics, on the chin would extend to this latest generation of citizens. Those assumptions died the death with Theo van Gogh's knife-pierced body lying in an Amsterdam street, assassinated by a Muslim zealot for making a film savagely and, in his eyes, indecently critical of the strictures of his religion. I've known the great, beautiful, raucous city for more than forty years and this is the first time that its humanism is on the defensive against competing waves of fear and fury.

But this too will pass, I believe. Amsterdam has endured fire and flood, armies sent to besiege it; an army of brutal occupation. It has always been able to sponge up trouble and wring it out again. Long after this essay is published, long after its author has been forgotten, there will still be crowds spilling out on to the evening streets, smoking, drinking and laughing while a carillon chimes and a convoy of bikes bounces along the cobbles, pedalled by the sheer elation of being an Amsterdammer.

Washington DC

An abridged version of this essay was published in John Julius Norwich's, *The Great Cities in History*, 2009

Are there any city avenues more inhumanly broad than those of Washington DC? For they are not really boulevards at all, these immense expanses at the centre of the institutional city. There are no sidewalk cafés with coffee-drinkers whiling away the time as they check out the evening strollers – and for the reason that there are no strollers. What there are, are Visitors to Our Nation's Capital, disgorged from tour buses, pointed at the Smithsonian Air and Space Museum, or the Washington Monument, and gathered up again when their business is done. Even new buildings like the East Wing of the National Gallery, perfectly beautiful on the interior, manage to have a broad, low stepped plaza in front of them, complete with massively monumental sculpture that sucks all human life out of the space. Bow your head, revere, and enter the temple; so the message goes. Mandatory solemnity at the expense of the human swarm was there right from the beginning. The engineer who drew up the first plan, Pierre Charles l'Enfant, prescribed avenues not less than 160 feet wide. That's what you get when you hire a French classicist; someone who doesn't notice that the place gets broiling in the summer and for whom narrower, densely tree-shaded streets might have been a kinder idea that might have encouraged some ease of street life. But what l'Enfant valued in his royal prospects were (in his endearingly strangled English) 'reciprocity of sight, variety of pleasant ride and being to ensure a rapide intercourse with all the part of the city which they will serve as does the main vains in the animal body to diffuse life through smaller vessels in quickening the active motion of the heart'.

Washington does have its true neighbourhoods where the beehive hums, people sit on stoops in the spring sunshine, and wander in and out of bars and jazzy cafés; where you can eat anything from

Ethiopian to Brazilian – Adams Morgan, for instance, where in season there is even a fine farmers' market, fruit and vegetables trucked in from farms in Maryland, Pennsylvania and Virginia, a reminder that there is true country out beyond the beltway. Or around U Street where African-American Washington comes alive near the Duke Ellington Theater. And the sense of a vast bureau-cratic-punditocratic savannah is broken by Washington's bosky places, the parks and gardens laid out after the recommendations of the McMillan Commission at the turn of the century. In Rock Creek Park joggers jog (although muggers mug); the Zoo nearby is where Washingtonians come as families, and the gardens of Dumb-arton Oaks, Harvard's institute of medieval and Byzantine studies, is shared between the philosophically contemplative and the bliss-fully amorous. But most of the young people who make up the clientele and who come to love the place aren't there because of the romance of the city, but because they need to live in an idea made architecturally visible: the idea of democratic government. That is at the beating heart of the place; the pulse of its body politic, but that same notion is also why 'Washington' in some quarters of Amer-ican life is not so much an actual city as a byword for bureaucratic remoteness and self-importance.

Its problems and its many genuine splendours are both products of the original split personality of the American Republic. For Thomas Jefferson (who nonetheless seized the opportunity to be President with robust eagerness), the true America lay in the myriad farms where the yeomen citizens, whom he believed were the life-blood of democracy, were building a truly new society and polity. George Washington, whose own plantation farm, Mount Vernon, is just fourteen miles south of the District, was more ambiguous. On the one hand, he too was averse to empty pomp; on the other hand, it mattered deeply to him that the United States hold its head high in a world of vainglorious monarchies; that a capital city, like the Roman Republic, be the visi-ble expression not just of the parity, but of the superiority of a democratic constitution. It helped foster those dreams of the New Rome that the eventual site had running through it a mucky creek grandly known as the Tiber. Washington, the city, is in fact very much the vision of Washington the man. Dolly Madison, the fourth President's wife, knew this when, on the approach of the British in 1814, she took a knife to Gilbert Stuart's beautiful portrait of Washington, cut it from its frame, rolled it and made haste with it to the soldiers' camp where she spent the night on the run from the invaders, watching the horizon flame with the ruins of the town.

The very characteristic of which self-designated conservatives (many established in Washington think tanks) complain – the artificiality of the city, its detachment from anything resembling a self-sustaining commercial economy – was precisely the reason why George Washington wanted such a capital in the first place. Metropolitan wens like London and Paris, were, he and Thomas Jefferson thought, the breeding places of idle fashion, vice and corruption. But a nation founded on the majesty of the people ought to have a great city custom-designed as a residence for democratic institutions. The relationship between the independent legislature and the governing executive, for example, ought to be made visible by their mile-long separation at opposite ends of Pennsylvania Avenue; the two, however, always in each other's sight. It was an American thing to ensure that it would be the legislature, not any executive residence, that would be the elevated structure, sitting on its eighty-foot hill, watching over the servants of the government beneath, keeping them accountable.

The very notion of a federal city originally came from necessity as much as ideology. Because of the moving theatre of peril during the revolutionary war, the itinerant Congress had shifted no fewer than eight times, and had sat in places as various as York Pennsylvania, Trenton New Jersey and the academic Nassau Hall at Princeton. To have a single, defensible site, perhaps no more than ten square miles, where law and governance were published and treasury accounts cleared, was obviously essential to the integrity and efficiency of government. A decision was taken almost as soon as the war was over in 1783, but a protracted debate then ensued as to where that site should be. The criteria were a location on a navigable river, but sufficiently far inland to be protected from the naval raids the founding fathers expected of the British – or, indeed, their ex-allies the French. The mid-Atlantic suggested itself as arbitrating between the already conflicting claims of the great sectional interests of the new republic – industrial, high-minded New England and the plantation slave world of the South. Two choice sites were on the Delaware in New Jersey or on the Potomac at the line separating Maryland and Virginia.

But even those choices were thought to favour, respectively, northern and southern preferences, so that for a few weeks two capitals, one on each site, were seriously contemplated, at least until Francis Wilkinson, in a burst of inspired ridicule, proposed building a gigantic trolley that could wheel the capital and its archives from one place to the other, along with an equestrian statue of Washington. Ultimately it was Washington himself – who had begun his career as a land surveyor – whose firm preference was for a city on the Potomac, surrounded by gentle hills and, as he thought, blessed with a benign climate, who decided the matter. When the land was plotted he rode it himself, charting its topography and imagining where, amidst the farmland and the river valley, would arise the grand buildings and monuments that would embody the vital social virtues of working democracy.

For a detailed plan Washington, in 1790, turned to Pierre Charles l'Enfant, a French military engineer who had been honourably wounded at the siege of Charleston (where the French lost the city) and had become a kind of official artist to the Continental Army. Not surprisingly l'Enfant's vision was formed by classical French urbanism from the reigns of the Sun King and Louis XV: central *grandes places*, each embellished with statuary, obelisks and monuments from which broad radial avenues would extend, along which the edifices of government would be aligned – Treasury, Department of War, Post Office (*very* important in the early Republic), Patent Office, etc. The Potomac and its Great Falls outside the city would provide (possibly by making more of the Tiber) a chain of watercourses, so that Washington would not just resemble classical Paris, but a little bit of Venice and Rome too, with a cascade falling down Capitol Hill and feeding handsome canals. Though l'Enfant ran foul of Congress, and the execution of a much-modified plan was carried out by the less grandiose Andrew Ellicott, much of his essential vision – the emblematic separation and connection of executive and legislature; the eminence of the latter, the gentility of the former; as well as those immense avenues – survived. It was the other great Enlightenment mind, that of Jefferson, who had the idea of calling the intersecting streets by letters and numbers and who made sure that both l'Enfant and Ellicott were supplied with plans of all the great European cities from Strasbourg to Amsterdam.

By 1800, when Jefferson moved into the President's House, there were just 3,000 inhabitants of the federal district, of whom a third were slave and free blacks. The House itself, resembling 'a country gentleman's dwelling' according to one visitor, already had its little colonnade and modest park and the East Room planned for state receptions, but most of it was unfinished. Abigail Adams, the first First Lady to attempt to run the House, complained of the expense of heating and lighting and the difficulty of finding thirty reliable servants who could be entrusted with its management. The Capitol was being built by the Boston architect Charles Bulfinch, who had created the domed Massachusetts State House and who provided for the nation's legislature another dome flanked by two pavilions. The ensemble when built was grand by American standards but, as the Republic grew, not ceremonious enough, resembling, as one wag put it, 'an upside-down sugar bowl between two tea chests'.

After the British burned Washington in the summer of 1814, it took time before rebuilding got under way, the eager and scientifically minded John Quincy Adams providing much of the impetus. But for decades Washington was jeered at in much of the country as the 'great Serbonian Bog' – a place of 'streets without buildings' – while its neighbour, the busy port of Georgetown, had 'buildings without streets'. The climate was more brutal than the First President imagined; mosquitoes devoured the population in the fetid summer; the water supply was foul and prone to delivering cholera to the city rather than the graceful torrents and limpid basins l'Enfant had envisioned. Hogs wandered the Mall, and at some distance from the grandeur, rickety taverns and disorderly houses made their contribution to the city's peculiar mix of solemnity and squalor; the emblems of liberty and the reality – in the persons of the unfree without whom the place would never have functioned – of slavery. Washington literally, but barely, held the line between two Americas rather than symbolising its unity.

And then in the early 1850s there arrived in town one of the most prodigious and still relatively unknown American heroes, the army engineer who as Quartermaster General of the Union would win the Civil War for the North quite as decisively as Lincoln, Grant and Sherman. Montgomery Meigs was first and foremost a builder. His spectacular brick Romanesque temple-like structure of the Pensions Building (created in the 1870s to provide welfare for old soldiers and memorialise the fallen), now the Buildings Museum, is one of the most extraordinary architectural achievements in the entire country. But it was Meigs who, throwing an immense masonry span over one gorge and an iron bridge over Rock Creek, created the aqueduct that carried, at last, a decent supply of fresh water (also imperative for the extinguishing of fires) from the Great Falls of the Potomac to the city. It was Meigs too, a regular tartar when it came to coming down hard on the dubious businessmen who saw in the growth of the District an opportunity for fat profits, who presided over the rebuilding of the Capitol to its present appearance and magnitude, and who replaced the Bulfinch sugar bowl with something taken instead from Brunelleschi, Michelangelo and Wren, but which had an iron fabric just in case the British decided to set fire to it again.

During the Civil War, Washington became a barracks — almost 100,000 troops camped there; bivouacs on the Mall, soldiers amidst the hogs and geese (for they had no intention of moving); beef and milk cattle grazing. In July 1864 the invalids and veterans under Meigs's command had to man forts and trenches at the advance of General Jubal Early, who, however, never made it. The wounded and mutilated were carried in carts and barges from the two battles of Bull Run, and some of those who perished were buried, on Meigs's orders, on the confiscated land of his former friend, Robert E. Lee, up on Arlington Heights. Meigs and Lincoln were always anxious that if the Confederacy took the Heights they would have a direct line of fire on both the White House and the Capitol, so that turning the proprietorial gentility of the Lee estate into the first national cemetery became, for them both, a matter of strategy as well as national symbolism.

Modern Washington, though, came to be in the years around the turn of the century. It was then that the old federal government buildings were replaced by the masonry-faced piles that house the Treasury, the Department of State and the rest. Every so often there were wonderful, eccentric exceptions like the Gothic Smithsonian 'castle' — the result of a legacy offered (and accepted by Congress in 1846) by English scientist James Smithson as an 'establishment for the increase of knowledge among men', a rubric sufficiently broad to extend, now, to fighter planes and space capsules as well as historical artefacts and treasures of American technology and invention. The Corcoran Gallery was intended as Washington's first art gallery, but the Beaux Arts building, designed by one of the city's mavericks, Renwick, stayed unrealised as its Confederate-leaning patron sat out the war from the safety of Paris. By the end of the century, the Corcoran and the Freer were home to spectacular collections, but it was only with the gifts of the Secretary of the Treasury, Andrew Mellon, and the Widener dynasty that the immense National Gallery was finally established on a scale befitting the collections in the 1930s. And the great memorial monuments that bookend the axis of the Mall – Washington, Lincoln and Jefferson – and which, for most visitors, along with the Capitol and the White House, *are* the 'Nation's Capital', took a long time coming. A Washington memorial of some sort was mooted almost as soon as the General-President was dead, at the end of 1799; and before long the idea of an equestrian statue was scrapped for a grander mausoleum, to house his remains, from which some sort of column or obelisk would sprout. The reluctance of the owner of Mount Vernon to release the sacred relics, the usual squabbling of interested parties *in situ*, and above all the cost of the structure meant that it took a century before, in 1885, the obelisk in its finished state was formally opened. Lincoln's great memorial with the seated figure sculpted by Daniel Chester French, the bare temple-like space decorated with the fallen hero's words and friezes of the emancipation of the slaves, was likewise a creation of the second half of the nineteenth century.

And now everyone wants a monument in Washington. Franklin Roosevelt, who specified he did *not* want one, got one anyway. A major memorial to the fallen of the Second World War, also on the Mall, is still being hotly debated. But sometimes a convergence of national passion and inspired design takes place and something gets built that transcends its own materials to become a place of true communing. Such of course is the profoundly eloquent Vietnam memorial created by Maya Lin: a basalt wall in a cut trench that rises and falls with the body count and the grief of the country.

Though Boston and New York have been my home towns, I feel I know this city well. I remember crossing the grilling breadth of Pennsylvania Avenue in 1964 to see an Assistant Secretary of Labor who became a friend and mentor, and who would well up in an impassioned Irish way at the thought of the slain Jack Kennedy not a year before; I remember the jazz piano bars in the tougher end of town around M Street and 14th; the rising hemispherical walls of Watergate; my first astounded sally into the glory of the Library of Congress Reading Room, as welcoming to a young student as the British Museum Reading Room (then) was chilly and difficult. I went back last year each week in November to give the Mellon Lectures at the National Gallery, beginning to make the white grandeur of Union Station and the amiably shouting directives of the taxi despatchers on the threshhold a kind of homecoming. I have friends, a daughter living there, all happily, all very much settled into the weave of the place; knowing its street corners and park benches, its dogs and ice cream. And there, when the cherry blossom is doing its shameless thing, and the streets of Adams Morgan are warming to the kids on the block, it's entirely possible to see Washington as not just DC, not just ideology made visible, but as an American community; and a good one at that.

Brazil

Financial Times, 22 November 2008

Mid-November . . . so it's spring, or it is in Brazil, which meant that that's where I had to be to get out of the way of autumn in New York: pumpkins, the dirge-like descent of leaves, a lot of suburban happy talk about crisp weather when I'm still lamenting the departure of uncrisp summer, the time of sweaty rot that's my idea of perfect climate. And it was just possible I'd said all I could ever say (for a while, at least) about Barack Obama, so time to change the subject and talk to 800 Brazilians about Picasso and Goya for a change. Well, they had asked for it.

'They' were the benevolent patrons of a university seminar in Porto Alegre, right on the southern border with Argentina and Uruguay, called 'Boundaries of Thought', across which, I assumed, one was invited to stride. Camille Paglia, a boundary-crosser if ever there was one, had been there last year talking about sex in art — for two-and-a-half hours, the sponsors said. They looked at me earnestly as they said it and winced, I thought, at that much sex from Professor Paglia. But my subject was calamity and an hour of that seemed more than enough.

I had been to Brazil ten years before to promote the translation of *Landscape and Memory* and was easily infatuated. Glimpses of heaven and hell opened up: tall women glided on the street rather than walked, as if they were tuning up their samba moves; herons and egrets nested amid sewage and detergent scum on the canal between the airport and São Paulo; the innocent intensity of journalists wanting to be told the history of a free press in Britain when they were still cagey about liberating theirs after the military dictatorship; being trapped happily in the embrace of an immense hulk of a man, glittering with sequins, who grinned and said: 'I am Roberto, king of the *favela*, now you must come and talk to us . . .'

'*Sim!*' I said, 'yes!', while my publisher, a sweet but fretful soul, swung his head from side to side while rolling his eyes (no small feat even for a Brazilian), which I gathered was a no. Despondent, Roberto planted a juicy kiss full on my mouth, which was a first for a book tour, but did nothing to alter the publisher's irrevocable ban. In Rio, at Ipanema, long-legged kids booted footballs on the beach while others demanded money when you parked the car, promising to 'look after it' – the alternative being not worth thinking about.

Oh, yes, I love Brazil, but Porto Alegre was different: less tropical; more, sigh, European. There is much talk about the Germans and the Italians who came there, and on to the plane came a pack of the former, drunk at noon; planting themselves wherever seats seemed to beckon, despising mere boarding-pass seat assignment; mighty shouts of 'Markus' and 'Thomas' roaring down the aisles for no particular reason anyone could make out except as an expression of *Kameradschaft* in the southern hemisphere. The plane skirted the Atlantic coast, breakers curling below while the flight attendants pretended to have run out of beer.

Porto Alegre is an instantly appealing place, foaming with blue jacaranda blossoms, merry with sidewalk cafés set between nineteenth-century Brazilian town houses, their gables as curly as a gaucho's whiskers with snazzy touches of crimson or gold paint. It was Sunday, which meant, even in the Sheraton, that *feijoada* was on; a gamut of darkly stewed meats together with the *manioc farofa* I remember loving on that first trip and did again: it's fluffy and gritty at the same time, which doesn't sound enticing, but somehow is. In the park, a boy pulled out his guitar and sang samba to impress, while a circle of capoeira devotees went through their clambering motions to a dull drum beat.

A book fair was in swing; not the kind boasting marquee events with the usual suspects, but a pretty, shady plaza laid out with fifty or so stalls, each the size of a *bouquiniste*, displaying the wares of local publishers and booksellers. The organisers were proud of the egalitarian principle, and it was astonishing in the age when the death of print is prematurely announced to find a smallish Brazilian city where little presses seemed to be around every corner. Charles Kiefer, the handsome professor with whom we had lunch, walked us over to one of the stalls and showed us the thirty-odd volumes that collected the fiction of his students. Another year, another volume, and the professor couldn't have been happier. If Brazilian fiction were ever in danger, it wouldn't be his fault. Myself, I was reading *The Adventures and Misadventures of Maqroll*, novellas by the Colombian author Alvaro Mutis so richly, spectacularly, sensually wondrous that you hate him for ever stopping. 'Ah,' said Kiefer, 'so good', as if he had filled his mouth with fine wine, and then, sighing a little, thought I might, in that case, enjoy a small exhibition over at the local bank devoted to Gilberto Freyre. Freyre! I hadn't thought about him for forty-odd years: a poet among historians; a romancer of the Brazilian difference: slavery and the Casa Grande, somehow made less brutal by miscegenation; the cradle of a mixed-blood culture. Oh sure. Samba slavery. Doesn't count. I had wised up to the fantasy a long time ago, but there was, nonetheless, something wickedly beautiful about Freyre's dreamy writing, and the show beneath the stained-glass ceiling advertising 'Prudence', 'Enterprise' and such like unerringly harvested the spell. Displays of Freyre's tropically coloured paintings were set above trays of sand; peeling cabinets with drawers were opened to reveal faded banquet menus, dog-eared photographs and diary entries. You entered the whole thing through the skirts of a giant carnival mannequin. Another Brazilian seduction; and I could feel my portion of northern scepticism draining away into the gentle afternoon.

The lecture was delivered: a generously receptive 800, most of whom seemed to want to ask questions, and most of them did. Eventually our hosts ushered us off to an upscale French restaurant where it would have been churlish to turn down the foie gras. It wasn't until our last night in São Paulo that we were taken, by Marcello Dantas, the designer of many of Brazil's most brilliant museums and exhibitions, to a place that boasted serious native cooking: Amazon fish ('neither salt nor freshwater,' said Dantas, beaming, 'just packed with big river nutrients'); fresh hearts of palm, warm and silky on the tongue; stupendously subtle banana ice cream (a contradiction in terms, but go figure). The place is called Brasil a Gosto. It's better than anywhere in London.

If you fly in to São Paulo from another Brazilian city, you'll land (if you use the local airport) in a startling place: bristling with tower blocks set close and white like the model for *Blade Runner*; a city 120 kilometres across; piled up *favela* slums; stunning fashion by designers such as Rosa Cha and Gloria Coelho, who does things with sequins that I can't begin to explain in the *Financial Times*. And yet, this wild, teeming antheap of a place has no billboards. The mayor, Gilberto Kassab, a Syrian-Paulista, decided they were 'visual pollution' and gave owners thirty days to get rid of them. The fine for failing to do so was 10,000 reals (about £2,500) a day. So the place throbs along beneath its pall of traffic fumes; just eleven million Paulistas trying to get to the end of the week. A place for heroes.

On the way back to New York, my nose in Alvaro Mutis's journeyings of *Maqroll the Lookout*, I'd look out myself to the fading shoreline of the tropic forest and feel wistful. Brazil is one of the places where your nerve-endings work overtime and you never want them to stop their dancing little hum and buzz.

Back in the Hudson Valley, everything decelerated. The farmers' market at the local train station was loaded with good stuff. People bustled autumnally, chirpy with the delight of a fine new president.

Comedy Meets Catastrophe:
On the Korean DMZ

Financial Times, 25 September 2009

On a late-summer afternoon, the last frontier of the Cold War, the Military Demarcation Line dividing the two Koreas, is picture-perfect: a romantic landscape painter's dream, provided of course you block out the barbed-wire fence running along the summit of the high hills. Indifferent to history, the dragonflies that are everywhere in Korea bob and flutter around the gun nests. A hundred metres down the steep hillside, the Imjin River loops through idyllic country which, fifty-nine years ago, was cratered with mortar fire. On the south bank, woods tangled with wild grape grow to the river's edge. The north bank, though, is deforested, and the South Korean soldiers at the observation post tell you this is not just for a clearer path of fire for their communist enemies, but to deter defections by their own men.

From time to time, soldiers from the North Korean People's Army come to the river to catch fish for their supper, or hunt the wild boar roaming the few coppices left on their side. The pigs scavenge trash discarded by the South Korean outposts, so that indirectly, courtesy of the porkers, the south feeds the north. Without the self-provisioning, so the South Koreans humorously say of their enemy counterparts, it's bark and grass soup for dinner. A North Korean invasion, they imply, is held at bay less by their barbed wire than by the fear that should the People's Army ever make it to Seoul, it would head straight for Burger King and not come out for a week.

Smugness aside, it's hard not to notice a telling contrast between the eroded, barren uplands to the north and the brilliant green rice and corn fields to the south. Local farmers here who found themselves trapped in the Demilitarised Zone are subsidised by the Joint Security Agency (United Nations and South Korea), and their land swept of the millions of mines left behind by the Chinese during their advances in the grim war of 1950–53. No pesticides are allowed on these crops, so 'DMZ' rice, the military will tell you, is the most fragrant in all of Korea.

Et in Arcadia ego. An island of gourmet organic rice surrounded by landmined woodlands sums up the bizarre adjacence between prosperity and paranoia that is the Korean front line. And as the Clinton mission which last month sprung two American women journalists from twelve years' hard (not to mention the occasional nuclear underground test) reminds us, sixty years after the war that few outside the region remember, Korea still matters. It's the zombie war that won't lie down and it's still ravenous for trouble. The Korean question is both relic and omen; an ideological conflict preserved in aspic and the hottest of hot sauces for a hard-pressed US president and his over-stretched military. Kim Jong-Il, the self-styled Dear Leader, is fond of reminding the world that his missiles can reach California. This should be a joke, but it isn't. Every time Pyongyang pounds its chest, Tokyo grins, but nervously.

Up at Observation Post Typhoon, a monarch butterfly, bigger than a humming bird, alights on a hemp sack dumped at the foot of the barbed wire. The good-natured soldier escorting us while we shoot footage for a documentary about Obama's foreign-policy challenges tells me the sacking contains a cluster bomb. Every two months or so, a lightning bolt from one of the big storms that roll through the mountains will set one off. 'The first time that happened I thought the war had started . . .'

On this late August day the servicemen seem more battle-ready to fight swine flu than the million soldiers of the KPA stationed the other side of the Demilitarised Zone. We pass platoons of them, sitting in trucks, their faces covered in protective sky-blue masks. They ask politely if they might take our temperature, a procedure they themselves observe four times a day. A soldier slides a thermometer under my armpit and, five minutes later, announces that I am in the best of health.

Comedy rubbing shoulders with catastrophe is on even more theatrical display fifty kilometres to the west at Panmunjom, where the United Nations Command Military Armistice Commission (UNCMAC) has had its base since the cessation of hostilities in 1953. Private First Class Anthony Hauch from Philadelphia reminds us –

easy ballpark cheer coming from his film-star looks – that, notwith-standing its official demilitarisation, we are in an Active Combat Zone. 'If you feel like getting off the bus and taking a leak at the side of the road, don't.' Those landmines, five million of them, are waiting for the unsuspecting. Do they, we ask, ever go off? 'Oh sure, they're Soviet old-style, pretty unstable. The deer land on them now and again.'

Those ancient minefields are not the only thing about the fifty-six-year armistice that's unstable. Every few years there is an 'incident' that sobers up the absurdity. In 1976 a tree-trimming patrol, deemed by the North Koreans to have violated the armistice, was attacked by a military axe gang, two officers hacked to death. Though Private Hauch won't say when the most recent 'incident' was, he hints that they are not infrequent. The Chinooks parked on the helipad look ready for action and the small troop of UN soldiers stay on high alert because of a not-unfounded sense that Kim Jong-Il can't be relied on to play by the usual rules, especially if reports of his ill health are true and a power struggle for succession is about to ensue.

For Kim Jong-Il wears the uniform of a Maoist, but runs his office like a gangster. Drug trafficking and counterfeiting supply revenue for the nuclear game. In an infuriated response to the UN's denunciation of this May's underground test (approximately the same grade as that dropped on Hiroshima), the Dear Leader declared on 27 May that North Korea was no longer bound by the armistice – which means, technically, that the war between North Korea and the UN has now gone hot.

Still, it's hard to go trembly two kilometres away on the actual *Duck Soup* character of the ritualised mutual nose-thumbing. It would need a combo of Joseph Heller, Voltaire and Jaroslav Hašek (the author of *The Good Soldier Svejk*) to do justice to its madness. Negotiations for the original armistice and any discussion of infringements are conducted in long low huts, painted respectively blue for the UN and aluminium silver for the North Koreans. Two large buildings face off in emblematic hostility. Ours, the South Korean, known as 'Freedom House', sports granite floors, polished chrome and glass doors. Theirs – optimistically named 'Welcome House' – is a number assembled from the Leonid Brezhnev Album of Architectural Style. When the Freedom House was seen to stand taller than its opposite number, the North Koreans lodged a protest and added a glass-walled storey to theirs. South Korean guards stand behind the blue huts, precisely half of their helmeted heads hidden by the walls, the other half exposed to the foe, fists clenched at their side, as if auditioning for a martial-arts movie. Their opposite numbers prowl the Welcome terrace, stopping to brandish a pair of aggressive binoculars in our direction. But, from the roof of Freedom House, you can peer through much bigger binoculars at them glaring right back at us. I must regretfully report that the enemy has a definite edge in tactical glowering.

All this is so fabulously loony, a living museum of Cold War craziness, that one has to remind oneself that behind the mutually assured scowling there is, in fact, something profoundly serious at stake, the moral significance of which is not depleted by its repetition in the mouths of blow-hard politicians, namely the price to be paid for the survival of freedom.

The sentry boxes beside the motorway that runs south along the Han River to Seoul might seem peripheral to the life or death of one of the most vibrant and complicated political societies in all of Asia, but they are not. No one believes the KPA is about to pour down Route 77 to the capital. But the point of North Korean military bluster is to remind the US – and probably Russia and China too – that as a mischief-maker, the last true communist dictatorship (not counting life-support Cuba), the country can create havoc, whether through covert relationships with terrorists, insurgent forces taking on the US in west Asia or outright anti-American governments like Iran.

Remote and esoteric though the Korean story may seem, it still represents a tutorial in the purposes and legitimacy of using military power to enable, protect and stabilise fragile democracies far from the West. As he ponders his narrowing options in Iraq and Afghanistan, Barack Obama could do worse than to ponder Korea's modern history. In January 1950, Harry Truman's usually canny Secretary of State Dean Acheson neglected to include Korea in a statement about the perimeter of indispensable defence in east Asia. This was the green light that allowed Kim Il-Sung and his patrons Stalin and Mao to believe North Korea could overrun the South without serious opposition. Truman's decision to send troops and the UN commitment to resist aggression amounted to a belief that the credibility of the American shield for the democracies emerging after the Second World War, in Europe, Asia and above all in Japan, would not survive the fall of South Korea.

Was Truman wrong? The war that ground to a bitter stalemate in 1953 took 36,000 American lives, tens of thousands of other UN troops, and 353,000 Korean military on both sides, as well as 2.5 million Korean civilians. It was, as David Halberstam reminds us in *The Coldest Winter* (2007), a pitiless horror. And, after it was over, it was not at all clear that the Korea south of the thirty-eighth parallel that had survived was, in any sense worthy of Truman's rhetoric, a truly free, rather than merely non-communist, state.

Cold War paranoia drove American policy to turn a blind eye to succeeding authoritarian governments in Seoul, and the persecution of any oppositional figures who could be stigmatised as leftist. Only belatedly did the American government come to the aid of champions of civil rights like the late South Korean President Kim Dae-Jung. It took the atrocity of the Kwangju massacre in 1980, and the recoil against the brutal suppression of the democracy movement, for South Koreans to reclaim the true fruits of their liberation. Whatever decisions are taken about the places where American power might be used to shield fledgling electoral democracies in the Middle East and Asia, similar torturous complications are bound to occur there too.

Which may not mean, however, that the effort might not be worth the sacrifice. The contrast between the wretched, cruel and self-eviscerating tyranny in North Korea and the dazzling economic and cultural energy of the South could not be more instructive. Despite the recession, the South Korean economy is a marvel of modern enterprise. Unlike most Western economies, it manufactures globally marketable cars, mobile phones and electronic goods. And if these achievements are bought through depressed labour costs, there's precious little sign of that on a Saturday night in downtown Seoul. The streets are packed with a raucous crowd, mostly young, hitting the espresso bars. Street vendors do a roaring trade, but so do the retailers selling trainers and casual wear, much of it in the juvenile pastels that Koreans seem to enjoy.

The unimpeded right to consume may not exactly be up there with Franklin Roosevelt's Four Freedoms as a reason to commit arms to resist authoritarianism. But the consumption is not just of trainers and jeans: it's the choice to buy or reject religion (church spires are everywhere in South Korea); the right to free and fair elections and to read and speak as one wishes, usually (though not invariably) unthreatened by police. And the right to inject traditional culture with modern temerity.

On a dogstar night in front of the Seoul City Hall, I sat with a big crowd and listened to a thrilling 'new-wave Korean' band – Noreum Machi – deliver new power to traditional percussion. A robed man who beat on an immense hanging vertical drum and four girl drummers delivered a violent and ecstatic sound into the velvety darkness. There was something apt about this explosion of sound for borderline Korea. The drum is the voice of an army, but on that night in that place, it was the beat of jubilant liberty too.

Testing Democracy

9/11

Guardian, 14 September 2001

It came, literally, out of a clear blue sky, one of those eye-poppingly beautiful mornings when you forgive autumn for polishing off summer. All around New York the last rituals of American innocence were being enacted: huddles of mums and dads at the roadside reassuring their seven-year-olds that there was nothing frightening about the big old yellow school bus lumbering towards them. A grey heron was dabbling in the mill pond in our Hudson-valley suburb, oblivious, like the rest of us, to the fact that American history, in the shape of its most irrepressibly ebullient city, and American power, in the shape of its fortress Pentagon, was about to take the hit of its life.

Two nights before, millions had watched the Spielberg-Tom Hanks Second World War TV epic, *Band of Brothers*, based on Steven Ambrose's history of a paratroop company in the Normandy invasion. Like *Saving Private Ryan*, its selling point was supposed to be the unsparing realism of its combat scenes; its willingness to concede pain and terror. Up to a point. The tobacco tint of the images told you this was history, inspirational, consoling. And a history in which everything worked out just fine. Some, at least, of the good guys would make it. And whole nations of bad guys would bite the dust.

The media, reaching for one of their war-horse clichés (the other being sports), were quick to chorus that what happened was beyond the imaginings of the most feverish disaster movie. But the truth is that if the script of Bloody Tuesday had been offered to a studio, it would have been turned down not for the scale of the horror, but for its failure to supply identifiable villains. America's only usable analogy, Pearl Harbor, 7 December 1941, is on everyone's lips, on the streets and in the news studios. But there was no rising sun — nor for that matter a crescent moon — painted on the fuselage of the airplanes which slammed into the World Trade Center on Tuesday. Their markings belonged instead to United Airlines, whose corporate logo welcomes passengers to 'The Friendly Skies'.

Franklin Roosevelt bunched up American anguish and fury in his big meaty fist and smacked it out again as a war launched against an identifiable foe. The high-voltage energy on which American culture runs could be harnessed right away on concrete, practical work. Enlistment lines stretched round the block. Rubber and aluminium drives got under way. Trepidation surrendered to resolution. It was all very clear-cut; the way America likes it.

But this time the go-and-get-em American responses are scrambled by the terrifying diffuseness of the threat and the inconvenience of the enemy not being any sort of discernible nation state. 'Should the President and Congress make a formal declaration of war?' asked one CNN correspondent last night to another. 'Against whom, exactly?' he reasonably replied. She wasn't listening. 'But shouldn't we declare war?' she repeated, pointlessly. 'How about carpet-bombing everything between Jordan and Nepal?' one of my downtown friends who had seen the towers collapse in front of his eyes sardonically asked a belligerent comrade-in-suffering. 'Well, yes, that might take care of it,' was his reply. America, as Alexis de Tocqueville noticed in the mid-nineteenth century, was founded, and runs, on impatience.

Allied to impatience and impetuousness, de Tocqueville thought, was an uncompromising individualism, the American religion of self-sufficiency before which any sense of community would always have to yield. And you would suppose that if self-interest is a national cult on this side of the Atlantic, New York, the Look-at-me metropolis, would be its cathedral. But you'd be wrong. Foreigners – especially perhaps Britons who, on the basis of very little first-hand experience, still think of America as some sort of petulant child liable to throw a thermonuclear tantrum when denied its ice cream – always get New York, not to say the rest of the republic over which they used to fly en route to a ski-lodge in Colorado or the Golden Gate Bridge, wrong. This is a loud city all right, but decibels have nothing to do with decency, or the lack of it, and in the ten years I've been here, I've seen countless acts of spontaneous humanity that belie New York's reputation for callous narcissism.

In our first winter here, we managed to blow a tyre in the midst of a snowstorm, right under the George Washington Bridge, the neighbourhood which at that time richly merited its reputation as the crack capital of the Western world, and with the burned-out hulks of what once had been cars ominously decorating the roadside. But the cops who came to our rescue not only asked what they could do, but went ahead and changed the tyre (perhaps instantly sizing me up as someone seriously challenged in the jack-and-lugnut department). Since then I've seen ordinary New Yorkers go out of their way to help out people who were ill, lost or distressed in street, subway and park.

Don't get me wrong. It's not that this is the real city of angels. It's just that it's a city where people want to be doing, and if good is what has to be done, it gets done. So if there was any doubt that New York wouldn't be able to 'take it' on the chin like blitzed London, or that its citizens were too pampered a bunch to respond to catastrophe with anything but a panicky stampede to save their designer-label jogging shoes, it ought to have been laid to rest, first by the grieving calm which characterised the city and then by the outpouring of mass volunteerism which followed hard on the heels of the inferno. So many lined up quietly to volunteer for anything they could be called on to do that they had to be turned away. Lines formed round the block, waiting for hours to give blood; even when, to everyone's sorrow, there seemed to be precious few to give blood to.

We already have our local heroes and 300 of them are dead – the firemen, police and paramedics who were on the scene attempting to get people out of the World Trade Center when the towers fell on them. Their graves are the twisted remains of fire engines, shrouded, like everything else below 14th Street in a thick pall of grey ash, much of it dense with asbestos. Entire ladder companies disappeared in that holocaust.

Even to card-carrying liberals like me who have sometimes had misgivings about his red-hot temper, Mayor Giuliani changed overnight from Mussolini to Mother Teresa, appearing everywhere, often putting himself in harm's way, to comfort the distraught, encourage the exhausted and, perhaps most important of all (especially at his press conferences), to tell the truth. A more inspiring example of common decency and instinctively practical humanity in public life you could not possibly imagine.

In glaring contrast, George Bush has yet to show his face on the island of Manhattan, lest a sooty cinder or two land on the smoothly shaved presidential chin. New Yorkers, who don't take kindly to being stood up, especially at times like this, are beginning to sound as though they might want to land something else, for all their initial basic instinct to rally round the flag and the man who is supposed to embody it.

Nor has the presidential performance on television been exactly Churchillian. Instead of bringing a traumatised country together as a family, united in shared grief and fortitude; instead of evoking the spirit of American trials past and how the republic has endured them, Bush (or his speechwriters, who need to get out of the East Wing and into the back yards of the bereft) has depended on warmed-up platitudes inherited, like much of the National Security cabinet, from the administration of Poppy and Reagan.

With every repetition of the fighting cliché, 'Make no mistake', the deeper the sinking feeling that neither he nor his administration has a clue about how to reboot their systems away from the comic-book obsession with 'missile defence' to actually protecting America from men with razor blades, box-cutters and Arabic flight-training manuals, much less an elementary degree in anthrax 101.

So instead of listening to cowboy pieties, or endlessly respooling video horror, or seeing in our mind's eye those twin towers as phantom, 110-storey tombstones, we turn to those who do, miraculously, know what they're supposed to say, feel and do: to Jeremy Glick who phoned his wife from the hijacked plane over Pennsylvania to tell her there had been a vote of all the men aboard to try to overpower the hijackers, even though they knew it would cost them all their lives, and who saved who-knows-how-many other lives by doing just that; to the son and daughter of one of the dead passengers letting themselves be interviewed on morning TV so they could appeal to the airlines to get their sister, marooned in London, back to the States for their father's funeral; to the handful of politicians who know when to speak and when to shut up; to all those in this suddenly, shockingly loving town who understand, especially when they hear the word 'revenge' thundered out by talk-show warriors, that the best, the only revenge, when you're fighting a cult that fetishises death, is life.

The Dead and the Guilty: 9/11 a year on

Guardian, 11 September 2002

For one afternoon, at least, it was grievously simple: Britons and Americans gathered, indivisibly, to mourn a shared massacre.

No terrorist attack in history had ever claimed more British lives: sixty-seven. So it seemed right that a dark Manchester drizzle was falling on Fifth Avenue on 20 September as mourners – and we were all mourners – climbed the steps of St Thomas's church, a piece of pure Barsetshire dropped into midtown Manhattan.

The usual suspects filed in: the Clintons, Kofi Annan, Mayor Giuliani, Governor Pataki. But before Tony and Cherie Blair arrived, a side door beside the choir opened and the British bereaved walked in to take their pews at the front of the church.

At once the brittle stylishness of the city collapsed into pathos. They were Britain: shapeless tweed jackets with leather elbow patches; reading glasses by Boots; Jermyn Street shirts for the upper crust. They looked lost in calamity; lost in New York. Bravery masked some faces; jaws set; staring straight ahead, afraid to blink.

Others bore the unmistakable marks of helpless, uncomprehending sorrow: red-rimmed eyes; cheeks pale with distraction, or bearing layers of repeatedly and hopelessly applied make-up. During the service, heads would suddenly bow as if bent with unsupportable feeling. At no point in particular, shoulders gently shook. An arm would reach round to do what it could.

Body language was everything that day and that week. Words had never seemed so redundant; so incapable of carrying the weight of trauma. Explicitly acknowledging this, knowing that simply showing up counted for more than any eloquence, the Prime Minister kept it brief.

A gaping, blackened ground zero had opened inside every New

Yorker (and everyone who had, through the catastrophe, become a New Yorker) and at the smoking core of the misery were, instead of words, images: spools of them, the ones you all know, looping mercilessly. The implausible glide into the steel; the blooming flower of flame; the slow, imploding crumple; the rolling tsunami of dust and shredded paperwork; the terrible drop of bodies, falling with heartbreaking grace like hunted birds.

Icons did the talking. The word means image, but also copy, and the iconology of 9/11, unlike the real thing which was utterly singular, drew on past images to guide instinctive response. Stored memories of the raising of the flag at Iwo Jima (itself an organised photo op) prompted the shot of firemen raising the flag on the torn steel ribs of the World Trade Center; a phoenix in the storm of dun ash.

The flags shouted, howled, roared. Tied as fluttering pennants to the radio antennae of Jeeps, they conquered the suburbs, as if driveby patriotism could of itself make things better.

But other icons wept. In the days and weeks after 9/11 the city was papered with home-made or office-copied posters, bearing photos of missing loved ones, a format hitherto reserved for lost pets. Some of them bore heart-rending pocket attributes as if their indisputable likeability ('she smiles a lot'; 'he has three-day stubble') would jog memories, help find them, bring them back safe and sound.

Quietness spoke volumes. Long lines of blood donors snaked round hospitals and clinics. Cartons of bottled water for rescue workers rose in charitable ziggurats outside police stations and schools.

And when words did finally return, they came back first as inspirational chorale: Irving Berlin's 'God Bless America' replacing 'Take Me Out to the Ballpark' as the anthem of the seventh-inning break when baseball fans get up and stre . . . tch.

In St Thomas's too, on the 20th, nothing was sung more fiercely than both national anthems, the Clintons singing 'God Save the Queen'; game Britons rising to the vocal and verbal challenge of 'The Star-Spangled Banner', a song composed during the 1812 war in which we burned Washington and the White House.

Speech returned, haltingly, in two guises: information from the inferno and pieties from the government. Rudolph Giuliani, often flanked by his commissioner of police and the fire department chief (who, respectively lost 80 and 343 of their men), mastered the first genre precisely because it was, for the mayor, a matter of common decency and practical necessity.

When George Bush began to vocalise again, it was with the pieties served up by his speechwriters, confident that his Manichaean declaration of war on evil also answered a deep need in the American public for moral clarity, spiritual consolation and recovered nerve.

He was not wrong about this. The homilies, not to mention the Waynesque vow to hunt the bad guys down – a promise yet to be fulfilled in the case of the al-Qaeda leadership – may have made Islington cringe, but then again Islington was not under attack.

The European press began to squirm uneasily at talk of evil, as if a wine-and-cheese party had suddenly turned into a Pentecostal revival meeting, and looked nervously round for the exit sign. Some of us, more accustomed to the religiosity of American life, had, and have, no problem whatever with using the e-word.

If the calculated mass murder of 3,000 innocent civilians, from eighty countries, many of them Muslims, just ordinary working people going about their business on a sunny September morning, was not an act of absolute evil, then I have no idea what is. The more serious problem with presidential rhetoric was that the Manichaean struggle between good and evil, freedom and terror, was not just the beginning, but apparently also the end of any sustained attempt to articulate just what, in this particular life-and-death struggle, was truly at stake.

Some weeks later Bill Clinton, both at Harvard and in the Richard Dimbleby lecture for the BBC, made exactly that effort. For obvious reasons the ex-president, now a New Yorker (in my very own neighbourhood), had been sparing with public commentary. But, struggling between prudence and thinly veiled exasperation, he emerged from silence, risking the wrath of patriotic blow-hards, to venture that a refusal to understand the roots of terrorism would be to guarantee its perpetuation.

Lest he be misunderstood, Clinton was also commendably clear on what the battle lines of the already bloody new century would be: the conflict between those who not only claimed a monopoly of wisdom, but the right to impose it on everyone else, against those who claimed neither. Put another way, the fight is between power based on revelation (and thus not open to argument) and power based on persuasion, and thus conditional on argument; militant theocracy against the tolerant Enlightenment.

Since the United States, notwithstanding the Pilgrims and the Great Awakening, was very much the child of the Enlightenment, one might have expected this case for tolerant, secular pluralism to be made in the most adamant and unapologetic fashion by the country's leadership.

But the shroud of mass reverence which enveloped everyone and everything after 9/11, and which once again is blanketing the anniversary, has succeeded in making secular debate about liberty into an act of indecency, disrespectful of the dead and disloyal to the flag.

The notion that the parliament of tongues is, in fact, our best vindication wins few hearts and minds right now. The centrepiece of Public Television's anniversary offerings was a *Frontline* documentary on how 9/11 had affected the religiosity of the nation.

The unsurprising answer is quite a lot. The steady drip of goodness and godliness (multi-faith, naturally) is a reminder of how impossible it seems, two and a half centuries later in America, for the magnitude of a calamity – in Voltaire's case, the Lisbon earthquake – to prompt awkward questions about either the competence or the benevolence of the Almighty.

More than one of the widows of 9/11, though, has been heard to say that she no longer talks to God; she talks to her dead husband. For the most part, though, to say out loud (as a few courageous souls have done) that religious revelation – Judaic and Christian as well as Muslim, not least the notion of a paradise for the pure – is the problem, is to risk immediate and irrevocable patriotic anathema.

Deist scepticism is, I'm sure, too cold a comfort to wish on the distraught, a mere year after the slaughter. As therapy for the traumatised, Bruce Springsteen's new hymnal, complete with gospel-choir backing and ringing with resurrectional themes of The Rising, will beat *Candide* every time. But the need to break clear from the suffocation of reverent togetherness is not just a matter of philosophical self-respect. The immediate future of the American Republic depends on it.

That the Bush administration would always prefer prayers to politics, avoiding at all costs debate, both within its own ranks and in the public arena, has long been apparent. Silence and secrecy, punctuated with disingenuousness, have consistently been its preferred modus operandi. (The problem with the Clintonites was something like the opposite: incontinent gabbiness.)

To this day, Dick Cheney, the most padlocked of all the senior members of the administration, refuses, even under legal pressure, to disclose to Congress the substance of what was discussed in closed meetings with energy-industry executives, leading to the formulation of a policy which corresponded precisely to the needs of business, rather than environmental lobbyists.

So we should not wonder at the aversion to debate, for the United States Inc. is currently being run by an oligarchy, conducting its affairs with a plutocratic effrontery which in comparison makes the age of the robber barons in the late nineteenth century seem a model of capitalist rectitude. The dominant managerial style of the oligarchy is golf-club chumminess; its messages exchanged along with hot stock tips by the mutual scratching and slapping of backs.

The corporations from which the government draws much of its personnel, including its chief executive, and which, on taking office, boasted of their business *savoir faire*, have not, in truth, produced very much, though some of them, like Dick Cheney's Halliburton, now under investigation by the Securities and Exchange Commission for creative accounting practices, have been past masters at converting political connections into corporate advantage and both into personal wealth.

The President himself owed his position at Harken Energy entirely to his name, and once there used it to get a stadium built from public funds for his Texas Rangers baseball team.

The Secretary of the Army, Thomas White – currently, one supposes, planning a war not a million miles away from a rich source of oil – was actually an executive of the spectacularly corrupt and incompetent Enron Corporation, whose implosion began the unravelling of scoundrel capitalism.

The administration's position on the scandals and follies of corporate America – essentially the world it comes from – is to flutter their fans in shock at the wickedness of Certain Individuals and to allow the selective distribution of scarlet letters while trumpeting ever more confidently the purity of the flock and the virtue of the Church. Nothing to do with us, heavens no. And it ploughs merrily ahead with policies expressly designed to come to the aid of distressed plutocracy.

Never mind that, thanks to the likes of the Secretary of the Army's and the Vice-President's old management practices, the stock exchange is mired in a debacle of broken confidence. Never mind that defenceless ex-employees of Enron, WorldCom and the like have seen their jobs and their stock-based pension plans evaporate, the President still thinks that privatisation of social security is the best way to ensure its future.

In a spin of breathtaking Orwellianism, the elimination of estate duties (paid only on fortunes of a quarter of a million dollars or more) is presented as the removal of a 'death tax', transforming a surrender of the public interest into a scene painted by Norman Rockwell with Mom or Pop able to breathe their last now that their legacy will safely pass to Junior unthreatened by the horny hand of bureaucratic brigands.

In the unedifying spectacle of the Sucker Economy, there is, as a mid-term election draws close, fuel for serious public contention; an argument, in fact, over the relative claims of community or corporation in post-9/11 America.

There are people to be held accountable, not least the oiligarch energy traders who, by manipulating demand, turn out to have caused the 2001 'energy crisis' in California which gave Republicans ammunition to pillory the Democratic governor of the state, Gray Davis. Though the hard-right ideologues who control Republican policy much more tenaciously than the smiley-face bonhomie of the President suggests want to identify the American Way, both at home and abroad, with the aggressive pursuit of self-interest, American history actually says otherwise.

It was Alexis de Tocqueville who, in the 1830s, first noticed the peculiar coexistence of a feverish, almost animal scramble for wealth, alongside a deep civic instinct; a feeling, in fact, for community.

The Republican rationalisation is to claim this as the exclusive territory of churches, but that is to ignore some of the most powerful urges in modern American life: the secular voluntarism and philanthropy which sustain museums, public broadcasting, libraries, conservation, even hospitals, and which flow not just from the rich but untold millions of middle-class Americans.

It is the same public spirit which drove the abolitionists of the nineteenth century and the Progressive movement of the early twentieth century. It moved Lady Bird Johnson to become an environmentalist and Jimmy Carter to build houses for the poor, and it is a social patriotism which is star-spangled Americanism at its most authentic.

And it has, already, made itself felt at Ground Zero. Plans to rebuild the site were initially subject to the New York port authority's requirement that the entirety of the thirteen million square feet of office and retail space lost to 9/11 be restored. Commercial rents and revenues were at stake.

This brief duly produced six architectural designs of such staggering banality, with mean little green spaces and walks shoehorned into spaces between bog-standard corporate towers. The public reaction was almost universal execration.

A series of town hall meetings made it overwhelmingly clear that the needs of civic rebirth and a memorial that would serve for lament, memory and meditation were a priority over business as usual. Starting over, the humane imagination, not a quality overvalued in oligarch America – though one which produced a deeply moving memorial at the site of the Oklahoma City bombing – has been called on to do its best.

This happened because voices were raised. The danger of the anniversary is that, out of respect for the dead and through a revisitation of shock, they will become, once again, reverently muffled. The administration is counting on just such a pious hush to bestow on its adventurism the odour of sanctity.

Apparently, the dead are owed another war. But they are not. What they are owed is a good, stand-up, bruising row over the fate of America; just who determines it and for what end?

The first and greatest weapon a democracy has for its own defence is the assumption of common equity; of shared sacrifice. That was what got us through the Blitz. It is, however, otherwise in oligarchic America. Those who are most eager to put young American lives on the line happen to be precisely those who have been greediest for the spoils.

The company run by the Vietnam draft-dodging ('I had other priorities') Cheney, Halliburton, has told the employees of one of its subsidiary companies (resold by Cheney) that the pension plans it was supposed to honour are now worth a fraction of what the workers had been counting on. On leaving the company in 2000 to run for Vice-President, however, Cheney himself was deemed to have 'retired' rather than resigned, thus walking away with a multimillion pension deal. So long, suckers.

Never have the ordinary people of America, the decent, working stiffs whose bodies lay in the hecatomb of Ground Zero, needed and deserved a great tribune more urgently. The greatest honour we could do them is to take back the voice of democracy from the plutocrats.

So it is altogether too bad that this Wednesday, Mayor Bloomberg and Governor Pataki, both liberal Republicans, both decent enough men, shrinking from the challenge to articulate such a debate, have decided instead to read from the Declaration of Independence, the Gettysburg Address and Franklin Roosevelt's 'Four Freedoms' speech. Those words – often sublime – derived their power from the urgency of the moment. To reiterate them merely to produce a moment of dependable veneration is to short-change both history and the present.

Though, in Britain, America is often ignorantly caricatured as a land of impoverished rhetoric, its public speech has often been the glory of its democracy.

And now it needs to sound off. Starting in New York, starting now, we need to do what the people of this astoundingly irrepressible city do best: stand up and make a hell of a noise.

The Civil War in the USA

Guardian, 5 November 2004

In the wee small hours of 3 November 2004, a new country appeared on the map of the modern world: the DSA, the Divided States of America. Oh yes, I know, the obligatory pieties about 'healing' have begun; not least from the lips of the noble Loser. This is music to the ears of the Victor of course, who wants nothing better than for us all to Come Together, a position otherwise known as unconditional surrender. Please, fellow curmudgeons and last ditchers, can someone on the losing side just for once not roll over and fall into a warm bath of patriotic platitudes at such moments, but toot the flute of battle instead; yell and holler and snarl just a wee bit? I don't want to heal the wound, I want to scratch the damned thing until it hurts and bleeds — and then maybe we'll have what it takes to get up from the mat. Do we think the far-right Republican candidate Barry Goldwater, in the ashy dawn of his annihilation in 1964, wanted to share? Don't think so. He wanted to win; sometime. And now, by God, he has.

'We are one nation,' the newborn star of the Democrats, Senator-elect Barack Obama, exclaimed, even as every salient fact of political life belied him. Well might he invoke Lincoln, for not since the Civil War has the fault line between its two halves been so glaringly clear, nor the chasm between its two cultures so starkly unbridgeable. Even territorially (with the exception of Florida, its peninsular finger pointing expectantly at tottering Cuba), the two Americas are topographically coherent and almost contiguous. One of those Americas is a perimeter, lying on the oceans or athwart the fuzzy boundary with the Canadian lakes, and is necessarily porous and outward-looking. The other America, whether montagnard or prairie, is solidly continental and landlocked, its tap roots of obstinate self-belief buried deep beneath the bluegrass and the high corn. It is time we called those two Americas something other than Republican and Democrat, for their mutual alienation and unforgiving contempt are closer to Sunni and Shia, or (in Indian terms) Muslim and Hindu. How about, then, Godly America and Worldly America?

Worldly America, which of course John Kerry won by a massive landslide, faces, well, the world on its Pacific and Atlantic coasts and freely engages, commercially and culturally, with Asia and Europe in the easy understanding that those continents are a dynamic synthesis of ancient cultures and modern social and economic practices. This truism is unthreatening to Worldly America, not least because so many of its people, in the crowded cities, are themselves products of the old-new ways of Korea, Japan, Ireland or Italy. In Worldly America – in San Francisco, Chicago, San Diego, New York – the foreigner is not an anxiety, but rather a necessity. Its America is polycultural, not Pollyanna.

Godly America, on the other hand, rock-ribbed in Dick Cheney's Wyoming, stretched out just as far as it pleases in Dubya's deeply drilled Texas, turns its back on that dangerous, promiscuous, impure world and proclaims to high heaven the indestructible endurance of the American Difference. If Worldly America is, beyond anything else, a city, a street, and a port, Godly America is, at its heart (the organ whose bidding invariably determines its votes over the cooler instructions of the head), a church, a farm and a barracks; places that are walled, fenced and consecrated. Worldly America is about finding civil ways to share crowded space, from a metro-bus to the planet; Godly America is about making over space in its image. One America makes room, the other America muscles in.

Worldly America is pragmatic, practical, rational and sceptical. In California it passed Proposition 71, funding embryonic stem-cell research beyond the restrictions imposed by Bush's federal policy. Godly America is mythic, messianic, conversionary, given to acts of public witness, hence the need – in Utah and Montana and a handful of other states – to poll the voters on amendments to their state constitution defining marriage as a union between the opposite sexes. But then Worldly America is said to feed the carnal vanities; Godly America banishes and punishes them. From time to time Godly America will descend on the fleshpots of Worldly America, from Gotham (it had its citadel-like Convention there after all) to Californication, will shop for T-shirts, take a sniff at the local pagans and then return to base-camp more convinced than ever that a time of Redemption and Repentance must be at hand. But if the stiff-necked transgressors cannot be persuaded, they can be cowed and conquered.

No wonder so many of us got the election so fabulously wrong even into the early hours of Tuesday evening, when the exit polls were apparently giving John Kerry a two- or three-point lead in both Florida and Ohio. For most of us purblind writers spend our days in Worldly America and think that Godly America is some sort of quaint anachronism, doomed to atrophy and disappear as the hypermodernity of the cyber age overtakes it, in whatever fastness of Kentucky or Montana it might still circle its wagons. The shock for the Worldlies is to discover that Godly America is its modernity; that so far from it withering before the advance of the blog and the zip drive, it is actually empowered by them. The tenacity with which Godly America insists the theory of evolution is just that – a theory – with no more validity than Creationism, or that Iraqis did, in fact, bring down the twin towers, is not in any way challenged by the digital pathways of the information age. In fact, such articles of faith are expedited and reinforced by them. Holy bloggers bloviate, Pentecostalists ornament their website with a nimbus of trembling electronic radiance and, for all I know, you can download Pastor John Ashcroft singing the Praises of the Lord right to your Godpod.

Nor, it transpires, is the exercise of the franchise a sure-fire way for the Democrats to prevail. The received wisdom in these Worldly parts (subscribed to by yours truly; mea culpa) was that a massively higher turnout would necessarily favour Kerry. P. Diddy's 'Vote or Die' campaign was credited with getting out young voters en masse who ignored the polls in 2000. We saw a lot of Springsteen and Bon Jovi and ecstatic upturned faces. Who could possibly match their mobilisation, we thought? Answer: Jehovah and his Faithful Servant St Karl the Rove. The biggest story of all in 2004 is the astounding success of the Republicans in shipping millions of white evangelicals to the polls who had also stayed at home four years earlier. We thought we were fired up with righteous indignation – against the deceits of the propaganda campaign for the Iraq war, against the gross inequities of the tax cuts – but our fire was just hot air compared to the jihad launched by the Godlies against the infamy of a tax rollback, of merely presuming to diss the Dear Leader in a time of war. And the battalions of Christian soldiers made the telling difference in the few critical places where

Godly and Worldly America do actually rub shoulders (or at least share a state), Ohio above all.

By the lights of the psephology manuals, Ohio ought to have been a natural for the Democrats: ageing industrial cities such as Akron and Dayton, with big concentrations of minorities, suffering prolonged economic pain from outsourced industries. Cleveland and Cincinnati are classic cities of the Worldly plain: half-decayed, incompletely revived; great art museums, a rock'n'roll hall of fame, a terrific symphony orchestra. But drive a bit and you're in deep Zion, where the Holsteins graze by billboards urging the sinful to return to the bosom of the Almighty, the church of Friday-night high-school football shouts its hosannas at the touchdowns, and Support Our Troops signs grow as thick as the rutabaga. At first sight there's not much distance between this world and western Pennsylvania, but were the state line to be marked in twenty-foot-high electrified fences, the frontier between the two Americas couldn't be sharper. The voters of the 'Buckeye State' cities did care about their jobs; they did listen when Kerry told them the rich had done disproportionately nicely from Bush's tax cut. But they were also listening when their preachers (both black and white) fulminated against the uncleanliness of Sodom and the murder of the unborn. In the end, those whose most serious anxieties were the state of the economy and the Mess-o-potamia were outvoted by those who told exit pollers their greatest concern in 2004 was 'moral values'.

Faith-driven politics may even have had a hand in delivering Florida to Bush by a surprising margin, since it seems possible that Jewish voters there who voted for 'my son the Vice-President' Joe Lieberman (not to mention Hadassah, oy what nachas) in 2000, actually switched sides as a result of the President's support for Ariel Sharon. It wasn't that the Kerry campaign didn't notice the confessional effect. It was just that they didn't know what to do about it. Making the candidate over as some sort of altar boy (notwithstanding directives from Rome instructing the faithful on the abhorrence of his position on abortion) would have been about as persuasive as kitting him out with gun, camouflage and dead Canada geese; a laboriously transparent exercise in damning insincerity.

In Godly America the politics of impassioned conviction inevitably trumped the politics of logical argument. On CNN a fuming James

Carville wondered out loud how a candidate declared by the voting public to have decisively won at least two of the three televised debates could have still been defeated. But the 'victory' in those debates was one of body language rather than reasoned discourse. It registered more deeply with the public that the President looked hunched and peevish than that he had been called by Kerry on the irrelevance of the war in Iraq to the threat of terror. And since the insight was one of appearance, not essence, it could just as easily be replaced by countless photo-ops of the President restored to soundbite affability. The charge that Bush and his second war had actually made America less, not more, safe, and had created, not flushed out, nests of terror, simply failed to register with the majority of those who put that issue at the top of their concerns.

Why? Because, the President had 'acted', meaning he had killed at least some Middle Eastern bad dudes in response to 9/11. That they might be the wrong ones, in the wrong place – as Kerry said over and over – was simply too complicated a truth to master. Forget the quiz in political geography, the electorate was saying (for the popular commitment to altruistic democratic reconstruction on the Tigris is, whatever the White House orthodoxy, less than Wolfowitzian), it's all sand and towel-heads anyway, right? Just smash 'them' (as one ardent Bush supporter put it on talk radio the other morning) 'like a ripe cantaloupe'. Who them? Who gives a shit? Just make the testosterone tingle all the way to the polls. Thus it was that the war veteran found himself demonised as vacillating compromiser, the Osama Candidate, while a pair of draft-dodgers who had sacrificed more than 1,100 young men and women to a quixotic levantine makeover, and one which I prophesy will be ignominiously wound up by next summer (the isolationists in the administration having routed the neocons), got off scot-free, lionised as the Fathers of Our Troops.

Well, the autumn leaves have, just this week, fallen from the trees up here in the Hudson Valley and the scales from the eyes of us deluded Worldlies. If there is to be any sort of serious political future for the Democrats, they have to do far more than merely trade on the shortcomings of the incumbents – and there will be opportunities galore in the witching years ahead (a military mire, a fiscal China syndrome and, hello, right before inauguration, a visit from al-Qaeda). The real challenge is to voice an alternative social gospel to the political liturgy of the Godlies; one that redefines patriotism as an American community, not just a collection of wealth-seeking individuals; one that refuses to play a zero-sum game between freedom and justice; one in which, as the last populist president put it just a week ago, thought and hope are not mutually exclusive. You want moral values? So do we, but let them come from the street, not the pulpit. And if a fresh beginning must be made — and it must — let it not begin with a healing, but with a fight.

Katrina and George Bush

Guardian, 12 September 2005

Slipstreaming behind the annual rituals of sorrow and reverence for 9/11, George W. Bush has decreed that, five days later, on the 16th, there is to be a further day of solemnities on which the nation will pray for the unnumbered victims of Hurricane Katrina. Prayers (like vacations) are the default mode for this president, who knows how to chuckle and bow the head in the midst of disaster but not, when it counts, how to govern or to command. If you feel the prickly heat of politics, summon a hymn to make it go away; make accountability seem a blasphemy. Thus has George Bush become the Archbishop of Washington even as his aura as lord protector slides into the putrid black lagoon, bobbing with cadavers and slick with oil, that has swallowed New Orleans. No doubt the born-again President is himself sincere about invoking the Almighty. But you can hear the muttered advice in the White House: Mr President, we were in trouble after 9/11; the unfortunate episode of the schoolroom, My Little Goat and all that. But do what you did then; set yourself once more at the centre of the nation; go to the epicentre of the horror and embrace its heroes; make yourself the country's patriotic invigorator and all may yet be well.

So this weekend it was predictable that the president would shamelessly invoke the spirit of 9/11 to cover his shamefully exposed rear end – 'resolve of nation . . . defend freedom . . . rebuild wounded city . . . care for our neighbours'. But comparisons with 9/11 – the fourth anniversary of which was marked in New York yesterday – will only serve now to reinforce the differences between what the two calamities said about America, and especially about those entrusted with its government. The carnage of 9/11 generated an intense surge of patriotic solidarity, even with America's Babylon, a city scandalously and notoriously indifferent to Heartland values. This was because the mass murders had been committed by people who defined foreignness: theocratic nihilists who equated pluralist democracy with depravity. A hard-ass city supposedly abandoned to the most brutal forms of aggressive individualism (a fiction it liked to cultivate) showed instead the face of American mutualism as volunteers poured into the smouldering toxic crater. Blood and food donations piled up and a mayor disregarded his personal safety to be where he had to be, in the thick of the inferno; his daily press conferences astoundingly bullshit-free, unafraid of bearing bad news; treating his fellow citizens, *mirabile dictu*, like grown-ups.

The rest of the country looked at Zoo York and, astoundingly, saw images and heard stories that made themselves feel good about being American: the flag of defiance flown by firemen amid the Gothic ruins; the countless tales of bravery and sacrifice among those trapped inside the towers. For all the horror, this could be made into a good epic of the American character. It was this redeeming sense of national community that protected the President from any kind of serious political scrutiny whenever he invoked 9/11 as the overwhelming reason for launching the invasion of Iraq. As John Kerry found to his cost, unexamined passion triumphed over reasoned argument. Bush won re-election simply by making debate a kind of treason; an offence against the entombed.

Out of the genuinely noble response to 9/11, then, came an unconscionable deceit. Out of the ignoble response to Katrina will come a salutary truth. For along with much of New Orleans, the hurricane has swept away, at last, the shameful American era of the fearfully buttoned lip. Television networks that have self-censored themselves into abject deference have not flinched from their responsibility to show corpses drifting in the water; lines of the forlorn and the abandoned sitting amid piles of garbage outside the Convention Centre; patients from Charity Hospital waiting in the broiling sun in vain for water and medical supplies; helicopters too frightened of armed looters to actually land, but throwing bottles of water down from their twenty-foot hover. Embarrassed by their ignorance of the cesspool that was the Convention Centre, members of the government protested that it was hard to know what was really going on 'on the ground'. All they had to do was to turn on the TV to find out.

Millions of ordinary Americans did. And what they saw, as so many of them have said, was the brutality, destitution, desperation and chaos of the Third World. Instead of instinctive solidarity and compassion, they have witnessed a descent into a Hobbesian state of nature; with Leviathan offering fly-by compassion, 30,000 feet up, and then, once returned to the White House, broadcasting a defensive laundry list of deliveries, few of which showed up when and where they were needed. Instead of acts of mutual succour, there was the police force of Gretna, south of New Orleans, sealing off a bridge against incoming evacuees, and turning them back under threats of gunfire. Instead of a ubiquitous mayor with his finger on the pulse, and the guts to tell the truth, enter Michael Brown, a pathetically inadequate director of the Federal Emergency Management Agency, Fema, hounded from his eleven-year tenure as supervisor of commissioners and stewards of the International Arabian Horse Association by legal proceedings. Instead of summarily firing 'Brownie', the President ostentatiously congratulated him on camera for doing 'a heck of a job'.

Only on Friday, in an attempt at damage control, was the hapless Brown 'recalled' to Washington, his position as Fema director intact.

And instead of an urban community of every conceivable race, religion and even class brought together by trauma, another kind of city, startlingly divided by race and fortune, has symbolised everything about America that makes its people uneasy, ashamed and, finally, perhaps lethally for the conservative ascendancy and its myths, angry. A faint but detectable whiff of mortality is steaming up, not just from the Louisiana mire, but from this Republican administration. Call me a cynic, but is it entirely a coincidence that suddenly the great black hope of moderate Republicanism, Colin Powell, is everywhere, publicly repenting of his speech to the UN (and by implication damning those who supplied him with unreliable intelligence), and offering, unbidden, his own lament for the institutional meltdown that followed the breach of the levee? The administration is already thought of as a turkey and the turkey vultures are starting to wheel.

Historians ought not to be in the prophecy business, but I'll venture this one: Katrina will be seen as a watershed in the public and political life of the US, because it has put back into play the profound question of American government. Ever since Ronald Reagan proclaimed that government was not the answer but the problem, conservatism has stigmatised public service as parasitically unpatriotic, an anomaly in the robust self-sufficiency of American life. For the most part, Democrats have been too supine, too embarrassed and too inarticulate to fight back with a coherent defence of the legitimacy of democratic government. Now, if ever, is their moment; not to revive the New Deal or the Great Society (though unapologetically preserving social security might be a start), but to stake a claim to being the party that delivers competent, humane, responsive government, the party of public trust.

For the most shocking difference between 9/11 and Katrina was in what might have been expected in the aftermath of disaster. For all the intelligence soundings, it was impossible to predict the ferocity, much less the timing, of the 9/11 attacks. But Katrina was the most anticipated catastrophe in modern American history. Perhaps the lowest point in Bush's abject performance last week was when he claimed that no one could have predicted the breach in the New Orleans levees, when report after report commissioned by him, not to mention a simulation just last year, had done precisely that. But he had cut the budget appropriation for maintaining flood defences by nearly 50 per cent, so that for the first time in thirty-seven years Louisiana was unable to supply the protection it knew it would need in the event of catastrophe. Likewise Fema, which under Bill Clinton had been a cabinet-level agency reporting directly to the President, had under his successor been turned into a hiring opportunity for political hacks and cronies and disappeared into the lumbering behemoth of Homeland Security. It was Fema that failed the Gulf; Fema which failed to secure the delivery of food, water, ice and medical supplies desperately asked for by the Mayor of New Orleans; and it was the President and his government-averse administration that had made Fema a bad joke.

In the last election campaign George W. Bush asked Americans to vote for him as the man who would best fulfil the most essential obligation of government: the impartial and vigilant protection of its citizens. Now the fraudulence of the claim has come back to haunt him, not in Baghdad, but in the drowned counties of Louisiana. In the recoil, disgust and fury felt by millions of Americans at this abdication of responsibility, the President — notwithstanding his comically self-serving promise to lead an inquiry into the fiasco — will assuredly reap the whirlwind.

Obama Rising: The Denver Speech

Guardian, 30 August 2008

Oh, how the McCain campaign must have chuckled when they got an inkling of what the Obama strategists had in mind as the backdrop for his acceptance speech in the stadium of the Denver Broncos, surmounted by an apparently neutered plaster stallion. Architrave alert! Fluted columns! Cecil B. DeMille Doric! What a gift to satirists who could lampoon Obama as a wannabe Demosthenes, so self-monumentalised that he seemed to be presumptuously rehearsing the inaugural oath on the Capitol steps. It's possible that, even after one of the most memorably dramatic speeches in modern American history, they may still be betting on what they think is an eloquence aversion out there in the heartland; the ingrained suspicion that fancy phrase-making is a fig leaf for lack of substance. Early in the primary season Hillary Clinton made much of the difference between words and deeds, as if high rhetoric was a tip-off to political inadequacy. Beware fine words, that unsubtle message ran, for they are gossamer, the pretty fabric you spin when you can't hack the hard stuff of power. By this reasoning, McCain is a shoo-in, not in spite of his shortcomings in the eloquence department, but because of them. The Hanoi Hilton, after all, was a place of terrifying silence, and aw shucks will beat silver tongue every time with the regular Joes and Janes.

But this year, the year of primal national scream in the US, is this smart politics? In the end the Republican posture of laconic authenticity, of Quiet Americans, may backfire. For what Obama delivered on Thursday night deliberately left pyrotechnics to the literal fireworks that brought the convention to an end. Instead he delivered severity; combative polemic over the hurting body of the republic; a gripping sense of the magnitude of the moment, without ever dropping his audience into resignation or pessimism. It was the least showy and, by some distance I think, the most moving and powerful of all his remarkable speeches, for its eschewal of rhetorical flamboyance was done in the service of a higher goal: the rebirth of what he called in his stirring peroration 'common purpose', meaning the reassertion of mutuality without the compromise of individuality.

It is this insistence of being one's brother's and sister's keeper as a pure American ideal, the questioning of what an 'ownership society' means, that was so heartening. What Obama seems to be after is not just the reawakening of national community, but altering what an election campaign actually is. 'You can make a big election small,' he said, witheringly, of the decades of Lee Atwater, Roger Ailes and Karl Rove. The time is too serious, the stakes too high, to tolerate that kind of politics. After cataloguing the Bush administration's manifold failures, something happened to his voice that, in the months that I have followed him since the Iowa caucuses, I have never heard: a ferocious roar of fury bellowed into the microphone. And the word that formed in the fire of his indignation was, simply: 'ENOUGH!' It was a Shakespearean moment that shook the 80,000 rigid, and ought to have disabused any Republicans of the idle assumption that they are taking on a remote, effete intellectual who doesn't have the wherewithal for bloody political combat.

So Obama is betting on the word's enduring power as a reformer of American life. Historically he has good reason for, from the beginning, words and texts have constructed American realities, not the other way round. The spell cast on Americans by the mantle of words goes all the way back to the first Great Awakening in the 1740s when flocks thrilled to Methodist preachers such as George Whitefield. Evangelical passion remains a brilliant strand in the weave of American discourse, but when it made way for the reasoning of the Enlightenment deists and unitarians who made the revolution, another element of American speech-power sounded loud and clear: the reverence for classical oratory.

The Republican bet is that all this is a thing of the past; that, self-evidently, we live in the age of images, and words are just the add-ons to the beguilement of the eye; that all we have are soundbites. Obama's is the more stunning gamble; that so far from the digital age killing off the reign of the word, it has actually given logos a whole new lease of life.

As I write this, the diapason of Martin Luther King's rhetoric on 28 August 1963 rolls over the stadium again, while beside me a row of bloggers writing for *blackamericaweb.com* tap their keyboards. In downtown Denver the places where energy spilled over were certainly not the citadels of CNN or the networks, but the spaces occupied by the Daily Kos, Wonkette and the rest. The blog and the great speech are the low and the high of the enduring dominion of American words; and Obama is betting that words still have the force to remake politics, and even government. Obama is Dick Cheney's worst nightmare, for he represents the antidote to the unanswerably laconic. Has there ever been a politician who revelled in deadly quietness quite so much as Cheney?

Ravelled up inside that gamble is another daring hunch: that, of all Americans, Obama is uniquely qualified to braid together the two great strands of national rhetoric. On the one hand, that of black redemption: saturated with scriptural passion; the eloquence of Martin Luther King (whom in a wonderful conceit Obama simply called 'the Preacher'); the language that altered what Lyndon Johnson believed and did. And on the other, the rhetoric of American classicism: Lincoln's, Franklin Roosevelt's and Jack Kennedy's. From these distinct threads he is hoping to make a new American fabric of speech.

On this evening, though, Obama knew he had to make his words do two things: go on unsparing attack against his opponent, and somehow become a natural extension of the everyday life of suffering Americans. The attack speech, delivered with sombre coldness, did the job. Taking his high concerns to regular Americans was the tougher assignment. Knowing there could be no point in making Obama sound like a trucker faced with foreclosure, the campaign hit on the clever device of having a parade of indisputably middle-class Americans, some long-time Republicans, deliver their grievances to camera. The populist voice comes right from the *populus*.

What Obama did is to touch the nerve of what he knows most Americans care about: old-fashioned virtues – the 'dignity of hard work'; the promise of fair reward for that work; patriotism; the 'promise' that if they live right and do right, their children will reap the reward of that promise. 'That's why I am here,' he said, 'that's what I think every time I tuck my children up at night.'

Suddenly Obama becomes not a politician but a dad, who needs no prompting to understand the heroism of everyday life. In another agile counterpunch at the Republican accusation that he is no more than a 'celebrity', Obama, speaking of the sacrifices of his mother and grand-parents, said: 'I don't know what kind of lives John McCain thinks that celebrities lead, but this has been mine. These are my heroes.' And equally suddenly McCain turns into the patrician who isn't sure how many homes he owns.

In contrast to Al Gore's sententiousness and John Kerry's high-minded elegance, Obama is light on his feet and deadly with his jabs, a pre-emptive warrior. A parade of generals and admirals attest to his fitness to be commander-in-chief, but more spunkily he says: 'If John McCain wants to have a debate about who has the temperament . . . to serve as the next commander-in-chief, that's a debate I'm ready to have.' From this unlikely investment of authority, he says to McCain: 'Let us agree that patriotism has no party . . . so I've got news for you . . . We all put our country first.'

Obama is staking the whole house on a belief that the times are so serious, the damage wrought in the past eight years so grave, that for once the American voters are hungry for a reborn sense of national community, and a president who embodies it. It's common-place that the problem for McCain is that he is too old, and for Obama that he's too young. But one of the transformations that happened in this speech was to make Obama seem a whole lot older, or at least more grown-up, than McCain. As he himself says, his call for a rekindled sense of common purpose can be written off as so much 'happy talk'. The campaign can go straight downhill to its customary depths. But the Republicans had better practise an unac-customed economy of derision, for after Obama's severe magnificence, an attack on his style carries the risk of churlishness: the grim snicker of the crabbed.

Bye-Bye, Dubya

Guardian, 3 November 2008

'Forgotten but not gone' was the way in which the supremo of Boston politics, Billy Bulger, liked to dismiss the human irritants he had crushed beneath his trim boot. The same could now be said for the hapless forty-third President of the United States as the daylight draws mercifully in on his reign of misfortune and calamity. How is he bearing up, one wonders, as the candidate from his own party treats him as the carrier of some sort of infectious political disease? How telling was it that the most impassioned moment in John McCain's performance in the final debate was when he declared: 'I am not George Bush.'

Where, O where, are you, Dubya, as the action passes you by like a jet skirting dirty weather? Are you roaming the lonely corridors of the White House in search of a friendly shoulder around which to clap your affable arm? Are you sweating it out on the treadmill, hurt and confused as to why the man everyone wanted to have a beer (or Coke) with, who swept to re-election four years ago, has been downgraded to all-time loser in presidential history, stuck there in the bush leagues along with the likes of James Buchanan and Warren Harding? Or are you whacking brush in Crawford, where the locals now make a point of telling visitors that George W. never really was from hereabouts anyroad.

Whatever else his legacy, the man who called himself 'the decider' has left some gripping history. The last eight years have been so rich in epic imperial hubris that it would take a reborn Gibbon to do justice to the fall. It should be said right away that amid the landscape of smoking craters there are one or two sprigs of decency that have been planted: record amounts of financial help given to Aids-blighted countries of Africa; immigration reform that would have offered an amnesty to illegals and given them a secure path to citizenship, had not those efforts hit the reef of intransigence in Bush's own party. And no one can argue with the fact that since 9/11 the United States has not been attacked on its home territory by jihadi terrorists; though whether or not that security is more illusory than real is, to put it mildly, open to debate.

But against that there is the matter of hundreds of thousands of Iraqi civilian casualties, more than 4,000 American troops dead, many times that gravely injured, not to mention the puncture wounds and mutilations inflicted on internationally agreed standards of humane conduct for prisoners – and on the protection of domestic liberties enshrined in the American constitution. If the Statue of Liberty were alive, she would be weeping tears of blood.

If Bush himself has been largely kept out of sight, his baleful legacy has been visible in the McCain campaign. McCain has made much of his credentials for independence of mind, a claim which once was credible given his support for immigration reform and opposition to Bush's tax cuts. But somewhere along the road to the Republican nomination, all of this became less important than the lessons of the Reagan-Bush-Rove political playbook which, with the exception of the Clinton election of 1992, seemed to have a track record of unbroken success.

McCain knew this from bitter personal experience, having been on the receiving end of Bush lowball politics in the South Carolina primary in 2000. Coming out of a convincing win against George Bush in New Hampshire, he was stopped in his tracks by a smear campaign conducted through push-poll phone calls in which people were asked whether they knew that the daughter McCain had adopted from Sri Lanka was in fact the illegitimate child of an affair with a woman of colour. Now you would think McCain could never reconcile himself to a politician capable of those kinds of tactics. But there he was in the campaign of 2004, stumping the country for the incumbent, ingratiating himself with the conservative base he knew he would need, even as his old Vietnam buddy, John Kerry, was being coated in slime by the Swift Boaters.

Whatever misgivings McCain might have had about adopting the hardball tactics of his 2000 adversary have long since disappeared before the blandishments of classic Bush-style operatives like Rick Davis and Stephen Schmidt. 'Do you want to be pure, or do you want to win?' they must have asked right after the nomination. Ditching Joe Lieberman as a running mate and unleashing pitbull Palin was his answer.

So even while George Bush is kept at arm's length from the campaign, his campaign style lives on as Obama is stigmatised as a terrorist-friendly stealth-socialist, too deeply un-American to be let anywhere near the Oval Office. 'He just doesn't see America as we do,' says Sarah Palin, trying to wink her way into Dick Cheney's seat. McCain is betting the house that this way of doing politics has at least one more hurrah left in it, and we will find out in the early hours of Wednesday morning whether he is right.

The Bush presidency is the spectre haunting the feast in more than tactics. Although every conservative administration since Ronald Reagan has promised to deliver, through supply-side stimulation, economic growth without bloated deficits, they have never been vindicated in their blind faith in what Bush senior once rashly called 'voodoo economics'. Consistently, they have brought the US Wall Street crashes and recessions along with massive deficits; and yet somehow, the stake that history attempts to drive through the heart of their economic theology never puts the ghoul away.

No weight of evidence to the contrary has ever shaken the totemic belief that tax cuts can grow the economy robustly enough to compensate for drastic shortfalls in revenue. George W. Bush clung to this belief even as the Clinton budget surplus was converted into a mountainous deficit, and John McCain continues to parrot the same belief with the shining face of a true believer.

Not even Gibbon could supply a story as fatefully bizarre as the ultimate consummation of Reagan-Bush conservatism, its last act: the most massive shift of financial power from the private to the public sector since the New Deal. Rather like the Pope deciding that all along he really wanted a bar mitzvah.

If you look at this saga as the history of a dynasty, it's come full circle. For, believe it or not, there once was a time when Bush politics was about centrist moderation. Dubya's revered granddad, Prescott Sheldon Bush, son of an Ohio railroad executive and Senator for Connecticut from 1952 to 1963, was punished in the Catholic towns of industrial Connecticut for his connection with Planned Parenthood. Not only that, but he was a trustee of the United Negro College Fund, the kind of institution that made the eventual career of Barack Obama conceivable.

- But the Bushes have always been selective about idealism. And even at the height of the Kennedy-Johnson apogee, Prescott and George Herbert Walker Bush were turning the pages of Barry Goldwater's *Conscience of a Conservative*. They could smell the wind-direction changing. The future of Republican money and Republican power lay elsewhere; with Texas oil. Hence the migration to Midland Texas of George Herbert Walker Bush and his makeover into a Texan who knew the ways of the corporate world; and how to bring about the Great Cosiness between government and business that seemed like the perfect feedback loop: money to power, power to money; tax breaks for the corporations; donations to those who might command the heights.

This is the politics George W. Bush inherited, and he has been its faithful disciple; to the point of purging it of any remaining traces of pragmatism. It is astounding to hear right-wing talk-show bloviators rant about the predicament of the Bush administration being caused by its failure to carry out the true conservative agenda. For there never has been and never will be a more doctrinally faithful instrument of the creed. Never mind the hanging chads of 2000, the Cheney-Bush administration seized the moment to bring on the Goldwater-Reagan Rapture in which government was once and for all got out of the way of business.

So it hasn't really been all George Bush's fault, the stupendous American fiasco. He came to power armed with an ideology that was about to crash and burn; that was, years before the present tumult, already fatally disconnected from historical reality. It was on his watch that American government needed reinventing. It was responsible government that was needed in Iraq and Afghanistan; government that was desperately needed in New Orleans after Katrina, while all George Bush could manage was a fly-by. It is government that this most anti-governmental of all American administrations is learning that is needed now to save the United States from a second Depression.

In his heart of hearts I actually think the shell-shocked Dubya, somewhere in the bowels of his presidency, knows this. But he is nowhere to be found, and so on goes the mad rant that healthcare reform and progressive taxes are the Trojan horse for socialist revolution. To which those who have another view altogether might want to say, fear not, for yours, as a Republican president once said, is a government of the people, by the people. And really it will not perish from the earth.

The British Election, 2005

Guardian, 5 May 2005

It was when Michael Howard shifted into the conditional mood that I knew which side of the Atlantic I was really on. 'On Friday,' he said, 'Britain could wake up to a brighter future.' COULD? You mean ... it might not happen? If this had been Detroit or San Diego or Dubuque, incredulous staffers would have rushed the candidate off the podium for emergency reprogramming. 'Will, Michael,' they would chant patiently at him until he Got It. 'Never, ever so much as breathe a possibility of defeat.' But this wasn't Dubuque, it was the Ashford Holiday Inn, and the Somewhat Beloved Leader was addressing the party faithful on how, probably, all things considered, he might, with any luck, and showery periods on Thursday, even the score by full time.

Howard's vision of a briskly spring-cleaned Albion was meant as a rousing clarion call, but it had all the resonance of a tinkling bicycle bell in a country lane. I was just a few hours off the jumbo from Newark, New Jersey, but it felt like dropping down the rabbit hole and emerging into parish-pump politics. Compared with the engorged rapture, the fully orchestrated Hollywood production numbers; the serried ranks of Raybanned Secret Service Men; the ululating good 'ole boys, the big-hair hoopla, the bra-popping, pompom-waggling cheerleaders, the Spandex highkicks; the tossing ocean of flags; the relentlessly inspirational gospel songs; the banners as big as a wall; the parade of uniforms (any uniform will do – firemen, police, marines, traffic wardens, apartment-house doormen); the descending chopper blades; the eventual appearance of the Awaited One to swoons of joy and exultant whoops of messianic acclaim; compared to the whole delirious cornball razzmatazz that passes for democratic politics in the great American empire, Ashford on a bank-holiday weekend was utter Ambridge. Thank God. Except he too was mercifully missing from the general election.

After the stifling incense-choked sanctimoniousness of American politics, getting back to Britain was like coming up for air. Or was I just nostalgic; childishly elated to be on the electoral roll for the first time, after twenty years of residential disenfranchisement? Maybe I was succumbing to antiquated memories of campaigns past: traipsing house to house for Harold Wilson in the brickier zones of Cambridge in 1964; exhilarated that we were at last on the threshold of seeing off the Tories who'd been Her Majesty's government ever since I'd become aware of politics. (Many years on, I'd seen The Enemy close up. Tripping over a rug in the Christ's College senior common room, I rose to find myself face to face with Harold Macmillan's whiskers. 'There there,' Supermac drawled, not missing a beat, 'gratitude understandable; prostration quite unnecessary.') Little did he know. In 1964 we were the New Model Army in Morris Minors, interrupting *Housewives' Choice* to drive aproned grannies to the polls, transforming, as we thought, a forelock-tugging squirearchical Britain into the bracing social democracy of George Brown, Barbara Castle and Roy Jenkins.

There had always been a streak of political feistiness in our family. Living in Margaret Thatcher's Finchley, my father had been so furious at the presumption of whomever it was that had put up a Conservative sign in front of his block of flats, suggesting collective allegiance, that he'd hung from the window balcony of number 26 the biggest Labour-party banner he could find. No one spoke to him in synagogue for months after that. So, yes, coming home politically probably meant returning to unrealistic expectations of face-to-face, high-street, argy-bargy oxygenated polemics. But even if it fell short, it would still feel like red meat compared to the white-bread pap I'd had to consume in the last election I'd covered for this paper: Bush v. Kerry, 2004; primetime-ready brand marketing, punctuated only by sleazebag character assassination.

I'd heard reports that British politics had been invaded by focus-group, market-tested campaigning. That, between Lynton Crosby and Maurice Saatchi, the Tories were playing the American game, eavesdropping on Basil Fawlty in the snug and turning his pet peeves into electoral policy. Are you drinking what I'm drinking, squire?

But if slick persuasiveness was the idea, Howard's performance at Ashford suggested there was more work to be done. After a sly warm-up speech by Damian Green, the local MP, the Somewhat Beloved Leader entered to the stirring chords of 'Victory at Sea', composed for television in the early 1960s by the true-blue American Richard Rodgers. Was this a good idea? Tory party as HMS *Victory*, fine. Pity about the 'At Sea' bit, though.

There then followed what in America would be called the Stump Speech, except that 'stump' with its evocation of cigar-pulling down-home wisdom, cookie-bake homilies and a feverish orgy of baby-kissing, isn't really mid-Kent. To rapt silence, broken only by aldermanic murmurs of assent, the SBL painted an apocalyptic picture of a New Labour Britain – *Blade Runner* with tea – in which pensioners no longer feel free to go to the shops in safety, where MRSA pullulates in hospitals unchecked by Matron, where a critical swab shortage holds up urgent surgery, a Britain where the police are doomed to standing around on street corners sucking on pencils as they complete interminable questionnaires while platoons of drunken yobs, Shauns of the Undead, run amok in the high street, pillaging Starbucks and sacking Boots.

Under his government, Howard pledged, the police would be liberated from pencil duty and set free to 'invade the personal physical space' of the yobs (protected, presumably, by rubber gloves obtained from Matron). SWABS not YOBS: who could possibly disagree?

Several times we were promised a government which would roll up its sleeves (though those of Howard's blue shirt remained elegantly buttoned). Then came the really worrying bit. SBL's voice dropped, the eyes moistened, the smile widened. Acute observers could instantly recognise the onset of a Sincerity Attack. 'I love my country.' Then he told us how he truly feels. About himself. About Britain. Proud. Immigrant roots. State school. Really proud. Work hard. Do well. What Britain's all about. Not layabout.

This sort of thing is of course obligatory for American campaigns where the 'story' of the candidate – a combination of autobiographical confession and patriotic profession – is the *sine qua non* of 'making a connection with the voters'. But in Ashford, among the flowery frocks and jackets flecked with dog-hair, the narrative seemed wetly embarrassing. Then exit to reprise of 'Victory at Sea' and sustained (if not exactly deafening) applause. The faithful were giddy with excitement. Well, almost all of them. One loyalist with a bottle-green flying-ducks tie was still barking over the State of the Country. 'Are you optimistic about Thursday?' I asked tentatively. 'I TRY to be,' he conceded, 'though I was going to desert the sinking ship.' 'Where to?' 'Montene-gro.' 'Montenegro?' 'Yes, Montenegro. Not many people know this, but the wine is wonderful and −' (he whispered confidentially) '− they have the most beautiful women in the world. Though, of course, they do tend to be a bit hairy.'

As indeed do the campaigns in these endgame days. Not that you'd guess it watching Howard taking a walkabout on his own patch. For once the sun shone benevolently on his progress. ('We arrive; it rains. It always rains,' said one campaign Eeyore on the battle bus.) Howard was bouncily affable as he trotted down Folkestone high street, a place inexplicably bereft of the roaming hordes of ruffians and mendicant asylum-seekers he says infest New Labour's derelict Britain. Surely he can't mean the ubiquitous Ecuadorian pan-pipers (are there any left in the Andes?) who warbled away while the SBL closed in on constituents, for an economical hand-pump (pensioners got a concerned left hand on their arm too) adroitly avoiding, in short order, the Green party table overstocked with belligerently pacifist eco-literature; giggly girls stuffed into jeans shouting their resolution to vote for the Official Monster Raving Loony party; and burps and hoots from acne-stricken yoofs dressed, bafflingly, in Boston Celtics kit.

As the Leader ducked into Celeste, 'A Taste of Heaven on Earth', for lunch, I was left marvelling at the village-green cosiness of it all; unthink-able in the United States where the candidate would be flanked by a wall of myrmidons with imperfectly concealed shoulder holsters, and would never ever be unplugged from the earpiece through which staff would prompt his every reply. ('Remember, Michael, WHEN we win, not IF!') As for the Monster Raving Loony party, they would be in a Secure Holding Facility, not munching on ham sandwiches ten feet away from the Leader. But in Folkestone, the sun glinted off the sea, vagrant scavenging gulls wheeled around the battle bus (send 'em home) and the violent grunge-hole of Howard's Albion seemed a long way away.

What is it that draws British politicians down to the sea? Confer-ences in Blackpool and Brighton; a rally for the Labour party in Hove? In America they go to the major markets: conventions, then, in Chicago, Los Angeles, New York, not Cape Cod or Virginia Beach. I was at the only exception, forty years ago, Lyndon Johnson's corona-tion in Atlantic City, where, amidst the toffee vendors on the boardwalk, porky-pink straw-boatered men from Mississippi with wilting bow ties pretended not to notice the civil-rights demonstrators. At the moment of apotheosis, LBJ, the Hidden One, rose majestically on to the stage on a hydraulic platform as thousands of minute plastic cowboys descended on parachutes from the convention-hall roof. 'All the Way with LBJ,' the Democrats roared. And they did; all the way to Hué and Saigon and the helicopters on the roof.

But whatever's wrong with this election, it isn't hubris. No one was shouting 'If you care, vote for Blair' in Hove last Sunday. In fact they weren't shouting at all. Everything and everyone, except David Blunkett, who gave new meaning to the word unrepentant, was a tad defensive, beginning with the lighting of the stage – not exactly shameless red, more softly fuchsia, the kind of ambient glow that lap dancers use to juice the tips.

The audience in Hove town hall resembled an almost ideological parade of domesticity: babies had tantrums; toddlers toddled, primary-schoolers kicked balls around the back with New Labour dads.

Blunkett eschewed altogether the much-vaunted masochism strategy in favour of unapologetic balls-of-brass: 'You know why they're attacking Tony Blair?' No, go on, tell us. 'Because Tony Blair is the greatest asset the Labour party has.' He even told a story against himself involving blindness and flirting, which somehow managed to make him endearing.

The comedian, Jo Brand, warming up for Blair, was rather more equivocal. She gave him just one stick-on star for achievement, but two for effort. She would vote Labour, she conceded, but there were some, well, a lot of really, things she wasn't too keen on – the small matter of a dodgy war, for instance. But, you know, you wouldn't want Michael Howard, would you?

Stateside, this less-than-ringing endorsement would be a cue for loud music and dimming of stage lights, while Brand was swiftly escorted from the podium and conveyed to a long and richly deserved vacation. Instead we got, by way of reminding us that someone in this outfit (Darth Campbell?) could play electoral hardball: a video evoking the Dark Side of the Tory leader; a brilliantly mixed little cocktail of malice (take one part Poll Tax and one part record unemployment, top with ice and shake) that could have had the campaign heavies in New York and Washington beaming with satisfaction that at last the Limeys have learned something about negative campaigning.

But what would they have made of the Prime Minister, next up, irradiated with the fuchsia glow, in full The Passion of the Tony, go-on-give-it-to-me mode. Look, he understands the three Disses: as in -enchantment, -agreement and -illusion. But really, come on, that's real life, not just politics. And there's so much to be proud of. The faithful agreed. Two rather small 'If you value it, vote for it' banners waved back in puppyish salutation.

But whatever elixir had been downed that night did the trick. By the Monday-morning press conference at, yes, a primary school, Blair was back in punchy, shoot-from-the-hip form, as he did what he likes doing best, pouring ridicule on the Tories' inability to do the sums; Howard's and Oliver Letwin's fitness to be CEOs of Britannia, Inc. The Prime Minister and the Chancellor then went into their alto and tenor sax riffs, the bright and the baggy, Blair at his most engaging, the Chancellor at his most solidly Gladstonian. As Brown upbraided the Tories for being insufficiently faithful to Margaret Thatcher's fiscal prudence, the map of Cuba on the classroom wall with its slogan of '*Socialismo o Muerte*' drawn in the Caribbean seemed to turn redder by the minute. Or perhaps I just imagined it.

Then followed questions from the press, the only feature of which that might have been recognisable to American reporters would have been the well-practised habit of leaders to disarm questioners by remembering their first names. In the White House press room (a calculatedly dismal prefab in the grounds) it might have the effect of defanging the journalists with mock camaraderie; but not in Wimbledon at nine in the morning. Even in the dress code of the press conference – jackets and ties for both party leaders (who'd suited up from the calculated, open-necked informality of the walkabouts) – there was the unspoken recognition of the ritualised, gladiatorial nature of the exchange. 'Right, James (or Brendan or Andrew).' 'Yes, well, going on about the danger of letting the Tories in if you vote Lib-Dem, isn't that the wife-beater sneering, "You'll stay, you've got nowhere else to go"?' To this kind of question, it's safe to say, the famous Dubya lightness would not have responded well. Instead: the telltale dilation of nostrils, the giveaway smirk behind which plans for No Future Admission would already be being finalised. Instead, both Brown and Blair laughed and it was not at all the laugh of someone about to be sick.

The ability to take this kind of take-no-prisoners irreverence on the chin; indeed, to expect it, is breathtaking to visiting reporters from the US, where oppositional politics (such as it is) is mired in a tar-pool of tepid glutinous reverence, where Democratic fury has been frightened into Milquetoast bleating by pre-emptive Republican accusations of 'divisiveness'. If John Humphrys is thinking of a late career move across the pond, he should forget it.

But then again, what must American observers make of the fact that it's Blair and Brown who are given to evoking the New Deal (albeit vintage 1997, not 1932) rather than Democrats who, with Bush prosecuting a deeply unpopular 'reform' (gutting) of social security, ought to be rallying to defend what little is left of it with their last breath? The spectacle of all three parties (for Howard, pledged to abolish student fees, would be identified as well to the American left-of-centre) campaigning on their own particular approaches to fine-tuning the welfare state is enough to fill the neutered American opposition with envious despair. They look at a government standing on a record of economic success, committed to defend public services – the mere mention of which, in the US, would likely trigger the opening of a File in the Department of Homeland Security – and, even with the long trail of muck leading from dubious intelligence reports and suspiciously altered legal advice about Iraq, they listen to the ferocity of Blairophobia and scratch their heads. (At which point perhaps they should remember LBJ for whom no amount of virtue prosecuting the great society exonerated the sins of Vietnam.) But if Blair wakes one morning and feels one prick of the pincushion too many, he might well consider a career move across the pond where he'd be a shoo-in for the next governor of New York. We're already assuming Mayor Clinton. The dynamic duo, then, reborn on the Hudson! Can't wait.

Most wondrous of all, perhaps, is the conspicuous absence in British hustings rhetoric of the one campaign helper without whose assistance no American candidate can possibly hope to prevail, namely God. But then the election is being held in a country where, unlike the US, it is assumed that Darwinian evolution is actually incontestable scientific fact, rather than just a wild hunch that has to compete with Creationism for space in textbooks and lessons. The G word finally got uttered in the Lib-Dems' last press conference before the election. 'So, Charles, do you think you'll be making another run as leader in 2009?' 'God – and my colleagues and constituents – willing,' Kennedy cheerfully replied, invoking the deity with no more theological conviction than if someone had sneezed and he'd said, 'God bless you.' And he would, wouldn't he? On parade at the press conference were all the virtues of his party and leadership: disarming honesty, cornflake-crisp optimism; milk-of-human-kindness concern for, inter alia, pensioners, students, the landscape of Britain and doubtless the Scotties and red deer that roam it.

Was I – after only a few days impersonating a political reporter – becoming, perish the thought, a tad cynical? Or was Kennedy's niceness somehow worrying? Lust for power? Not a sniff. Killer instinct? I don't think so. Even an attempt to congratulate him on the decapitation strategy provoked a denial that he'd ever thought of any term so brutal. If he doesn't want to be confused with Robespierre, perhaps Kennedy ought to spend a little time with Machiavelli. At the press conference, I asked whether he was happy to go into the election positioned as the true centre-left party. He smiled and said well, yes, the Lib-Dems were indeed progressive. Progressive as in heirs to the great reforming post-war Labour government and the bitterly unrealised dreams of the Wilson years? Well, yes, he acknowledged, apparently quite happy to slip into history tutorial mode, but I should remember that those achievements were built on the foundation of the Liberal-party reforms of the people's budget, old-age pensions, Lloyd-George/Churchill years before the First World War. Back to the future then with the Lib-Dems!

It was fabulous, this sit-down chinwag as if we were both sipping pints. And perhaps that's what Kennedy likes doing in his crofter fastness. Jean-Jacques Rousseau would have endorsed this pastoral version of politics, for he warned that while popular democracy was the only right and just political system, it could only prosper in republics of 25,000 or fewer – the size of eighteenth-century Geneva. However low the turnout today, it will be rather more than that. But coming from America where the manipulation of the millions presupposes the priority of commodity marketing, massive up-front investment, saturation advertising, the reduction of politics to the soundbite and the photo-op, a British election looks rather closer to Rousseau's ideal. In these few days I've heard colleagues say they've never seen an election more remote from the people, to which I can only reply: try coming to Baltimore or Minneapolis.

There was, though, at least one big American-pie mob scene to sample: Howard's monster rally out in Docklands. There, I met America's most prolific and famous blogger, Markos Moulitsas, who has never seen British politics at first hand before. He marvelled at the absence from the proceedings, not just of the big campaigner in the sky, but also of flags, bands, the whole pumped-up operation of patriotic euphoria and snake-oil pitches, without which the business of American politics is just so much grey newsprint and paid-for televenom.

Not that this event was low-key. Since Ashford, the SBL had had a slight but telling makeover. The shirt-cuffs now were definitely open; the shirt itself was pink; the tie had been banished. He was ACTION MAN with the ACTION PLAN! He was ready to be ACCOUNTABLE, and to prove it he announced a calendar of achievements, designed with wonderfully meaningless specificity. On 6 June 2006, mark my words and your diaries, the British Border Patrol WILL start patrolling! (What's wrong with 5 June?)

But this heady vision of a new Britain got the crowd on its feet, and, yes, they were cheering. For the new Britain turned out, in fact, to be the old Britain: cricket and courtesy, picnics and politeness, yob-free, swabs aplenty, and to prove it, as the SBL unburdened himself once more of a profession of love of country, there began the low rumble of unmistakably British Music. He ended unequivocally. The backroom boys had done their job. There will, after all, be a brighter tomorrow, starting Friday. The cheers got as riotous as English cheers can get. Elgar's 'Nimrod' powered up and Howard drank in the glory, rode the crescendo all the way to the exit, for one sovereign moment, elated, omnipotent and wholly unconditional.

Virtual Annihilation: Anti-Semitism on the Web

From Ron Rosenbaum, *Those Who Forget the Past: The Question of Anti-Semitism*, 2004

How was your Mother's Day this year? Mine didn't go so well. Call mother. What's up? 386 headstones is what's up, she says: Plashet Cemetery, East Ham, yesterday. Perpetrators arrested. A shock, I say. I'm not shocked any more, she says. And she's right.

Why should we be surprised that the ancient paranoia – or, rather, the proper Jewish anxiety about anti-Semitism – should have survived both the reasonings of modernity and the testimony of history? This is, after all, a time (and a country) where, or so opinion polls tell us, more people than not reject the scientific validity of the theory of evolution. (In some quarters, Darwinism is regarded, along with secular humanism, as another conspiracy of the Elders of Zion.) But then America is not the only country in which children are made precociously knowing, while adults are made credulous. It was a French book, after all, that recently became a best-seller by asserting that the al-Qaeda attack on the Pentagon never happened and that photographs which suggested it happened had been digitally doctored by the CIA. Where once it was naively supposed that 'images never lie', the sovereign assumption of the digital age is that they never tell the truth. Truth morphs; Elvis is alive; there were no gas chambers at Auschwitz.

The digital communications technology that was once imagined as a universe of transparent and perpetual illumination, in which cancerous falsehoods would perish beneath a saturation bombardment of irradiating data, has instead generated a much murkier and verification-free habitat where a google-generated search will deliver an electronic page in which links to lies and lunacy appear in identical format as those to truths and sanity. But why should we ever have assumed that technology and reason would be mutually self-reinforcing? The quickest visit to, say, a site called *Stormfront* will persuade you that the demonic is in fact the best customer of the electronic.

It is only in America that we imagine history as a series of cultural supercessions, each one comprehensively victorious in the totality of its effacements. Thus, in this processional view of the past, Native American society is supposed to have been obliterated by a colonialism which in turn yields to individualist and capitalist democracy. Except, of course, that it doesn't, not entirely; and much time is spent, and blood oft times spilled, tidying up the inconvenient anachronisms. In Europe, on the other hand, especially at the end of the last century, so rigidly serial an approach to cultural alteration has been suspected to be not much more than textbook convenience.

In Europe, ghosts have an impolite way of muscling their way into times and places where they are unexpected – which is why, for example, the cultural emblem of the first great industrial society in the world, Victorian Britain, imprinted on railway-station design and museums of arts, crafts and science, was the medieval pointed arch. It was, to be sure, an emblem of resistance as much as appreciation. So the pointiest of the champions of Christian Perpendicular England – Thomas Carlyle – unsurprisingly also turns out to be the fiercest in his hatred of (his words) Niggers and Jews. The great and the good of Victorian Britain could take both the friends and the enemies of the machine age in its stride. So the age that fetishised rootedness, while at the same time making fortunes by displacing mass populations, made the wilfully deracinated, the *juif errant*, the special target of its disingenuousness. Bonjour, M. Melmotte. Hello, Henry Ford.

To grow up British and Jewish is, by definition, not to be especially confounded at the obstinacy of atavisms refusing to lie down in the tomb of their redundancy. The protean persistence of anti-Semitism came home to me early. I was just seven, I think, when I first saw the writing on the wall. The wall in question was one of those crumbling red-brick affairs blocking off a view of the tracks on the Fenchurch Street line connecting London with the Essex villages lining the north bank of the Thames estuary. They were not quite suburban, though Jewish businessmen like my father had moved there out of the burnt-out wreckage of the city and the East End where they still kept warehouses and offices. They were part fishing villages, part seaside towns, part dormitory cottages and mansions; yellow broom in the spring, blowsy cabbage roses in the summer; the smell of the unloading shrimp boats and the laden winkle carts dangerously, excitingly *treif* drifting over the tide. But every morning those Jewish businessmen would take the Fenchurch Street train, and one morning my father took me as far as the station. And there on that wall, in white letters, faint and fugitive, but, since the day was cloudy (as they often are in the Estuary), glaring in the grey morning light, two cryptic letters: 'PJ'.

Nothing more; no 'PJ loves ST'; just the letters alone. So of course I asked my father about their meaning, and I remember him reddening briefly and telling me it was just some old *khazarei* – to forget about it, it didn't matter any more. This, of course, made me determined to decode the crypt, and it was, I think, my cheder teacher Mrs Marks, the same teacher who got me to dress up in miniature tuxedo as Mr Shabba (the eight-year-old bride was Mrs Balabooster), who looked me in the eye and told me that it stood for 'Perish Judah'; and that it was a relic of some bad old days in the 1930s when the fascists and Arnold Leese's Britons had marched not just in Stepney and Whitechapel and Mile End, but right down to the end of the line, to where the Jews had dared penetrate the sanctum sanctorum of Englishness: pebble-dashed, herbaceous bordered, tea-pouring Westcliff and Leigh on Sea.

'PJ' scared the hell out of me not because it smelled faintly of Zyklon B (I'm not sure I knew much about that in 1952, despite the missing relatives on my mother's side), but because my generation, born in the last years of the war, would only get their crash course on the Holocaust a little later in the London *shul* library, where Lord Russell of Liverpool's *Scourge of the Swastika*, with its obscenely unsparing photography of bulldozed naked bodies, opened and shut our eyes. But I had read *Ivanhoe*, indeed I had seen Elizabeth Taylor as Rebecca, and so the archaic, declamatory quality of the graffito spoke to me of the massacres at York, the canonisation of little St Hugh of Lincoln, Richard I's coronation slaughter in London in 1199. The persistence of the uglier strain of medieval paranoia in my island culture seemed, while not exactly fish and chips, not something wholly alien from British tradition, notwithstanding Disraeli, *Daniel Deronda*, and the Victorian high hats and morning coats that for some reason marked the official Shabba morning dress of the notables of our synagogue. Some of the same writers I most enthusiastically read as a child – Hilaire Belloc, G. K. Chesterton, John Buchan, all of them armoured warriors for holy tradition – turned out a bit later, on closer inspection, to be also the most relentless perpetuators of anti-Semitic demonologies.

Still, there was a moment of innocence. It came in 1951, in the cheerfully technocratic Festival of Britain, which seemed to announce an exorcism of barbarian phantoms. Never mind that it coincided with the first panicky revival of racist fascism in Britain, mobilised against Caribbean immigration. We were told that technology – and especially new kinds of communications technology – would diffuse knowledge, and knowledge would chase away superstition, destitution and disease. It would fall to our generation, the most confidently booming of the Baby Boomers, to make good on the promises of the Enlightenment – of Voltaire, Franklin and above all Condorcet. Modernism's start in the first half of the twentieth century had somehow fallen foul of red-fanged tribalism, but we were the children of techne, of the dream machines of the *philosophes.* I remember one of my history teachers, who, in fact, bore a startling resemblance to Voltaire, saying to our class of thirteen-year-olds, 'Well, lads, we don't know what the rest of the twentieth century has in store, but I guarantee that two of the old legacies are finally done for – revealed religion and ethnic nationalism.' So much for history's predictive power.

And looking so much like Voltaire as he did, he should perhaps have known better, since Voltaire, as we know from Arthur Hertzberg, Peter Gay and others, was the prime case of a *philosophe* who thought one way and felt another; who positively nursed the worm in the bud; who believed in the transformative power of reason up to a point, and that point was where it concerned Jews. It was not just that Voltaire believed that the condition of being able to treat Jews humanely was the mass abandonment of their Judaism by the Jews, and that he was understandably pessimistic that this would ever happen; it was also that *au fond* he believed that, even if the Jews could be persuaded to discard what made them religiously and culturally Jews, there would always be some sort of insuperable racial or even biological obstacle to true assimilation.

The notion that the benevolent illuminations of the Enlightenment

would in due course be bound to eradicate superstition and prejudice
– both those said to be held by the Jews and those undoubtedly held
against them – was compromised not just by the disingenuousness of
its apostles, but by the feebly mechanical nature of their prescience.
What failed them was their dependence on wordiness; their belief in
the inevitable and permanent supremacy of textual logic; their faith
in the unconditional surrender of fables to the irrefutably documented
proof. He who could command critical reading – and critical writing
– would, in such a world of logically driven discourse, command the
future, and that future would be one in which rational demonstration would always prevail over emotive spectacle; just as the same
epistemologists thought that the Protestant logos had vanquished
Catholic charisma. But of course it hadn't. Nor did the Enlightenment
banish the fairy-tale so much as become, in the hands of the brothers
Grimm, its most psychologically aggressive reinventor. What would
unfold, in the age of the industrial machine that ensued, was precisely
the astonishing capacity of technology to promote and to project
fantastic mythologies, rather than to dispel them.

From the outset, of course, the machinery of sensationalist stupefaction – the dioramas, and panoramas, the Eidophusikon – was the
natural handmaid of the sublime and the terrible. As Victorian Britain
became more colonised by industry, so its public became greedier for
spectacles of disaster, brought to them as visceral entertainment: the
simulacra of Vesuvian eruptions; the collapse of the Tay Bridge; an
avalanche in the Simplon. More ominously, the paradox of a modernist
technology co-opted to attack modernism became, in the hands of its
most adroit practitioners, no longer so paradoxical. D. W. Griffith, who
specialised in the manipulation of immense crowds and the apocalyptic collapse of imperial hubris, was all of a piece with the chivalric
romancer of the Ku Klux Klan. Mussolini simultaneously embraced
the piston-pumped ecstasies of Marinettian Futurism and the most
preposterous, Cinecittà-fabricated colossalism of Roman nostalgia.
Ultimately, of course, Albert Speer would deliver for Hitler a Cathedral of Light, where annihilationist rant would be bathed in arc-lit
effulgence; and Leni Riefenstahl would begin her epiphany with a
kind of aerial-cinematic Annunciation, the Angel of the Totenkopf
moving through the skies and casting an immaculately shadowed
simulacrum down on the ancestral sod.

From which it is surely just a hop, a skip and a click to the consummation of cyberhatred – to the welcoming page, for example, of the Czech-based *Jew-Rats*, where its designers, appreciative of their predecessors' knack for cutting-edge media, proudly declare, rather as if they were offering a year's warranty, that 'National Socialism was always known for its all-round, quality propaganda.' At *Jew-Rats* you can download not only the old favourites, *Der Ewige Jude* and *Triumph of the Will*, and elegiac interviews with George Lincoln Rockwell, but also try your hand at games such as *S. A. Mann, Rattenjagd* and *Ghetto Blaster*. Or try the home page of Resistance Records, which features a video game called 'Ethnic Cleansing' whose champions are Terminator-style armoured gladiators and whose targets, helpfully visualised at the top of the page (lest casual visitors confuse them with, say, Muslims or Bosnians) are Julius Streicher caricatures of Jews, complete with standard-issue *Der Stürmer*-ish extruded lips and hooked proboscis.

Just as Romantic-Gothic sensationalism fed on the victories that the optical scored over the textual, so the creative forte of digital media has been the projection of electronic violence and encrypted runes, the most archaic motifs of human culture – Manichaean battle, objects of occult veneration and ecstatic, occasionally hallucinatory vision – all delivered in liquid-crystal read-outs. One kind of elemental plasma is translated into quite another kind. The online game *Nazi Doom* is, in fact, just an adapted (and slightly pirated) version of the emphatically non-scientific Gothic Space Fantasy Games, *Doom, Final Doom* and the rather oxymoronic *Final Doom II*. The optimistic dream of the Enlightenment that technology and addictive fantasy would be in some sort of zero-sum game relationship turns out, as Walter Benjamin predicted, to be precisely the opposite case.

I do not mean to suggest, of course, that the digital world is typified by the engineered delivery of the irrational; only that it is not exactly inhospitable to its propagation. Cyberspace is itself the work of much cerebration, but its most elaborate fabulists are certainly devoted to the primacy of the visceral over the logical. They know their market. Against instantly summoned, electronically pulsing apparitions – the Celtic crosses of the White Power organisations such as Aryan Resistance, or *Stormfront*, the mid-1990s creation of the ex-Klansman Don Black – reasoned argument is handicapped, especially in any competition for the attention of alienated adolescents, for whom the appeal of barbarian action is precisely its violent rejection of bookishness. The ultimate Gothic fantasists, the mass murderers of Columbine High School, are known to have been visitors to these websites.

It is a commonplace now to observe, with Jay Bolter, that the triumph of the Web represents the overthrow — for good or for ill — not just of linear narratives, but also of the entire system of Baconian and Cartesian systems of classification, with their explicit commitment to hierarchies of knowledge. The universe of deep cyberspace is akin to whatever lies way beyond the orderly alignment of the planets in our own relatively parochial solar system. Instead it launches the traveller along pathways of links to indeterminate destinations, to the wormholes of epistemology; and along the route the digital argonaut is exposed to a furiously oncoming welter of incoherently arrayed bodies of information. The engineers of hate-sites know this, and they depend on catching the aimless surfer who might stumble, for example, on an ostensibly orientalist health site called *Bamboo Delight*, including (really) the *Skinny Buddha Weight Loss Method*, and be directed through a single link to the neo-Nazi *Police Patriot* site designed by Jew Watch and Stormfront.

The Web is, by its very nature, uncritically omnivorous. All it asks is to be fed with information. It has the capacity to monitor its input only through the clumsy and ethically controversial means of censorship, so that (I am told) in Germany, when asked for sites responding to the search 'Mengele', the Web will refuse to deliver them to the user. But the notion that any sites can somehow be adequately scrutinised, much less policed for misinformation, fraud and lies, is already both electronically and institutionally impossible. If you search Google or *www.alltheweb.com* for the Protocols of the Elders of Zion, you will be greeted on the first page by many hundreds of entries (many of which are now devoted to reporting and debating the Egyptian television series called *Horse Without a Rider*, which notoriously treated them as an historical event), not by the Anti-Defamation League, but by Radio Islam's invitation to download the entire foul and forged text, along with *The Jewish Conspiracy against the Muslim World* and Henry Ford's *The International Jew*. The Church of True Israel, and the anti-New World Order ravings of Henry Makow, Ph.D. (inventor of the word game Scruples), website *www.Savethemales.com*, regard Judaism as a mask to disguise the international hegemony of the Khazars. All these will line up for the attention of the unwary long before any sort of critical commentary is reached.

Nor could anything possibly be further away from the epistemological conventions, according to which arguments are tested against critical challenges, than the Net's characteristic form of chat, which overwhelmingly takes the form of mere call and response to which there is never any resolution, or conclusion, merely a string of unadjudicated utterances and ejaculations. Digital allegiances can be formed, then, not through any sort of sifting of truth and falsehood, but in response to, or in defence against, a kind of cognitive battering. And the virtual reality of the Internet, as Sherry Turkle, Les Back and others have pointed out, has been a gift to both the purveyors and the consumers of paranoia. It offers an electronic habitat that is simultaneously furtive and exhibitionist; structurally molecular but capable, as the user is emboldened, of forming itself into an electronic community of the like-minded. It is then perfectly engineered, in other words, for Leaderless Resistance and the Lone Wolf, the recommended model for zealous racists, Neo-Nazis and White Power warriors who are hunting, like Timothy McVeigh, in solitude or in very small and temporarily linked packs. Instead of slogging up to the camp in Idaho and Montana, digital Stormtroopers can assemble in their very own virtual Idaho, download the Horst Wessel *Lied* and electronically bond.

The Web is also, of course, a mine of useful information for the aspiring neo-Nazi, not just in the selection of human and institutional targets, but also in the resources needed to strike them: everything from artisanal ammonium nitrate to the much more wired offensives against the race enemy, involving intensive electronic jamming known as 'digital bombing' to targeted systems of contamination and sabotage. Taken together, the 500 or so websites in the United States built to proselytise for anti-Semitic and racist causes constitute a virtual universe of hatred, protean enough to hunker down or to reach out as the moment requires, encrypting, when necessary, its most bilious messages so that they become accessible only to those with the decrypting keys (a tactic adored by the secrecy fetishists), or aggressively and openly campaigning when that seems to be the priority. Once inside the net, you can log on to Resistance Records and download White

Power music or order CDs from the online catalogue; you can link to the ostensibly more mainstream racist organisations like the British National Party (who have just trebled their representation in local government elections); you can reassure yourself that the HoloCost or the Holohoax never happened and is just another disinformation conspiracy designed to channel reparations to the ever-open maw of the international conspiracy of Jew Bankers. You can order up your Nazi memorabilia or Aryan Nation warm-up jacket with all the ease of someone going shopping for Yankee souvenirs. And most ominously of all, out there in cyberspace you can act out games of virtual annihilations, with none of the risks or consequences you would incur in the actual world of body space.

In the circumstances, it is perhaps reassuring that, according to the best and most recent estimates, active regular visitors and inhabitants of anti-Semitic and racist websites may amount to no more than 50,000 or 100,000 at most. It is possible to argue, I suppose, that it is better that the paranoids lock themselves away in the black holes of poisoned cyberspace than act out their aggressions and delusions in the world of actual flesh-and-blood humanity; but that is to assume that Stormfront troopers and crusaders of the Church of True Israel will never make the leap from clicking to shooting. If there is anything that we have learned from this peculiarly delusional moment in our history, surely it is that today's media fantasy may turn into tomorrow's cultural virus. And in the world of wired terror, head-counts are no guide to the possibility of trouble, which comes, as we have already learned to our dreadful cost, very much in single terrorists rather than in battalions.

However abhorrent, the real threat posed by electronic hatred may not in fact, I suspect, be the hard-core of rabidly delusional anti-Semites and racists, who may, alas, always be with us. It is rather from the electronic extension of the paranoid style to much bigger constituencies of the aggrieved, who see in its basic world view – a global conspiracy of money, secular and sexual corruption – a perennial explanation for their own misfortune, for their own sense of beleaguered alienation. The transpositions then become easy. For the Rothschilds, read Goldman Sachs and the IMF; for the Illuminati, read the Council on Foreign Relations. As Henry Ford said of the *Protocols of the Elders of Zion*, 'All I know is that it fits events.' Nor is this habitual imprinting of the old template on contemporary events a monopoly of the left or right. In fact, *les extrêmes se touchent*: anti-globalisers meet the anti-immigrants; anti-Americanism meets America First; America First meets America Only.

What they share is a freshening and quickening of the rhetoric of violence, the poisoning of the airwaves as well as cyberspace. Ultra-chauvinist blow-hards habitually demonise on air those whom they take as insufficiently patriotic as 'scum' or 'vermin', who need in whatever manner to be locked up, deported or generally done away with. 'Who are these contaminating aliens lodged in the bloodstream of the body politic?' Lovers of multilateralism or the United Nations, and any sort of faggoty liberal intellectual who professes a self-evidently diseased scepticism and exercises a disguised but claw-like grip over the media. Jews? Goodness no. Just people who happen to talk too much and think too highly of reason.

Talking and
Listening

TBM and John

First published in Peter Mandler and Susan Pedersen's,
Private Conscience and Public Duty in Modern Britain, 1994

You always remember where it was that you first read the books that changed your life.

I first read *Macaulay: The Shaping of the Historian* in September 1976 in rocky, Medusa-infested coves on the Aegean islands of Hydra and Spetsai. While Macaulay was storming the Whig citadel of Holland House, Mavrocordatos and his fellow pan-Hellenes were launching armed fishing boats from those thyme-scented bays against the Turkish fleet. But such was the spell cast by John Clive's book that my imagination did not drift towards Messolonghi or Navarino. It was elsewhere, in virtuous Clapham, industrious Leeds and pullulating Calcutta. Later, John would give me a respectable cloth-bound signed edition of his book. But it is the dog-eared, suntan-oil-stained paperback hauled around the islands that I truly cherish. For it was in its pages that I first began to comprehend the deep wells that produced the glorious gush of Macaulay's famous *vehemence*. And it was in its pages that I first encountered John Clive.

It is the mark of a truly powerful biography to leave the reader vexed with the author for ending it, robbing him of a companion with whom he has become easily familiar. And by the time I reached 'In more ways than one, Zachary had cast a long shadow' I was all the more sorry to have Macaulay abruptly removed after a mere 500 pages of close acquaintance, especially since I longed to dog his footsteps through Italy; eavesdrop on his Cabinet gossip in 1840; commiserate with his electoral defeat in Edinburgh; sample his rich satisfaction at the record sales of the *History*; listen as he recited his rhymes to his niece Baba Trevelyan and marched the children past the giraffes of Regent's Park, the waxworks of Madame Tussaud's or (to little George Otto Trevelyan's bored dismay) the masterpieces of Eastlake's National Gallery.

I consoled myself with the knowledge that before too long I would meet the famous National Book Award-winning author whom I supposed I already knew pretty well. The jacket carried no photograph, but from the elegant, penetrating prose, the controlled sympathy shown towards Macaulay, the rigorous analysis of his intellectual formation, the shrewd delineation of his life as a political and social animal, I assumed that John Clive would turn out to be an understated, impeccably turned-out Harvard professor. His sense of humour, I thought, would be gentle and loftily Jamesian; someone who carried his colonial name with an air of Brahminical Bostonian *savoir faire*. The biographer's relationship with his subject, whose public mask he had removed to expose the conflicted, passionate and often troubled private man beneath, had to be, I supposed, that of a sympathetic doctor who would calmly listen and offer spoonfuls of cool understanding to his distracted patient.

So much for my powers of literary deduction. Two months later, John knocked (or rather pounded) on the doors of my rooms in Brasenose, tripped over the door-sill and fell spread-eagled on my couch. After we had exchanged flustered apologies, it took about five minutes and a cup of tea (which John drank as if it were a famous vintage, enquiring after brand, store of origin, length of brew) for me to see how spectacularly wrong I had been. The name 'Clive' remained mysterious (as it did for many years), but it didn't take a genius to see that my rumpled guest, who was enjoying his tea and cake so visibly, was hardly a representative of the Boston class, famous for its cool detachment and sensuous self-denial. By the end of an hour I was in a state of delighted amazement that the historian whose extraordinary work I had so admired had also become an immediate friend. After John departed (without further hazard) I ran through the character description which now replaced my hopelessly misjudged extrapolation from his prose style. The historian I had met was warm-hearted, affectionate, voluble; mischievously hilarious, gossipy; clumsy, and self-indulgent. His speech moved from embarrassed stammering to flights of eloquence, the sentences broken with puns and rhymes and even snatches of song performed with exaggerated operatic trills. In the mouldy dimness of the Oxford room his large eyes sparkled with pleasure at a well-taken idea or a well-turned phrase and, at the delicious prospect of routing a common enemy, he would smack a fist into his palm with boyish exultation.

But I had run through this anatomy of a personality before, hadn't I? It was John's account of Macaulay.

The best thing I know on the problems of biography is Richard Holmes's *Footsteps*. Its premise is the inescapable *glissade* between biography and autobiography. Are there any biographers who never ask themselves why they have chosen their subjects; whether, indeed, their subjects have not in some disconcerting sense chosen *them*? Why indeed, you might ask yourselves, have the contributors to this very volume adopted their own particular historical doppelgängers?

Among the many virtues of Holmes's book is that it makes these conundrums explicit. Its confessional voice, tracking Robert Louis Stevenson through the Cévennes (albeit without donkey), Shelley in Lerici, Mary Wollstonecraft and Gerard de Nerval in Paris, is made tolerable by Holmes's own acute self-consciousness of the naivety of these pursuits. In one of the most powerful passages of the book, the denial of total identification is suggested to him by the belated discovery of the very bridge over which Stevenson had crossed the Allier River to reach the little country town of Langogne. It was visible but unattainable, 'crumbling and covered with ivy'. The biographer's efforts to overtake the footsteps of his subject would always be thwarted by such obstacles. The best that could be expected was 'to produce the living effect while remaining true to the dead fact . . . You stood at the end of the broken bridge and looked across carefully, objectively into the unattainable past on the other side. You brought it alive, brought it back, by other sorts of skills and crafts and sensible magic.'

Yet part of that 'sensible magic', Holmes concludes at the end of his Stevenson essay, is the willingness to experience a 'haunting' of the kind he himself went through in 1964 in the Cévennes. This means not only approaching the life of the subject as closely as possible, but actually inventing a continuous dialogue between biographer and subject; a sustained conversation with the writer 'talking back' to his alter ego. Such a process necessarily involves identification and projection for, Holmes says with disconcerting candour, 'If you are not in love with them you will not follow them – not very far, anyway.' And, to be sure, those biographies designed from beginning to end as combat most often end as a vehicle for the author, rather than an exposure of the life, or else simply co-opt their subject as endorsements for the author's favourite cause. No one could ever accuse Richard Holmes of that kind of literary hijacking. But his claim that the biographer should become a virtual literary twin of the subject, distinct yet extremely closely related, is of a piece with the attempt to recover the contingencies that shape a life, not to see it from its birth as somehow predestined to follow a particular path. Only if the subject can be disentombed from his obituary can the unpredictable turns, which John often reminded his readers could somehow be the crucial determinants of a life, be given their real due.

Holmes knows, of course, that this close engagement can never be the whole story. For if the biographer must pursue identification for his story to have inner truth and conviction, he must also disengage if it is to have coherence and understanding. This is especially true of historical biography where authors are inescapably caught in a notoriously tight hermeneutic circle. For while their subject's career is necessarily, and to some degree, the product of his culture and society, it may well, during his own lifetime, have decisively shaped the character of that culture.

So whom had I met on that Oxford autumn day in 1976: the biographer or the biographee? Was my own imagination still so imprinted with his image of Macaulay that I was now fancying it perpetuated in the person of the historian's historian? Had John Clive's own life been so leased out to Macaulay to create his book that it had been returned to him decisively altered by the encounter? Or was it just that this was a literary marriage made on Parnassus, the perfect fit, a miraculous transfer of intelligence and sympathy from one Cambridge to the other?

How close were those natural affinities? In the Clapham Sect little Tom had been celebrated as an extraordinary prodigy, composing Latin poems and assuming a precociously grave manner. To Lady Waldegrave's solicitous enquiry after he had had hot coffee spilled over him by her maid, he replied, 'Thank you, Madam, the agony has somewhat abated.' The instantaneous completeness of his memory was found startling; his quickfire speech almost an excited gabble; his appetite for learning apparently insatiable. Yet his natural exuberance gave his father, Zachary, cause for concern that it might lead him into acts of abomination like reading novels. Hence the energies of the boy were contained within a high stockade of grim Evangelical righteousness.

The little boy with the fair hair and chubby cheeks who hung on the least sign of affection from his mother Selina, and gloried in the performance of parlour recitations, was first entrusted to the zealous Hannah More for the right mixture of godliness and good learning. Then, at twelve, he was packed off to an austerely correct Evangelical boarding school at Little Shelford, near Cambridge, where he suffered agonies of homesickness and discovered that not all Wilberforces, especially not the small thug-like representative at Reverend Preston's School, were paragons of Christian piety. To letters that John Clive describes as 'blotted with tears' Zachary responded with cold consolation. 'He did not find any comfort in Zachary's reminder that Christ had left His father for thirty years and had encountered many troubles yet faced them cheerfully.'

In the Berlin of the 1920s and '30s, Hans Kleyff grew up in almost the opposite atmosphere of patriotic assimilation: Biedermeyer furniture; *Küchen, Kinder und Kultur*. Where Macaulay's cultural performances were in essence always dramatic and rhetorical, in the kind of house typified by the Kleyffs the highest expression of *Bildung* would necessarily have been musical. (The first prize that John won was for music and both he and his brother Geoffrey were accomplished performers.) While Zachary Macaulay's exacting and fervent faith coloured his entire public life, and was a creed drummed relentlessly into the head of his son, Bruno Kleyff's relaxed Judaism barely intruded at all into the social rituals of his metropolitan, professional world. Synagogue, John often recalled, was principally the occasion for his father to sport the Iron Cross he had received for his service in the First World War. And that belief in the civilised compatibility of German culture and Jewish origins remained obstinately in place (as it did for so many of that community), even as the monstrous savagery of National Socialism began to proclaim it a biological impossibility. So where Zachary and Selina Macaulay *chose* to embrace the moral identity of Outsiders, saints walking upright among the sinners of the slave-holding empire, the Kleyffs were turned into fugitives only by the most violent horrors the century had to offer.

For John it was the Fatherland, not the father, that stripped him of the familiar assurances of a bourgeois childhood. Though he would experience the harrowing ordeal of his father's arrest, it was a boyish humiliation that brought home to him the true nature of the punishing barbarism of the Third Reich. For inevitably, the Nuremberg laws caught up with the traditions of the *Gymnasium* and John, along with other Jewish boys, was forbidden to go on the annual boat outing on the Spree. Wounded by the ostracism, burning with tears, John always remembered that day as the beginning of exile.

Did his family's experience at the hands of the Nazis make John warm to the Whig whose maiden speech in the House of Commons was an appeal to remove the bar against Jewish Members of Parliament? In fact, Macaulay took the subject further by writing an eloquent and influential essay in the *Edinburgh Review* against 'the Civil Disabilities of the Jews'. Yet John's treatment of the whole topic is tantalisingly and uncharacteristically sketchy. And given his extraordinary critical penetration of almost every *other* aspect of the young Macaulay's life, it is also strangely incurious. The speech and the essay may well, as he claims, show 'at their best [the author's] commonsense', but whether they also 'get to the root of the matter' is more debatable. For although Macaulay characteristically punctures the most fatuous prejudices against the Jews, and especially those that implied their unassimilability in English society, he is not without decided prejudices of his own. He does not, for example, follow the lead of the French revolutionary legislators who argued for emancipation on the grounds that its consequence would be to dissolve the separateness of the Jews within the political nation. (Indeed it may be to Macaulay's credit that he baulked at this patronising liberalism.) But he argued instead that *since* the Jews had so much property and economic power it was inexpedient to deny them the political influence that went with them. Of course this 'interest group' reform Whiggism was of a piece with his view on extending representation to incorporate industrial constituencies, and he may well have felt about the burghers of Leeds whom he would represent as he did about the Goldsmids and the Rothschilds. But then again, possibly not.

In any case there is one revealing piece of evidence about Macaulay's real attitudes towards the Jews, in the form of a letter written to his sister Hannah at virtually the same time (the summer of 1831) that he was writing his essay for the *Edinburgh Review*. It describes a costume party given by a wealthy Jew to which Macaulay went in ordinary dinner dress, and it shows the young lion of Whig society at his worst, sniggering in corners with the likes of Strutt and Romilly at the ridiculous parvenus got up as Turks and Persians. Occasionally the patricians would take time off from condescension to ogle the 'Israelitish women' like the 'angel of a Jewess in a Highland plaid'. And even when he got to bed that night, Macaulay writes to Hannah, it 'was some time before I could get to sleep. The sound of fiddles was in mine ears and gaudy dresses and black hair and Jewish noses were fluctuating up and down before mine eyes.'

For some reason John Clive's account omits this incident entirely, even though George Otto Trevelyan's *Life and Letters* includes the letter and though it had exactly the kind of brilliant historical colour that he splashed over the pages of his biography. Indeed when he was reminded of the letter by a friend and colleague, John's first instinct was to express scepticism about whether any such letter or any such event existed. Could it have been that his own feeling for London and Oxford as tolerant worlds, where the 'Whig grandees' of his own time mixed on easy terms with the inner circle of German Jewish intellectuals who made up the core of John's favourite *Stammtisch*, softened the edges of Anglo-Jewish history?

Certainly John looked back on his asylum in England as a crucial moment in the trajectory of his whole life, even though he seldom talked about its details. His family lived in Buxton, the old spa town of the Derbyshire Peaks near Matlock (that Macaulay knew very well), and where other German Jews had settled, sometimes under a kind of official surveillance, designated, however absurdly given their circumstances, as 'enemy aliens'. John went to school at Buxton and at some point in these years Hans Leo Kleyff turned into John Leonard Clive, his grandly imperial name some protection at least from the predictable misfortunes of being a Jewish refugee with a German accent in an English public school. Was it at this time that he fell in love with English (rather than British) culture, with its patterns of speech and the sounds of its voices, with the stuttering horsiness and the plummy gentility that he loved to mimic later on?

In any event Buxton was not, for John Clive, what Cambridge was for Macaulay: the place where a fresh social and intellectual identity was established *against* the grain of his family background. Periods of real hardship followed in New York, where at one point the Clives made ends meet by stapling teabag tags, possibly the only manual craft that John ever mastered. The gutsy vitality of New York, even in wartime, encouraged another side of his personality: earthy, pleasure-seeking and flamboyant. To the pianist who played (and sang in a husky baritone) Schubert lieder, and who could pound out choruses of the Victorian hymns, was now added the ivory-tickler of Cole Porter and Gershwin standards. In our house ''S Wonderful' or 'You're the Top' got the full cabaret treatment while a large pastrami on rye waited on top of the upright.

By an amazing quirk of fate, the institution that really had the same formative impact on John as Cambridge had for Macaulay, was the US Army, or rather the not especially typical research unit of the OSS assigned to analyse German politics and strategy for military intelligence. That unit, as Barry Katz's fine book has shown, was staffed with historians, many of whom were to remain John's closest friends and, in other crucial respects, his intellectual mentors and peers: Felix Gilbert, Carl Schorske, Stuart Hughes and Franklin Ford. At the University of North Carolina, as a student on a special scholarship, he had mostly read English literature. But in the OSS he was brought directly into the company of a whole group of distinguished and brilliant historians in the making. It was, moreover, a group that deployed their analytical and critical faculties for an incontrovertible political good. The fact that a crucial inner core were all, like John, refugees from the great German-Jewish culture obliterated by the Nazis only added to their solidarity. It also reinforced an urgent Thucydidean sense that history could speak directly and decisively to the most powerful crises of the human condition.

Thucydides also remained Macaulay's ideal historian: analytically concentrated, critically sharp; unapologetic about history as the origins of the contemporary; unsurpassed as a narrative craftsman and rhetorician. At the age of twenty-eight (roughly the age graduate students now complete their doctorates) Macaulay was cocksure enough to announce just what history was, what was wrong with its modern practice; and to prescribe how it might be improved. That improvement would, in his view, be essentially literary since history was 'a debatable land. It lies on the confines of two distinct territories. It is under the jurisdiction of two hostile powers . . . Instead of being equally shared between its two rulers Reason and the Imagination it falls alternately under the sole and absolute dominion of each.' (Later the same year in his essay on Hallam, Macaulay would characterise the division of history as one part poetry, one part philosophy, or in yet another formulation of the same idea, as part map-making, part landscape-painting.)

John shared exactly Macaulay's notion that 'History in its state of ideal perfection' should be both poetical and philosophical. But he did not always have Macaulay's ebullient confidence that the reconciliation of those two sensibilities could be accomplished, osmotically, by a Scottian immersion in the texture of sources. Though it is hard to think of any historical biography which more brilliantly accomplished this synthesis of literary craft and historical analysis than his *Macaulay*, the union of skills did not come effortlessly. When he enrolled in David Owen's seminar in British history as a first-year graduate student at Harvard in 1946, he thought he might work on Disraeli's novels (a subject which would, I think, have been a perfect choice). But the professor, whose work had principally been in the field of local government and Victorian philanthropy and whose temper was, by turns, mordantly sardonic and austerely remote, rapidly disabused him. The young Clive was instead set to work on the Poor Law Amendment Act of 1834 since that, as he himself explained in a Foreword to a posthumously published book of Owen's, was a way to 'get you into parliamentary papers'. Seeing his student immediately crestfallen, Owen urged him to 'Cheer up, you'll be reading the London *Times* as well.'

In the same essay John expresses gratitude to Owen for emphasising the historian's necessary engagement with institutional and political sources. But though he plunged into research for both his major books with the most painstaking thoroughness, he sometimes felt it more duty than pleasure, especially when compared with the speculative and playful qualities of free historical writing that came to him with such grace and brilliance. Even in his first book, *Scotch Reviewers* (1957), that deals with the early history of the *Edinburgh Review*, it is the passages that sketch the personality of its great editor, the pint-sized and pugnacious Francis Jeffreys, that dart from the printed page.

So however conscientious he wanted to be in respect of mastering the most intricate historical circumstances – and in Macaulay's political heyday in the 1830s and '40s, they were to a layman phenomenally complicated – it was always likely that the power of John's biography would be that of a gripping human history. He was also fortunate, as he was the first to admit, that in G. O. Trevelyan's famous *Life and Letters* he had a wonderful springboard from which to launch his own enquiry. As a nephew of Macaulay and a Victorian Eminence in his own right, Trevelyan discreetly circumnavigated some of the most delicate aspects of his uncle's life. But in many places he is surprisingly forthright about his uncle's mercurial personality. Indeed Trevelyan's declared purpose in writing his book was to show that the Statesman and Historian conventionally accused of righteous self-satisfaction, both with himself and with his Times, was in fact a man of the most exacting and often self-mortifying passions.

There were, however, certain moments in Macaulay's life from which Trevelyan not only averted his own gaze, but directly informed the reader he would pass on to more seemly and edifying matters. Together with the superlative and exhaustive job of editing Macaulay's papers done by Thomas Pinney, this left John in a perfect position from which to revisit the storms and stresses of the career. Where Trevelyan had presented Macaulay's turbulent emotional life as a darkened background to his public life, John made it the *clavis interpretandi*. Above all it was to be a family history, as those closing words about Zachary suggest, and one written with all the engagement, compassion and insight of one of the great Mitteleuropa sagas of bourgeois dynasties: Mann, Fontane, Schnitzler and Zweig, as it were, come to visit the Clapham Sect.

And Sigmund Freud too, of course. Not that John's reading of Macaulay's relationships with his mother, father and sisters is in any sense mechanically Freudian. But given his gathering revolt against Zachary's moral authoritarianism, his adoring devotion to his mother Selina and above all his disturbingly inflamed love for his sisters, the central drama of the book could not help but be acutely psychological.

Neither Tom nor John ever married. After his father died, the centre of John's personal life was his older brother Geoffrey, a philosophy professor and, by all accounts, an accomplished cellist. But Geoffrey Clive was also a diabetic who suffered a brutally withering form of the disorder, going blind before dying in 1975. I don't mean to make crass analogies here between John's devotion to Geoffrey, which in any case I only knew of as part of his memory, and Macaulay's almost operatic possessiveness towards Hannah and Margaret. But it seems to me inconceivable that the closeness of the brothers did not, to some degree, enrich the compassion and depth of understanding that John had for Macaulay's own intense sibling relationships.

At the heart of that relationship, John makes clear, was the overgrown boy Tom's craving to find a domestic nest that would give him the emotional and even physical succour that the bleak righteousness of Zachary and Selina's Clapham virtue had denied. With Hannah (whom he even rebaptised as 'Nancy') and Margaret, he was able to do all the prohibited things: joke, caper, confess weakness; show off; preen himself on his brilliance, chastise himself on his inadequacies, and, both on paper and in person, talk on and on and on, mostly on the subject of Tom, without fear of interruption or contradiction. The bonds which attached his sisters to his own life were, then, intensely selfish. Macaulay felt that his entertainment value, the reflected light that shone from his own political and literary brilliance, and his repeated utterances (all perfectly sincere) of passionate and undiluted love, were enough recompense for all they were supposed to do for him. But those kindnesses and services comprised a long list: from tending his political wounds, humouring his caprices, invariably endorsing his prejudices and, not least, keeping house.

Self-conscious to the point of obsession with what he thought was his ugliness and corpulence (neither of which appears especially offputting in any of the known likenesses), Macaulay decided, fairly early on, that he would eschew a sexual or conjugal relationship. Those energies that might be dangerously compromised by such tangles would instead be harnessed to the drive of his political and literary career. And as for love, of which he truly possessed a natural abundance, that would find expression in what he imagined to be the purest possible form: that of a brother for his sisters.

It is quite impossible for a modern reader to take in the elemental passion of many of those letters and not find them, at many points, implicitly incestuous. Macaulay's tone to both of them is, in the idiom of the time, that of a lover who goes well beyond the norms of brotherly affection. When Margaret became engaged, his response (expressed to the other sister) was one of jealous outrage and hurt.

For the most part John's biography surveys these storms and stresses with humane precision, often allowing the extraordinary correspondence to speak for itself. In fact at times authorial intervention seems almost excessively suppressed, given the drama unfolding in the letters. In 1834, for instance, Macaulay decided that he would have to accept the post of one of the Secretaries-in-Council to the Governor-General of the East India Company in Calcutta, for purely financial reasons. Announcing this fact to the remaining single sister Hannah (his 'Nancy'), he also asks her to go with him to India, a request that was in fact an act of outrageous selfishness and which was initially greeted with horrified disbelief. Of course, Macaulay couches his request in such a way that it would be *possible* for her to deny him, but only at the prohibitive price of reneging on her own loyalty and love. All in all, the letter is a classic of moral blackmail.

The biographer refrains from saying anything like this. Perhaps he knows full well that Macaulay would be punished many times over for his selfishness when Hannah finds *her* own husband in Charles Trevelyan, one of Tom's colleagues in the civil administration in Calcutta. Moreover, the letter he sends on this occasion back to Margaret in England, full of despairing (if belated) self-knowledge about the futility of the idyll he had created for himself, unmarried sisters ministering for ever to the needs of their genius brother, is so tragically dark as to make any editorialising gratuitous. But is it possible, also, that John, who lived his life in a series of surrogate families, who was virtually adopted by them as an honorary brother and uncle, ate at their table, sang to their children, watched ball games and movies with them, was fed and cared for by them, understood this heavy loneliness at an emotional and psychological depth that could not be registered in the conventions of an historical biography?

Though Margaret's death in 1835 threatened for a while to throw Macaulay into an abyss of depression, this is not a story of unrelenting sorrow – the sad face beneath the public mask of Victorian good cheer. Macaulay never recovered the gregariousness of his Holland House days in the 1820s when he had been the toast of Whig Westminster. But much of his life, until his death in 1852, was spent in the domestic circle of Hannah and Charles Trevelyan and their children to whom he was the irrepressibly high-spirited uncle, regaling them with poems and stories and outings and treats. At one point Macaulay even attributed his ability to make history popular to the fact that he spent so much time talking to small children. That he could do this with a magically assured touch, utterly without condescension, was because there was always a large, overgrown child in the adult Macaulay himself: greedy for affection and praise; easily stung and wounded; just as easily delighted and excited; lavish with his emotions and wicked with his literary nose-thumbing.

John never got to write of this Macaulay: the 'Uncle Tom' whom his first biographer George, when still little 'Georgie' Trevelyan, had no idea was in any way famous or distinguished beyond the fact that he now and then wrote books. But my own children got to know and love their 'Uncle John'; to hear *his* poems, and stories, and songs; laugh at his jokes; humour his rituals; tease him with the threat of his most detested foods (a long list that included honey, olives and any vegetables unknown to his mother's kitchen in the Berlin of the 1930s). Once when I attempted to cook him his favourite dessert, Salzburgernockerln, an impossibly oxymoronic confection of ice and hot custardy interior, I saw my daughter Chloë catching John in an expression of shut-eyed rapture and later asking me, 'Daddy, what did you *put* in that?' For them he was utterly memorable; a child-man; a walking explosion of affectionate and wonderfully uncoordinated humanity.

One of his very closest friends and colleagues has noted that John had a great genius for friendship. And though we who still bitterly miss him understand this first of all as something he added to our personal and domestic lives, it might be argued that that gift actually had powerful and positive consequences for his historical writing. In one of the most dazzling essays in his last book, 'The Great Historians in the Age of Cliometrics', he has Gibbon, Macaulay and Carlyle, each in their own manner, discuss the cutting-edge issue of correlations between sibling numbers and the incidence of baldness among Ohio clockmakers. The pastiches are realised with deadly precision. But as hilarious as they are, they could only have been produced by someone who had become an affectionate familiar of the great men; had listened carefully to the mannerisms of their diction; whose impersonations would then be marked by loving attentiveness.

In another essay in *Not By Fact Alone* (1989) John does his best to give cogent intellectual reasons why we should go on reading the great historians: as exemplars of narrative, tacticians of argument and so on. But in the end he always reverted to the sheer pleasure of their company. Burckhardt, Michelet, Parkman, Henry Adams, Tocqueville and even Marx made up this precious *Stammtisch* of great historians, along with the British writers. The delight with which he samples them, follows their moves, relishes their ingenuity, wallows in their eccentricity, basks in the warmth of their vitality, was much the same as the unalloyed happiness he exuded at a table of eloquent, gabbling, laughing friends. By the same token he would roll his eyes in despair when banal monotony engulfed any sort of institutional meeting, which meant that there was a good deal of eye-rolling from his corner along with a peculiar gesture of taking off his wristwatch and dangling it by the strap, as if he could see his life ticking away in inconsequential tedium.

Yet there was much more to this than a kind of intellectual epicureanism. For at heart John believed that historical wisdom only deserved to endure if it had a proper quotient of wit, force and literary power. That was why he was so depressed by the vast cargo of drab, congested and hectoring prose that he thought weighed down the learned journals. By contrast there was obviously something irresistibly joyous even in the most outrageous adolescent crowing of the young Macaulay who announced a new publication (*The Etonian*) thus:

> Some of us have no occupation, some of us have no money, some of us are desperately in love, some of us are desperately in debt; many of us are very clever and wish to convince the public of that fact . . . we will go forth to the world once a quarter in high spirits and handsome type and a modest dress of drab with verse and prose criticism and witticism, fond love and loud laughter . . . Our food shall be of the spicy curry and the glistening champagne — our inspiration shall be the thanks of pleasant voices and the smiles of sparkling eyes.

When I arrived at Harvard in 1980 I myself thought John's reverence for these past masters exaggerated and his determination to pass on their legacy to his students, a gently old-fashioned kind of work, canonical and aesthetic, not at all in keeping with the vogue for cultural history done by those roaming the jungles of symbolic anthropology. How callow and obtuse I was! For even before he died, and certainly ever since, I can think of nothing more important than to convey the enduring power and wisdom, form and substance of the great masters. Far from cramping the style of students, direct contact with the immense range of creative imagination inscribed in their texts liberates them for any and all possibilities of historical expression. To my belated delight I have found that most undergraduates would gladly trade all the dense theoretical discussions of 'narrative strategy' and 'cultural methodology' for a few pages of the seductive gossip of Herodotus or the dazzling mischief of Edward Gibbon. For as long as this matters, historians and many others will read John Clive with huge pleasure and instruction.

Isaiah Berlin

Review of Isaiah Berlin: *Flourishing: Letters 1928–1946*,
edited by Henry Hardy, *New Republic*, 31 January 2005

In February 1942, Isaiah Berlin, thirty-two years old, sat in a Jewish
religious court in New York City, listening intently to the case of a
one-legged octogenarian *schnorrer* whose amputated limb had gone
missing after surgery. This, as Berlin recognised, was no joke. Unless
the leg was buried in hallowed ground, preferably close to the rest of
the old boy, come the return of the Messiah, it could not be reunited
with the rest of him. A while without his leg, he said, he didn't mind;
fifty years, say, okay, even 100, 200 maybe, but to go around on a
wooden leg for all eternity? Understandably bemused, the judges (one
of whom Berlin noted was called, sublimely, Justice Null) wondered
out loud what the court could do about it. 'That's what I want to know,'
the *schnorrer* replied. After deliberation the rabbi and the justice came
up with a solution. A token piece of the old man – a fingernail, say –
would be buried with due solemnity declaring that, in the unavoid-
able circumstances, it would stand in for the leg. On the day of
resurrection, the Almighty, surely impressed by the judgement of the
court, would accept the substitution, and the reassembled man would,
with any luck, stride off into the everlasting.

In the letter to his parents, back in solid Hampstead, Berlin, famous
for his relish of the human comedy, described the scene without a trace
of condescension, much less farce. 'The thing was really most pathetic,'
he wrote, using that last word literally. 'A man condemned to wander
about on one leg for eternity, unenviable even in Paradise.' But what
touched Berlin was not just the plight of the old man, but the inspired
improvisation of the two judges, faced with an apparently impossible
request. Short of the ideal solution – the recovery of the missing leg –
their task was to find some way in which the pain and fear of the sufferer
could be eased, and this they satisfactorily accomplished. By Berlin's

lights, this was humane intelligence operating exactly as it should; authority applied to its supreme duty: that of minimising suffering.

If reading this glorious collection of Berlin's letters is, predictably, a heady experience, it is also hearty. Not in the British sense of cheery muscularity (definitely not Berlin's thing), but in the sense that the letters reveal an intellectual sensibility in which uncompromising analytical clarity was uniquely married to an unshakable faith in the moral instincts of humanity. Abstract ideas, free-floating in their own rarefied sphere of discourse, unmoored from historical place and moment (the philosophical fashion when he arrived in Oxford in the early 1930s), became, for him, a kind of high intellectual aesthetics. In the hands of its nimblest practitioners, like J. L. Austin, the performance was a marvellous thing to behold, but in the end, as Berlin realised while crossing the Atlantic in the belly of a bomber in 1944, it was play, not work; at any rate not his kind of work. So while *Flourishing*, packed with letters which, on top form, put Isaiah Berlin in the same rank of epistolary artists as Evelyn Waugh or Kenneth Tynan, can be enjoyed as the most delicious kind of literary and intellectual confectionery (a form of nourishment Isaiah was the last to discount), the book is best read as a *Bildungsroman* of the twentieth century; the strenuous journey of an exceptional mind towards its own self-realisation.

Isaiah Berlin is most famously remembered (especially in Britain) as an unparalleled intellectual phenomenon: the encyclopaedic memory and prodigious intellect delivering high-velocity aperçus, at a rate that left audiences gasping: a bassoon on speed. The first time I saw him lecture in the late 1960s, on the tortured relationship between Tolstoy and Turgenev, he prefaced his remarks by declaring: 'Ladies and Gentlemen, I must warn you that I speak very low and very fast, so if you fail to understand me, would you please indicate this by some eccentricity of behaviour.' Since the caveat was itself delivered the same way, no one took him up. All of Berlin's most dazzling qualities were on pyrotechnic display that evening: the sharp-focused illumination of literature as social thought; the representation (almost a re-enactment) of the cultural world from which that literature had sprung; the poignant incommensurability of ultimately irreconcilable tempers (a Berlin speciality, whether of writers or nations). As he warmed to the subject – as usual without a note, much less a text, the eloquence unfaltering – his expansiveness lit the wintry Cambridge evening. (It had been a prophetic choice when he had named the high-school magazine he founded at St Paul's: *The Radiator*.) Narrating some of Tolstoy's high moral absurdities, Berlin mugged, his broad face turning impishly deadpan, shamelessly milking the laughs. As for his two protagonists, especially Turgenev, who functioned as a ghostly (and sometimes disturbingly close) alter ego for his own anxieties and insecurities, Berlin not so much explored their personae as inhabited them; the basso profundo turning less, or more, emphatic depending on which of the two was getting his moment: the head shaking in mock disbelief; a hand tucked into the vest of his three-piece suit, then emerging in mildly Ciceronian gestures of advocacy. As a performance of the drama of ideas, the lecture was for the connoisseur of the genre, delectably operatic.

Which, some recent critics claim, is all that there really ever was. Reviewed coolly, without benefit of the sentimental reverence generated by a rich body of Berlin anecdotal lore, his whole body of work is said to amount to less than the sum of its parts. This demurral, offered as an astringent reaction against the excesses of Isaiolatry, was entirely predictable, especially in Britain where dimming haloes, especially posthumously, is something of a national pastime, but it could hardly be more obtuse. Far from Berlin's central intellectual preoccupations havering weakly between the hard poles of analytical philosophy and political practice, they can be seen, now more than ever, as unerringly located, precisely at the point where ideas catch dangerous fire: in the realm of social religion. Far from the issues with which he struggled – the tragic irreconcilability of liberty and equality; the social and psychological roots of tribal and national allegiance, to name but two – being extended footnotes to the long nineteenth century (where, certainly, Berlin felt at home), they could hardly be more germane to the tortured perplexities of our own immediate and future situation. When Tony Blair asked Berlin whether he truly believed 'negative liberty' (the removal of coercive constraint) sufficed without the complement of 'positive liberty' (a universally agreed good, reachable through collective rational self-determination), he was paying homage, rather than lip service, to the perennial importance of the distinction first essayed in Berlin's *Two Concepts of Liberty*. Doubtless Berlin would have answered, 'You may well be right', but even supposing you are, not to recognise the pursuit of whatever greater good the Prime Minister might have in mind would entail the sacrifice of some element of liberty, would be to bury his head in the deepest dune.

Nor is there anything about 2005 which would have made Isaiah Berlin repent of the insistence, reiterated in so much of his work, on the historicity of ideas; their particularity in time and place; their obstinate resistance to universalisation. The naive fancy that one-size-fits-all democracy could be transported from the Potomac to the Tigris; or that any sort of system of ideas could be held to be objectively 'timeless' and thus deliverable independently of specific cultural circumstances, would have filled him with grim disbelief. The notion that a *war* might be fought on such deeply mistaken premises would have left him shaking his head (and he did this as rapidly as his speech patterns) in dire dismay.

Though I'm not sure he would have welcomed the classification, Berlin was, in his way, an anthropologist of cultural allegiance; prepared to engage seriously with precisely the kind of ideas which ought to have repelled him: those which were the least cosmopolitan, the least rational, the least amenable to easy resolution through agreed ends. It would have been easy enough for him to write about Voltaire or Benjamin Constant. Instead he gave Counter-Enlightenment anti-rationalist writers like Joseph de Maistre and J. G. Hamann their full due. It was the airy thinness of mechanistic Enlightenment rationality, its failure to speak to the deeper impulses of memory, language and mythology, which, however alien to his own cast of mind, Berlin recognised as potent epistemological facts and which sent him to Vico and Herder. Those exasperated by the reluctance of Sunni Iraqis to be reasonable and take their coming electorally rendered punishment on the chin could do worse than to read Berlin on the tenacity of social magic in the allure of tribal nationalism.

Not that the message would be cheering. Early on in his stay in the United States, where he arrived first in 1940, hoping to move on to Moscow (via Japan), Berlin realised that his sceptical, tragic view of history made him a cultural misfit. In both New York, where Berlin was employed at the British Press Service in Manhattan, and in Washington, where he became Head of the Political Survey section at the embassy, he blinked at the sunlit intensity of American optimism.

Though he genuinely admired American energy and forthrightness, the mistaken conviction that exhaustive iteration was the same thing as understanding depressed him. Ultimately he thought that the national passion for the unequivocal could only be sustained through an exercise of eye-shutting make-believe akin to a children's party game; the conversion of the world from what it was to what America wished (fingers crossed and scarlet slippers clicked) it would be. If not actually inhuman, this optimisation of the world, he thought, was nonetheless a willed self-deception about the reality of human behaviour, namely that there were no conflicts which, with the application of enough goodwill, money and robust determination, could not be resolved.

But for Berlin, even then, it was the beginning of public wisdom to accept that there were indeed a multitude of evils which, in fact, were not open to resolution since arguments of persuasively equal validity could be made for each side. Hello Belfast, hello Jerusalem. Accordingly, the job of statecraft was not to liquidate those differences (for that would seldom happen), but to contain them; to find a space in which *acceptance* of irreconcilability would not require mutual annihilation. However unarguable as historical fact and however timely for our own instruction, this, it need hardly be said, is not the kind of message likely to feature in American inaugural addresses. Better the vacuous uplift of the inspirational nostrum than the sobering descent of the incontrovertible truth.

Not surprisingly, then, there is some mischievous Berlinian ambiguity to the title that his exemplary editor, Henry Hardy, has given to this book of letters. 'Flourishing' was Berlin's habitual communiqué to his parents, Mendel and Marie, to calm their perpetual anxieties about his health and fortunes. In these repeated reassurances he was the touchingly dutiful Jewish son; so much so that, on occasion, Isaiah actually reproached *them* for not writing, cabling, calling. But sometimes, especially from New York, he signalled 'flourishing' when he was anything but. Stuck in his British Press Office on the thirtieth floor of the Rockefeller Center, appointed to liaise with American Jews and Labour Organisations, Berlin missed the banter and gossip of his Oxford friends so desperately and became so despondently guilty about the triviality, as he then saw it, of his contribution to the war effort that at one point his feelings turned suicidal. On another occasion, discovered by his parents to have been hospitalised with pneumonia while sending off yet another 'flourishing' letter, Berlin protested that in fact he *had* flourished before he hadn't, and that, in any case, a New York hospital bed was an enviable idyll: terrific food, nothing to do but read, no one bothering him.

Yet of course Isaiah Berlin did *flourish*, not just in the sense of thriving as Mendel and Marie Berlin hoped, but in the sense of delivering a bravura passage of brass in the reedy plainsong that was philosophical Oxford in the 1930s. Though he happily plunged into a post-Wittgensteinian ethos, drunk on the over-excited discovery that language and the unstable apparatus of cognition might constitute the only available reality, Berlin – who hardly lacked for speech-acts – registered his presence substantively, not just rhetorically. When Isaiah was in a room, no one needed to ask, in the E. M. Forster parody of J. L. Austin, yes, but how do we know he was *really* there? Not that the pleasure he had in being 'Shaya' made Berlin in any sense a *flâneur*. He detested narcissism almost as much as philistinism. And in some aspects of his life, not least his early relationships with women, he could be brutally self-protective: happier as their non-stop cuddly talking bear than as their lover.

As the letters make plain, the epicurean jauntiness came early. The headlong rush of talk on which the equally fast flow of ideas would be borne; the exhilarated delight in gossip as art form; the long steeping in music, especially Mozart, the composer who, for Berlin, ideally married hard-edged classical brilliance with passionate sublimity; the voracious pleasure taken in food, all the indulgent wallowing in the small quotidian happinesses of life like a hippo in warmly gurgling mud, aligned him with his hero Alexander Herzen who believed (along with at least half of Tolstoy's brain) that the point of life was the daily living of it.

He was, in fact, that unlikely thing: a seriously happy Jew. It may well be, as some biographers have suggested, that the eight-year-old Isaiah was afforded his pessimistic view of history, and his aversion to immediate misery inflicted in the name of a proclaimed future good, by witnessing the 1917 revolution in Petrograd. But there's little sign that the triangulation of his personality between its Russian, Jewish and English components ever made him uneasy about the wholeness of his identity. Identities, he would have scoffed, are seldom whole, not the interesting ones, anyway. It may be, as it seemed to Guy de Rothschild, that he 'floated inside his clothes', but there's no doubt that Isaiah Berlin was perfectly comfortable in the solid suiting of a middle-class, north-west London English Jew. The synagogues he attended with his parents, in Bayswater, Hampstead and Golders Green, were, architecturally and socially, testaments to the determination with which bourgeois Anglo-Jews staked their claim to a stable place within the institutions of late-imperial Britain. The interiors were (and are) oak-panelled; the windows neo-Victorian stained glass; the '*yad*' pointer for the Torah readings made from Hatton Garden sterling silver; and the synagogue's official notables, the 'wardens', dressed in black silk top hats and seated in their very own closed pew, the 'box' – solemnly opened and shut each time one of them emerged to mount the steps to the ark.

There was no reason, then, for Isaiah, or his parents, to suppose that doors would be barred against him, provided, that is, he was sensible about which to knock on. So no Eton or Winchester for Isaiah, but the day-school of St Paul's, in London, itself an intense forcing house of intellectual distinction; then Oxford, but not the aristocratic preserves of Christ Church or Magdalen, but Corpus Christi, neither the most dazzling of the colleges nor the drabbest. After graduating (first in Classics 'Greats'; then in Politics, Philosophy and Economics, both with Firsts), Berlin moved smoothly to a lectureship in philosophy at New College. Although in later life he would often say (usually when he was out of Oxford) that he was never happier than in academic life, like many of the most gifted, he paused at the crossroads, not least because he thought New College a depressingly dull place and also because he was tantalised by what seemed, for a while, to be a job offer on the *Manchester Guardian*. When, to his acute disappointment, the job failed to materialise, Berlin took the bull by the horns and entered the notoriously stiff fellowship examination for All Souls, the only Oxford college with no students. No Jew had ever been elected to All Souls, and Berlin's own father attempted to cool his son's expectations by telling him it would be a miracle if it happened. It did. *The Jewish Chronicle* heralded the achievement as another hurdle vaulted; the Chief Rabbi of Britain, Dr Herz, a famous pillar of the conservative establishment, sent congratulations (albeit addressed to 'Irving' Berlin).

Isaiah was already The Phenomenon: unstoppably voluble, eloquent; notoriously ardent; playfully poetic rather than drily cerebral in his intellectual enthusiasms. No wonder so many of his earliest, best friends were Irish: the Lynd sisters, Sigle and Maire, daughters of a writer whom Berlin had met when they had been living in the Warden's Lodge at New College. They were clever, fine-boned, fair-haired, wistful, sardonic, playful; with a good deal of steel beneath the rain-soft complexions. (Both Lynd sisters ended up in the Communist party.) How could the owlish, portly, intense young Jew not fall? He did. Sigle was the first of his real passions, though apparently not so much as a touch passed between them. Her younger sister, Maire, became a lifelong intimate: someone more than a friend and less than a lover; someone to whom Berlin could pour out the contents of his heart as well as his head from time to time. That Maire liked to be known as 'B. J' — for 'Baby Junior' — gives an accurate sense of the circle in which Isaiah felt happiest in the mid-thirties: teasing, faux-worldly, companionable; a fizzing cocktail of chummy brilliance laced with a dash of backbiting bitters at the expense of those judged Not Really Us: among them the relentlessly self-promoting historian A. L. Rowse; the blustering, bullying Richard Crossman, not yet a Labour party politician, whom Isaiah hated and later diagnosed as a 'left-wing fascist'.

His letters at this time occasionally give the uncomfortable impression of playing to the gallery: I Say, I Say-er doing his turn as Entertaining Pet Hebrew ('my dear, you know how *frightfully* clever they all are'):

Dear John,

Not a breath passes here where all is very still. I am about to write a tractate on God chasing his own predictions for you but am so idiotically busy that I haven't been able to find a cool hour yet . . . The only piece of really stimulating gossip there is the unmentionable fact [do be careful] that the President being weak and dying demands blood. The Fellows gallantly offered theirs . . . Hardie was found to have none to offer. Pidduck and Phelps though something was running furiously in their veins were discovered in its not being blood but some sharper, inferior liquid.

But this was June 1933 and through the rest of the decade, ugly political reality kept breaking into the glaring brightness. When Adam von Trott (later executed as one of the July 1944 Rastenburg bomb plotters) defended the Third Reich against charges of persecuting the Jews, Isaiah was at first incredulous and then indignant. On one of his summer pilgrimages to Salzburg he ran into his first authentic Nazi: 'a great corpulent creature in the official brown uniform, with a red & black Swastika on his sleeve, & wearing a small black demi-astrakhan hat with silver symbols embroidered thereon: he was very drunk, rolled into my café, and was led out by 3 waiters'. Yet there is still a disconcerting lightness to his tone when he writes of such things. (Von Trott is given a mild reproof; the brownshirt treated as an amusing curiosity.)

But the acutely observant Berlin is nonetheless beginning to sharpen his focus, both about those at whom he looked as well as himself. In Palestine he described the kibbutzniks to Felix and Marion Frankfurter as 'the old 1848 idealist type of person who somehow do work the land by day & read poetry by night without making it seem impossibly arty and affected. I like them better than I've ever liked any body of men, tho I couldn't live among them, they are too noble, simple and oppressively good.' Much of the surliness of British officials (neither malevolent nor benevolent) towards the Jews, Berlin diagnosed as stemming from a resentment of their usual imperial role of *Kulturträger* to the natives having been usurped by dentists from Cracow, demoting the pukka pashas to the status of glorified traffic cops. Hence the romantic eagerness of the British to adopt the role of protector of the noble Arabs *against* the pushily disruptive Jews and their Mitteleuropa culture of coffee, cake and *Kinder*.

The Frankfurters, whom Berlin met in Oxford, were among the correspondents who provoked him to take the letters to an altogether different plane than that of mercurially entertaining tongue-wagger. For the young Stephen Spender, Berlin became an acute and ruthlessly honest literary critic (not least of Spender's own work), nailing Aldous Huxley's disingenuousness at contriving sinister moments:

> we are used to war horrors, consequently he produces a scene in which the mangled remains of a terrier plop down from an aeroplane on two lovers naked on a roof & spatter them with blood. Quiet horror is a speciality of the French in the last century but whereas Baudelaire and Huysmans do so for purely artistic reasons & standing aloof from it present it without comment, Huxley, a puritan moralist makes a sort

of propaganda of it & merely lowers & sordidifies [*sic*] the scene. One is touched or nauseated or pierced in some way but not moved or at all profoundly affected or made capable of seeing something or understanding anything save abstract general propositions.

No one brought out the best in Berlin's letter-writing as consistently as the Anglo-Irish novelist, Elizabeth Bowen, whom Isaiah first met when, on one of his trips to Ireland with his Anglo-Irish Oxford girlfriends, he was taken to her house in County Cork. Much later, Isaiah would himself contribute to the deflation of Bowen's reputation by claiming that he had always found her novels unreadable: a doubly unbelievable disclaimer, since at the time he waxed feverishly enthusiastic about *The House in Paris* and *Death of the Heart* ('your novel robs me of sleep at nights; it is colossally absorbing') and with good reason for they are two of the strongest books Bowen ever wrote, glittering with precisely the kind of gritty physical characterisation and unflinching psychological insight that Berlin admired.

So when he wrote to Elizabeth Bowen, he raised his own writing to Bowenite heights, often producing literary scene-painting that resembled some of the more confessionally autobiographical moments from Tolstoy or Svevo. Extracting himself at the Paris zoo 'opposite the Python' from the pathetically attached Rachel 'Tips' Walker, a former pupil, whom Isaiah had very definitely Led On, he wrote to Bowen with self-dramatising candour:

We went on aiming at each other, missing mostly, with desperate gravity. Dear me. I can't possibly marry her. She thinks I can. We should be miserable at once. The last scene in which I forced myself to be sensible & pedestrian & analyse the situation calmly & declare that I must stop was awful beyond words. I always found I had to begin afresh & talked almost of the weather, to begin with. Then a silence. Then I would get up & make as if to go. We both felt that something had to be said. We gulped and floundered & I felt unscrupulous & a cad. The climax was reached when she inquired how far my recent declarations resembled my final end with Sigle Lynd? It was past all bearing.

The women Berlin most admired were the opposite of poor 'Tips' (who ended in a mental hospital): strong-minded; unabashed;

verbally quick on the draw, like 'B. J' Lynd; Bowen (whom, Isaiah believed, could hold her own with doubtful types in London and Dublin pubs), Virginia Woolf, who intimidated him with what he thought was the most beautiful face he had ever seen in his life; and Gertrude Stein, who took the smirk right off the face of Oxford undergraduates by telling 'them what was wrong with their lives, asked them what schools they were at, embarrassed them, trampled on them and winked a great deal at Alice B. Toklas'. Bowen's Court improbably became a kind of home from home for the Russian-Jewish Oxford philosophy don, who got into his wellies and even onto a horse to trot along the 'violent green' lanes. It was there in the summer of 1938, while Neville Chamberlain was shuttling back and forth to Berchtesgaden, that Berlin finally completed his short book on Marx, commissioned five years earlier by H. A. L. Fisher for the Home University Library. In the intervening years the work had become an ordeal since Berlin was simultaneously mesmerised and repelled by Marx himself: aghast at recognising traits of single-minded ferocity combined with thin-skinned sensitivity that he acknowledged in himself; deeply alienated by Marx's determinism at the same time as he was in awe of the adamantine coherence of the philosophical edifice he had constructed. For summers on end he procrastinated his way around Europe: the south of France; Dublin; Venice ('so delightful and silly to go in a gondola through a fairly squalid canal & realise this is like a v. second rate novel & then suddenly hear Chopin played from the window of a not very beautiful palazzo & realize that one is part of a sentimental and ridiculous film set'), conspicuously not polishing off the manuscript. But while evading the hairy, chilling presence of Marx somewhere over his shoulder, Berlin fired off volleys, usually to Elizabeth Bowen, of dead-on observations about almost everything else – the problem of defining a highbrow when only highbrows did; Stuart Hampshire's affair with Freddie Ayer's wife Renée; his thrilling discovery of Herzen (who functioned as a kind of anti-Marx for Berlin through the Russian's ironic 'gentlemanliness' and 'unsqualid disillusionment'); the ultimately alienating quality of Henry James's characters, 'all jittering because their private world may be taken away from them (the ultimate tragedy is when it is)'; James's unwitting reinforcement of the stereotype that 'we – the intellectuals, the sensitives, the observers, the persons who discuss – are all cripples; able to peer from all sorts of unusual angles . . . but thereby we deprive ourselves of the right of life which James vaguely accords to the rare normal figures who occur at the edge of his world . . . Everything he [James] says is true, piecemeal, so to speak but false in the aggregate.'

The odd thing is that Berlin was, finally, buckling down to his Marx book while so many of his friends were, perforce, choosing sides; Stephen Spender joining the Lynds in the British Communist party; others taking the Spanish Civil War as a litmus test of allegiance. But Berlin thought and wrote about Marx as if he was encountering him in the middle of the nineteenth century. This had the intellectual virtue of not anachronistically projecting back on to Marx everything that had been done in his name, but it gave the book – which appeared after the war had begun – an inevitable air of over-detachment from the monstrous historical drama that was being played out in Europe.

Ayer and Hampshire went off to war. Berlin, who had always been an unequivocal and impassioned anti-appeaser, was rejected as physically unfit for military service and chafed at the unreality of donning endlessly on (more Kant, more Locke) as one country after another fell to the Blitzkrieg. He soothed his frustration somewhat by recording, Waugh-like, witty reports from the ivory battlements. 'Maurice (Bowra), if in a lower-keyed register, is still making the same jokes as before . . . He is in charge, I believe, of some 160 postal workers. So our mails are safe at any rate. David Cecil still runs in and out with a voice like a crate of hens carried across a field.' Striking in the letters of this time is the total absence of any sort of apprehensiveness, much less panic, as Britain was finally left alone to face the apparently invincible Third Reich. To American friends like the Frankfurters he insisted that England was absolutely not done for, and let those like Auden (who had scuttled away while pretending some act of cultural diplomacy) have it:

Personal survival is no doubt a legitimate end; one fights while one can & then one either dies or escapes. I am not a soldier & can't be one and am in certain respects highly exposed, if only because I am a Jew & have written on Marx: I shd do my best not to be caught: if I could induce some institution in the US to invite me I would. But cold blooded flight is monstrous. And indifference to a conflict on the outcome of which all art and thought depend, repulsive and stupid ... I perceive that I am being violent and unusually public minded. That is perhaps a genuine change. The private world has cracked in numerous places. I should terribly like to help in the great historical process in some way.

The way, however, proved elusive. Berlin, usually nobody's fool, was comprehensively suckered by one of British history's flashier wicked jesters, the amoral, bibulously charismatic Guy Burgess, already in the stable of Soviet intelligence (along with Anthony Blunt and Donald Maclean, whom Berlin also knew without any suspicion that they were communists, much less agents). Eager to get to Moscow himself, Burgess concocted a scheme by which he and Berlin would go together, the latter as a Russian-fluent press attaché-cum-local-expert who might report back to the Foreign Office in London, perhaps on the prospects of detaching the Soviet Union from the non-aggression pact. For Berlin, this seemed just the ticket, and talks with other acquaintances in the Foreign Office in London were encouraging enough for him, paradoxically, to book a passage west to Washington from where, it was said, the trip to Russia would be arranged. In the event, someone smelled something not quite right (Burgess's notorious intimacy, not with the NKVD, but with the whisky bottle perhaps) and Berlin's own credentials were compromised along with his dodgy friend. Instructions came from London. Do not, repeat, not send B and B.

The ignominious collapse of his Russian mission left Berlin stranded, first in Washington, then in New York, and much chastened in temper – both by the starkness of the world crisis in 1940 and 1941, envisioning the flames of the Blitz at home, and feeling guiltily fretful about his distance from it. His sparkly correspondents dim and disappear into the night of the war; no more letters to Stephen Spender or Elizabeth Bowen. Overwhelmingly, the letters that survive throughout Berlin's war years in the United States are to his parents and, after the habitual reassurances of his continuing to flourish, assume a graver, more straightforward tone. They also, quite often, tell pardonable whoppers (as children will do) about his true state of mind, which was deeply homesick for England and often sharply alienated from the America in which he found himself. It was not only his parents whom he benignly misled. To Marion Frankfurter, in August 1940, Berlin drew a contrast between Anglo-French over-sophistication and American directness wholly flattering to the latter. 'I am myself a little disturbed by this terrific [American] clarity and emphasis,' he conceded, 'where nothing is taken for granted, everything is stated in so many unambiguous terms, no secret seasoning is tasteable . . . But it is superior to the nuances and evasions of England and France. Aesthetically inferior but morally superior. It destroys art but conduces to life, liberty and the pursuit of happiness.' To one of his old Oxford pals, Shiela Grant Duff, however, he wrote more candidly that 'I cling to the English desperately. I passionately long to come home. England is *infinitely* preferable to the best discoverable here.' More poetically telling, Berlin often compared himself to a melancholy holdover from the *eighteenth* century, confronted with the raw factual world of the nineteenth, unable to withhold his admiration for its iron grip on the future, yet at the same time deeply repelled by a version of mankind which somehow had edited out precisely the weaknesses and contradictions that were, for him (as for Turgenev and Herzen), the essence of being human.

Which is to say, of course, the essence of being Isaiah. For both the views expressed to Marion Frankfurter as well as those to Shiela Grant Duff were authentic Berlin. The inability to reconcile these two halves of his cultural personality, or to have one prevail over the other, and, finally, his hostility to any *reason* why one or the other should triumph, marks not only Berlin's liberation from his long captivity, toiling in the dense and gloomy woods of the Marxist dialectic, but also an early inkling of what would become the hallmark of his own prudentially pessimistic pluralism. The fact that Berlin would go on to articulate a prescriptive philosophical ethic born of his own autobiography does not, of course, necessarily weaken its claim to truth; just the contrary, as the obstinately Romantic half of him would doubtless insist.

This did not mean, though, that the 'daily living' of these contradictions was, for Berlin, especially easy. A brief period of leave in England in 1940 ('the happiest months of my life') only made the distance between British and American values seem more oceanic than ever. Returned to New York, to the job with the British Information

Service, Berlin acknowledged that since 'I wish to help with the war' he had no choice but to apply himself to the job at hand – of enlisting American Jews to use their influence in assisting FDR's undeclared war – he nonetheless declared himself to Maire Gaster as 'nearer to dissolution in my life than ever before'.

More than anyone else it was Chaim Weizmann, the President of the World Zionist Organisation (and Manchester University chemist), who arguably saved Isaiah from a more serious crack-up and who exemplified, to a degree that Berlin came to find heroic, the historical necessity of suppressing the pangs of *Weltschmerz* and Just Getting On With It. On first meeting Weizmann in England, Berlin was curiously unimpressed. Perhaps the Zionist was too much the unreconstructed Russian Jew, relatively (compared to Isaiah himself) unvarnished with the patina of Oxford Common Room cleverness, for Berlin to warm to him right away. However, witnessing Weizmann's inexhaustible determination to make the aims of the Allied war effort congruent with the establishment of a Jewish national homeland; his relentless campaigning and the infallible passion and eloquence he brought to it; the shrewdness of his pragmatism sustained without compromising the nobility of his ideals, Berlin inevitably became lost in admiration. Here was, he thought, an indisputably great man, someone out of the nineteenth century, with the looks of a 'very distinguished, rather tragic camel', but the charisma of a Mazzini or a Garibaldi. Most of all Berlin saw in Weizmann – whose cautionary gradualism was born of an intense devotion to Britain, which in no way diluted his commitment to Jewish self-determination – the perfect exemplar of the man of felicitously mixed feelings. Well before the war was over – and those mixed feelings became precisely the reason why Weizmann would become marginalised by more militant nationalists like David Ben-Gurion – Berlin was defending him against their impatience. Anti-British policies that seemed to have the virtue of urgency, Berlin thought, would, in the end, turn out to be more damaging than beneficial to the long-term interests of Jewish Palestine.

Pearl Harbor made the work of championing the cause of British survival to American-Jewish opinion redundant. Berlin was moved to the embassy in Washington with the reverse commission of explaining American policy and politics in weekly reports sent to the Foreign

Office (and sometimes, as it transpired, to Churchill). His style – and reputation for brilliant candour – was set in July 1942 in a justifiably famous early report, listing in twenty-three paragraphs just what it was about the British which, notwithstanding the hero-worship of Churchill and the near-universal admiration for their behaviour during the Blitz, made his countrymen so unappealing in some quarters of American opinion. Berlin's talent for cultural summary, deployed for the good of the alliance, was on brilliant display here, especially penetrating when it cut to the quick of English cultural snobbery. Contradictions being, of course, at the heart of every stereotype, Americans managed to dislike Britain for being *both* trapped in a rigid class structure and for 'going red'; for being both too 'adroit for simple, honest Americans' at the same time that they were rigid in their defence of obsolete empire. The British were both nervously reserved about 'treading on American corns' and yet too free with 'over-civilised English accents', aggravating the American suspicion of being patronised by a country that supposed itself culturally superior.

And so on. Just what policy-makers were supposed to do with these insights, of course, was another matter. Nonetheless, the incisiveness of Berlin's weekly reports became legendary in London and the reason for the famous conversation at lunch at Downing Street, in which Churchill quizzed the understandably startled Irving Berlin on his views about American politics and the state of the world in general. Disabused of the mistake, Churchill dined out on the story and Isaiah himself thought it wonderful, the wonderfulness decreasing every time the British Ambassador, Halifax, repeated it, sometimes forcing Berlin to tell the tale himself.

In Washington Berlin settled into a routine, much of which was using dinner parties as a listening post, the gleanings from which would be converted into his reports. Provided he actually got to the dinners (a hilarious letter of apology to a Brazilian diplomat chronicles an evening of unparalleled haplessness at failing to find her address), Berlin revelled in his lionising as the wittiest, smartest fellow in town. No wonder, for only Isaiah Berlin could dispel exaggerated fears that Harold Laski was the *éminence rouge* at the heart of a sinister socialist Jesuitry by telling Americans that Laski was merely 'a harmless megalomaniac'.

As the war wound to its end, Berlin's reputation for analytical acuity made him in demand for a post-war job in government. Arnold Toynbee, whose historical outlook (not to mention his anti-Zionism) was the polar opposite of Berlin's, offered him a place in the Foreign Office Research Department: a prospect which he rejected right away as an existence toiling in 'the sunless cave of inhibited professors'. Towards the end of 1945 he finally got his wish to go to Russia, where, in Leningrad, he had the encounter with Anna Akhmatova, sexless (for she was no longer the startling, bird-like beauty of earlier years) but nonetheless love-struck, a meeting which changed both their lives and to mark which Akhmatova inscribed a poem for Isaiah.

The letters from Russia, though, are the only major disappointment in the book: entertaining on the antics of Randolph Churchill, but strangely silent on almost everything that mattered. On the social and material ruin of Leningrad after the siege, there is little; of the enormity of Soviet tyranny, then playing out the spasms of its most insane cruelties, nothing at all. Akhmatova herself appears more an item of cultural tourism than the heart-stopping epiphany their meeting actually was.

But then Isaiah Berlin's future had been set, and it was not going to be in America or Russia (though he was now uniquely placed to write something of global significance about the fate of British culture between the two colossi). It was in that bomber, going back to England in 1944, forbidden to sleep 'because there was some danger of falling on the oxygen pipe and so suffocating', that he found his true vocation. 'There was no light and therefore one couldn't read,' he later told Henry Hardy, in one of the interposed spoken commentaries which wind beautifully through the book like a twist of silk, 'one was therefore reduced to a most terrible thing – to having to think, and I had to think for seven or eight hours . . . from Canada to England.'

What Berlin thought, above all, was that 'I really wanted to know more at the end of my life than at the beginning' and that pure philosophy 'which taxed the intelligence of man to the highest degree' was not somehow for him. 'I didn't want the answers to these philosophical questions with that degree of urgency with which a true philosopher must want them.' Instead he had discovered that he wanted to reconstruct how social and political ideas became generated in a particular place and time and then how they operated in the flesh-and-blood world of history.

And he also knew, with the decisiveness that his immersion in history had brought, that the last places such illumination would be yielded were in official research departments, where humane intelligence toiled for the powerful. He would, then, go back to Oxford.

And there Isaiah Berlin stayed for the rest of his life, unrepentant of the decision, dismissive of the view that in so doing (to the chagrin of Weizmann among others) he had somehow turned his back on real political engagement. For Berlin, the academy would never be a site of mere cultural gaming. It was, rather, the place where liberty – defined as freedom from any sort of coercion – could be lived; and where the challenge of choosing between life's contradictory impulses could be faced with clear-eyed courage.

J. H. Plumb

Foreword to *The Death of the Past*, 2003

The past may or may not have been dead when J. H. Plumb pronounced its obsequies, but to those of us who were taught by him in Cambridge in the 1960s, the author was unforgettably, alarmingly, alive. What-ever stereotypes those of us arriving at Christ's College in 1963 might have had about history dons, a first encounter with Jack Plumb in his rooms – a small man with a perfectly round, bald head, seated in a big armchair, nattily dressed in a three-piece, crisply tailored suit, a high-coloured Jermyn Street striped shirt and bow tie – swiftly saw off the cliché of tweeds and amontillado. Display cases poured brilliant light on to Sèvres porcelain in kingfisher blue and rose pink. The walls were filled with Dutch still-life and genre paintings: a young man with a weak chin and get-me whiskers; a mournful bar-girl with too much sallow cleavage; an arrangement for hock and lemons. Not a bottle of sherry to be seen, but decanters of Château Figeac, often. When Plumb spoke, and especially when he chuckled, as he often did, the effect of Voltaire in the Fens was complete. But there was, however, a serious price to be paid for all this epicurean dazzlement bestowed on clever but slightly stunned youth: intellectual survival under intense and unsparing fire.

Plumb was famously, tigerishly, combative; though also affable and witty, his conversation punctuated by bursts of laughter at the follies of humanity past and present, of which academia itself, he made clear, offered the richest trove. His temper was naturally quizzical, sardonic, gleeful. But it was impossible, amidst the gales of irony that swept through the room on the subject of some hapless figure, not to be nerv-ous that one might be next for the Treatment. The slightly exophthalmic eyes, glittering from behind his spectacles, would fix steadily and expec-tantly on whomever a Plumb question, joke or challenge alighted. Abashed thoughtfulness was not a possible response, nor was any sort of laboured earnestness. Anyone suspected of Being Serious About Religion was subjected to a philosophical barrage of teasing which could sometimes turn punishingly picador. Most of the wounding, though, happened in the intense hour or so of history supervisions in those rooms, when we read our essays, our hearts sinking to our boots should Jack begin to fidget ominously in the yellow-upholstered armchair. When it went well, the praise was fulsome and went straight to our giddy heads like champagne. But for some, it seldom did go well. Come six in the evening, the remains of large undergraduates (for this was then a rugby college) could be seen collapsed in trembling exhaustion in the College Buttery after an unhappy hour with Plumb, dosing themselves with healing pints of Watneys, repenting solecisms uttered on the Merovingians (for Plumb loved teaching outside his speciality) and swearing never to go through it again.

But of course we invariably did. There was, for a start, always the prospect of the occasional magical supervision, when he would spend half an hour analysing the form, as well as the content, of a paragraph or two; juggling, like the nimblest editor, with the rhetorical structure of the essay, suggesting how it could gain more punch and conviction were paragraph four to have been the opening, and so on. Towards the end, sometimes over those hard-earned glasses of claret, an encyclopaedic range of bibliographic suggestions would tumble out, many of them eccentrically original. A tentative essay on the cultural backwash of the discovery of the New World drew from him amazement that I had read neither Redcliffe Salaman's *History of the Potato*, nor Geoffroy Atkinson's *Nouveaux Horizons de la Renaissance française*, the latter a book which lived up to the winning peculiarity of its author's name by tackling Montaigne and the *Pléiade* via a lengthy discussion of the implications of Indian nudity for the theology of the Catholic reform movement.

Our own trials by fire culminated in the ritual of the Plumb after-dinner seminar. The seriousness of the event was marked by its being convened, not in the sitting room, but on the other side of the stairs of 'O' staircase, in Jack's dining room. A Sheraton table, the polish high enough for us to see our fretful faces embarrassingly reflected, was laid with a tall Paul de Lamerie silver candelabrum. Silver bowls brimmed with fruit, including a strangely incongruous banana. Two decanters of claret rested on the sideboard which, once the speaker had finished his paper, would be brought to the table to do the rounds. For forty minutes or so either Roy Porter, Geoffrey Parker, Andrew Wheatcroft, John Barber or I would hammer and stammer through our stuff, each of us using whatever kind of rhetorical persuasiveness we could muster amidst the intimidating antiques. Roy's speciality was jokes at which he'd be the first to chortle (and they were usually very funny). Geoffrey Parker fortified himself with armour of unassailable and esoteric scholarship. Schama, as usual, depended overmuch on adjectival overload and overwrought atmospherics to conceal the shakiness of his hypotheses. (*Plus ça change.*) In the candle-lit glow one always knew if things were going well. JHP's not twanging an elastic band, for instance, was definitely a good sign, as was his not turning his chair sideways to commune with the smirking likeness of Sir Robert Walpole on the wall.

After the reading came the listeners' turn to respond, or else. The claret and fruit circulated (Porter and I usually doing unspeakable things with the grape scissors, an instrument for which London lower-middle-class life had inadequately prepared us). The diplomatic psychology of the discussion was tricky: too fierce in our criticism and we would sacrifice a friendship; too cosy or indulgent, then we risked disbelief and raillery from Plumb. So we generally told the truth. At the end of the circle of comments, Jack would supply his own, and belie his reputation for fierceness by generous helpings of praise for the student's research and his grip on the subject, even while raising questions about both evidence and analysis which not infrequently turned the whole exercise inside out and upside down. Whatever else happened in those seminars, we all learned the art of vigilantly sympathetic attentiveness, which has stood me, at any rate, in good stead in over thirty years of teaching.

But aside from pedagogic style, was there a 'Plumb' philosophy of history, evident in these bracing hours of instruction, and faithfully represented in *The Death of the Past*? In the mid-1960s, it seemed to be an obligation for every historian worth his salt to make some sort of utterance on what history was and wasn't, many of them a response to, and exasperated refutation of, E. H. Carr's *What is History?*, a book which its countless critics (all of them in the right) see as the mailed fist of determinism lurking in the velvet glove of a faux-scepticism. Herbert Butterfield, G. R. Elton (Plumb's particular nemesis) and many others had all put their methodological oars in, but what is strik-ing about so many of these *professions de foi* is their un-self-examined address to the converted. Their working assumption (fair enough in the 1960s, when the escalator from A-level history to undergraduate history to graduate history to that first Research Fellowship was serenely uninterrupted by anything resembling a power outage from the employment *Zeitgeist*) was that academic history would continue to be the dominant discipline of both the humanities and the social sciences; its scholarly gravitas weightier than the study of literature, yet somehow more imaginatively creative than sociology or econom-ics. For Elton, the question 'who cares?' would have been not so much impertinent as unthinkable. The issue was not to legitimise the disci-pline so much as to issue a stringent manual for its professional practice.

For the worldly Plumb, though, with his relish for, and brilliance at, popular history writing and journalism, especially in America where he was the leading literary light of *Horizon* magazine, there was no question of history resting smugly on its laurels. Dragged inside the professional stockade, he believed, history would atrophy into an arid scholasticism. 'What do they of history know,' I remember him borrowing from E. M. Forster (who had in turn creatively pilfered Kipling), 'who know only other historians?' For Plumb, history was either a public craft or it was nothing; and in this spirit he was constantly urging on us books he cherished which had been written by historians either rejected by the academy or who had chosen to work outside it. Iris Origo's *Merchant of Prato*, Barbara Tuchman's *The Guns of August* and Frances Yates's work on neo-Platonist hermetics (very much an eccentricity in the 1960s) all come to mind. While others cringed at the belletrism they imputed to C. V. Wedg-wood, Plumb welcomed her to High Table and introduced us personally to that elegant, surprisingly astringent mind.

The battle lines were decisively drawn for us at Christ's: the ency-clopaedic and the omnivorous (us) versus the arid and the parochial (them); history seen as an enquiry into the human condition (us) versus history assumed to be the unfolding epic of English (not even British) governing institutions (them); history which embraced the literary and the imaginative without ever forsaking the hard tests of documentary evidence (us) versus history which treated strong writing as a fig-leaf for analytical mushiness (them). And while Plumb was adamant about the indispensability of the archive, neither did he fetishise it. The archive was, he insisted, startlingly anticipating Arlette Farge and Pierre Bourdieu, a social institution, with its own invented practices, hierarchies of significance, both human and documentary, and which was as much the product of a particular culture as its shaper. *Caveat lector!* The notion that the historian's task consisted entirely of archaeological self-effacement before the bedrock of archival truth – a mole-like digger of nuggets and gobbets – he found not so much professionally deluded as betraying an almost pathetic want of critical self-consciousness.

Yet it was precisely Plumb's abiding and unapologetic sense that history lived for others, not just for itself – that it was, at root, a civic vocation, not a monastic profession – which snared him in all kinds of contradictions, some of which are exposed, others glossed over in *The Death of the Past*. The central message of the book – that history, practised as a truly critical discipline, was the enemy of a 'past' in which liberty of thought and action was forever in thrall to the claimed authority of ancestral prescription – actually pointed its readers in two directions at once. On the one hand, history, construed as the study of human society, needed the input of professionals, saturated in, and invigorated by, the methodologies of the Annales school, especially Bloch and Braudel, if it were to break free, simultaneously from a culture of sentimental deference to heritage and from the airless claustrophobia of Gobbet Land. On the other hand, none of that would make any difference to the survival of history as a public craft, unless that new professionalism could be translated into genuinely popular writing. In principle, there was no reason why this little miracle should not happen, and Plumb's ambitious multi-volume *History of Human Society* attempted to do just that. But as an advertisement for a new, yet genuinely popular, history, the series never really took off, not least because the quality of its writing, while seldom exactly pedestrian, never really made for page-turning, either. The project, stalled before its ambitions could be realised, remained obstinately encyclopaedic rather than genuinely innovative. Several volumes only brought home the truism that Braudels, Blochs and Febvres, capable of achieving a synthesis of narrative and social analysis, of ethnography and textual exegesis, were painfully scarce.

Narrative drive and the force of events – precisely the history repudiated by Braudel as the artifice of dull practitioners in favour of the slow heave and shift of tectonic-plate forces – were in fact the *sine qua non* of bringing readers back to history and thus liberating them from 'the past'.

And Plumb, a supremely accomplished narrator, knew this. However much he may have asserted the equivalence of the history of the potato with the history of the British (or American) Civil Wars, in his heart of hearts he didn't believe it. In fact, at the height of the mode for social history in the Annales style, Plumb could be found insisting on the power of speech-acts to shake and shape the destiny of communities and nations. If, in some of his great lecture performances (as in his work on Walpole), he might suggest that parliamentary rhetoric was a veil behind which the grind of monied interest did its business, on other days he would impersonate the histrionics of a Fox or a Chatham with precisely the opposite conclusion in mind. His considering intellect, then, may have pointed him away from the power of argument and ideology, but the vitality of his temperament and his deep engagement with the mystery of language pointed, always, towards it. That, indeed, was the gravamen of his ferocious argument against Lewis Namier, whose obsession with interest over ideology Plumb thought a simple mistake about how humans behave.

None of which prevented Plumb from accomplishing an important and even lasting little polemic in *The Death of the Past*. But as so often with him (as with many of the finest historians) what he says is less significant than the way that he says it. Though Plumb clung to the notion that history had to be more than just the exercise of the pleasure principle; more than merely the inspection of the generations of humanity; that it ought, really, to bring about some sort of epistemological and cultural alteration; he was actually hard-pressed to define what such an alteration might be. While all his pupils would agree that a world without critical history would be dangerously worse off, in the end, Plumb, like many of us, remained stymied by an aesthetic in search of a didactic.

Rescuing Churchill

Review of *Churchill* by Roy Jenkins, *New York Review of Books*, 28 February 2002

The last thing George Orwell published was a May 1949 review of Volume Two of Winston Churchill's memoirs of the Second World War, *Their Finest Hour*. You might expect him to have been allergic to its chest-thumping patriotism, its flights of empurpled rhetoric; but not a bit of it. Churchill's writings, Orwell observed, bestowing the most meaningful accolade he could manage, were 'more like those of a human being than of a public figure'. Though in 1939 Orwell had been suspicious of Churchill's belligerent rhetoric and ominous potential for a personality cult of his own, by the time he came to write *1984*, it was not Big Brother who would be baptised Winston, but the doomed renegade, 'the last man'.

Churchill may have been born in Blenheim Palace, but Orwell was right to grant him the gift of the common touch. When the Prime Minister toured the scorched and shattered remains of Bristol after a particularly hellish air raid in April 1941, a woman who had lost everything and was awash with raging tears, on seeing the jowly face and cigar, stopped crying and waved her hanky, shouting herself hoarse, 'Hooray, hooray!' Along with the millions of his compatriots, Orwell believed that, more than any political, or military, gifts, it had been Winston's exuberant humanity – egotistical, erratic, histrionic – as well as his long career as a word-warrior, that had taken a people, shaking with trepidation, and made of them comrades in arms.

Of a piece with that humanity was Churchill's large capacity for self-mockery. Orwell also recycled the story that Churchill followed up 'we will fight on the beaches' with 'we'll throw bottles at the b———s, it's about all we've got left', but that the candid addition was buzzed out by the quick hand of the BBC censor just in time. The story was apocryphal, but the point was that such Churchilliana existed at all. No leader who made jokes against himself was in much danger of turning dictator. In the same vein, Clement Attlee, the Labour party leader who served in his War Cabinet and who could, at times, be a fierce critic, commented not long after Churchill's death that he was 'a supremely fortunate mortal', but that 'the most warming thing about him was that he never ceased to say so'.

But the comedian and the tragedian lived within the same surprisingly delicate skin. The challenge facing any biography added to the groaning shelves of Churchill histories is somehow to do full justice to the Promethean character of its subject, the richly lived (not to say gluttonously engorged) career, without ever being a slave to its mystique. Mere character delineation – easy enough in Churchill's case – won't suffice. The hard work is to demonstrate exactly *how* the outsize Churchillian personality, so truculent, so impulsive, so often profoundly wrongheaded, became, in the dark spring of 1940, just what was needed for national survival. There's no doubt that Roy Jenkins has risen splendidly to this challenge, succeeding, much better than many biographers before him, in bringing to life Churchill the political animal, whose impatient appetite for power, and strenuous exertions to secure it, are often hidden beneath the grand opera of his speechifying. He was smoke, certainly, but he was also mirrors. And Jenkins catches Churchill's studied self-inspection with the sure-shot sharpness of an expert portraitist, a Karsh who has the cheek to stare back.

His big book appears at a doubly interesting moment. The popularity of biographies of heroic but unimpeachably democratic leaders on both sides of the Atlantic owes something, obviously, to the present craving for both public reassurance and political education. The temptation is to return Karl Rove's call and deliver an anatomy of charisma, stripped down to interchangeable parts, available for selective cannibalisation, and rebuilt to cope with the Crisis of the Week, the very stuff (as Churchill might have said) of that most egregious waste of time and money: leadership seminars. Perennially shrewd politician (even, or rather especially, in his eighties) though Lord Jenkins is, he also knows that the cloth from which Churchill was cut is deeply unsuited for modern imitations. (Who, these days, writes his own speeches, much less has the guts to begin one: 'The news . . . is *very* bad'?) So he preserves and celebrates Churchill in all his titanic, unreproducible peculiarity; the storms of petulant fury rage along with the cherubic smiles. Jenkins's angle of vision is that of undeluded, critically intelligent appreciation, wisely informed by his own lifetime of governing experience, neither adulatory nor hyper-sceptical.

His biography also coincides, though, with a moment when Churchill revisionism shows signs, perhaps welcome, of running out of steam. The genre began with the most cumulatively powerful and perceptive book ever written on the daunting subject, *Churchill: Four Faces and the Man*, published in 1968, only three years after his death, when the marble at Bladon churchyard was still shining white. Such collections usually suffer from curate's-egg syndrome, with some good pieces and some bad; not, however, when its authors are A. J. P. Taylor (on the statesman), Robert Rhodes James (on the politician), J. H. Plumb (on the historian), Basil Liddell Hart (on the war leader) and Anthony Storr (on the 'Black Dog' bipolar depressive). While the memorable book was in no way a hatchet job, the authors were nonetheless determined to look at their subject without stars, or tears, in their eyes. While they all acknowledged his indispensability, they were equally forthright (as was Churchill himself) about his many failings. For Plumb (notwithstanding the fact that he had worked on the proofs of the last volume of *The History of the English-Speaking Peoples*), the histories that won Churchill the Nobel Prize for Literature were just so many anachronistic swashbuckling failures, Gibbon's orotundity married to Macaulay's complacent insularity. Liddell Hart thought he had been excessively criticised for disasters in the First World War, but not nearly enough for the Second World War, not least because he had rewritten its history so selectively. And A. J. P. Taylor pointed out with typically unsparing sharpness that the man who, during the 1930s, had so obstinately and so noisily resisted the demise of empire, especially in Asia, actually guaranteed its collapse in 1941 by starving its defences of fighter planes, warships and manpower, in favour of the North African theatre and, less forgivably, the catastrophic attempt to take on the Germans in Crete.

As the tomes of Martin Gilbert's multi-volume Churchilliad arose in the 1970s and '80s like some massive biographical Stonehenge, revisionists, as if in resistance, became correspondingly more audacious. Robert Rhodes James's book *Churchill: A Study in Failure, 1900–1939* made the fair point that had, in fact, the taxi that struck Churchill on Fifth Avenue in 1930 hit with lethal force, his career would indeed have been judged on its impulsive blunders (the Dardanelles in 1915) and its quixotic devotion to deservedly doomed causes – the gold standard, the British Raj in India, the constitutional viability of King Edward VIII. Likewise, Paul Addison's fine scholarly history of Churchill's career in domestic politics and government pulled no punches about his tendency to favour trigger-happy solutions for difficult problems – calling out the troops in 1911 and 1926 to deal with industrial strikes, for example.

A step very definitely too far, however, was taken by John Charmley, whose *Churchill: The End of Glory* (1993) was the most ambitious attempt yet to reach up and pull the giant from his pedestal, but which succeeded only in having his full weight collapse back on the author. Starting with Taylor's insight that the most intransigent defender of the Raj had ironically ended up being the inadvertent instrument of its downfall, Charmley added to it fresh research about the tentative suggestions mooted in the War Cabinet by Lord Halifax in the gloomy days of late May 1940, when France was on the point of collapse, for an approach through Mussolini, to discover what Hitler's terms might be.

The premise of any such negotiations was the proposition, raised as early as 1937 by von Ribbentrop in a private conversation with Churchill when the latter was still just an MP, that Hitler would be prepared to leave Britain's insular sovereignty and its empire intact, in return for a free hand in Eastern Europe. By 1940 this hegemony was to be extended through the whole continent, and Churchill's response – superlatively chronicled in John Lukacs's moving *Five Days in London, May 1940* was the same as it had been three years earlier: indignant categorical rejection.

Charmley, appealing (as self-appointed revisionists invariably do) to the calculus of national interest rather than to 'emotive' morality, argued that if imperial self-preservation, not to mention freedom from post-war economic and military dependence on the United States, was British policy, it might have been better to take the deal. But as Geoffrey Best's excellent, concise new biography (which has had the bad luck to appear at the same time as Jenkins's) points out, even supposing that British national independence, courtesy of the Third Reich, would have fared any better than the French, especially when it came to the little matter of saving Jews from the gas chambers, there is an air of quaintly naive parochialism about Charmley's assumption that the Raj (already exposed by Gandhi as intrinsically ungovernable) would somehow have been granted a stay of execution thanks to the Swastika and the Rising

Sun. It is, in fact, to Churchill's imperishable credit that, faced with the alternatives of hanging on to the scraps of empire, courtesy of Adolf Hitler, or fighting to the end, whatever long-term damage might accrue to British power, he unhesitatingly opted for the latter. Even for its most conspicuous eulogist, better by far an 'end of glory' than the end of freedom.

What, then, moved Lord Jenkins, at a time in his life when less compulsively prolific souls would be booking their poolside loungers in the Bahamas, to enter this crowded fray? According to his own disconcerting admission, he was moved less by any gladiatorial impulse or by the discovery of new information than by the avoidance of anticlimax in his literary résumé following his richly merited success with *Gladstone*. Then, too, there seems to have been the desire to decide whether or not Churchill was indeed Top Prime Minister, a determination made at the very end of the book with Jenkins duly awarding him prime space in the pantheon. Whatever the motives, Jenkins's qualifications are unarguable. Like Churchill, he has been very much a cat who has walked on his own. Both were long kept at arm's length from their party's leadership by suspicion about their loyalty to its core principles. (Arguably Churchill would never have been Prime Minister but for the war.)

Both also put ideas above party allegiance, and they were, in fact, the not dissimilar ideals of anti-Marxist liberalism and state-sponsored social reform, a combination once thought to be an anomaly in the polarised struggle between capitalism and labour, but which, a century after its birth in the early twentieth century, actually looks very much like becoming, at least in Europe, king of the zeitgeist. Churchill was a penal reformer; Jenkins an early campaigner against capital punishment. Both men suffered at the hands of the more puritanical elders of their respective parties for their unapologetic celebration of the pleasures of the table and the cellar. It's hard not to believe that Churchill wouldn't have been pleased by this most epicurean biography, in whose pages no memorable bottle ever goes uncorked. It's certainly the only Churchill biography in which the phrase 'a very remarkable Liebfraumilch', quoted from the recitation by Churchill's aide Jock Colville of the menu on the *Queen Mary* in 1944, seems as inevitable as 'blood, toil, tears and sweat'.

But one affinity beyond all others seems to tie the knot between author and subject: their intertwined careers as both historian and politician, which make the distinction between history as lived event and history as report of that event moot. Nor, in either case, has this been a matter of alternative vocations; the writing used as compensation, both psychological and pecuniary, for the loss of office and power (as it was with Clarendon). Jenkins's career as a thoughtful, elegantly readable political historian goes back almost fifty years. As a schoolboy in the late 1950s, I read and admired his biography of Charles Dilke, the nineteenth-century radical imperialist who self-destructed in a sexual scandal, and his brilliant account of the Liberal government's onslaught on the House of Lords, *Mr Balfour's Poodle*, before I knew much about Jenkins as a rising Labour party politician. Virtually all his books (until this one) have been, one way or another, commentaries on one of the two issues which have most engaged him in public life: the complicated, sometimes tortured, relationship between liberal democracy and social justice, and Britain's relationship with Europe. The writing has informed the career and vice versa.

So too with Churchill. Before 1945, it had emphatically not been a case of the politician exploiting his reputation to launch a literary career; rather the other way around. From the time he went to Cuba in 1896 to his exploits on the north-west Indian frontier, Sudan and South Africa, shamelessly exploiting his and his mother's social connections to put himself on the front line over the objections of local commanders, Churchill reinvented the war correspondent as both fighter and writer. And the more he scripted his destiny, the more outlandishly heroic it conveniently became, culminating in his escape from a Boer prisoner-of-war camp in Pretoria, followed by a trek through the veldt to liberty, before, it goes without saying, re-enlisting.

Copy flowed from his pen to popular British newspapers like *The Daily Graphic* and was then expanded into three substantial books in which Churchill, perfectly judging his readership, managed to combine ripping yarns with romantic laments for the nobly fallen foe. (He was moved to indignant protest when, after the battle of Omdurman, during which he'd taken part in the famous, nearly suicidal charge of the 21st Lancers, he learned that the commander, Lord Kitchener, had desecrated the tomb of the defeated Islamic jihad leader, the Mahdi, mutilated his body and used his skull as an inkwell.)

Recognising a fellow compulsive scribbler, Jenkins can't help be impressed by the single-mindedness with which Churchill went after contracts and royalties, and the adroitness with which he translated his maverick persona into bankable political capital. But when he returns to Churchill's later work, it's more to register his entrepreneurial savvy, running battalions of researchers and landing fat advances to pay for the country house at Chartwell, than to ponder with much sustained curiosity how history profoundly shaped his sense of political purpose. No British statesman since William Pitt the Elder was more deeply marked by so providential a view of his nation's past, and by extension a conviction that his own political life was to be spent in its perpetuation. His account, to be sure, is the conventional sea-girt epic of Protestant parliamentary liberty, unfolding as if through divine dispensation from Magna Carta to Mr Gladstone and related by Macaulay and Henry Hallam, whose books Churchill first greedily consumed between sets of polo in India.

The history was national rather than monarchic and, despite Churchill's birth, not especially aristocratic. (As a Liberal colleague of Lloyd George's attack on the veto power of the House of Lords, Churchill was hot to press for its abolition as an absurd anachronism.) This history was Churchill's religion. Its saints and martyrs spoke to him on a daily basis. When he met with Franklin Roosevelt on board HMS *Prince of Wales* in Placentia Bay in Newfoundland, in 1941, Churchill chose, for the concluding hymn, sung by the mingled ranks of American and British sailors, 'O God, Our Help in Ages Past'. The reason was that it had been sung by Cromwell's Ironsides as they buried the parliamentary tax resister John Hampden, killed in action against the royalists. *That* was his reply to the 'Horst Wessel Lied'.

It's fashionable, not to say mandatory, for serious, critical historiography to write off English parliamentary history as so much 'elitist', self-congratulatory, Whig teleology. But when Churchill returned again and again to the Manichaean confrontation between liberty and tyranny, and to the canonical moments in the British past when despotism had been resisted (the Armada in 1588; the Camp de Boulogne in 1803), those convictions were infectious, not just because they were so heroically articulated, but because they were not, in fact, false. If people wish to know why exactly we are fighting, he told his listeners in 1941, let them abandon the war and they will very soon find out!

In the service of these — to Churchill — self-evident historical truths, he could resort to outrageous acts of casuistry, characterising, for example, Britain's terrifying isolation after the fall of France as the 'honour' which had fallen to Britain of being Germany's 'foremost foe'. His strategy was to compliment his listeners – whether on the BBC or in the House of Commons – by always assuming that they all shared this lofty ideal, when for many millions the main aim of the war was to get through it in one piece, preferably without one's house in rubble. The flattery worked (as it did on FDR, who was co-opted by correspondence as a fellow defender of democracy). In no time at all, the British public *did* come to believe that on its resolve turned the fate not just of national survival, but the fate of democracy. It's this fundamental Churchillian generosity, half-cunning, half-instinctive, which also accounts for the otherwise inexplicable failure to tell the truth in his war memoirs about the deep divisions in the War Cabinet over whether to go it alone or to sound out 'Signor Mussolini'. In 1948, with Neville Chamberlain dead, Churchill could so easily have taken the personal credit due for stifling the last gasp of the appeasers, but he preferred instead to pretend that they were, in their heart of hearts, always on his side.

Roy Jenkins's jaunty narrative seldom pauses for reflections of this kind, much less to give Churchill's eloquence the kind of close analytical scrutiny offered in, for example David Cannadine's illuminating preface to the Penguin edition of the speeches, or the extraordinary essay by Isaiah Berlin entitled 'Mr Churchill in 1940', which doesn't even rate an appearance in Jenkins's bibliography. 'If somebody asked me what exactly Winston did to win the war,' Clement Attlee wrote, 'I would say, "Talk about it."' And although it was important that Churchill attended to the supply of ships and planes and men that would defeat the Axis, he was also the only leader who could take on the Führer's manic logorrhoea and wipe the floor with it. Jenkins has a tendency to take at face value the weaponry of Churchill's oratory, a unique, at times almost Shakespearean marriage between the grandiloquent and the puckishly conversational, even though these spoken masterpieces were the product of countless hours of labour. (His friend F. E. Smith joked that Winston spent the best part of his life preparing impromptu speeches.) As a writer he could be either flat-footed or twinkle-toed, but when he was on song he was unbeatable. Who else would have described the collapse of the old monarchies in 1918 as a 'drizzle of empires falling through the air'? At Harrow, wrote Churchill in his dazzling and often funny *My Early Life*, 'I got into my bones the essential structure of the ordinary British sentence – which is a noble thing.' But Jenkins sometimes betrays a tin ear for the succinct earthiness which, even at its most theatrically lime-lit moments, made it, as Orwell recognised, a true language of the people. Compare the two on his stint in the Cuban war in 1895. Churchill writes, 'We are on our horses, in uniform; our revolvers are loaded. In the dusk and half-light, long files of armed and laden men are shuffling off towards the enemy.' Jenkins writes of Churchill's being 'under mild fire' on his twenty-first birthday: 'This he regarded as a very satisfactory concatenation.'

Nor would Lord Jenkins be seen dead in the company of psycho-biographers, so don't go looking here for speculation about Churchill's reliance on silk underwear, his invention of the velveteen siren suit, essentially, as startled witnesses reported, overgrown baby rompers, the oral fixation of the cigar, lit or unlit, or the strenuous over-compensation (as with Theodore Roosevelt) for the thirty-one-inch, hairless chest, or the pursuit of oratory as a campaign of conquest over the stammer and the lisp.

There's a clubby smoothness about Jenkins's prose, which isn't much interested, either, in walking the growling Black Dog of Churchill's fits of self-annihilating depression, or pondering his moments of truly apocalyptic pessimism, both before and after the Second World War, when he imagined bombs raining from the sky in an immense, even universal immolation. While Jenkins duly notes the baleful influence of Churchill's father, the glowering, embittered Lord Randolph, on the insecure, physically delicate boy, he omits the one story that most dramatically conveys the pathetic intensity of Churchill's efforts to prove himself worthy in the eyes of his unspeakable parent.

Writing from Sandhurst Royal Military Academy (where he'd been sent, having been judged too stupid and idle to amount to anything in the law), Winston confessed, in a state of abject terror, that he had wrecked the gold watch his father had given him, not once (when another cadet ran into him), but twice (when it had fallen from his fob pocket into a pond). Correctly anticipating the cannonade of cold fury, the denunciations for incompetence, irresponsibility and all-around worthlessness that would come his way, Winston mounted a desperate salvage operation with the same manic energy with which he would later conduct world wars – mobilising a company of infantry, then a fire engine, to dredge the pond, finally diverting the headwaters before retrieving the mud-caked timepiece, irreparably ruined. All he could do was to prostrate himself before his father's wrath in one of the saddest letters he ever wrote. To his father's implacable denunciation, 'I would not believe you could be such a young stupid. It is clear you are not to be trusted', Winston bleated: 'Please don't judge me entirely on the strength of the watch. I am very very sorry about it.' More than sixty years later, after his Nobel Prize and his elaborately hagiographic biography of Lord Randolph, he was still trying to justify his life to the bug-eyed bully. One of the last pieces he ever published – mentioned by Jenkins – was 'The Dream', in which a phantom Lord Randolph materialises in front of Winston as he dabs at a canvas, the father baffled by the inexplicable affluence of the wastrel's house until the son proudly recounts the history of his prodigious career.

This still leaves a lot of Churchill's hectic life for Roy Jenkins to write wonderfully about, and he unquestionably does. Few writers know more about the heady days of the great reforming Liberal governments of 1906–16 than the author of an earlier, fine biography of H. H. Asquith, and Jenkins lucidly charts Churchill's desertion of the Tories followed by his meteoric rise through ministerial ranks from a colonial Under-Secretary to the Board of Trade, to Home Secretary and, finally, the Admiralty. Jenkins gives the tyro proper credit, along with his friend and mentor Lloyd George, for pushing through a raft of progressive reforms – labour exchanges, unemployment insurance, mine inspection improvements.

But like Robert Rhodes James and Geoffrey Best, he rightly points out that more than once in his career in government Churchill was the author of policies he later attacked as short-sighted. Thrice he was the impassioned advocate of reduced arms expenditure, as Tory, Liberal and Tory again, and thrice again (in the naval arms race immediately before the First World War, in the 1930s and in the Cold War) he was gung-ho for rearmament. Though he took the lion's share of blame (not altogether without justification) for the catastrophically botched attempt to force the Dardanelles in 1915, he somehow escaped whipping entirely for the almost equally appalling fiasco of the Norwegian campaign of 1940.

Field Marshal Alanbrooke, his bird-watching, pious Chief of Imperial General Staff, in his withering private diaries, often portrays

Churchill as strategically incompetent, deaf to informed counsel, violently abusive to subordinates, and pig-headed in standing by opinions all too often arrived at without even a modicum of familiarity with their logistical implications. Sometimes – as when he claims Churchill's famous 'Action This Day' memoranda suggested greater familiarity with detail than was actually the case – Alanbrooke is unduly harsh. But it is true that, from 1943, the relentless comings and goings over the Atlantic, along with equally gruelling trips to Russia and North Africa, took a toll on Churchill's clarity and grip. In Cabinet meetings his attention wandered and he was capable of rambling on to no particular point, bluffing his way through matters he had failed to prepare for by reading the proper papers. Pushed beyond endurance by this lackadaisical inattentiveness, the normally equable Attlee was goaded into sending Churchill a memorandum of disgusted protest and reproach. Increasingly fatalistic about Britain's inevitable subordination to American and Russian global power, Churchill enjoyed victory much less than he had anticipated.

But unlike his opposite number in the Bunker, much less the man in the Kremlin, Churchill took the criticism on the chin and would snap out of his brandy-lubricated bouts of gloom, summoning ministers to his bedside for morning conferences where he would hold forth, deep in breakfast crumbs and war maps, attired in his red-and-gold dragon robe like some omnipotent mandarin. And as even his most severe critics conceded, all his shortcomings were as nothing compared with the supreme accomplishment of giving Britain the collective will to fight at the time no one else would or could, and when opinionated observers like Ambassador Joseph Kennedy assumed it was not a case of whether the country would capitulate, but when. Alanbrooke would be on the verge of speaking his mind and then Churchill would have him to dine and he would marvel at the Prime Minister's buoyant courage and iron resolve.

What he may have lacked in micro-managerial attentiveness he more than compensated for by moral clarity. During the 1930s, when it was the political norm among the appeasers to hold their noses and turn a blind eye to what the Nazis were doing to the Jews, commenting, in effect, that doubtless it was all very deplorable, but what did one expect in a world which also boasted Mussolini and Stalin, Churchill understood the incommensurability of Nazi bestiality and unhesitatingly said so, over and over again. After Kristallnacht he was unembarrassed to shed tears while describing the torments in a culture which looked on such demonstrations of emotion as dreadfully bad form.

But then, one of the many reasons to be grateful to Roy Jenkins's fine book is to be reminded of Churchill's fundamental decency, the quality that made Orwell forgive him his anti-socialism and his sentimental imperialism. Though limited in education and social experience, Churchill nonetheless had no difficulty in translating his own romantic feeling for nationality to the aspirations of other cultures. It was natural, then, for him to end up the friend of Michael Collins as well as F. E. Smith, Chaim Weizmann as well as Emir (later King) Abdullah, and to see that a two-state solution in both Ireland and Palestine was the only way to satisfy equally legitimate longings for homeland.

In this, as in so many other aspects of the twentieth century, Churchill was a good deal more prescient than the clichés about his octogenarian dotage usually allow. Arguably the very best chapters of Jenkins's book are the last ones dealing with the late 1940s and '50s, after the victorious war leader had been rewarded with the stinging electoral defeat of 1945. Jenkins argues persuasively that even if, when re-elected in 1951, at the age of seventy-seven, Churchill did have a tendency to treat his 'Auld Lang Syne' government as a reunion, he had adjusted his historicist insularity to envision a Britain both enthusiastically pan-European and committed to the Atlantic alliance. The latest chapter of the providentialist story, then, was Britain's indispensable bridge-making between Europe and America.

His last cause, motivated by the certainty that any kind of nuclear exchange would presage the end of human history, was the diplomatic campaign fought doggedly but fruitlessly between 1953 and 1955 to defuse the Cold War. His last speech to the House of Commons before retiring as Prime Minister, ostensibly devoted to a White Paper on Defence, was prepared with excruciating care and was full of dark visions fitfully lit by flashes of optimism, the 'zigzag lightning' which Asquith had identified as the sign of his genius. Its rhythmically intoned peroration sounded, as Churchillian rhetoric had so many times before, the mighty chimes of his call to perseverance: 'Never flinch; never weary; never despair.' It's the achievement of Roy Jenkins's book to let us hear this voice again; to liberate the man from the mausoleum.

Churchill as Orator

Guardian, 20 April 2007

It was well after midnight on 7 February 1787 when Richard Brinsley Sheridan, MP, got up in the House of Commons to flay the hide off Warren Hastings, the impeached governor of Bengal.

The chamber was packed to the rafters, notwithstanding the fifty-guinea price for tickets. By the time Sheridan was done, it was six in the morning and no one had moved.

But virtuoso marathons of oratory weren't at all unusual in that distant golden age of eloquence (and they were a lot more fun than the Castro all-nighter).

Arguing for law reform in 1828, another celebrated silver-tongue, Henry Brougham, clocked six hours and three minutes and again no one budged. But then they both knew their spellbinding craft backwards.

Brougham had written essays on oratory (his favourite being Demosthenes) and at Edinburgh University had heard the great master of rhetoric, Hugh Blair, whose published lectures supplemented Cicero's *De Oratore* as the two great primers of studied eloquence, ancient and modern.

Sheridan took his stagecraft into the chamber, fulfilling Cicero's ideal that the orator should resemble Rome's star tragedian Roscius: 'When people hear he is to speak all the benches are taken . . . when he needs to speak silence is signalled by the crowd followed by repeated applause and much admiration. They laugh when he wishes, when he wishes they cry.'

When did you last hear a speech that good? Tony Blair's epideictic performance at the Labour-party conference last year won admiration even from his foes, but by and large the digital age is cool to rhetoric and, as the enthronement of the blogger suggests, prizes incoherent impulse over the Ciceronian arts of the exordium and the peroration.

State of the Nation addresses to the US Congress – that theatre of sob-sisters and ra-ra patriotism – most usually confuse passion with sentimentality, and since they are worked up by industrial teams of speechwriters, lack one of the elements thought indispensable to great oratory: integrity of personal conviction, the sound of what Cicero, following the Greeks, called ethos.

The robotically choreographed antics in which Democrats and Republicans alternate standing ovations every five minutes is the opposite of the free-spirited audiences Cicero had in mind submitting themselves to the persuader's art.

True public eloquence presupposes a citizen-audience gathered into a republic of listening. But our oral age is iPodded for our customised egos, an audience of one. Headphone listening seals us off, cuts connections.

Then there is that peculiarly British thing about grandiloquence, happier, for the most part, absorbing it in the theatre than in the public realm, where, as Winston Churchill found for most of his career, it was thought a symptom of his showy shallowness, his inconstancy, his addiction to hyperbole; in short, everything a man of sound policy was not.

But of course, speeches were what he did supremely well. Self-conscious that he'd never been through the upper-class nursery of eloquence, the Oxbridge Unions, Churchill fed off the great tradition of British politicians who had prevailed over the laws of understatement and pragmatic sobriety.

He communed with Cromwell, Chatham, Burke and Fox, Brougham, Macaulay and Gladstone, studying their master speeches for instruction on the oral economy of vehemence; when to let pathos, the appeal to passion, rip, and when, as Hugh Blair insisted, to make it retreat. And in one moment, the catastrophic late spring of 1940, this lifetime of rhetorical education and mercurial performance finally paid off.

Churchill's words went to war when Britain's armed forces seemed to be going under and had less wordy politicians like Halifax scurrying for a compromise with the triumphant Axis.

But, though he felt 'physically sick' at the Cabinet meeting of 26 May, when the horrifying magnitude of the German sweep to the Channel, coupled with King Leopold's Belgian capitulation, was sinking in, Churchill was adamant.

'No such discussions are to be permitted' was his response to suggestions to evacuate the royal family to some distant dominion of the empire.

When Kenneth Clark proposed taking the cream of the National Gallery's collection to Canada, Churchill shot back: 'No. Bury them in caves and cellars. None must go. We are going to beat them.'

The rehearsal for his great performance in the House of Commons on 4 June was to the full Cabinet (helpfully minus Halifax) in which Churchill passionately declaimed, 'We shall go on and we shall fight it out here or elsewhere and if at the last the long story is at an end it were better it should end, not through surrender but only when we are rolling senseless on the ground.' (Hugh Dalton added that Churchill had actually said 'when each of us lies choking in his own blood'.)

Ministers thumped fists on the table; some rose and patted him on the back. Defeatism – for the moment – had been held at bay. The long speech to the House of Commons a week later was meant to pre-empt any further thoughts of compromise with the 'Nahzies' (a wonderfully, calculatedly dismissive pronunciation) and to turn the mood of the country from despair to resolution.

Josiah Wedgwood thought it was worth 'a thousand guns and a thousand years' and he was right. It embodied both ethos (noble candour) and pathos (vehement passion) in equal degree and its inspirational persuasion depended fundamentally on one rhetorical tactic: honesty.

Unusually, Churchill dispensed with an introductory exordium and went straight to his narrative of the German blitzkrieg on the north, as if he were writing one of his military histories.

No one minded the mixed metaphor 'the German eruption swept like a scythe stroke'. Interspersed amid the lengthy storytelling was heroic relief, albeit in tragic mood: the futile four days of resistance in Calais (ordered by him). 'Cheers' reported the *Guardian*.

Then followed, in Churchill's instinctively archaic manner, what he thought would have been – and what still sounded like – 'hard and heavy tidings' of the encirclement. He trowelled on the despair, 'the whole root and core and brain of the British army . . . seemed about to perish on the air'. But the 'about', of course, allowed his transition to the 'miracle of deliverance' account of Dunkirk for which Churchill switched tenses, consciously emulating the Chorus from

Henry V: 'Now suddenly the scene is clear and the crash and thunder has if only for a moment died away.'

'Wars are not won by evacuations,' he cautioned, but then followed another of his romances of the 'island home'; the valiant airmen compared to whom 'the Knights of the Round Table, the Crusaders – they all fall back into the prosaic past'.

Each time Churchill appeared to be describing calamity, he made sure to punctuate it with gestures of improbable defiance. There had been 'a colossal military disaster', but 'we shall not be content with a defensive war' (cheers).

He could not guarantee there would be no invasion, but he summoned up the Clio again to remind the House that Napoleon too had been a victim of that delusion.

Even that might have gone differently had the winds in the Channel veered differently. But as the great speech moved to its unforgettable peroration, Churchill was giving all who heard it and beyond the sense of historical vocation, a calling against tyranny, that he felt so deeply himself. 'We cannot flag or fail', and from his Cabinet speech: 'We shall go on to the end', followed by the incantatory lines: 'We shall fight on the seas and oceans', and the rest. To hear the recording of the speech is to be amazed all over again at the fine-tuning of the performance since Churchill deliberately lowers his pitch for much of the 'we shall fight' repetitions, in softly heroic lament, a reproach, perhaps, to the unhinged vocal histrionics of his arch-enemy.

Only with 'we shall never surrender' did the voice suddenly produce a mighty Churchillian growly roar; the full-throated resonance of the roused beast.

It is still magically easy to conjure him up: the glasses down the nose; the bottom lip protruding in pouty determination, shoulders stooped, his very un-Ciceronian body language of patting both hands, all five fingers extended, against his chest, then, as Harold Nicolson reported, down his stomach all the way to his groin.

Standing like that, he looked, Nicolson wrote, like 'a solid, obstinate ploughman' as if the earth of Britain itself defied the worst that Hitler could throw at it.

Nicolson's wife, Vita Sackville-West, wrote to him that even when recited by a news announcer, the speech sent 'shivers' (of the right kind) 'down my spine'.

The reason, she wrote, 'why one is stirred by his Elizabethan phrases, that one feels the whole massive backing of powerful resolve behind them, like a fortress, [is that] they are never words for words' sake'.

She was right. They were words for everyone's sake. They were the lifeboat and the blood transfusion. They turned the tide.

The Fate of Eloquence in the
Age of The Osbournes

Phi Beta Kappa Oration, Harvard University, 3 June 2002

The extraordinary honour of being asked to deliver the oration to the Phi Beta Kappa chapter, and so become part of a tradition that runs from Ralph Waldo Emerson to Anthony Appiah, was only *slightly* qualified by being misinformed by the Dean of Undergraduate Education that her own Phi Beta Kappa orator had been Kermit the Frog. Now since I manifestly lack both the philosophical depth of Kermit and the wisecracking irreverence of Appiah, I wondered what could have possessed whichever guardians of the chapter to imagine that I could do the job? To another Harvard graduate I wondered out loud, in fact, and he gave me the answer, which I'm still not sure is a compliment. 'You do,' he said, 'have a certain way with the spoken word.'

Quite what that way might be remains to be seen, or heard, but I'm prepared to concede that this might be so, since I was told this at a very early age by my father who thought that, however I'd come by it, I'd got what in Britain was called the 'gift of the gab'. He had it himself in abundant measure, having done his time as a soapbox orator in Hyde Park and the East End of London in the 1930s, where he carried on talking and talking as Oswald Mosley's fascist blackshirts pelted him with rotten eggs and the occasional rock. 'A Jew's ultimate weapon is his mouth,' he insisted, even though my mother added that the ultimate weapon was, just occasionally and of course temporarily, disarmed by its collision with a large hairy fascist fist.

I was about ten when I began to be drilled in the bootcamp of public rhetoric, beginning with a trip to the theatre to see Richard Burton play Henry V. Though there were no Harfleurs in our neck of London to attack, a few weeks later there I was, in grey flannel short trousers, perched perilously on a chair in our living room waving a broom handle around, and lustily urging the troops to hurl themselves against the breach 'or fill the walls up with our English dead'. When this was recited at our elementary-school concert, between items understandably thought more suitable, or at least less bloodthirsty, for ten-year-olds, the reaction, when I finished, was one of stunned silence broken by furious applause from my actor-manager father. Some years earlier I had responded to all this voice-work by hitting him where I knew it would hurt most. I went on speech strike, going Trappist – for about five months, I seem to recall, remaining defiantly taciturn through a procession of speech therapists and psychotherapists, verbalising only to the gardener and swearing him to silence.

There are those who will tell you I've not shut up since. But this precocious sense of being afflicted with a pretty much incurable case of logorrhoea has actually left me with mixed feelings about the condition. On the one hand, it's hard not to relish the exhilaration of doing one's thing as a language animal. 'Nothing is so akin to our natural feelings as the rhythms and sounds of voices,' says Cicero in *De Oratore*, 'they rouse and inflame us, calm us and soothe us and often lead us to joy and sadness.' 'SPEECH! Speech!' wrote one of the greatest of all its American practitioners, Frederick Douglass, reflecting how he himself had been virtually reborn and certainly emancipated through his own dawning self-consciousness of being a natural orator, and how he had gone on to revolutionise public diction: 'the live, calm, grave, clear, pointed, warm, sweet, melodious human voice . . . humanity, justice, liberty demand the service of the living voice.' But it's precisely those for whom eloquence at the service of truth is an indispensable condition of a free society who are also most likely to fret at its apparent atrophy. The eloquent, of course, have been complaining about this at least since Quintilian (in the second century AD). Rhetoric that was both beautiful and virtuous, they lamented, was degenerating into either self-serving demagoguery, florid ornamentalism or the stumblings and mumblings of the inarticulate – Osbournes in togas – all of which heralded, in the most pessimistic view, the onset of a kind of slavery; the captivity of the powers of speech and the freedom of audience by the forces of diction-management. Listen to a culture flooded by platitude or vastly amused by grunts of dopey incoherence, they would say, and you will hear the bleating of the doomed.

Are we ourselves in that peril? Are we a culture washed in cacophonic fury, but signifying not a whole lot? Can Eminem or a gangsta rapper get away with what they get away with because the barked and shouted violence mocks and deafens any kind of response? Are *we* (as distinct from the licensed manufacturers of presidential rhetoric) even *capable* – especially in a moment of danger – of articulating to ourselves, to the nation, to the world, just what it is that's worth arguing over, fighting for or defending? Is the designed discontinuity of contemporary life – the indispensability of programmed obsolescence; fashion-turnover; the machinery of the market; the obsession with speed (faster, computer, *faster*); with instant drive-through gratification (I want that cheeseburger and I want it NOW); with the disposable over the durable; the strobe-lit subliminally registered broken-faceted reception of sensation – hopelessly incompatible with the voiced thoughtfulness we need if we are to figure out what it is exactly that holds us together against terror? If we can only articulate the meaning of calamity through the waving of flags and choruses of 'America the Beautiful', does this mean that tragedy has a short shelf-life? Would it have been better for all of *you* – made even better citizens of you – if you had been required to take not Expository Writing, but Expository Speaking?

It's a fair bet your forebears of Phi Beta Kappa thought so. For the chapter/fraternity was established as a community of spoken thought and debate; for the express purpose of sustaining classical scholarly values inside and, more urgently, outside the academy. An *American* scholar, it optimistically presupposed, was someone for whom the pursuit of knowledge was conditional not on escape from the contamination of the public world, but active engagement with it. Browse the forbidding pages of the published Phi Beta Kappa orations – not just at Harvard, but at Chicago, Columbia, Cornell – and you'll step into an ongoing Platonic symposium on civic virtue. Now this kind of wisdom does not, of course, come in soundbites. A roughly calculated average running time for those orations was, I would say, an hour and a half (so those of you nodding off at the back, count yourself lucky that my masters today shackled me to twenty-five minutes). On the other hand, those nineteenth-century brethren of yours were treated, quite often, to really scintillating, opening exordia. Try this zinger from Harvard's best – President Charles Eliot in 1888: 'I purpose to

examine some parts of the experience of the American Democracy
with the intention of suggesting the answers to certain theoretical
objections which have been urged against democracy in general and
of showing, in part, what makes the strength of the democratic form
of government . . .'

Eliot's turgid earnestness was actually out of character with
Harvard's traditions – especially Phi Beta Kappa traditions – which
perhaps more than anywhere else in the young Republic personified
the truism that, as the first Boylston Professor of Rhetoric and
Oratory from 1806 to 1809, John Quincy Adams, put it, 'eloquence is
power'. Adams believed that the young Republic was in an historical
state of political grace – something he could dream about in post-
revolutionary eastern Massachusetts – akin to fifth-century Athens
or the halcyon years of the Roman Republic; where voices which
allied rhetoric to virtue could prevail over faction and brute force.
'Where prejudice [has] not acquired an uncontrolled ascendancy,' he
wrote, 'the voice of eloquence will not be heard in vain.' Though, like
most of his generation of Harvard graduates, Adams had been
trained in rhetoric through the works of Hugh Blair and the eighteenth-century Scot Lord Kames, his own manual for modern orators
turned away from the belletristic manner back to what he thought
of as a neo-Ciceronian flinty vernacular; designed to plead before the
courts or sway a crowd. The tragedy of his life was that although he
was nicknamed 'Old Man Eloquent' and although he *looked* as though
you could set his bust alongside Demosthenes and Cato the Elder, and
although his speaking style was with 'kindled eyes and tremulous
frame', the organ itself was apparently shrill and piercing. In an age
of the honey-smooth oratory of the young Daniel Webster and John
Calhoun, Adams's presidential speeches, which sounded fine when
he rehearsed them before the Cabinet – his Farewell to Lafayette or
the panegyric to the Erie Canal – seemed barked at, rather than
voiced to, the public. And as a President who stood accused of getting
the office by a back-door Electoral College manoeuvre, John Quincy
was a perfect target for the oncoming Andrew Jackson, who made an
issue precisely of Adams's high-pitched classical diction, targeting it
with his own populist anti-highfalutin Hickory-Military vernacular.
A century and more before the equally glistening dome of Adlai
Stevenson (the spiritual descendant of Adams) was attacked as

eggheadedly un-American by another no-nonsense ex-general, Dwight Eisenhower, Adams too suffered from seeing what he'd always imagined to be the virtues of the detached, incorruptible proconsul stood on their head as symptoms of effete loftiness.

Now Adams got his faith in the persuasive power of eloquence directly from his father John, the second President, who would drill him in Cicero and Pericles whether walking the farm tracks at Quincy or the canal footpaths in revolutionary Amsterdam. And John Adams, as lawyer, schoolmaster and politician, felt himself to be the guardian of a long tradition of inspirational rhetoric which went all the way back to the Calvinist sermons of Thomas Hooker and the Great Awakening performances of Jonathan Edwards. The power of that charismatic preaching came from the faith that eloquence was saved from egotism, in so far as the mouth that was its instrument was merely a sounding board for the word of God. Moses, of course, had been a stammerer before that word had touched him. Likewise the Great Awakeners were no more than the organ of some higher natural truth. For John Adams's generation coming of age in the Boston of the 1760s, prophecy and politics became fused. It was not so much injustice that they saw in British policy as iniquity. In the unlikely figure of James Otis and the even unlikelier cause of writs of assistance – the legal warrants used by the British to search for contraband – Adams thought he heard and saw a vision of reborn civic virtue. Otis was then thirty-six, his style of speech as he argued against the writs before the heavily wigged and robed justices 'quick and elastic', 'his apprehension as quick as his temper'. For Adams, his was the voice of the natural American; the lost voice of Ciceronian virtue. The fact that Otis's 'passions were painted in his face' seemed to correspond precisely to Quintilian's doctrine that the speaker must feel, emotively, the truth of what he utters if he is to persuade his listeners. Had Otis worn a virtuously dishevelled toga, he could not have won Adams more completely.

All the great orators of the revolutionary age – Sam Adams, Patrick Henry in Virginia, and the first great rhetorician of the post-revolutionary House of Representatives, the now-forgotten Harvard graduate Fisher Ames, said to be the most silver-tongued of all – were famous for their controlled flamboyance; the calculation of a manner that was said to be 'natural' or 'easy', but which managed to achieve often outrageous theatricality without being accused of affectation. They were hams – think of that invisible dagger Patrick Henry plunged over and again into his breast – but they were hams for liberty.

Winning 'hearts and minds', as Adams claimed had been the case, was not *just* the victory of liberty over imperial coercion; it was the vindication, as he and Jefferson believed, of classical republican rhetoric over brute military muscle. The critical role played by French military power – inconveniently the product of a self-interested Catholic despotism – was underplayed in favour of the legend of the mass mobilisation of the people through the sonorities of virtue. And the vocal Founding Fathers believed they were redeeming, among other things, the tradition of Greco-Roman eloquence itself, which in Britain had degenerated into ornamental disingenuousness. Latter-day Ciceros like Edmund Burke – significantly Irish, not English – had attempted to stop the rot. But public diction had decayed into luxury. For the austerely civic Americans it was, on the contrary, a necessity, their first line of defence. An entire generation thought of themselves as 'Massacre' orators, after the Boston Massacre (in which an accident was transformed by indignant oratory into an emblematic confrontation between innocence and occupation).

To that generation, American eloquence worked because it so obviously exemplified Quintilian's definition of an orator as a *good* man who speaks well. They also subscribed to the Aristotelian assumption that the power of rhetoric was in inverse relationship to the self-sufficiency of brute force. Where that force was coercive, mouths and ears were shut. Sparta was taciturn; Athens eloquent. The ideal Athenian leader was the hero who spoke beautiful and impassioned truths – Pericles. But their American descendants also cherished the tradition because the power of eloquence presupposed the freedom to be persuaded; to be reasoned with; to be moved. Cicero's natural theatre was the Senate in which those of like mind would literally stand together, and the job of the orator was, equally literally, to *move* them to a different position. A vote was, of course, a voice. For Cicero, for the Adamses, for Jefferson – and of course for the Lincoln of the Lincoln-Douglas debates – a republic which took the arts of persuasion seriously was not just a free state, but one which could contain difference of belief without resort to mutual extermination. The opposite to that humanely pluralist eloquence is commandment authorised by fiat or revelation and executed through coercion. Terror is, in every sense, dumb.

If the preservation of a public life tolerant of difference is one reason why we should cherish eloquence, the second reason, scarcely less important, and the logical outcome of the first, is that it reconstitutes community without sacrificing liberty. If the founding fathers of public American speech were concerned, in the first instance, to use it to differentiate a free from a tyrannised society, their heirs in the nineteenth century worried about the republic falling apart, either in fratricidal division or into a mere aggregate of mutually conflicting interests.

The great moments of nineteenth-century public eloquence were when orators believed – and made their listeners believe – that for the duration of their discourse, using all the tools that Isocrates, Demosthenes, Cicero and Quintilian had given them – they could reconstitute a mere crowd, a gathering of individuals, into a community; and that that supra-individualist cohesion would survive their dispersal. This is what converted individual abolitionists into a shoulder-to-shoulder brethren; and what Frederick Douglass, who had learned some of his rhetorical magic from them and from his own reading and practising, took on his travels, not least to Britain in 1845–7 where, in Cork, Belfast, Dundee and London, he tried to persuade his listeners that they were part of an indivisible movement to extirpate an abomination from the face of the earth. The most sublimely enduring speech which took, as its mission, the attempt to remake national community over the partially buried bodies of those who had died for it, was of course Lincoln's Gettysburg address – its two minutes preceded by Edward Everett's two-hour performance. (It had been Everett, not Lincoln, who had been the star attraction and for whom the event had been postponed from 23 October 1863 to 19 November in order to give the Harvard President and ex-Secretary of State adequate time to prepare.)

Doomed to be remembered as Lincoln's interminable warm-up act, Everett's speech is, in fact, in its own way – a recitation of the narrative of the battle followed by an appeal for eventual reconciliation – not half bad. But arguably, one of the great and now completely forgotten moments when eloquence was summoned to mobilise national community took place here, at the Phi Beta Kappa Alpha chapter of Harvard, almost exactly 140 years ago, when George William Curtis – *Harper's* journalist and war veteran – delivered the oration on 17 July 1862, a speech which we know was repeated at least forty times around New England that grave autumn. Curtis's aim was to insist on the indivisibility of liberty and equality; to take away from the seceding states their claim to the rhetoric of freedom, which he characterised as fraudulent since it was inseparable from the preservation of slavery, and restore that rhetoric to true American nationality: an inclusive nationality based on the assumption of common humanity. To *be* American was to celebrate this. If this had never before been achieved, the enterprise only grew in significance:

> The achievement of all other nations should be only wings to American feet that they may hasten to heights that Greeks and Romans, that Englishmen and Frenchmen and Germans never trod. Were they wise? Let us be wiser. Were they noble? Let us be nobler. Were they just? Let us be juster. Were they free? Let our very air be freedom . . . Let those who will, despair of that perfect liberty with which God made us all free. But let us now, here, in the solemn moments which are deciding if there is to BE a distinctive America, resolve that even were the American system to fade from history, the American principle should survive immortal in our hearts . . .

Freedom, Curtis insisted, was the natural right of all, not some, men – and he came out swinging against discrimination on grounds of sex as well as race. 'We will never again forget, God help us,' he ended, 'that the cause of the United States is the cause of human nature, and the permanent life of the nation is the liberty of *all* its children.'

Now if this speech and its orator have been relegated to the realms of the unremarkable, perhaps it's just because for the generations when eloquence *was* power, rhetoric of this degree of truth and power *was* actually unremarkable; or at least those who could practise it were, if not exactly two a penny, then thick on the ground. Can we say this of our own time? Is the question absurd when the 'arts of communication' (and God knows there are abundant seminars going by that name) presupposes the shortest of attention spans? Go to Widener Library and look under 'elocution' or 'oratory' and you will be led to the Miss Havisham of the public arts: tome after tome gathering dust; relics of a time when mastery of rhetoric was not just a sign of the educated citizen, but also the ladder, as Frederick Douglass found, of true social mobility. If you want to learn the arts of persuasion now, you go not to Cicero and Quintilian, but the Business School Library where you can pick up the latest technique of negative advertising. Some of the greatest of the twentieth-century rhetoricians saw this coming. In 1912, Teddy Roosevelt waxed eloquent on the need, above all, to outlaw corporate money donated to political campaigns (as well as the critical need to regulate the accounting practices of big business and use state power to conserve the environment).

It was the management of persuasion in the interests of corporations which struck Roosevelt as most ominous for the fate of democracy. Implicit in his anxieties was the prophecy of synthetic eloquence; not the mobilisation of active, participatory citizenship, but its opposite: its convenient abdication to professional opinion-formers. Of course there is nothing wicked about professional speechwriters. The Greeks had rhetores who for payment produced speeches for public orators. Andrew Jackson's best stuff was written by Chief Justice Roger Taney. And Samuel Rosenmann turned them out for Franklin Roosevelt. But there is, I think, a difference between the collaboration of say, Seward and Lincoln, on drafts of his speeches, and the industrial fabrication of purpose-designed speeches, produced by White House Nibelungen toiling in the mines of rhetorical gold – eight full-time writers for Ronald Reagan and a complete staff of fourteen. If we were to take a contemporary check on Cicero's famous five constituents of oratory, what would we find? An *inventio* – the main idea dreamed up and carefully monitored by the staff; *dispositio* – the arrangement, tailor-made for television and punctuated by gestures to 'real-life' heroes inserted into the gallery; *memoria* – supplied by the invisible teleprompter; *actio* – style, the oxymoronic down-home gravitas, studded with reassuring simplicities; and finally *elocutio* – delivery, finely judged to reassure that the incumbent can complete sentences, but equally finely judged to make them short. 'I want four-letter words,' demanded Lyndon Johnson of Richard Goodwin, 'and paragraphs four sentences long.'

And who is to say that they are wrong? If I'm right that the survival of eloquence is the condition of both a free political society and a coherent community, we do need to cherish it. But we also need to hotwire it to contemporary diction, without, I hasten to say, turning into the kind of political rap parodied by Warren Beatty's last film: a public discourse that lies somewhere between Demosthenes and Ozzy Osbourne. And one of the most powerful qualities of such a discourse will be, as Lincoln knew at Gettysburg, knowing just when to stop.

Barack Obama

Independent, 23 January 2009

'They said this day would never come,' he began as he faced the ecstatic throng in the downtown Convention Centre in Des Moines on 3 January 2008. This was the night Barack Obama became a force to be reckoned with. It was a party without food or drink, but no one needed either. They were juiced with jubilation, the din of it bouncing off the precast concrete. The packed crowd, hooting and hollering, was mostly (this was Iowa) white: all shapes, ages and classes. But amid them were plenty of African-Americans, schoolkids in buttercup-yellow T-shirts, silver-haired matrons, tall college boys, who, before the appearance of the candidate, had been rocking and rapping and singing and swaying. They were the gospel choir of The One and the crowd rode the elation as if this was a revival meeting, which in its way it was, the body revived being that of the United States of America.

Obama can play heart and he can play head. He's the classical orator as well as the preacher of call-and-response. That evening he was pitch-perfect; letting the emotional electricity surge before cooling the voltage. He spoke in calculated measures, light on his feet, the basketballing candidate with the nifty jump shot, head turned slightly aside as if tuning in to history's promptings: 'I hear you, Abe, I hear you, Martin; message coming in loud and clear.' Then square on again to the crowd, the gaunt gravity broken by a flashing collusive grin; everybody a brother and sister. Right now he owns American rhetoric. And until he came along the standard response of the hacks was to say he's welcome to it, who cares?

In the age of the television spot and the Web, formal speeches seemed a redundant luxury; so much embellishment; nothing to do with the engineering of power. But lo and behold, it turned out that words were the fuel that turned the pistons after all. George W. Bush's inadequacies with language had stopped being a sign of sterling inner strength, or even an endearing comedy. In the age of Hurricane Katrina and the war in Iraq, words failed him and so he failed America. The country, it turned out, hungered for *logos*, but not the pabulum of standard operating procedure for election campaigns, much less talk radio rant. What it wanted were words to bind up America's wounds; words such as Lincoln and Franklin D. Roosevelt managed; words which, in the midst of calamity, could remind the nation of the resilience of its history; the possibilities of a decent future.

So Obama is both blog and blarney; the melder of old and new in American democracy. His footsoldiers leave no email address undisturbed, but they also knock on doors to get voters registered; veterans to the polls. They can spin a sharp slogan with the best, but their man knows how to be Cicero when the occasion begs for it. That evening in Des Moines, the rhythm of the sentences was scrupulously scored. The last word of that opening sentence, counter-intuitively falling in a downbeat, the irony allowed to register, throwing the crowd its hit of underdog glee.

'They' who thought the 'day would never come' were the thunderstruck operatives of what, until this very evening, had been assumed to be the unstoppable Hillary machine. But it was also the media hacks who had long awarded her the nomination and had written off Obama as too professorial, too liberal, too black and yet not black enough. (The Clintons still had the allegiance of most of the black Democratic leadership.) Obama's campaign, the conventional wisdom had it, would be the candidacy of doomed wholesomeness: losers' granola; the Bill Bradley of 2008. Obama was Campus Man, catnip for the sophomores, all finesse and no killer instinct, who would fold as soon as he realised politics was a contact sport. 'They' were even some of the Obama campaign people themselves, who, not quite predicting the magnitude of the result in Iowa, had failed to organise any security for the celebration. No metal detectors, no watchful men in metallically bulked suits. He was, after all, still a 'Hopeful'. Best not to get deluded. Give it a shot, end up with the second spot on the ticket? Not so bad.

'They' were the Republican opinion-makers who had been salivating at the opportunity of a Clinton nomination. Dirt-diggers primed and raring to go, who resented this inexplicable, irritating disruption to their plans. But this was the greatest wrong-footing in post-war electoral history. Beneath all the prime-time bloviation that night, the dismissals of the Iowa result as nothing more than a web-geek wonder, you could pick up a faint but unmistakable tremor of unease. Could it be that something stupendously unsettling in the political order was actually taking place? What was that sudden subsidence beneath the feet? Just an untoward event or a political sinkhole about to swallow the entire Roveian Republican ascendancy, along with the doomed Bush presidency? Were things really that *weird*? Was it all up with the Age of Reagan? As the campaign rolled on through Hillary's fighting comeback, Obama's capacity to brush off everything thrown at him and his unmistakable growth into presidential suit-size drew reluctant admiration from his foes. This was serious. This was real.

There is no point asking whether Obama would have made it were the times not so out of whack. History made him and he made history. It's the test of a formidable politician that he or she can smell opportunity in unfolding disaster and has the resolution to brush aside those who live by more conventional timetables. It has already been said that it's Obama's misfortune to be the first African-American president at a time of acute national crisis. But you can bet he doesn't see it that way; rather as the gift of challenge. Sometimes — as in 1860 with Abraham Lincoln and 1932 with Franklin D. Roosevelt — the man and the moment do meet. This is one of those occasions, all the more miraculous for occurring at a juncture when the United States must urgently accomplish two goals usually supposed to be in mutual contradiction. On the one hand, America has to rediscover common national purpose; on the other, it must re-engage with the world. Matters have moved so far and so fast from the sovereign assumption of George W. Bush's presidency — that America needed to shrug off the diplomatic niceties of the rest of the world if it was to assert its national interest and protect its security — that the active reintegration of the United States into the global community is now held to be a *condition* of American recovery.

The woeful side of interdependence has been exposed by financial debacle; but it's now Obama's task to turn it into a strength. Obama's mantra has been that, historically, mutual regard has been as much the American way as rugged individualism. Acknowledgement that we are our brothers' and sisters' keepers, he often says, is what we owe to those who want to stand on their own two feet, but who have been disabled by circumstances not of their doing, whether that is a missing father, a neglected school or a catastrophic spike in unemployment. That same truism could be applied from the developed to the developing world; and to the need for concerted international action to arrest climate change. After a long period when attending to others' concerns has been stigmatised as a soft aversion to the exercise of power, Obama wants to reassert mutuality not just as a bona-fide American ideal in the tradition of Wilson, Franklin D. Roosevelt and George Marshall, but one that serves American interests more reliably and more morally than military heft.

It is burden enough that he has to carry the desperate expectations of a damaged United States on his shoulders, but Obama can scarcely avoid a sense around the world that he is the answer to its prayers as well. That somehow he can manage to be a miracle-worker in the Middle East, in Afghanistan and in Latin America. The impossible assignment comes along with what he has wryly called his 'funny name'. For better or worse he is supposed to be President of the planet. Through Barack Hussein Obama run culture lines that connect Kenya with Kansas; ethnically complicated Polynesian-Asian Hawaii with black south Chicago; Scots-Irish bloodlines with a touch of Cherokee on his maternal grandmother's side. His and Michelle's daughters, Malia and Sasha, bring together west and east Africa; the atrocity of the slave ships with his Luo father's voluntary immigration. It's safe to say that he was not elected President because of this cosmopolitan richness. But it's equally true – and remarkable evidence of the American capacity for national redefinition – that it did Obama no harm, either. Once they had recovered from their shock at not getting Hillary Clinton as their long-desired Democratic nominee, the movers and shakers of the Republican party must have gleefully assumed that Obama's name – along with the rich possibilities for its branding him as un-American, not to mention his skin colour, his association with radical preachers and an unrepentant anti-Vietnam-War underground militant – precluded any possibilties of his actually winning the presidential election. Americans, ran the received wisdom, might flirt with his exoticism (the usual code word for race) and his intellectual elitism, but they would never actually put him in the White House. Whatever they now said about George W. Bush, they *had* wanted to have a beer with him, had valued and voted the affability factor, the reassuring sense that somehow he was 'one of them'. Would regular white folks in the heartlands of Indiana, Colorado and North Carolina really think Obama was one of them?

Perhaps the most astonishing fact about the election of 2008 was that by an emphatic majority, if not a landslide, American voters judged someone called Barack Hussein Obama, whose complexion in no way resembled the preceding forty-three presidents of the United States, to be the patriot to whom they wished to entrust the fate of the country at a time of grave peril. Instead of the decorated Vietnam prisoner of war with the hero's story, the public voted into power a lanky African-American intellectual. On the eve of his inauguration, close to three-quarters of the population – a number far greater than those who voted for him – expressed confidence in the prospects of his leadership and administration. Obama's goal of transcending bitter partisanship, of leaving behind the triviality of mutual abuse for a politics of substance – the stance that in every campaign has been discounted as naive – turned out to voice a national craving that, with the avalanche of disasters falling on America, became simply irresistible. The idealistic visionary turned out to be the smart politician.

Whether this delicate flower of national solidarity will survive the deepening recession or a war gone bad in Afghanistan remains to be seen. But even before a word of what must be the most anticipated inaugural speech since John F. Kennedy in 1961 has been uttered, Obama has accomplished something indispensable for the immediate condition of the country: he has restored public trust in the integrity and competence of American government. Against the self-accelerating disintegration of confidence in institutions assumed, as a matter of course, to be more or less dependable – banks, insurance, the stock market, the property market – the mere fact of the Obama administration offers a fixed point around which belief in American reinvention can make a credible stand. Given the ignominy into which the Bush-Cheney administration has fallen, its almost complete loss of legitimacy and credibility, would this have been the case with *any* incoming administration? Almost certainly not, for the manifold crises that have befallen the United States have had at their core a resistance to the notion that there could be any virtue in acts of the federal government other than those undertaken to secure American power. George W. Bush's fatal alternation between contempt for government and panic-stricken plunges into its arms are the logical consummation of the philosophy of Jeffersonian individualism paramount since Reagan. The undisguised masterplan was to use deficits to starve reprehensible (and, as the conservatives saw them, self-perpetuating) public institutions – such as Public Broadcasting, the Department of Education, the Environmental Protection Agency – of funds and so doom them to such impotence that they could be liquidated to nary a bleat of protest. Thus the bureaucratic behemoth would be shrunk to its irreducible minimum – and lo, in the burial ground of the New Deal, a thousand flowers of enterprise would bloom unimpeded by the thorns and tares of regulation.

So ran the true religion of the right. So it was hardly a surprise that the Iraq invasion followed the same game plan. As this view insists that the default mode for every culture worldwide is democracy and capitalism, once the Baath party and Saddam Hussein were removed, the allegedly Western-leaning, enterprise-oriented Iraqi culture would vault to dynamic liberation and its stability and prosperity would become self-sustaining. The feedback loop was unarguable. Freedom would ensure integrity; infrastructure – and temporary security needs – would be funded by oil revenues; and a nucleus of Western entrepreneurial culture would take hold in the benighted autocratic, theocratic Middle East. The stagnant pond in which the insects of al-Qaeda bred would be drained and life would be grand in Mesopotamia.

It's hard to think of a moment in American history when ideological blinkers got more fatally in the way of an administration's capacity to see the true direction of national history. Iraq desperately needed more and better government, not less. What it got, for many years following the invasion, was an exploded infrastructure in which masters of outsourcing roamed at will. As the United States has learned to its bitter cost, financial institutions needed more careful regulation, not less. A cyclone of economic imperatives has swept away the bad odour hanging over government since Ronald Reagan declared it to be the problem, not the solution. Ask Detroit's automobile-makers and you will find that Bill Clinton's declaration that 'the era of big government is over' turns out to be premature. Government has been recalled, presided over by a chief executive who is unapologetic about its obligations to the socially vulnerable while being under no illusion that its long-term job is to manufacture automobiles or run the banks.

Republican attempts to demonise Obama as a stealth socialist about to impose a radically alien welfare state on the land of the free failed to strike a chord with a majority of American voters. The reason was that, unlike John Kerry, Obama avoided being boxed into the stereotype of the remote patrician intellectual aloof from the mundane hurts of the average Joe and Jane. Paradoxically, Obama escaped this snare (also eluded by the authentically down-home, chicken-fried Bill Clinton) by not pretending he was something he wasn't. No one was going to buy a version of Obama that was NASCAR and Bud six-pack. But the tried and true conservative tactic of unleashing the mistrust of cleverness, of tarring it as suspiciously metropolitan, failed them. Not only because the results of its most glaring counter-example in the forty-third President were all too fresh, but also because Obama embodied a politics that reflected 'the way people actually live their lives', as he put it in *The Audacity of Hope*. Palin kept yelling that Obama hadn't actually *done* anything, other than strutting his Harvard Law School stuff into the Senate, and in the debate with Joe Biden she turned his record of 'community service' into a joke, as if it were no more than a liberal cookie-bake sale. Obama (though not the street-tough Biden from Scranton, Pennsylvania) was oddly passive in response, but nonetheless the message got across that in south Chicago he had organised tenants to demand basic decencies of life from the Housing Authority.

Those were not trivial matters: removal of asbestos; provision of dependable sewerage; minimal security against the predation of drug gangs; public schools that were invested in learning rather than being teenage holding pens. This was why in Iowa a television-crew driver, raised as a farm boy on a small spread in the south of the state, described Obama's appeal to me as 'down-to-earth'. A way with words, the sharp mind, didn't undercut that impression. They are of a piece with his conviction that intelligence is not necessarily unpatriotic, that education is an American liberation, and that no government need apologise for securing for its least-fortunate citizens the education and healthcare that make the realisation of the American dream something more than an empty piety.

Two places provided Barack Obama with his unfashionable belief in the possibility of a doctrine of public justice and social benevolence that would accord with, rather than betray (as the right had it), American idealism. Those places are Hawaii and the urban black church. They were the making of Barack Obama, though neither of them has been of much interest to commentators on this side of the ocean who, when they pay any attention, dismiss them as two symptoms of American fantasy: the loud shirt and the credulous hallelujah. But fail to understand them and you will never get the forty-fourth President.

Hawaii was as formative for Obama as rural Illinois was for Lincoln. It's the state that regularly appears in the top deck of administrations spending most per capita on education, healthcare, public transport; a state unembarrassed about government activism. None of which makes Hawaii any sort of social paradise. It's precisely because the ethnic wound opened when the kingdom was annexed in 1898 (largely at the behest of the pineapple mogul Sanford Dole) refuses to heal – because the relationship between natives and *haole* whites remains that of colonised victims and imperialists – that the challenge for government to close the gap between extremes of wealth and poverty has remained perenially urgent. The brutality of modern Hawaiian history makes for a state with a restless conscience. All the historical ingredients that made mainland Americans allergic to civic government – above all, the frontier that allowed pioneers to indulge their fantasies of Jeffersonian self-sufficiency – were glaringly absent from modern Hawaiian history. If the islands weren't quite Sweden in mid-Pacific, nor were they the wilder West.

They were, in fact, as much Eastern as Western. Native codes of *kapu* – what was forbidden and the power of traditional law to enforce punishment and maintain asylum – followed by the Asian devotion to family paternalism and governing omniscience, generated a different kind of attitude to public ethics than in the rest of the United States. And although the colonising presence of industrial farming and ranching companies followed the classic pattern of unregulated capitalism, even Sanford Dole and his heirs affected the Hawaiian manner of paternalist obligation. Two other institutions – the strong presence of both Protestant and Catholic church missions and their schools; and the American Armed Forces – only reinforced this unembarrassed sense of an ethical order containing the excesses of an entrepreneurial culture. If anything, Hawaii's reputation as a pleasure dome only made the public determination to contain its hedonism within the bounds of social regulation stronger. Hawaii's story runs counter to American mythologies in so many ways. Instead of unlimited space and a fiction of permanent abundance, it has always been aware of the pressure of population on limited space and finite natural resources. Though there has been ecological havoc wrought by both dense settlement and the destruction of native species by animal colonisation, the Hawaiian way has been to be aware of the costs of the damage and to take steps to arrest it. Tourists get confined to their beach pens on Waikiki, so the last Nene geese can make it on the rainforest hills of western Kauai. Anyone familiar with the wasted terrain of Lana'l and western Moloka'l with its black plastic sheets, torn and blowing in the wind, relics of pineapple plantations long since abandoned, will understand Obama's passion about the stewardship of the global environment. You could scarcely imagine anyone with a background less like the oil drillers of Midland, Texas.

Then, too, Hawaii scrambles the ethnic game in ways that would always make Barry Obama, as he was then, ultimately impervious to the obligations of race-identity politics. Oahu, the island of Obama's upbringing, means 'The Gathering Place', but those who were gathered were exceptionally complicated in their cultural identity. Portuguese and Basque whalers fetched up in Hawaii, as did the Russians and British. The islands are imprinted with Asian strains, but none of them match, much less meld; even though Filipinos and the first wave of Japanese migrants came in virtual bondage as sugarcane workers. Some of those who toiled under indentures were Chinese, but they gravitated quickly (as they did on the Pacific coast of the mainland) to dry-goods stores, launderers, road-builders and cooks. Different generations of Japanese wear the distinctions of their history carefully and precisely; the earliest immigrants now a cut above (rather like convict chic in Australia) later cohorts, including those patriotic Americans who suffered the humiliation and privation of internment after Pearl Harbor, often condescending to the hordes of tourists from Tokyo and Osaka who flood the islands at vacation time. One thing, however, the many Asian-Pacific cultures did share and that was the twinned belief in unremitting bootstrap hard work and the pricelessness of learning.

Growing up black in Hawaii was a whole lot more auspicious than in, say, Alabama or south-central Los Angeles, but it was certainly no picnic. Nearly all of those Asian cultures rubbing up against each other shared a disdain for Africans, distinct from white American racism, but an affliction all the more rankling in what, day by day, must have seemed the easy-going pace of Oahu society. What came as a particular blessing to Obama then was the simple fact of cherishing parentage, meaning his mother and grandparents. Barack Obama Sr and Ann (real name Stanley) Dunham could fall in love at university in Honolulu and their union be relatively uncontroversial compared with states where black–white marriages were still a criminal offence, because Hawaii's attitude was relaxed in such matters. In his gripping autobiography, *Dreams from My Father* (a book so beautifully written that it seems inconceivable it came from the hand of a politician, which, at the time he wrote it, he was not), Obama is unsentimentally clear-eyed about all this. His father and mother, in their respective ways, embodied authentic, if ultimately contradictory, beliefs about American redemption. Barack Sr, the son of a goat-herding Luo chief, came to the United States as the epitome of upward mobility through the American opportunity. But it was the pursuit of that same goal that took him away from the conjugal nest when he was offered another scholarship, this time to Harvard. What he left was not so much an African-American as American-African son, just four years old. Ann, on the other hand, represented something like the opposite instinct: that of America as a liberal commonwealth of social conscience. (Her mother, Obama's 'Toot', characterised Ann as an Adlai Stevenson liberal Democrat, secular and utopian.) In her own passion for America as school project, Ann reached back to the ideals of Emerson, Bronson Alcott and New England instruction, even though she and her parents were from the world of the Great Plains. During her second marriage in Indonesia, she would rouse the small Barack – seven or eight years old – at four in the morning for crash lessons that would supplement the shortcomings of local schooling.

Obama's education was formative in more than a purely pedagogical sense. It made him wonder: was he to be Barry or Barack? What *was* the relationship of a child of Kansas and Kenya to the history of African-Americans; their slavery, persecution, segregation and liberation? Should he escape that history or embrace it? Could *America* escape or embrace it? Oahu's elite schools owed something to the British model as much as the American: uniforms; loyalty codes; heavy-duty homework; and when his mother sent him back to the island to live with Gramps, the moody, unfulfilled furniture salesman and the indomitable, dynamic Toot, Obama went to one of Hawaii's most serious hothouses of talent, Punahou School. Amid the white shirts and dark ties, teenage self-romance was bound to go black and so he did, complete with Afro, basketball, hard music and a smattering of dope. *Dreams from My Father* is pre-emptively candid about all this. Scoring off the forty-second President's procrastinations on the same subject, Obama writes: 'I did inhale. That was the point.' The abrupt and very brief reappearance in Hawaii of Barack Sr, who threw his weight around in Gramps and Toot's Honolulu apartment like some visiting district collector from the British Empire, must have only made the boy's role confusion worse. Was he supposed to admire the missing patriarch or drive a stake through his heart?

At Occidental College in California (chosen because a girlfriend had gone there), Barack got the uppermost of Barry. Black politics and Malcolm the charismatic martyr were irresistible. But what Obama took from Malcolm X (he must have *read* the autobiography rather than just invoking it) was the slain leader's resistance to role-assignments for Black Men: by black Islam, by militant radicalism or by Martin Luther King's Christian exhortation. Obama began to see the addiction to victim-rage as a liability. It was unclear, though, what might replace it. Columbia University, where he transferred for his junior and senior year, doesn't seem to have given him the answer he was looking for. There were more great books; a headlong dive into political theory. But although Harlem was on his doorstep and part of him wanted to lose his doubts east of Morningside Park, his black and white angels continued to wrestle in his head. For some months after graduation, Obama worked as an apprentice consultant to a business corporation in Manhattan. He suited up and bought the briefcase. Hair neatly cropped, he was the African-American In the Office. When he shared his yearning to do something that brought him closer to the tough realities of black life in the cities, the African-Americans who worked at the low-paid cleaning jobs told him they didn't need any more social workers – what they needed were brothers who 'made it', who brought the bacon home to the hood.

Barack came of age with the news of his father's death. Obama was twenty-one, living a mournful, solitary life on a block of East Harlem 'treeless and barren, lined with soot-coloured walk-ups'. Later, he would learn from his half-sister that there had been a sorry decline.

Barack Sr, the gifted goatherd's son who had made it to Harvard, had been an oil-company executive, then a government economic advisor in independent Kenya. But he had paid a heavy price for standing up to Jomo Kenyatta over the Kikuyu monopolisation of offices at the expense of the Luo. His own job had gone; penury and depression followed and in their train, inevitably, multiple women and heavy drinking. By the time he managed a sad, slow climb back, he had been consumed by humiliation and resentment. The tragic picture liberated Obama from that indeterminate vision of the missing but charismatic father on whom he could project some sort of heroic wishful thinking. Now he knew he needed solid connection; the 'hunger for community' that later he would accurately believe America itself craved.

He would find it in south Chicago, though the road to solidarity and success was hardly paved with yellow bricks. Working for the Developing Communities Project, run by a Jewish convert to Catholicism, Jerry Kellman, in the tough projects of Roseland and Altgeld Gardens was an apprenticeship in heartbreak. Trying to mobilise tenants to claim rights to basic services, Obama endured empty meeting halls; hardened cynicism from the city; disbelief among the black churchmen who wrote him off as another naive, over-educated kid who would high-tail it back to a fancy job when he realised he couldn't build Jerusalem overnight on the south side of Chicago. But just the fact that the first black mayor, Harold Washington, was in office, along with deep reserves of tenacity and the famous Obama unflappability, along with the refusal to back off from the improbable, got him through many of these trials. He earned respect the hard way. And through working with the churches – the vital link to the neighbourhoods – Obama found religion the social way, with Jesus the ethical teacher. Once inside, he made the instinctive, historical connection with the entire history of black self-determination, from the secret slave churches in the south through to the great temple establishments that ran schools and cared for the sick and pretty much everything during the century of Jim Crow segregation. He began to tune in to its melodies and cadences; the music itself, but also the mighty instrument of its preaching, without which the civil-rights leaders would have been muffled or distant apostles. From being a listener, he became a speaker, so that when the accusations against

Jeremiah Wright's unhinged anger threatened to derail his campaign in March 2008, it was the most natural thing in the world for Obama to deliver the finest of all his speeches, in Philadelphia, in which he undertook to help white America face and understand the long history through which race, religion and the politics of salvation were all braided up together.

So Barack Obama became an interlocutor, discovering that without compromising his own history he could disarm paranoia and make people of opposite minds and backgrounds listen to each other. At Harvard Law School, where he had gone to acquire the sharp knowledge he would need, whether he stayed in community work or, as his inner voices (and friends) were telling him, tested the waters of politics, he became the first elected black president of the *Harvard Law Review* because he was already seen as someone who transcended partisan alignments. In a bitterly divided institution, Obama was elected with the help of conservatives who saw him as a maker of consensus rather than someone who endorsed radical positions as a duty to his race.

This is how it has gone on ever since. Stereotyped over and again as a presumptuous outsider whose unapologetic reverence for knowledge somehow was supposed to make him tone-deaf to the needs of regular people, Obama has mobilised those who were tired of hearing that the way things had to be was the way they had always been. That went as much for black city and state politics as for the kind of presidential campaign his own was organised to confound. When he went back to Chicago, taking a job in a law firm specialising in civil-rights cases, rather than the high-paying corporate position that would have been offered on a plate, there was no question about either his understanding of, or his credibility with, the districts of south Chicago. Marriage to Michelle Robinson, who had gone from a working-class background to Princeton, did no harm to perceptions of Obama as someone whose understanding of, and credibility with, neighbourhood politics was unimpeachable.

It's true that astonishing breaks have come his way. During the campaign for the United States Senate in 2004, first his Democratic opponent, the billionaire Blair Hull, became terminally mired in a bad divorce; then his Republican opponent, Jack Ryan, was exposed as forcing his wife to have sex in public in heavily equipped swinger clubs. This did not go down well with the party faithful. More often, though, Obama has made his own luck. Taking on a veteran black politician, Alice Palmer, for a seat in the Illinois Senate seemed a wild gamble designed to separate him for good from exactly the constituency he would have to count on for any kind of political career beyond the city. But time and again, he has caught the change in wind-direction, projected himself as new life for an enervated body politic, whether city, state or country, and time and again he has managed to put together a coalition of support across race, class and the cultures that are presumed to divide the United States into two permanently alienated warring camps. Last year, Indiana was in his column.

He is not all mouth and mind. Though his opponents liked to caricature him as someone who talked the talk while ducking votes, his time in the Illinois Assembly and his shorter tenure in the Senate were certainly not short of evidence that he knows how to deliver legislation that makes a concrete difference to people's lives. In Illinois, hundreds of bills bore his sponsorship and many of them, though unglamorous, were of the utmost importance: securing state funding for free mammograms and prostate screening, for example. In the Senate, he teamed up with the pillar of orthodox Republican foreign policy, Richard Lugar, to sponsor legislation dealing with the security of nuclear waste and to tighten oversight of nuclear materials that might have gone astray inside or outside the United States. What could be more important than that? Well, saving the nation, I suppose. (Let's leave the world out of it for the moment, shall we?) No election campaign or no curriculum vitae could guarantee he is up to the task. But last October, when everything fell apart and the dread phrase 'uncharted waters' kept on issuing from the lips of stricken veterans of US political and financial life, Americans recognised a stark difference in the capacity of the two men they were being offered as potential presidents. John McCain imploded in meaningless histrionics, suspended his campaign and marched to Washington to do, as it turned out, nothing in particular. Obama kept his cool. When he opened his mouth it was to say things that, on the whole, made sense to the confused and the panicky. It was a good enough omen to win him the White House.

Calm intelligence will be the necessary but insufficient condition of bringing the United States out of its economic trough. At a time when public faith in those who were entrusted with money, power, credit and weapons has utterly collapsed, it falls to Barack Obama to restore belief in the history and destiny of the American experiment. Who could conceivably be in a stronger position to do that?

So as he took the oath of office on the Bible that Abraham Lincoln used in 1861, Obama at last began wiping clean American history of its ancient taint: the promise of equality and liberty, made by the Founding Fathers at the same time that it was denied to its slaves and their shamefully oppressed descendants. A day later, on 21 January, his government was installed on the fiftieth anniversary of Martin Luther King's great Washington speech, and Obama can now say to whoever will listen that it is truly a dream no longer postponed. All of America can be embraced in that recognition, just as all of America, those who voted for him and those who did not, was uplifted by his election.

None of which guarantees he will be the President his country and the world is hoping for. But I'm prepared to take a bet he will.

Performing

Richard II

Almeida programme, 2002

The word 'theatre', in our modern sense of a playhouse, makes its debut in English literature in Act V, Scene II of *Richard II*. Reporting on the drastically different reception given by Londoners to the ascendant Bolingbroke and the fallen Richard, the Duke of York thinks of them as competing performers:

> As in a theatre, the eyes of men
> After a well-grac'd actor leaves the stage
> Are idly bent on him that enters next
> Thinking his prattle to be tedious
> Even so, or with much more contempt, men's eyes
> Did scowl on Richard.

And this is apt because *Richard II* is intensely concerned with the performance of sovereignty: the relationship between stage presence and authority. The play asks its lead to act the part of someone who is, himself, acutely conscious of the need to act, and who, in his Big Moments, is overcome, not so much by stage fright as by a paralysing insight into his own mortal humanity. On the battlements of Flint castle in Act III, York is momentarily struck by the fact that, despite his dire predicament, Richard still looks the part of a king: 'his eye, / as bright as is the eagle's, lightens forth, /Controlling majesty; alack, alack, for woe, / That any harm should stain so fair a show.' But after thundering at the presumptuous Northumberland and delivering one of the play's many accurate prophecies that his deposition would inaugurate generations of slaughter, the grass bedewed 'with faithful English blood', Richard collapses, almost incomprehensibly, into a vision of his own annihilation, buried beneath the king's highway 'where subjects' feet / May hourly trample on their sovereign's head'.

Flooded with a sickening understanding of the false consciousness of majesty, Richard, whose entire life up to that point had been conditioned by it, surrenders the crown to Bolingbroke who (until the very last lines of the play) is plainly not much bothered by self-knowledge. In York's chilling account of the London procession, it is evident that Bolingbroke has become an overnight impresario of political bullshit, marketing his fake humility before the adoring throng.

> Whilst he, from one side to the other turning,
> Bare-headed, lower than his proud steed's neck,
> Bespake them thus 'I thank you countrymen.'

From very early on in its performance history, *King Richard II* spoke to an issue on contemporaries' minds: the difficult contrivance of 'majesty' – a title which the historical Richard was the first English king to require of his subjects. Too little of it, and the country as well as the person was demeaned; too much, and the country would be governed by megalomania rather than justice. 'I am Richard the Second Know ye not that?' Elizabeth told the antiquary and geographer William Lambarde when he presented her with his *Pandecta*, a compilation of rolls and muniments stored in the Tower of London. The utterance sounds oracular, but it was actually delivered in a rare moment of touching vulnerability. A few months before, the aged queen had survived a botched rebellion, led by her sometime favourite the Earl of Essex. He had gone to the block, but the crisis must still have been very much on her mind for when her gaze caught Richard II's name on Lambarde's list of kings, she reminded him that one of Essex's supporters, Gellie Meyrick, had paid to have the play performed 'forty times in streets and open houses' as a way of softening up the public for a deposition. It's possible that this was not Shakespeare's version, since the astrologer Simon Forman reported in 1611 having seen a *Richard II* which, unlike Shakespeare's play, featured scenes from the Peasants' Revolt. But Elizabeth was defensive enough about the whole subject of the ill-starred king to send Sir John Haywarde, whose history of Henry IV contained an account of the deposition, to prison for his pains in 1599.

Not surprisingly, then, as long as the Queen was alive, Shakespeare took care to publish the play without the great deposition scene in Act

IV. But he would certainly have been aware when he was writing the play in the mid-1590s that many contemporaries thought the catalogue of miseries in that dreadful decade to be a replay of the 1390s. Once again, England seemed militarily weak with a new Armada in the offing. Once again, punitive taxes were being imposed while a succession of catastrophic harvests had sent food prices sky-high. There were food riots in London and other towns in 1596. And once again England seemed ruled by a sovereign who had lost touch with reality, preferring to listen to the drooling encomia of court flatterers while Faerie-Land was sewn with gibbets. In the same year that Shakespeare probably completed the play – 1596 – a man in Kent was arrested for declaring it would 'never be a merry world until her Majesty was dead'. No one could hear John of Gaunt's bitter death-bed complaint about an England 'leas'd out' and its king become 'landlord of England' without thinking of the furious protests against monopolies and patents sold off by the crown in the last years of Elizabeth's reign.

But if the Queen had ignored her low-boiling point long enough to read, or actually see, Shakespeare's play, she could hardly have taken it as a blank cheque for deposition.

Following Raphael Holinshed's *Chronicles* (in their second augmented edition) Shakespeare dutifully goes through the case for his removal – the arbitrary dispossession of the Lancastrian inheritance, and the indulgence of flatterers who are said to have come between Richard and his conjugal duty to sire an heir. (There's not a shred of evidence, other than his childlessness, that the historical Richard was gay, although I suppose any monarch who commissions a cookbook and insists that his courtiers eat with their spoons was bound to be thought suspiciously un-English.) But except perhaps for his jocular callousness towards the dying John of Gaunt (in reality a far more detested figure than the King), Shakespeare is at his least convincing when labouring to turn Richard into a ruthless land-grabber who deserves his come-uppance. Disaster falls on England and on the King for nothing much more serious than bad refereeing, bad timing (the Irish expedition) and for having the cheek to use the Lancastrian inheritance to finance it. As soon as matters go swiftly downhill, the play picks up pace and persuasiveness. Much more compelling than the extended 'sceptred isle' travel-bureau panegyric orated by Gaunt is its rhetorical bookend: the Bishop of Carlisle's apocalyptic vision of the fatal consequences of usurpation: a country drowning in blood:

> Disorder, horror, fear and mutiny,
> Shall here inhabit, and this land be call'd
> The field of Golgotha and dead men's skulls.

Death is everywhere in the play – 'graves, worms and epitaphs' already on Richard's mind when he is barely back on dry land. In fact, the drama is perhaps best thought (especially by the sixty-something Queen Elizabeth) as an *Ars Moriendi*: a preparatory treatise on how to die, wholly right for a history set in the world of the Black Death. Richard learns the hard way. But he does learn, and near the end asks his weeping queen also to 'learn, good soul,/To think our former state a happy dream'. Richard's eagerness to embrace his Christ-like sacrificial martyrdom was a logical end for the historical ruler, who did indeed suffer more than somewhat from a Messiah complex, understandable (if not forgivable) in an age desperate for saviours. It's a pity, really, that Shakespeare opted for the predictable thug-attack to polish him off, since the more historically plausible end of the King – death by starvation – would have given Richard a chance to meditate more fully on the provisional nature of majesty, indeed of earthly life itself, and to become absorbed most completely into his transfiguration as a Plantagenet Buddha.

Henry IV, Part II

Note for the Royal Shakespeare Company production, 2008

Among the Histories this is The tragedy. It is, not least in the cool
tightness of its writing, right up there with Dane, Moor and Scot. At
its pitiless end, no bodies litter the stage. Something much worse has
happened: the annihilation of hope; the banishment not just of plump
Jack Falstaff, but of delusion. What remains? The naked machinery
of power in all its grinding metallic cruelty; the tinny blare of trum-
pets tuning up for the new king's murderous cross-Channel excursion,
courtesy of his father's deathbed counsel. And Shakespeare appearing as himself at the very end offering a mordant shrug, 'My tongue
is weary; when my legs are too, I will bid you good night.'

Only those half-asleep in the stalls imagine that *Henry IV,* Part II
is somehow an 'add-on' to Part I. It certainly is woodwind to I's brass,
but the plaintive minor key that plays throughout is the tip-off to II's
darker profundity. II needs I to set up the vanities – history, amity,
loyalty, appetite, mirth, battle – because II's job is to rip them all to
shreds. The muscular heft of history gets collapsed into rumour, false
comfort, ill tidings. Unlike I, not only is there no point to the plots and
rebellions, but those who enact them know there is no point, except
some sort of remorseless execution of a fatal cycle. So the protagonists
on both sides – the dying king, the melancholy Archbishop of York –
spend time wrestling with the unquiet ghost of Richard II, whose
deposition and murder have condemned them all to stumble around
forever sleepless like the grimly insomniac king.

Not a hoot, then, even with Falstaff at its heart? No, but something
important remains amid the cold political ashes: memory. Part II is
better called a memory play than a history; it is the most lyrical Shakespeare ever wrote. And it needs the most delicate touch in its direction
and acting to draw out the autumnal pathos. The most heartbreakingly
vivid scenes come from the mouths of the old as they spirit themselves

back beyond the ache of their brittle bones to the lusty lads and lasses they still feel themselves to be. Whatever else ails them, their memories are as bright as gems: 'Thou didst swear to me upon a parcel-gilt goblet sitting in my Dolphin-chamber at the round table, by a sea-coal fire, upon Wednesday in Wheeson week when the prince broke thy head for liking his father to a singing man of Windsor . . .' prattles Mistress Quickly, never forgetting Falstaff's promise of betrothal – and we see the moment in all its hopeless glory. 'Then was Jack Falstaff, now Sir John, a boy and page to Thomas Mowbray, Duke of Norfolk,' reminisces Shallow to Silence, and we suddenly see the juvenile, perhaps slender Jack. Time rustles in the lines like fallen leaves.

What makes all this bearable is a scene of intense sweetness, a love scene all the more tender for being ostensibly dressed in farce, and the purer for being set in Mistress Quickly's brothel. After the raillery – and brutal it is, with much talk of diseases – between Falstaff and Doll Tearsheet, they become creakily amorous for old time's sake: 'Come I'll be friends with thee Jack; thou art going to the wars and whether I shall ever see thee again or no there is nobody cares.'

Falstaff defends Doll against the rampaging Pistol, then verbally sets about the Prince and his friend Ned Poins, 'a weak mind and an able body', not knowing they are listening in disguise. The affronted then get their satisfaction by cackling at the ancient venery:

> Poins: Let's beat him before his whore.
> Prince: Look, whether the withered elder hath not his poll clawed like a parrot.
> Poins: Is it not strange that desire should so many years outlive performance?

To which Falstaff, oblivious, gives the retort that redeems the entire play from the cynicism that sometimes seems to chill it, a single moment of instinctive, unembarrassed humanity: 'Kiss me, Doll.' And she does, for unlike princes and kings, the whore is true: 'By my troth, I kiss thee with a most constant heart.'

Martin Scorsese: Good-Fella

Financial Times, 30 October 2009

It's just as well that the couch I'm sitting on is plump and hospitable or I might have fallen off it when Martin Scorsese tells me that the real inspiration for the tone and voice of *Goodfellas* was not *Scarface* or *Public Enemy*, but *Kind Hearts and Coronets*. Oh, right, Alec Guinness in drag, Joe Pesci in murderous hysterics, I see. But then, when you think about it for a minute, the revelation makes perfect sense. The note of black glee in Ray Liotta's interior monologues ('As far back as I can remember I always wanted to be a gangster') is not that far away from Dennis Price's cool plan to murder his way into the landed class that presumes to despise him. They share the smirk of superior knowledge, the contempt for the chumps who do things the regular way. Mayhem and chuckling are never far apart in either the British post-war comedies or Scorsese's opera of mischief. Stick a fedora on Dennis Price or Alastair Sim, unclip the accent and they could breeze downtown. The wiseguys in *Goodfellas* spend even more time laughing than killing. Sometimes the uproar is so unhinged that it looks like de Niro, Liotta and Pesci will dislocate their jaws, like pythons guffawing as they digest a goat.

In his sixties, Scorsese is at the height of his powers, which is saying something. After a long day in the cutting room working on a pilot for a television drama series about Prohibition-era Atlantic City, his conversation is still high-octane, the enthusiasms sparks, that catch the weighty pack of his idea-loaded imagination. Lately, he's got a lot to be happy about. His new movie, *Shutter Island*, based on a thriller by Dennis Lehane, scheduled for release early in 2010, is set in an institution for the criminally insane off the Massachusetts coast, a pile that makes the hotel in *The Shining* or Motel Bates look like day-trips to Disneyland. Scorsese built the set around the shell of the old hospital. The gurneys were still there, the stainless steel of the cafeteria giving off a bad glint. 'You walked in and you could feel it, the disturbance,' he says. Ben

Kingsley and Leonardo di Caprio (doing most of his own stunts) stalk and scuttle through it like cat and rat, and the storm-blasted island turns in a performance of thunderously Calvinist gloom. If there were an Oscar for best acting role by a landscape, Shutter Island would be a shoo-in. For the first time Scorsese had to work with those pesky extras, trees. 'Never worked in a forest before. Hard to get the shots, no room for dollies and tracks.' In many ways the movie, a crazy quilt of dreams and terrors, was a tall order. A week into filming the director realised what he was up against, the fiendishly complicated layering of Lehane's story asking him to 'make three films at the same time'. Maybe Scorsese works best when most stretched, for the result of all the perfectionist head-scratching and pitch-in ensemble acting is a triumph of what you might call heavy entertainment, but only in the sense that bits of *King Lear* are too.

And like everything Martin Scorsese does, *Shutter Island* is enriched by its director's encylopaedic memory of the cinema. Nothing so laborious as 'homage' gets inserted; there are no billboarded visual quotations, but it's as though Scorsese has internalised the entire history of the medium, turning himself into a one-man archive on which he can draw for inspiration in whichever genre he happens to be working. Sometimes even the admirers forget his astounding range. The same director who made the agonised *Raging Bull* and the manic, temple-pounding *Bringing Out the Dead* also made the exquisitely patient *Kundun*, the camera letting a small boy come at his own pace to the realisation of what it meant to be the Dalai Lama. The guiding light of Satyajit Ray seemed to be at Scorsese's shoulder when he dissolved the camera into the chosen boy's point of view. So which movies guided him this time? 'Oh, for the atmospherics, the way of setting mood: *Cat People*, *I Walked with a Zombie* and *Out of the Past*,' he says, as if I was bound to know all about the work of Jacques Tourneur. Caught out like an undergraduate claiming to have 'looked' at the assignment rather than actually to have done it, I make a quick hit on YouTube after our meeting and there are the Tourneur films, moodily off-kilter, tautly scripted, nagging little shards in the psyche.

This total immersion works curatorially. Scorsese doesn't just make individual movies, chasing box-office and the annual-award madness, though he'd be inhuman not to want both. But he has always felt lucky to be able to work in the art to which he's been addicted since, as a bronchial altar boy, he sat bewitched in the Saturday-morning movie theatre darkness, or watching on black-and-white television (as I did an ocean away in London) Alexander Korda costume movies like *The Private Life of Henry VIII* or David Lean's *Great Expectations*, in which John Mills was scared pipless by Magwitch and Jean Simmons as Estella stomped on our balls even before we had any.

Never taking this good fortune for granted (it was an outrageously long time before The Movies finally returned the favour with Oscars), Scorsese has done everything he could to look after the memory bank. He has been a major force in the conservation and restoration of decaying and damaged film; devoting special care to films which meant a lot to his own education as student and practitioner. Olivier's *Richard III* he first saw in a black-and-white television broadcast, but it was shot in a process called VistaVision, and he is currently restoring a surviving print to its original splendour. The winter of discontent will never look so sunny. Meanwhile, the 'crawl' that opens the film, 'England, 1485 . . .' etc., sits in his personal treasure trove in New York along with the Red Shoes from Michael Powell's masterpiece. In between feature films he and his long-time friend and editor-collaborator Thelma Schoonmaker, who was married to Powell and whose perfect touch is all over *Shutter Island*, are putting together a documentary chronicle of the British cinema from the late 1940s to the gritty neo-realist films of the early '60s: Karel Reisz's *Saturday Night and Sunday Morning*, Tony Richardson's *Loneliness of the Long Distance Runner* and Lindsay Anderson's *This Sporting Life*. Like his Italian documentary, the work will be unapologetically personal and when I hear him summon up the shade of Ian Carmichael (*I'm Alright Jack* is a favourite), the improbability of the young Scorsese, spending time in the world of the Lawrentian slagheaps and the two-ups, two-downs, strikes me all over again. But for Scorsese, the fried eggs and rolled-down nylons, footy in the smoke and puke in the pubs, brought a scuffed-up truth of documentary realism to Ealing, Pinewood and Elstree, much as Rossellini, de Sica and Visconti did for the fantasy world of Italian films. He may be the only director who can invoke *Rocco and His Brothers* and *This Sporting Life* in the same sentence, as if it were obvious they were rivers flowing into the same deep sea of social drama. Talking about them, I have a presumptuous hunch and wonder out loud if the bone-crunching sound track of the rugby-league movie, with Richard Harris's skull smashing against other mangled faces, had any influence on the way Scorsese recorded and shot the boxing devastation of de Niro's Jake la Motta in *Raging Bull*? A pause. Ever the tactful gent, he replies, 'Maybe, yes, maybe!'

Sure. But generosity comes naturally to Scorsese. So it shouldn't be surprising that he agreed to participate in the Rolex Mentor and Protégé Arts Initiative – one of a group (other distinguished mentors work in theatre, literature, dance, music and the visual arts) – that gives younger artists the opportunity to learn something about their vocation by directly experiencing a work-in-progress. (Stephen Frears was a Rolex Mentor in 2008.) The lucky young director who got to spend precious time, months of it, with Scorsese at work on *Shutter Island* is Celina Murgan, an Argentinian with two films already on her résumé. Scorsese chose her from a shortlist of three, impressed by a film she had made about teenagers doing their thing in a gated community after the parents had gone. 'I sat there, and around twenty-five minutes into it, I realised this was something; that, almost casually, she had created a world that already seemed to have been there, no starting, no stopping.' A benevolent chuckle and 'Of course that's a different sensibility, not the way *I* work, but . . .' And it was exactly because he does things differently, generates the worlds he creates out of the plot, that Scorsese, so open to other ways, picked his lucky protégé. Murgan got to go to the shoot of *Shutter Island* as often as she wanted and must have seen the toughest of movie-making challenges bloom into something extraordinary; the actors reaching hard; the director revising and revising again as things went along. Could she talk about particular shots? 'Sure, sometimes, to the assistant director.' She was welcomed to the cutting room, to the sound mix and, exceptionally, even to rushes – 'not always . . . I like to speak freely to Thelma'.

There's a back story to this great gift. Murgan – and many others, it turns out – are getting the chance that the young Scorsese was himself denied. In the 1960s, a young film student in NYU School of the Arts, Scorsese badly wanted to get experience first-hand from a master. Elia Kazan – whose *On the Waterfront* and *East of Eden* were just the kind of epics of social pain he revered – was visiting the school. Scorsese, script in hand, made an appointment. He arrived ten minutes late at the great man's office. Kazan had his coat on, listened to the young enthusiast, riffled cursorily through the script and wished him luck. Indies hardly existed in New York, other than John Cassavetes's company that produced

Shadows. There was nowhere to go and no one to help a novice through an apprenticeship. Scorsese, without any ill will, thought at that moment, 'If ever I was in Kazan's position, I'd do something to help.' So starting with *Taxi Driver*, he brought novices onto the set, sometimes youngsters with absolutely no experience of film-making beforehand, and into the crew as apprentices, 'So long as they didn't get in the way of the actors and knew when not to speak up.' Some of them decided film wasn't for them, but others began their career this way and went on to make good features and stay in touch. I'd never heard of such a thing, directors normally being ruthless about keeping 'outsiders' away from the set. But Scorsese was, and is, different. He makes outsiders insiders and all he asks for is rapt attentiveness. So, I ask him, which films after *Taxi Driver* did he open to this kind of apprenticeship. 'All of them,' he says. 'Anyone else do this kind of thing that you know of?' Scorsese smiles, shrugs.

Which only reminds me that to spend any time with him is to be in the presence of someone for whom his hard craft is an exacting labour of love. He burns with the anxiety and pleasure of that knowledge like a perpetually glowing coal. And some lucky people get to draw close to the warmth. His ten-year-old daughter Francesca, for example, to whom he's showing the British comedies of the 1950s that still fill him with delight. 'Does she get it, the wickedness?' I ask. 'Oh, *The Ladykillers*, she and her friends they all love it. There's this moment when there's a fight going on and the little old lady comes in and they *stop fighting*! They *stop*!' Scorsese laughs like the connoisseur of mischief that he is – and like the ten-year-old he once was, watching that malarkey unfold for the first time. One thing is for certain; he's the *perpetuum mobile*; he doesn't do stop.

Charlotte Rampling

Harper's Bazaar, January 2010

There's a crunchy moment in *The Night Porter* when Charlotte Rampling lays a trap for her ex-concentration-camp guard, played by Dirk Bogarde, which involves him walking over broken glass. He does so and smiles. Ten minutes into the interview with her and I know how he felt. The lacerations are minor, the attractions powerful. But there are moments when it feels bloody. It's not that Rampling is openly hostile; just giving off waves of someone enduring a minor indignity, like a dental check-up. To be fair, she had been perfectly frank about her distaste for interviews, telling me that one reason she doesn't do many films is that she finds 'the exposure' tawdry. 'There are so many things I hate,' she says, offering a steely smile. I grin back weakly, hoping I'm not the most recent addition to what's obviously a long list.

Call me a cynic, but is there not a smidgen of disingenuousness here? Is she not – for all her smouldering disdain through photoshoots – just the teeniest bit complicit in this perennial curiosity about whether she still has 'the Look'? (She does.) Doesn't she actually enjoy the gasps of disbelief that the body which in the 1970s turned men into warm puddles on the floor is still, at sixty-three, a thing of beauty? Probably. But you believe her when, tightening her lip a little and making a face as though she's swallowed something dodgy, she talks wanly of the rounds of film promotion – talks, that is, while avoiding eye contact and mostly directing her words diagonally across me to the restaurant wall. Still, at the start of a year that promises a number of high-profile Rampling performances – in films including an adaptation this September of Kazuo Ishiguro's *Never Let Me Go*, co-starring Keira Knightley and Carey Mulligan; Danny Moynihan's satire on the London art scene, *Boogie Woogie*, in spring; and, coming this autumn, the latest from American auteur Todd Solondz, *Life During Wartime* – she will surely have to gird herself for the inevitable run of 'exposure'.

For a time, installed in a corner booth at the upscale London restaurant where we have agreed to meet, we just contend in awkwardness; she doing her cat impersonation, me the floppy old terrier who just wants to woof and play. But then, when I ask her in earnest (for this is what actually interests me) about how she came to be the mind-blowingly great actress she is, she emerges from under the hedge of her frowning, and turns directly towards me as if surprised that anyone – for a *magazine* article – would want to talk about how she came by her craft.

Then it suddenly becomes a very different story; a story, in fact, of how her life and art have flowed into each other, for she's not shy about talking about some chapters – at least of her own family history, rather than her married life and loves – weighted though it is with trouble and sorrow.

Her father Godfrey Rampling died last year (aged 100), and no degree in advanced psychoanalysis is needed to understand that he was the true north on Rampling's compass. It was from him she got her backbone and physical bravery. 'Made you climb walls, did he?' 'Oh, everything,' she says, 'We [she and her sister] couldn't be wimps.' He saw in Charlotte the tomboy; the fighter, the one who in some way might be an athlete. Godfrey ran the second leg in the 400-metres relay at the notorious Berlin Olympics of 1936, and is captured in Leni Riefenstahl's *Olympia* winning the gold for Britain. The runner immediately behind him had fallen ill and was way behind when Godfrey took the baton and carved his way through the pack. 'He *was* beautiful,' Rampling emphasises, looking wistfully into the distance. 'They said he ran like a god, and they were right.' He paid a price for his heroics. A leg went out, and was never quite the same again.

Rampling was born ten years later, in Sturmer, Essex (I greet her as a fellow Essexian and she smiles in mildly snobbish surprise, 'Really?'). Her father had already become remote or, in her own word, 'frightening', disappearing into silent distances that seem to have translated into emotional intimidation. In fact, he was as much frightened as the frightener. 'Of what?' 'A haunting,' says Rampling, sighing a little. 'He began to carry the weight of the world on his shoulders.' The load of it crushed him into periodic depressions, which his daughter felt the burden of, growing up first in Fontainebleau, where her father was stationed for NATO as a lieutenant colonel with the Royal Artillery (and where she was part-educated, becoming fluent in French); and perhaps even later, at a distance, at the girls' boarding school St Hilda's in Bushey, Hertfordshire.

The playpen of the late Sixties was, of course, the antidote to all this patriarchal gloom, and like so many other cool stunners, Rampling played hard. 'I did everything very young,' she says. She worked as a model before being spotted in a Cadbury commercial and cast in Silvio Narizzano's 1966 classic *Georgy Girl* as the impossibly fine-boned, hard, hot number, against Lynn Redgrave's adorable dumpy duckling who eventually gets the man.

Then came the shattering moment when the Swinging stopped. Her twenty-three-year-old older sister Sarah fell ill while pregnant, gave birth prematurely, fell into a steep depression and shot herself. Shortly after, their mother, who had always been very close to Sarah, suffered a stroke, and was left severely disabled. In a matter of weeks, Rampling, now in her early twenties and with the world about to be at her feet, was robbed of the two people she loved most in the world. (Her grief was disrupted by her father's insistence, so as not to upset her mother during her long, painful rehabilitation, that the truth of Sarah's suicide remain a secret. The official version would be that she suffered a cerebral haemorrhage.)

It's not surprising that acting became a way of changing the subject, moving into someone else's skin. If the part called for it, Rampling would do pain, not be its victim. It was while she was shooting an Italian film with Gianfranco Mingozzi in 1968 that Luchino Visconti spotted her and cast her in *The Damned*, his epic tale of dynastic corruption at the beginning of the Third Reich. As the Jewish daughter-in-law of the only liberal scion of the family, Rampling was pitch-perfect: tender, poignant and desperate (a rebuttal to those who think of her as mostly sexy-tough). I tell her that I've always thought one of the remarkable things about her career has been its range; and though it's the truth, this is not something she's used to hearing.

It's a paradox. On the one hand, she insists that somehow there has to be something in the part that is also of her. On the other hand, she was crucially guided by Visconti to understand the psychological morphing needed to make a performance credible. (We enjoy a brief Visconti love-in when I reveal that some of my earliest movie passions as a teenager were *La Terra Trema* and, especially, *Rocco and His*

Brothers, which took me weeks – if ever – to get over.) When she murmurs of his charisma and handsome, Marxist-aristo charm, it's obvious that he became for her the warm-blooded fatherly mentor. When, in *The Damned*, she had to play a scene pleading for the life of her children, she went to Visconti in despair, saying she had no idea how to do it, that she couldn't do it. 'Listen, Charlotte,' he said, 'you don't have to have *done* anything like this. You must just *believe* you have done it.' Later, standing right beside the camera as she acted, he urged her: 'See behind the eyes. See behind the eyes . . .'

Without Visconti's guiding hand, then, there would have been no *Night Porter* and no international fame. It was Dirk Bogarde, the tortured male lead in *The Damned*, who saw she could play something quite different, and working with the director Liliana Cavani devised the script and plot for the strange, terrifying, sadomasochistic fantasy that became *The Night Porter*. Rampling recalls putting Visconti's advice to the test early by having to do, right at the start of the shoot, 'the fucking concentration-camp scene. I had to *sing*.'

For all the thunderstruck acclaim she received for the film, life was not altogether plain sailing. Many parts came along, many of them mediocre. Her first marriage (to actor Bryan Southcombe) broke up when she fell headlong for rock composer Jean Michel Jarre. It was mega-force love, and articles regularly appeared about the Beautiful Couple's romantic life in Paris. But every so often, in the 1980s, she would hit a reef, falling into what sounds like the same depression experienced by her father. Being cared for by her husband, she'd recover, only to sink into the terror of its return.

There must have been a moment when Jarre had had enough, as he took up with a younger civil servant, and in 1997 Rampling's second marriage ended. Then, in 2001, her mother died, and it freed something up in her. She became much closer to her father, moved by his kindness and love for her mother. ('It was his redemption,' she says.) And, when the truth about her sister's suicide was let out, she was at last allowed to grieve.

The join between Rampling's emotional life and working life became sewn together by the great French indie director François Ozon. She says, looking back on her career, that her best films have been 'a documentary of me'. (Indeed, without the deep stain of her personal drama, her acting would just be an affectation, the calculated projection of 'the Look'.) But in her two films for Ozon, *Under the Sand* (2000) and *Swimming Pool* (2003), she reached for, and achieved, something much more profound: the sensuality of melancholy; the embodiment of the angry wound.

In *Under the Sand* especially, in which she plays a childless, affectionate wife whose husband disappears on a beach in south-west France while she has her eyes closed sunbathing, Rampling's capacity to play the light moments – bursts of wilt-inducing laughter in the midst of sex, breezy certainty in the gathering distress – give the drama its full tragic force.

She also loved playing Miss Havisham in a BBC adaptation of *Great Expectations*, reading Dickens and looking up David Lean's classic to prep; and had the part of graceful, sexually potent middle age nailed. 'They suited me,' she says of roles in films like Laurent Cantet's 2005 *Heading South*, about a professor who travels to Haiti for sex with the local young men.

But you somehow don't want Rampling just to corner the market in sexually compulsive crosspatches, though she is said to perform brilliantly in a hotel-bedroom scene as a rich, unhappy sexual predator in the upcoming *Life During Wartime*. Still, the work she has done lately – including a feature about street dancers in England called *StreetDance; Never Let Me Go*, in which she plays the enigmatic and haunted headmistress Miss Emily; and a comic turn in *Boogie Woogie* – seems to draw on that capacity for range that Visconti first saw in her. 'But I just don't get that many parts,' she says, 'not the scripts I can be bothered with.' After her sister died, she swore she would not make films 'just to entertain'. And if there have been projects in the past that have fallen short of that lofty principle, there's no doubt that, in her early sixties, she no longer has truck with the mediocre.

It's dark now, out there on the rain-slick London street; and gradually the lights are being dimmed in the Italian restaurant. The tape recorder goes off. I order glasses of white wine. She demurs for a second and then is happy when I overrule her. She is off later to see her friend Kevin Spacey's play of *Inherit the Wind* at the Old Vic. With her velvety voice, it's not surprising she has done theatre both in London and Paris – a Marivaux and the unedited, terrifying version of Strindberg's *Dance of Death*. But now she wants to talk a bit about my childhood, not hers, and we do, friendliness replacing professional curiosity. She has stopped looking at the wall. 'What am I going to do to pass the time?' she teases, giving me the full-on charm. I am speechless. Then the angel passes, and back comes a self-satirising version of Grumpy Puss. 'Will it be good?' she worries of the play. It's the audience, not the actors, she's already taking exception to. The massed sitting, the clapping . . . 'You know I *hate* places where people all do the same thing.' The fact that she laughs at her own vehemence is a sure sign she really means it.

Clio at the Multiplex

New Yorker, 19 January 1998

'We have come to understand that who we are is who we were,' says Anthony Hopkins, impersonating John Quincy Adams at the climactic moment of Steven Spielberg's *Amistad*. He says this in front of a bust of his father, John Adams, seen in soft focus. A muted trumpet sounds over the rhetoric, vaguely invoking patriotic sacrifice. Hearts around the theatre swell like popcorn. In reality, Adams's address to the bench on behalf of the abducted Africans of the *Amistad* took eight hours, spread over two days. Spielberg works on a broad canvas, but not that broad. His movie boils the speech down to a five-minute appeal to the Founding Fathers, and, in particular, a cheerful assertion of the compatibility of liberty and equality enshrined in the Declaration of Independence. When Jefferson duly appears (in bust form), we are evidently *not* meant to think of the unrepentant Virginia slave-holder. In fact, since the closing speech does little else but make that ringing appeal to ancestor worship, we're asked to believe that it was enough to sway the justices (the majority of them slave-holders) into upholding the decision of the Connecticut court, thereby freeing the captives.

As a clinching argument about the legality of treating the Africans as born slaves or born free, this makes no sense, not least because the case turned neither on the morality nor on the legality of slavery in America, but on the slave *trade* on the high seas. The *Amistad* Africans had been abducted from a British protectorate and shipped to a Spanish colony in clear violation of a treaty between the two kingdoms which prohibited the traffic. John Quincy Adams did end his great address with an appeal to the past, but it was an appeal to the independence of the Supreme Court, and invoked John Marshall and his colleagues, men apparently with too little name-recognition for Hollywood. As for his peroration, 'I can only ejaculate a fervent petition to

Heaven that every member [of the Court] may go to his final account with as little of earthly frailty to answer for as those illustrious dead', it, too, may not have the ring of the box office, but it was a master-piece of psychological cunning. One of the most odiously adamant of the Southern Justices, Philip Barbour, died in his sleep between the beginning and the end of Adams's speech, thus presenting Adams with a perfect opportunity to remind the rest of the bench of an even Supre-mer Court waiting for them.

It's an opportunity that Spielberg passes up. Instead, he concocts the feel-good fantasy that JQA's appeal to ancestry was borrowed from Cinque, the leader of the shipboard slave rising – that between the Mende wise man and the Massachusetts rationalist (the two never met) there existed the unspoken bond of warriors for freedom. Possi-bly the most important moment in the movie is also the most fabulously fictitious. Cinque, sitting in Adams's library (in those far-off days presidential libraries were places where ex-presidents actually read books), reassures his champion that they will not go into court alone. 'No, no, we have right at our side,' Adams says hurriedly. '*No*,' Cinque gently admonishes the ex-President. 'I meant my ancestors . . . I will call into the past . . . and beg them to come . . . And they must come, for at this moment, I am the whole reason they have existed at all.' Adams stares back at Cinque, mutely grateful for the insight. His eyes water with deferential illumination. Spielberg holds the shot and holds the shot, flagging its Significance.

You can't altogether blame Steven Spielberg for the piety. As a rela-tively recent convert to ancestor worship himself, he seems to have realised that in late-second-millennium America he has his work cut out for him, and he has applied his brilliance as a storyteller to getting it done. But lining up a row of busts of the Founding Fathers as a way of cueing up patriotic nostalgia only brings the difficulty of history-in-America into sharper focus. After all, those same patriarchs were in the business of repudiating, not venerating, the past – of creating a nation that was conspicuously liberated from the weight of the past's authority. And at the same time that the film invokes the need to keep the memory of national history alive, it has a lot of fun with Amer-ica's invention of political modernity. Martin Van Buren, looking like an affable chipmunk in Nigel Hawthorne's enactment (the real Adams, dedicated to vigorous swims in the Potomac, called Van Buren 'inordinately fat'), is gleefully depicted as the archetypal creature of the hustings, complete with baby-kissing and Nixonian full-arm salutes, a deliberate contrast with the flinty, philosophical JQA. Yet Adams, after his own blighted presidential tenure, showed himself to be a belated but adept convert to political populism, jumping into the muckiest popular campaign of his day – anti-Masonry.

So when Hollywood history claims that in ancestor veneration lies our redemption from the culture of the short shelf life, it only sort of means it. *Amistad* is just the most recent, and most impressive, example of filmed history as costume civics, chronicles of latter-day saints and martyrs, right in line with *Glory*, *Malcolm X* and *Michael Collins*. If movie history is to get produced as box office with a conscience, it must serve one of two purposes: explain the Origins of Us or act as Augury of What Is to Come. But this kind of history, whether designed as the genealogy of identity politics or as prudential political-investment service, seldom escapes the contemporary world that it claims to transcend. Even in a production as painstakingly researched as *Amistad*, entrapment within the contemporary is suggested by a multiplicity of careless details, not enough in themselves for any except the most pedantically correct historian to get steamed over, but cumulatively betraying a tin ear for the obstinate otherness of the past. While both the nocturnal shipboard musical party that sails past the newly liberated *Amistad* and the velocipede that rides past the astonished Africans who thought themselves home carry a certificate of impeccable research, the film's writers hardly notice (any more, I guess, than the audience does) utterances inconceivable in 1839. 'Sure you do,' Pete Postlethwaite says when Cinque denies knowing anything much about African domestic slavery. *'Yesss!'* the defence team cheers when it wins its verdict in court. 'Is there anything as pathetic as an ex-President?' jeers a member of Van Buren's entourage, meaning John Quincy Adams. In 1839, that would have been an expression of sympathy, not of derision.

But perhaps the writers did notice all these details and intend them to narrow the distance between the past and the present, making history more user-friendly. This would explain the relentless tide of tepidly inspirational chorales that washes over the action, much like the musical accompaniment to a Party Convention bio-documentary eulogising the nominee: Sigh here. Weep here. Chuckle here. A*men!*

here. Hence, too, some of the casting, which recycles familiar faces in the roles to which previous Hollywood productions have assigned them. Meet Morgan Freeman once again as the noble but uneasy intermediary between white and black culture. Say hello to Matthew McConaughey as the cutely presumptuous lawyer, whose courtroom savvy is belied by his rumpled but winsome demeanour. (The real Roger Baldwin was a distinguished advocate, a Yale man, and the grandson of a signer of the Declaration of Independence.) Most peculiar of all, the urge for familiarity seems to involve the assumption that history, especially American history, calls for Brits in costume, Masterpiece thespians, thereby giving the unintended impression that the Revolution never actually happened.

Historians ought not to gripe too much about these anomalies. A recent and excellent anthology of their commentaries on historical movies, *Past Imperfect*, edited by Mark Carnes, is a litany of complaint about distortion (*A Man for All Seasons*), naive lack of interpretation (*Gandhi*), and the passing-off of conspiracy theory as documented evidence (*JFK*). But if 'historical consultant' has generally come to mean a low-rent databank for producers in a hurry, rather than any real conceptual or creative role in the shaping of a credible historical narrative, the academy must take at least some of the blame, for having largely abandoned, until recently, the importance of story-telling as the elementary condition of historical explanation. Story-telling (aside from its exacting formal demands) lies at the heart of historical teaching and ought to be as much a part of the training of young historians as the acquisition of analytical skills. When the historian Natalie Zemon Davis, for example, who is herself gifted at and sensitive to the subtleties of narrative, got involved in the making of Daniel Vigne's *The Return of Martin Guerre*, that involvement was apparent in every frame, in the way the actors wore their village clothes – not clothes fresh from the wardrobe department or soiled for the day, but evidently lived-in, frayed and patched hand-me-downs. Vigne and Davis reconstructed the texture of rural provincial life in sixteenth-century France, its rites of passage and its rough justice as remote from modern experience as if the story had been African, rather than European. As a result, the crucial trial scene, at the end of the movie, was a long way from being Perry Mason in doublet and hose, yet lost nothing of its dramatic power for being historically credible.

A true feeling for period, then, should never be confused with pedantically correct costume-and-decor detail. It's possible to get all the minutiae right and still get the dramatic core of a history wrong. And here's a trade secret. The right stuff, whether the historian is trawling through the archives or prowling the set, is to have a hunch for the illuminating power of the incidental detail. At the climax of the true *Amistad* history, Spielberg missed, somehow, an astounding story that ought to have been a director's dream. Just as John Quincy Adams, a few days before he was to argue the case before the Supreme Court, alighted from his carriage in front of the Capitol (still, incidentally, *without* its dome), a violent burst of gunfire made his horses bolt. The first demonstration of the Colt repeating rifle was being performed in the Capitol yard. Adams's coachman was thrown to the ground, and the following day he died of his injuries. For the devoutly religious statesman, there could have been no more shocking witness that Providence was watching over the unfolding drama. Colts, carriage horses and Calvinism – the kind of historical collision undreamed of in scriptwriters' fiction.

All history is a negotiation between familiarity and strangeness. No one put it better than Thomas Babington Macaulay when, in 1828, at the ripe old age of twenty-seven, in a famous book review (which the omnivorous John Quincy Adams is likely to have read in *The Edinburgh Review*), he presumed to define history as divided between reason and imagination: 'a compound of poetry and philosophy'. What Macaulay yearned for was a perfect marriage between those two contrasting modes of apprehending the past. But he was not optimistic about seeing that ambition realised, even in his own dazzling and exuberant prose. Instead, he viewed history as a relentlessly contested battleground between regiments of analysts and story-tellers, with him stuck in a no-man's-land as the polemical bullets whistled over his head. In the meantime, he lamented, the best stories were being told to the biggest audiences by historical novelists, the auteurs of their day, and none of them more accomplished than Sir Walter Scott, the Spielberg of the Tweed Valley, whom most academic historians disdained, but whom Macaulay deeply envied and admired. In a beautiful aside, Macaulay compared Scott to the apprentice of a medieval master of stained-glass windows working in Lincoln Cathedral. The spurned apprentice went about collecting the shards and fragments discarded as worthless by his master, and assembled them in a window of such blazing splendour that the master not only acknowledged the superior genius of his pupil, but killed himself out of humbled mortification. Scott, Macaulay says, is the inspired opportunist who understands how to use the materials despised as trivially anecdotal by the philosophical historians. And, while Macaulay yielded to no Cambridge don in his insistence on the indispensability of reasoned interpretation, he saw the fate of history in popular culture as conditional on its self-appointed masters being prepared to reacquaint themselves with the imaginative skills of the story-teller.

Macaulay knew that both treatments of history — 'map' and 'painted landscape', as he characterised them — were hallowed by venerable pedigrees. He acknowledged Thucydides, for all his powerful narrative art, to be the founding father of history as the political science of the past, unapologetically engaged in explaining the great crisis of his age: the Peloponnesian War. Like Spielberg's writers, Thucydides had no hesitation in putting in the mouths of protagonists such as Pericles the sentiments he *thought* they would have uttered even if there was no record of their speeches, or any recollection on his part of what had been said. Neither for Macaulay nor for Thucydides was there the slightest anxiety that the record of the past might be fatally distorted by the enthusiasms and preoccupations of the present, or that the primary mission of history was indeed to explain and recount the Origins of Us.

But Macaulay knew that there was another kind of history, a history that emphasised, poetically, the otherness of the past, its obstinate unfamiliarity, the integrity of its remoteness. Indeed, he knew that the great exemplar of this kind of history; with its naive sense of wonder and its promiscuous muddling of myth and ritual, report and document, was Herodotus, the figure whom Thucydides acidly criticised as forfeiting credibility through an indiscriminate use of sources, and whom Macaulay, neatly standing the title of patriarch on its head, adroitly characterised as a 'delightful child'. Most historical writers, both inside and outside the academy, will, I think, own up to both styles — the rational and the poetic — and perhaps even acknowledge that the original attraction was as much romantic as analytical. For some of us, it's the byways, rather than the highways, that unexpectedly turn out to be the more profound routes of illumination. And those of us who are prepared to surrender to the informing detour cherish history, as the late Dame Veronica Wedgwood confessed, for its 'delightful undermining of certainty'.

If American culture is suspicious of candid confessions of uncertainty, Hollywood's history-makers, by and large, have wanted nothing to do with it. Who needs story lines that don't know where they're going, a cast of characters in which the nice and the nasty seem disconcertingly indistinguishable, and where the business at hand seems to have nothing to say to the issues of the day? Outside Hollywood, though, there have been powerful history movies, created in the poetic, not the instructional, mode. These are the films that have respected the strangeness of the past, and have accepted that the historical illumination of the human condition is not necessarily going to be an edifying exercise and that memory is not always identical with consolation. These are also films that embrace history for its power to complicate, rather than clarify, and warn the time traveller that he is entering a place where he may well lose the thread rather than get the gist. Worse yet, the decor of the poetic history movies, while rich in authenticity, is often bleak and raw in aspect, resistant to the glossy patina of its antique furniture.

The best movies in this mode – Luchino Visconti's *The Leopard* (1963), Miklós Jancsó's *The Round-Up* (1965), Roberto Rossellini's *The Rise to Power of Louis XIV* (1966), Andrei Tarkovsky's *Andrei Rublev* (1966), Werner Herzog's *Aguirre: The Wrath of God* (1972) and Yves Angelo's *Le Colonel Chabert* (1994) – not only are dedicated to reconstructing vanished worlds, in all their unruly completeness, but challenge the truisms of linear history, where the order of events is progressive in both a temporal and a moral sense. In curmudgeonly fashion, they hint that later is not necessarily better. Equally, though, such films accept the unavoidability of the past, the thinness of the soil in which our forebears lie buried. They don't so much reach out and grab the past in the name of the present as perform miracles in the opposite direction: have the present waylaid by the past. Rossellini's film used amateur actors in its faithfully ritualised tableaux of court life at Versailles, so that the 'performance' of Jean-Marie Patte as Louis XIV eating alone on his dais with the public watching was utterly remote from a star turn, something that seems unlikely when, any day now, Leonardo DiCaprio does the Sun King at your multiplex. It was the genius of Visconti to cast Burt Lancaster against type, as the fatalistic Sicilian aristocrat in *The Leopard*, so that his previous screen personae simply disappeared without a trace into the world of nineteenth-century Risorgimento Italy. Those are the kinds of movie history that enjoy confounding expectations, roughing up the neatness of our contemporary self-satisfaction. And, as often as not, they have something to say about what is at the back of every historian's mind: the relationship between the living and the dead.

The most eloquent of recent films to have done all this is Yves Angelo's tour de force *Le Colonel Chabert*, based on a novella by Balzac. Angelo was the cinematographer for another remarkably faithful historical reconstruction, *Tous les Matins du Monde*, the story of the seventeenth-century bass violist and composer Marin Marais, and is blessed with perfect historical pitch. Like *The Return of Martin Guerre*, *Le Colonel Chabert* concerns a figure who, having been presumed dead on the battlefield of Eylau, in 1807, returns a decade later and attempts to have his survival acknowledged in law and in society. Unlike the sixteenth-century peasant, though, Chabert (played, again, by Gérard Depardieu, who must have worn the clothes of every generation after the Black Death) is repudiated by his wife. She has survived the debacle of the Napoleonic Empire and has made her peace with the Restoration by marrying an ambitious aristocrat with a squandered fortune but an ancient pedigree. She wants nothing to do with the tattered phantom of her past, a social embarrassment and a political peril.

No one knows an *historical* establishing shot like Yves Angelo. The first frames of *Le Colonel Chabert* transport the viewer directly and shockingly into a vanished world (while also announcing the story's theme: the battle between entombment and endurance), and they do so by annihilating a cliché of cinema history, the gorgeousness of Napoleonic military spectacle. Grimy fingers, seen in close-up, scrabble through uniforms encrusted with mud and blood, ripping the frogging, hunting the valuables. It is Eylau, the day after. A piano plays an adagio from a chamber piece. Mutilated horses are thrown on bonfires. Boots, sabres, helmets and cuirasses pile up in tarnished hecatombs. The camera knowingly quotes from the period's own representations of disaster the Napoleonic hagiography of Baron Gros, Géricault's severed limbs and heads, Goya's puddles of blood and sightless eyes – but without any preciousness or pedantry. Eventually, the camera tracks back to a panorama of death, almost casually observed, peasants busily scavenging the corpses amid the dirty snow, surviving officers dragging bodies to communal burial pits.

In the greatest ten minutes of Depardieu's career, Chabert tells his story to the lawyer he wants to recruit to his cause. Left for dead, he was buried in a mass grave. His mind flickers back and forth between the Napoleonic glory days and the squalid nightmare of their eclipse, and he speaks of the horror of being taken for mad, of incarceration in German asylums. Angelo has no need to picture these on camera, but he must provide convincing reconstructions of two historical milieus: the world Chabert has left, and the world in which he now finds himself marooned – that of Restoration France, in which the first condition of legitimacy is selective forgetfulness. That world, pitilessly cynical, and governed by an ex-émigré culture that is grossly venal and preposterously snobbish, is sketched with a fidelity both to Balzac and to historical truth. Mme Chabert, now a countess, adjusts an earring of grey jasper decorated with a Greek-revival figure, revealing a taste more of the Empire than of the Restoration. The destitute children of army officers killed on the battlefield are taught sabre slashes with wooden sticks by an unrepentant and impoverished Bonapartist who befriends Chabert. An entire world is conjured up on the narrow fault line between victory and calamity, between recall and oblivion. There are no heroes, no tear-pricking diapasons of grandiose music. When Napoleonic military brass sounds, its metallic bravura has the jangling noise of history's black jokes.

Is it possible for an American movie-maker to produce anything remotely like *Le Colonel Chabert*? Is anyone at DreamWorks up for, say, *The War of 1812*, where British and American governments compete in a meaningless carnival of folly and hubris while the White House burns and men's lives are sacrificed for no reason at all?

The question of what befalls a history movie that nonetheless hews more to the poetic than to the instructional mode of historical narration is raised by the case of *Kundun*, Martin Scorsese's undersung masterpiece. *Kundun* may have begun its life being as much of a good-cause movie as *Amistad*. Its central figure, after all, is the unquestionably heroic, Nobelised figure of the Dalai Lama. And even though we're unlikely to see Michael Eisner in saffron any time soon, the atmosphere of Buddhist worthiness circulating in Hollywood can hardly have hurt its chances of being taken on by Disney.

But what Scorsese has accomplished is a work that has absolutely nothing to do with its ostensible billing as 'epic'. Like all great movies made in the poetic mode, it approaches its subject indirectly, backing into history rather than declaiming the theme. Its real story is about the abrupt *arrival* of history, both in the life of a small child and in the life of the culture he is supposed to personify. These linked narratives turn on the loss of innocence and the loss of freedom, not themes calculated to ingratiate themselves with the American movie-goer.

Like Angelo, Scorsese has invented a disconcerting visual language that flows naturally from his subject and does the necessary work of shaking the audience loose from habitual expectations of what a history movie is. The film is painted in the brilliant colours of the sand mandala, an ideogram of Buddhist contemplation, with Nirvana at its centre. The reconstitution and dissolution of the mandala, part of the Buddhist belief in the chain of existence, at the movie's poignant end becomes a metaphor for the fate of traditional Tibet itself. There is a dreamlike, ritualised quality to Roger Deakin's cinematography, and the non-actors who speak Melissa Mathison's deceptively simple lines do so with an integrity that takes the film out of the realm of produced enactment and into that of orally transmitted chronicle – the beginning of history itself. 'Tell me,' the two-year-old future Kundun says, insisting on hearing yet again the story of his birth, and Scorsese, as much as the child's family, obliges.

Like Angelo, Scorsese can't resist quoting history, but in his case it's the history he lives in: the archive of the cinema. There are elements of Satyajit Ray in the infant's-eye-view of the world at the beginning; clattering footage from a Méliès fantasy to punctuate the growing up; the brutal Agincourt scene from Olivier's *Henry V* playing as the walls of history press in on the young man; a tragic variation on the Atlanta crane shot from *Gone with the Wind* as the Dalai Lama dreams of slaughtered monks. While Tibet is pulled inexorably, as a captive, into the modern world of war and propaganda, the camera angle adjusts to modern necessities, but still halts on the far side of movie conventions. The sympathetically embarrassed Chinese general attempts to converse with the Dalai Lama, but is met with impassive silence. The debris of the modern world now gets mixed with the wreckage of tradition. Newspapers are read, but a living oracle, shrieking and hissing in prophetic convulsions, indicates the route of escape.

Throughout the movie, there are shots of startlingly compressed eloquence: a child Dalai Lama is literally framed against a high window of the Potala palace, simultaneously eminence and prisoner; a rat lapping at the water during a ceremony is allowed under Buddhist principles to continue his business undisturbed while the priests go about theirs; the Dalai Lama in his robes, summoned from a Peking bathroom to an audience with Chairman Mao, wipes his spectacles (inherited from the previous incarnation) before patiently attending to the wisdoms of the Great Helmsman, delivered from a well-upholstered couch. These are the pictures from which history is constructed, with the kind of intuitive delicacy that only a natural narrator understands.

The most enduring historians have always valued the necessary alliance between picture-making and argument. Sometimes they have relied on actual illustrations, like the unknown maker of the Bayeux Tapestry, and the propaganda genius who in 1803, 800 years later, decided to exhibit the tapestry as part of Napoleon's attempt to represent himself as the latter coming of William the Conqueror in the planned invasion of perfidious Albion. As often as not, though, historians have been content to shoot their scenes and paint their pictures in their writing. These were the histories that imprinted themselves on my mind when I began to get the history bug. Sometimes such auteurs worked in improbable places. The Venerable Bede, in his monastery at Jarrow, tells the seventh-century story of the West Saxon assassin sent to kill the virtuous King Edwin of Northumbria. To make sure the contract is done right, the hit man paints his double-edged dagger with poison. But at the last instant, faster than you can say 'Secret Service', a loyal thane throws himself in the way of the killer. The dagger passes right through the body of the retainer and pierces the King, who nonetheless survives to become a Christian convert.

To option this story, please contact <u>Bedeworks@Clio.edu</u>. Yes, that's right, edu.

True Confessions of a History Boy

National Theatre programme essay for Alan Bennett's *The History Boys*, May 2004

Yes I was, and still am. I blame it on my teachers whom we always called masters. One of them still writes to me, spotting egregious errors on a page or a TV script and gently correcting them at which point I revert to the 12-year-old dunce in grey flannels and snake belt, and go stand in the corner, flushed with shame.

The first master, at primary school, was a man of gaunt, wolfish features who reserved his occasional smile for History Boys of Promise and who thought it all right if I really wanted to do a history of the Royal Navy, the main point of which were the cigarette card illustrations: Golden Hind, Victory, Ark Royal, WD & HO Wills, Gallagher, Dunhill. He was followed at secondary school — one of the Oxbridge hatcheries Alan Bennett's Headmaster yearns to rival — by a history master committed to having us all experience, at first hand, the terror of the Dark Ages. Dressed in RAF uniform, he would bring a heavy metal ruler down on the desks of inattentive 'toads': Hengist and Horsa, boy, WHACK, Ethelred the Unready, boy, SLAM! One day, when his aim was off, a toad got it right on the knuckles while looking out of the window during the Battle of Hastings. We couldn't wait for the Renaissance to arrive but apparently it wouldn't until the Third Form.

The history masters of the Upper School divided into the Wise-crackers and the Uncles and both were magic. The Uncles really cared; perhaps about their part in the hatchery production quota, but what they cared most about was our distant kinship with the shades. In their charge we got to know Mazzini and William Jennings Bryan and Masaryk as if they were in the room. Hullo, Tamas, pull up a chair and tell us what really happened. With the wisecrackers (including the deutero-Voltaire) we chuckled at the antics of the mighty — that Charles I, what a ninny — and specialised in the foibles that brought them down to earth. It was bliss to know that Pitt the Younger couldn't hold his drink (especially in the House of Commons) and dawn to be alive when we learned that Bismarck's voice was falsetto. 'Blut und Eisen' we would shriek as we headed for the Fives Courts for a quick fag (of the nicotine not the pubescent kind).

But the Love That Dared Not Speak Its Name was certainly around in Cricklewood where the school stood (though its official address for the Headmasters' Conference was, needless to say, 'Hampstead'). A brilliant and gentle geography master was suddenly removed from teaching the climate and produce of Indonesia and then from the staff altogether. He was, the Head announced at assembly, 'not well' and so not well that no-one should attempt to communicate with him, even though he undoubtedly deserved our sympathy.

And we were lucky enough to have our own unforgettable, incomparable, Hector; erotically ambiguous, effortlessly charismatic, dazzlingly erudite. And like Hector, all the history he thought we would ever need, and much more besides, was in the literature he set before us. He didn't enter the lives of the History Boys until the school had made a move from the grit and grunge of Cricklewood to a suburban pastoral farther north, where it instantly invented a pukka public school 'house' for boarders. This was the last straw for us urban cowboys, already in grief and shock at being exiled from the Beeferie (Willesden Green) and from the House on the Corner which we were sure was an Irish brothel. (Why we lurked there, I'm not sure; possibly on the off-chance that someone would emerge one day and announce a Schoolboys' Discount?)

Public schoolboys we emphatically did not want to be. They were the enemy. There was a real one up the road, and when its inmates, on parole, came to our History Club our hearts went out to them for they were an anaemic, pimply-gangly bunch, all snot and blazers, evidently cast down by their incarceration in bosky Hertfordshire. Though our Hector had come to us from a Real Public School, and though he was, in fact, a deep-dyed aristocrat with actual land and an eccentric pa who did himself in with an ancient hunting gun while we were reading A-Level *Hamlet*, Hector was, for us The Glamour of the World. He had toiled in Greek bauxite mines, had been a Scots Guard, had sat at the feet of the immortal Leavis, all of which made us pay attention when he spoke of Empson and Eliot and Donne and

Dryden. His voice, a baritone as smooth and dark as buffed porphyry, could explode, when amused (and he was, a lot) into a girlish giggle. It was not Golders Green. It was not even Hampstead. Nor were his clothes. Leather-patched tweed and flannels and our Hector were strangers to each other. When we opened the door to our first class we beheld (rather than saw) a figure, dressed entirely in black (this was well before black was Black), perched, cross-legged on a table. The face was startlingly handsome; the nose Roman, the eyes blazing. Rows of desks had been replaced by a circle. He was, naturally, in the centre.

Yes it was an act, but we all signed up for parts: the shy but bookish closet philosopher (not me); the worldly tough-guy (not me); the versifying sixth form pseudo-Thom Gunn (not me); in fact, the Dakin, the Posner, the Scripps (or rather the Rebbe Shkripovich) (not me). And, my God, we worked for our prince of letters: if the essay was Donne, we damned well gave him Herbert too; if the essay was Shelley, we showed off our intimacy with Keats's prose. Without warning, entire lessons would be replaced by sessions listening to the Sanctus from different Masses: Bach, Brahms, Fauré. We went to hear the Czech Philharmonic with him and there was a party at his flat in Kensington (or was it Belgravia?). He was romantic, dangerous and perhaps a bit much, but we couldn't get enough of him.

But I was a History Boy, and come A-Level and Oxbridge time, I made my choice, albeit with some torment. Hector took it badly as if betrayed, and barely spoke to me for months; the flashing smile replaced by a thin-lipped expression of indifference which cut to the quick. Many years later at a garden party I told him that much of the rest of my life had been spent trying to make the choice between literature and history moot, and reminding him of Carlyle's dictum that 'history is the only poetry were we but to get it right'. He smiled the old smile, benevolently unconvinced.

Picturing

The Matter of the Unripe Nectarine:
High Ground/Low Ground and
Ruskin's Prejudices

Christ Church Symposium, on the centenary of Ruskin's
death, Oxford, 7 April 2000

I suppose we don't expect our prophets to be reasonable, which is just
as well, since this is the way that Ruskin offered his considered judgement, in the first volume of *Modern Painters*, on Dutch landscape
painting:

> The great body of them is merely to display manual dexterities of
> one kind or another and their effect on the public mind is so totally
> for evil that though I do not deny the advantage an artist of real judge-
> ment may derive from the study of some of them, I conceive the best
> patronage that any monarch could possibly bestow upon the arts would
> be to collect the whole body of them into a grand gallery and burn it
> to the ground.

Why *did* Ruskin hate Dutch painting so much, and with a vehemence
and intensity he sustained over many years, returning to the subject in
volume five of *Modern Painters* as a way of constructing a portrait of
everything he believed art should not be? It's no mystery, of course,
that his attacks on Dutch art were of a piece with his deeply felt anti-
commercialism. But it's worth noting at the outset that Ruskin's equation
of Dutch painting with ignobility, with the amoral reproduction of
mechanically derived effects, those '*manual dexterities*', was emphatically *not* the view of critics elsewhere in Europe, especially in France,
who otherwise did share much of Ruskin's hostility to capitalist philistinism. And in this respect at least, the prophet turned out to be false,
for the one thing that *Modern Painters* did not generate was modern

painting, and what Ruskin has to say about Dutch painting almost inadvertently tells us why. Authentically modern art – that is to say, and here I'm following Clement Greenberg's famous definition, painting that embraced its two-dimensional flatness, painting that self-consciously *rejected* a transparent relationship between objects and their representation – was not the child of Ruskinian criticism, but of the French critical tradition in which all the things that Ruskin most hated – the indifferent rendering of contemporary material life – turned out to drive the modernist revolution. In that respect at least, 1900 has to be seen as the last year of an old, rather than the first year of the new modernist century.

For Ruskin, of course, painting was normative or it was nothing. Its reach to beauty was only possible to the degree to which it also reached for truth. With this in mind he launched his attack on Dutch painting, as the epitome of stale meretriciousness. He was withering about seventeenth-century Dutch art in general, the 'various van somethings and Back somethings', seeing it as devoted to the mechanical reproduction of cheap lighting effects, the random accumulation of mindless anecdote. He complained of its vacancy of ideas and, most damning of all, its reduction of a calling to the status of a *trade*. Potter, Berchem, Backhuizen, Willem van de Velde the Younger and, most surprisingly, Jacob van Ruisdael (so passionately admired in Germany and France) all came in for a beating at the hands of Ruskin's big stick. Rubens was taken to task in a very particular and telling way, and Rembrandt seldom alluded to at all, although Ruskin evidently liked the master's landscape etchings and drawings, as well he might. Of Rembrandt's paintings he had virtually nothing to say except that he thought the greatest of all was the self-portrait of the artist and his wife in Dresden, which we now know to represent Rembrandt and Saskia as the Prodigal Son and his Whore in a Tavern, but which Ruskin, in keeping with his pathetic innocence about the nature of connubial bliss, believed to be the artist and his wife 'in a state of ideal happiness. He sits at supper with his wife on his knee flourishing a glass of champagne with a roast peacock on the table.'

Ruskin's most savage denunciations, though, were reserved for his particular bête noire, Aelbert Cuyp. Perhaps this was because Cuyps were represented in the Dulwich Picture Gallery, which, close to Ruskin's paternal home, must have been an exceptionally important place of initiation for him, assembling as it did so many more paintings than Eastlake's fledgling National Gallery. It was there that Ruskin saw one particular Cuyp and read William Hazlitt's description of it, which raised his hackles. In the chapter on 'The Truth of Skies' in volume I of *Modern Painters*, Ruskin let Cuyp and Hazlitt both have it. Skies were, after all, a crucial subject for Ruskin, for whom the perception and description of sky was a contact point between painterly practice and intimations of the celestial, which inspired some of his most beautiful drawings. Just before getting on Cuyp's case he cites the lovely remark made by Dickens in his *American Notes*, when lying on a barge deck and looking, as Dickens felt, not at but *through* a pure blue sky. Ruskin too was exacting in his account, not just of blue skies, but of what happened to those skies when they were flooded by different kinds of radiance, at dawn, at sunset, at high noon. He certainly knew that when commonplace admiration was voiced about Cuyp's grand production numbers, sooner or later it was his skies – their tonal warmth; their golden saturation – which was supposed to clinch the matter. So it was precisely this quality in which all of Cuyp's habitual meretriciousness was he thought exposed, on which Ruskin concentrated his critical gaze:

Look at the large Cuyp in the Dulwich Gallery, which Mr Hazlitt considers 'the finest in the world' and of which he very complimentarily says 'The tender green of the valleys, the gleaming lake, the purple light of the hills have an effect like the *down* [Ruskin italicises this for full withering effect] on an unripe nectarine!' I ought to have apologized before now, for not having studied sufficiently in Covent Garden to be provided with terms of correct and classical criticism. One of my friends begged me to observe the other day that Claude was 'pulpy', another added the yet more gratifying information that he was 'juicy' and it is now happily discovered that Cuyp is 'downy'. Now I dare say that the sky of this first-rate Cuyp [Ruskin had no more damningly backhanded compliment than a 'first-rate Cuyp'] *is very like an unripe nectarine: all that I have to say about it is, that it is exceedingly unlike a sky.'*

Perhaps Ruskin *should* in fact have spent some time in Covent Garden, in which case he might have noticed – and it would still have served his purpose in attacking Hazlitt – that nectarines (unless Victorian fruit was different from our own) are conspicuously smooth and un-downy on their skins, and that it was the red-golden colour, not the texture of their surface, that Hazlitt was after, in coining his doomed simile. But the producer of fake sunsets, compounded by the egregiously inattentive critic, epitomised for Ruskin everything that was wrong about conventional bourgeois taste – the craving for gaudy theatrical effects not found in nature, the willingness of the technically proficient painter to supply them, and the complicity of the critic in praising them. 'It is difficult to conceive how any man calling himself a painter could impose such a thing on the public and still more how the public can receive it.'

It is odd, though – or then again perhaps it is calculated – that in all his diatribes against Cuyp, Ruskin should have failed to notice or say anything about the fact of his hero Turner's immense and glaringly obvious debt to the very same detestable Cuyp. If the *point* of harping on about Cuyp was precisely to achieve a *dissociation* between Turner and the Dutch master – that Ruskin felt was inappropriately lodged in the public mind – then he completely, and quite uncharacteristically, fails to address the issue specifically. It's much more likely, I think, that Ruskin failed to register the awkward fact that so far from Turner understanding the Dutch tradition as something to be aggressively discarded in pursuit of the higher truths of his own landscape painting, he repeatedly turned back to it as a source of deep interpretative inspiration. Unlike Ruskin, who did his best to avoid the Low Countries, except in so far as he was obliged to disembark en route to the High Countries where his heart lay, Turner returned to Holland again and again: the first time in 1817, then in 1825; and in 1840–42, just prior to the publication of the first volume of *Modern Painters*, in 1843. Turner had been there for three successive years, not just as a traveller of course, but as a working artist, his sketchbook filling up with drawings. Paintings which drew deeply on Dutch art for their inspiration, and composition, punctuated crucial moments in Turner's career. The very first painting that he had ever shown in public, in 1796, a marine painting of fishermen, was famously closely modelled on a Willem van de Velde the Younger. The painting with which he gained a public following when it was exhibited at the British Institution in 1801, *Dutch Boats in a Gale, Fishermen Endeavouring to Put Their Fish on Board*, was likewise indebted to van de Velde, and was in fact commissioned by the Third Earl of Bridgewater (a huge fan and collector of Dutch marine paintings) to hang alongside his own van de Velde.

Of course Ruskin might well have retorted that it was precisely the taste of a canal-builder like Bridgewater which had deformed, happily not fatally, the young Turner's early prospects and healthy sense of independence. But he would have had a harder time with the painting exhibited in 1818 as a direct result of Turner's first journey to Holland the year before, and which justifiably won him an even greater fame: *Dort, or Dordrecht. The Dort Packet-Boat from Rotterdam Becalmed*. For it was blindingly obvious that the great picture, immediately and expensively bought by Turner's most devoted patron Walter Fawkes and hung in the music room of his Yorkshire house, was a fulsome act of homage to Aelbert Cuyp. Turner had seen Cuyp's *Maas at Dordrecht* when it was shown at the British Institution in 1815 and it may well have been that he was so struck by it as to make a pilgrimage (for there was no other reason to go to Dordrecht, which was quite out of the way for a British traveller), to the very site at the junction of the Scheldt and Maas from which Cuyp (and van Goyen) habitually painted their estuarine scenes.

Turner's painting ought to have been absolutely abhorrent to Ruskin, for, quite apart from its reproducing a classically Cuypian late-afternoon blue-gold sky, it was, after all, a picture of people, a very *low* kind of people by Ruskin's standards, reduced to doing absolutely nothing in the absence of wind. That is of course the magic of the piece: the sense of utter stillness in a world that was habitually busy. The twin emblems of the painting's play on movement and immobility are the bird skimming across the surface and an item straight from Ruskin's worst nightmares of Covent Garden – a single cabbage floating imperturbably on the oily surface of the river.

And there were plenty more 'Dutch' Turners to come: a whole sequence of them in the 1830s and '40s, in which the paragon was not Cuyp, but Jacob van Ruisdael. It doesn't say a lot for Ruskin's own attentiveness to, or familiarity with, the whole range of Dutch painting that he regrets that Ruisdael never turned his hand to painting rough water, when in fact English collections had countless examples of Ruisdaels in precisely this vein and which were so clearly the departure point for many of Turner's most powerful choppy-seas pictures, including the stunning *Port Ruysdael* of 1827, now in the Mellon Center for British Art at Yale. (How much of a gesture of homage did Turner have to make before Ruskin would acknowledge it?)

There was another aspect of these sea paintings which was obviously inconvenient for Ruskin's determination to make Turner the embodiment of everything Dutch art was not: namely their Whiggism. *The Prince of Orange, William III Embarked from Holland and Landed at Torbay, November 4th 1688 after a Stormy Passage* was exhibited at the Royal Academy in 1832 and was thought then – and now – to be an allegory of the Parliamentary Reform Act of the same year, a campaign into which Turner's patron, Walter Fawkes, MP, threw everything he had. Whether or not William III's 'stormy passage', dramatically sketched in on the left of the picture, did refer to the proceedings in Parliament, there's no doubt at all that Turner meant to make a connection between the canonical scripture of the Glorious Revolution and the consummation of that tradition of Whig liberty in the act of 1832. The picture, then, is a supreme instance of Turner doing something which Ruskin's view of him precluded: drawing inspiration from the tradition of Dutch painting, especially its dramas of light and darkness, in order to make visible an historical theme which, at least in the terms of its sympathetic protagonists, was morally and constitutionally heroic.

When Ruskin returned to the attack in volume V of *Modern Painters*, published of course in 1860, he had not seen any reason to moderate his hostility. Quite the opposite in fact. The last part of the book, 'Of Inventions Spiritual', which contains some of Ruskin's most wonderful literary pyrotechnics, is a critical review of the landscape tradition in European painting, beginning with the lofty heroes – Titian and Veronese – and ending with the low villains, or rather the clowns, as Ruskin calls them more than once, not just Cuyp but new targets of his excoriation: Teniers and Wouwermans. Rubens, who gets to share a chapter with Cuyp, is not treated to quite the same roasting, but he is patronised by Ruskin in, if possible, an even more deadly manner, as 'a healthy, worthy, kind-hearted courtly-phrased Animal – without any clearly perceptible traces of a soul except when he paints his children'. And it is not just in Rubens, but in Dutch painting generally, this obstinate earthiness, which for Ruskin makes Netherlandish art finally so irredeemable. The whole *point* of art being, for Ruskin, the transcendence of the material conditions of its production, Netherlandish painting was something which remained locked up in so much pigment, canvas and linseed oil. It was only to be expected, then, that when Dutch painters turned to animals, they should treat them as so much material stock-in-trade, the seventeenth-century equivalent of air-brushed lustrous advertising copy: 'Paul Potter their best herd and cattle painter does not care even for sheep but for wool; regards not cows but cowhide', incapable of perceiving 'any condition of an animal's mind except when it is grazing'. Veronese, on the other hand, seems to have a direct line to what Ruskin calls 'the spiritual view of the dog's nature', while 'the dog is used by Teniers and many other Hollanders merely to obtain unclean jest; while by the more powerful men, Rubens, Snyders, Rembrandt it is painted only in savage chase or butchered agony'.

The two chapters which follow are best summed up by Ruskin's opening of chapter VIII in which he contrasts Wouwermans and Fra Angelico – 'Having determined the general nature of vulgarity we are now able to close our view of the character of the Dutch school.' And Ruskin's preceding chapter on distinguishing between vulgarity and gentility is one of the least rewarding and tendentious in the entirety of *Modern Painters*, soaked in a kind of moral snobbery which on the page at least reads even more odiously than the regular social kind. But by this point there is absolutely no stopping him in his Manichaean opposition between the forces of good and wickedness. The 'Hollanders', as he calls them, turn out to be defective painters because they lived in a defective world: a world of cabbages and wool. It is a stupid world, bound to create stupid art in the literal sense of inducing stupor in those who behold it: Cuyp, of course, a 'brewer by trade' whose work 'will make you feel marvellously drowsy'; a world, too, from which God has been completely banished. In their 'pastoral landscape we lose not only all faith in religion but all remembrance of it. Absolutely now at last we find ourselves without sight of God in all the world.' As a view of Jacob van Ruisdael's mature landscapes, this reading would be forgivable in its obtuseness, I suppose, if the overwhelmingly self-evident spirituality of so many of those great paintings, most obviously of course with the two versions of the *Jewish Cemetery*, remained generally obscure to nineteenth-century critics. But of course they didn't. At least since Goethe and Hegel, if not before, Ruisdael's obvious transcendentalism had been the subject of innumerable essays and critical investigations: none of them, I suppose, read or at least taken on board by Ruskin. But as he warms to his task Ruskin reveals himself, I think, to be part of that strain, not entirely pleasant in nineteenth-century moral criticism, which is intent on pinning down and pinning the blame on specific historical moments when the Christian inheritance was sold off for pieces of silver. It's worth quoting this extraordinary passage in full: 'being without God in all the world,' then:

> So far as I can hear or read, this is an entirely new and wonderful state of things achieved by the Hollanders. The human being never got wholly quit of the terror of spiritual being before. Persian, Egyptian, Assyrian, Hindoo, Chinese, all kept some dim, appalling record of what they called 'gods.' Farthest savages had – and still have – their Great Spirit or, in extremity, their feather idols, large-eyed, but here in Holland we have at last got utterly done with it all. Our only idol glitters dimly in tangible shape of a pint pot and all the incense thereto comes out of a small censer or bowl at the end of a pipe. Of deities or virtues, angels, principalities or powers in the name of our ditches, no more. Let us have cattle and market vegetables.

Perhaps none of this would matter for Ruskin, had not this art of cattle and vegetables managed to infect landscape painting ever since, nowhere more completely than in England. Perhaps he was thinking of Crome and the Norwich school; perhaps Gainsborough. In any event Ruskin declares, 'the whole school . . . inherently mortal to all its admirers having by its influence in England destroyed our perception of the purposes of painting' (in particular a proper sense of colour; Ruskin was adamant that in a land without sunshine it was only to be expected that the only colour interest would be to extract 'greyness' and 'shininess').

Something had happened between writing volume I and volume V of *Modern Painters* to make Ruskin apopleptic about the Dutch disease in landscape. It happened, I believe, in 1857: the year of the Manchester lectures which became *Unto This Last*, Ruskin's headlong assault on the barbarities of liberal capitalism, and also the year when he began to work on the completion of *Modern Painters*. And the event was the mother of all blockbusters, held on the old cricket ground at Old Trafford and known as *The Art Treasures of the United Kingdom* (although an enormous number of works were in fact lent from abroad, as well as the cream of private collections within Britain itself). Evidently designed to be a riposte to the Paris Exposition Universelle of 1855, in what had become an alarming competition of exhibitionist one-upmanship, the Manchester exhibition was, for the art world, what the Great Exhibition of 1851 was for everyone else. The scale itself was gargantuan: 2,000 paintings, 1,200 of them Old Masters, from Byzantine icons all the way to Turner, as well as sculpture, decorative art – ceramics, enamels, terracottas, bronzes, glass, armour, ivories; watercolours, drawings, etchings and photographs. A railway line and station had been constructed expressly to transport visitors to the show (without, however, a four-hour wait on opening day) and disembarked them right in front of the exhibition. A great processional boulevard led to the immense iron-and-glass cathedral of art (just the sort of architecture, of course, abominated by Ruskin), the 'nave', as it were, 700 feet long by 200 wide, each branch of the crossing 400 feet long, with galleries running around them and a huge ceremonial space for a full orchestra at the crossing itself. A hundred thousand meals were served daily, 300 roast chickens an hour, a feat duly applauded in the national press. Once Queen Victoria and Prince Albert had lent their names to the organising committee, the £75,000 needed to underwrite the show appeared magically from the Bank of England. Ten thousand two-guinea season tickets had sold before opening day on 5 May. The Queen herself arrived on the twentieth anniversary exactly of her accession, on 30 June, together with the Prince Consort and a number of her children, including Vicky and her betrothed, the Crown Prince of Prussia. It was, of course, raining. This was Old Trafford in June after all.

The ceremonial centrepiece of the show was, naturally, a procession of historical portraits celebrating the grand continuities of British history: kings and queens to be sure (including Holbein's sublime miniature of Anne of Cleves, which Horace Walpole thought his greatest masterpiece), but also of course the great pantheon of cultural worthies: Shakespeare, Newton, Locke, Dr Johnson and, rather surprisingly, Oliver Cromwell and John Hampden. But the curator in charge of the Old Masters' collection, culled from the great and the good among the British aristocracy and plutocracy – the dukes of Devonshire, Buccleuch, Richmond, Northumberland; from Scotland: Breadalbane, Lothian; and on and on (and occasionally plain citizen collectors like John Walter, the journalist writing for *The Times*) – was none other than Gustaf Waagen, the director of the Berlin Museum, who in 1854 had been publishing

his exhaustive inventories of the Old Master paintings in private collections – still an extraordinary source for our understanding of the history
of taste. And although Waagen ensured an astonishing representation
of Italian painting – Giotto, Pollaiuolo, Mantegna, Masaccio, Leonardo,
Michelangelo, Dürer, Titian, Tintoretto, the Caracci and so on – it was
northern painting which really excited him, and which he mustered at
Manchester in profusion and quality. Twenty-eight of what were then
thought to be Rembrandts: three from the Queen, four from the Marquis
of Hertford (core of the Wallace Collection), the double portrait of Jean
Pellicorne and Susanna van Collen, the great grisaille of *John the Baptist
Preaching* (now in Berlin), *Floris Soop* and so on. But also a huge haul
of precisely the pictures for which Ruskin had such deep repugnance –
a crowd of Cuyps including the great view of Nijmegen from Woburn
Abbey, Queen's Hunters; also a mass of Hobbema, Potter animal pieces
and the execrated Wouwermans. And twenty Jacob van Ruisdaels,
including the *View of Bentheim* in John Walter's collection; the
pollarded oak, and marsh and waterfalls as well as a whole number of
stormy marine paintings which would have confirmed for Ruskin the
connection between the Dutch master and Turner.

The list, of course, is not the point. It goes on and on. What the
Manchester show affirmed, to a degree that must have set Ruskin's teeth
on edge (despite the inclusion of a *hundred* Turners) and sent him back
to further rounds of denunciation, was the pride of place given to
precisely the kind of paintings that he believed were destroying the
vitality of *true* painting in England. The Manchester exhibition must
have seemed to Ruskin, despite all those Turners and a sprinkling of
the Pre-Raphaelites, a repeat performance of the tawdry vulgarity of
the Great Exhibition six years before, but perhaps even worse because
it suggested so eloquently the essential imperviousness of English taste
to the sacred reawakening launched by the Pre-Raphaelites: the tyranny
of polish. The immense presence of Dutch art could only have
confirmed him in his judgement that it was, essentially, manufactured
interior decoration for the plutocracy. It's hard not to read *Unto This
Last* and not see it as Ruskin's specific counterblast to the orgy of vulgarity, the loss of gentility represented by the iron-and-glass cathedral at
Old Trafford.

Nor does it come as a surprise to learn that incomparably the best –
not necessarily the most exhaustive, but certainly the most perceptive

— report on the Manchester exhibition comes from the pen of a French critic, then living in exile in Holland under the adopted name of 'Willem Bürger' — Bill Citizen — and that critic was of course the great Théophile Thoré. (It's odd that no one has thought to write a parallel life of Ruskin and Thoré, since their passions were so similar and their influence almost equally profound.) Though they're slight in length, Thoré's two introductory chapters to his *Trésors d'Art en Angleterre* (published at amazing speed in London — in French — in 1858) are little gems of insight, since he sees right away to the social argument made by the *fact* of the Manchester show. Faux-naïf, he begins by asking why — at least for the convenience of foreigners — such an important exhibition wasn't located in London, a mere two hours' train journey from Dover, and then of course answers his own question. The idea is a parade of the *educational* pretensions of industrial capitalism in its own back yard, specifically a kind of pedagogical gift donated from capital to labour, from the entrepreneur to the worker. And it must be an expressly *British* enterprise at that — hence the deliberate distance, so Thoré thinks, from the Channel and the North Sea, and the enormous prominent space given to historical portraiture, historical miniatures and artefacts illustrating the continuity of British history. In continental Europe, the implication is, according to Thoré, you have revolutions. In Britain we have exhibitions. This ostensible union of classes is made all the more solid by the fact that the community of collectors increasingly cut across the formal stratifications of class in England — as far as owning great Dutch paintings is concerned, the journalist John Walter and Sir Robert Peel (or, rather, by 1857, his widow) were every bit the peer of the aristocratic Cavendishes, Grosvenors and Russells.

Thoré evidently has mixed feelings about all this, because while he's genuinely lost in admiration at the smoothness with which this propaganda stunt is handled by the businessmen of Manchester, in alliance with the broad acres of the rest of England, the old revolutionary in him rankles at '*his*' favourite art — Dutch art — being shamelessly exploited as an emollient for discontent. For it was not fortuitous that Thoré had chosen the Kingdom of the Netherlands for his place of exile (rather than Victor Hugo's Guernsey) from the police state of the Second Empire. It was not just Dutch art that was the attraction — although that was of immense importance to him — but the kind of society Thoré, in common with many other old revolutionaries, believed to have survived in the Netherlands, a society at the opposite pole of the metropolitan corruptions of Paris and London, or the industrial brutalities of Lille and Manchester. The best account of this French vision of the Netherlands is in an extraordinary book written by a now undeservedly forgotten writer, Alphonse Esquiros, who spent 1855 in Holland and who published *La Néerlande et la Vie Hollandaise* four years later. Esquiros was an old revolutionary comrade of Thoré, a cell-mate at Sainte-Pélagie where they had both done time for offending the censors under the July monarchy. Though his family was well-to-do haute bourgeoisie, the paternal house remained right in the centre of the Faubourg Saint-Antoine and thus in the middle of the bloodiest action of the June days in 1848. While Thoré was editing *La Vraie République* together with George Sand and the Saint-Simonien Pierre Leroux and contributing liberation manifestos to the *République des Arts*, Esquiros was opening his house to the wounded and dying hauled directly from the barricades.

After it was all over, and the warriors of the new France were all either in prison, exile or discreet silence, they cast around for some sort of light in the general darkness and, perhaps improbably, perhaps not, saw in Holland a culture in which bitter social division, plutocratic hegemony, cultural intolerance and the bureaucratic state were all miraculously absent. The northern Netherlands seem to have missed out altogether on the Industrial Revolution (in contrast to Belgium). Its little towns – Haarlem, Delft, Rotterdam and Gouda – all little miracles, so they thought, of self-government. In the writing not only of Esquiros but another utterly infatuated admirer of the Dutch, Jules Michelet, the *trekschuit*, the tow-barge, became the symbolic opposite of the railway locomotive. In the slow, horse-drawn barge, time and space, they thought, remained astonishingly in balance, its languid schedules utterly incompatible with the urgent clock of industrial production; and within the *trekschuit* were accommodated all types and conditions, with none of the glaringly inegalitarian class separations that marked the compartments of the railway train. The first thing that all the Francophone pilgrims did on disembarking from the train (in which, perforce, they were compelled to arrive in Holland) was to get on the *trekschuit*. Likewise the individual cargo-barge symbolised something else of supreme significance for the French Hollandophiles: the sanctity and autonomy of the nuclear family on which they believed true social happiness depended. (It's striking how little Ruskin has to say about this issue.) Jules Michelet, another of the most passionate devotees of the Dutch, and a personal friend of the great archivist historian Groen van Prinsterer, described the tow-barge (in a purple passage which in places almost anticipates the *bateau ivre*) as a 'Noah's ark': '*C'est l'arché de Noë, qui doit contenir toute une famille, homme, femme, enfants, animaux.*'

To these writers and critics, then, Holland was an unforced, organically cohesive community; precisely in fact the kind of society which Ruskin, and before him Pugin, imagined had existed in Christian medieval England and which he wanted to reintroduce through the Guild of St George. But in reinstating, as they imagined, the integrity of the medieval craft guilds along with neo-medieval design and painting, Ruskin, the Pre-Raphaelites and the Guild Socialists were reaching back across a great span of time in which the actual lived experience of work and worship had been irrevocably lost. But the French enthusiasts of small-town Dutch culture were, they supposed, witnessing a continuity they thought had never actually been broken. And granting a large degree of wishful thinking – especially in respect of the larger cities like Amsterdam – they were not entirely wrong. The northern Netherlands was one of the very last cultures in western Europe to experience the Industrial Revolution. Compared with Holland, Ruskin's Switzerland was Coketown.

The eulogists of Holland had not arrived at their improbable social epiphany overnight. What makes their position so diametrically opposite from Ruskin's is that while our Prophet read what he supposed to be the essentially prosaic and (his favourite word) 'carnal' nature of Dutch painting to be evidence of a hopelessly debased and vulgar culture, immune to any possibility of the spiritual life, French writers in whom art criticism, social evangelism and political activism were married to at least the same degree as Ruskin, came to precisely the opposite conclusion from the same evidence! Years before they were eyewitnesses and reporters on Dutch society, these critics, banded together as *Jeune France*, were impassioned devotees of its art, including its landscape painting.

Many of those who would become the champions of Dutch painting in France in the 1830s were first exposed to it when they were very young in the great aristocratic collections which passed, sometimes by force, to the new Louvre – the collection of the Marquis de Vaudreuil, for example – as well as in the loot brought to Paris by the wagons of Napoleonic triumph. It was through that more doubtful route that the great treasures from the Stadholder William V's collection, including the great Potter in The Hague and a number of Ruisdaels, were first seen by Michelet who never forgot them. After 1815 these canonical works disappeared in two directions: the expropriated works properly repatriated back to the royal collection in The Hague (the nucleus of the Mauritshuis) and in much greater numbers (from, for example, the Prince de Conti and the Choiseuls) into the collections of the aristocratic magnates of Britain, via the auctions and sales inventoried by John Smith.

So when the writers, poets and artists of *Jeune France* were looking for counter-paradigms around which they could rally against the academy, the lost treasures of Dutch art were one of their first thoughts. Though they might come to despise it in the end (and not all did), the railway train got them from Paris to Antwerp and eventually to Utrecht by the late 1830s and early '40s. And another crucial technological breakthrough – lithography – helped them publish the works of the Dutch masters in their periodicals, none more important than Arsène Houssaye's *L'Artiste*, which published art criticism by Théophile Gautier, Gérard de Nerval, Félix Pyat, Petrus Borel, Eugène Delacroix and of course the young Thoré.

The qualities which these writers saw in Dutch art, and which they held to be socially and morally redemptive, were precisely those which Ruskin read as evidence of the degenerate vulgarity of the culture: namely its earthiness, its rejection of grand or sacred narrative; its rejection of received assumptions about the beautiful and the ugly; the willingness of artists to consider themselves as proximate to their subjects, however drunk or debauched or dirty or violent those subjects might be. They also, of course, indulged in a great deal of wishful thinking – nourished by the anecdotal early eighteenth-century biographies of Dutch artists by Arnold Houbraken – as to their autodidact background. Rembrandt – their favorite farouche – was firmly lodged in their imagination as the miller's son with flour in his hair, marrying the peasant girl Saskia. And in keeping with Romantic assumptions about the indivisibility of personal temper and painterly style, they also read imaginary connections between those biographies and aspects of handling – van Goyen's notorious propensity for gambling thus became an explanation for the loose sketchiness of his style and his rejection (as was then thought) of under-drawing; Dou's apparent manic fastidiousness was of a piece with the gem-like licked finish of his genre paintings and still lifes, and so on.

Most important of all, though, the writers of *Jeune France* were attracted to the greatest work of Dutch art for what they called its '*poésie*': and here again both Potter and Jacob van Ruisdael played a crucial role. Poesy (for which these writers were at least in part indebted to their readings of German idealism) meant the intimation of unworldly things from the close inspection of the worldly; the implication of interiors from the avid description of surfaces. So that while Ruskin took Potter's cows to be evidence that all the Dutch cared for was a kind of merchant's inventory of leather on the hoof, Arsène Houssaye could write of the same painting that Potter 'fixes nature itself on the canvas as if it were a mirror . . . he [Potter] proves triumphantly that cattle have a soul, a spirit, even a mind (*pensée*), that these animals speak to you with their eyes, their movement, their postures (*attitudes*)'. Lammenais, the arch Christian mystic socialist in this company, felt precisely the same way. Jacob van Ruisdael was, just as Goethe had thought (Houssaye again), '*le poète des coeurs blessés* . . . the poet of wounded hearts; he is not just copying nature; he is giving it its soul'. Ruisdael is 'sad, dreamer, poet above all'. Thoré went even further. In 1844 he compared Ruisdael's *Little Tree* with Michelangelo's sculpture for Lorenzo de Medici known as *The Thinker* – so that the '*petit buisson*' attempting to find some peace amidst the agitations of nature became anthropomorphised as a tragic hero – an association which, it's safe to say, definitely would not have occurred to Ruskin.

But then Thoré had already decided – as he wrote in an essay on Adriaen van Ostade in 1847 – that Dutch painters of the golden age exhibited a kind of peculiar mysticism, suspended between the material and the immaterial worlds: 'The Dutch of Ostade are . . . more Christian than one would ever imagine, practising the spirit of the Gospel, the detachment from earthly vanities, equality and fraternity.' So while, for Ruskin, Dutch painters betrayed their shallow attachment to the surface appearances of this world through their vulgar concern with finish, for his French contemporary art critics, they were the pioneers not of the finite but the infinite world.

These two stances, about as opposite as one might imagine, were I suppose partly conditioned by the nature of the enemy to be attacked. In France, in the 1840s and '50s, it was still, by and large, classical academicism, or the stale posturings of the *style troubadour*. The earthiness of Dutch painting, by contrast, became obviously important for the painters who set themselves most resolutely *against* the grandiose histories and florid portraiture of the official Salons – painters as diverse as Daumier and Millet, and the *plein air* Barbizons (Corot and Rousseau). Dutch pictures were as yet very thinly displayed in the Louvre and even scarcer in the grand collections of the plutocracy. The late 1850s were the time when both of those situations changed. In England, on the other hand, the enemy was to be found in the bourgeois and aristocratic houses, which were positively stuffed full of Dutch art since the auctions of the post-Waterloo years. And it was in that over-upholstered milieu that Ruskin believed the taste for Cuyp and Ruisdael had deadened both private and public sensibility.

Whatever the reason for these strikingly opposed responses, their effects on the critical discourse about the nature of Dutch art were, I think, serious and long-lasting. Ruskin's brutal dismissal of Dutch art as, at best, so many painted lies about nature and, at worst, the painterly equivalent of the forces of Antichrist, deserving nothing better than being consigned to a great incineration, in effect left the field to writers like Mrs Anna Jameson, whose massively popular books on painting measured Dutch art for the degree to which it was 'charming' or not. Unshakably established as part of moneyed taste, writing about Dutch painting in England became (as it certainly had not been in the eighteenth century) almost exclusively a matter of disputes about authentication, and the development of simple chronologies of style from 'early' to 'late'. It was quite unthinkable, for example, that a serious study of Dutch art should play any part at all in the meditations of those critical communities which seemed in the year of Ruskin's death, a century ago, to be pointing towards the future – the aesthetic movement and Arts and Crafts. As far as Dutch painting was concerned, Ruskin had done something much more fatal than burned the lot of it – he had made its study the exclusive province of connoisseurs. It had become an intellectual dead end, the subject of parlour talk.

Across the Channel, something like the opposite was true. The early and acute insights of Thoré, Houssaye and Esquiros had blossomed in two extremely powerful ways. First, Thoré's own impassioned promotion of the work of Frans Hals generated a completely new understanding of his portraiture (close in many ways to Riegl), and his rediscovery of Vermeer had led him to see hard archival-based documentation as the next step towards proper historical reconstruction of the lives and working conditions of the artists which he himself realised he had over-idealised. The first major archival publications about Dutch painting that I know of were thus the production of a French specialist and friend of Thoré's, Henri Havard. Second, and perhaps in the end more fundamental to the future of thinking and practising art, the critical insight that Dutch art did *not* thrive on a transparent or literal relationship between the objective material world and the manner of its representation, but rather posed an enormous question mark over that representation, was astonishingly fertile for thinking about the function of painting in general. It was, in ways incomprehensible to Ruskin, who insisted over and over again that the painter's job was to do no more but no less than represent the truth of nature, the bud of modernism. It was in precisely the artificiality – the 'lies' told about nature in so much Dutch painting – that the way forward actually, for better or worse, lay. And in this respect, forgive me for saying, it was Jacob van Ruisdael, Rembrandt van Rijn and Théophile Thoré, and not John Ruskin, who turned out to be the real prophets of Modern Painting.

Dutch Courage

Guardian, 23 June 2007

Feeling conjugally challenged? Look at Frans Hals's double portrait of Isaac Massa and Beatrix van der Laen in the National Gallery's forth-coming *Dutch Portraits* show and, instantly, all will be right with your corner of the world. The graceful painting, silvery with intimate affec-tion, documents one of the great changes in the history of European marriage: the possibility of the shared smile – the *glimlach* revolu-tion. Not that lipwork had hitherto been out of the question for portraiture. But *La Joconde* she isn't. Leonardo's thinly knowing smirk implies private knowledge, to be decoded only through the proprieto-rial collusion of patron and painter. But Hals's newly married couple, Beatrix sporting both betrothal and wedding rings on her right hand, advertise their mutual pleasure openly for our shared celebration. They incline to each other and, through their self-identification as a harmo-nious pair, radiate that sympathy outwards through the picture plane towards us. Behold, the painting says, as Isaac holds his hand to his heart, the very picture of proper Christian marriage in which duty also happens to be pleasure.

To gauge the magnitude of that alteration you can look at Jan Claesz's twin portraits in the exhibition of a married couple from the first decade of the seventeenth century. The figures are still rigid with conventions of social duty, above all that of engendering, the human bond entirely subsumed by the obligations of decorum.

Precisely because, during the seventeenth century, the Dutch trav-elled that journey from iconic formalism, through a period of easygoing naturalism, back to refined family ensembles dressed to display patri-cian rank and classical taste, the National Gallery show is an opportunity to reflect on the evolution of the genre itself. As patrons reminded painters (including Rembrandt) whom they thought had been altogether too free with artistic licence, likeness was their first duty. But as Richard Brilliant argued in his elegant book, *Portraiture*, the artist has often interpreted that job as the likeness of an idea, a sense of a person, rather than the laborious imitation of physiognomic detail. Roger Fry complained of a Sargent portrait of a British general that he couldn't see the man for the likeness. He was commenting at a time when a portrait was thought to be the capture of a bundle of psychological characteristics stamping the unique quality of a person, which could be read through facial expression and body language, and then transcribed on to the canvas as a sign of essential self. This was no more than a subjective hunch about a person, masquerading as some deeper objective reality. But it meant that modern portraiture has generally been imitation complicated by interpretation.

Centuries earlier, before the Romantics inaugurated the cult of the unrepeatable self, the work of the portraitist was to represent the imagined mask of, say, the scholar (Holbein's Erasmus), the Doge (Titian's Andrea Gritti) or the virtuoso courtier (Raphael's Castiglione); all of them personifications rather than revelations. But between the normative icon of the Renaissance and the naked ego-show of the nineteenth century, bolder portraitists such as Hals nudged the decorous expectations of their patrons towards informality while never quite disobeying the obligation to represent something (wealth garnered in virtue, for instance) as well as someone. Then, enter the Haarlem smile, hallmarked not just by Hals, but by followers such as Jan de Bray, whose happy couple, the printer Abraham Casteleyn and his wife Margriet de Bancken, perpetuate the Halsian manner well into the 1660s, with the adoring *huisvrouw* (housewife) leaning towards her husband, while he gestures with creamy complacency towards us.

Just why Haarlem should have broken the solemnity barrier is a mystery, though perhaps the conjunction of breweries and textiles, both giving a glossy shine to things, the humanist slant of its academies removed from Calvinist-canting Leiden, had something to do with it. But the Haarlem painters also knew that the line between the sympathetic smile and the coarse grin, with teeth exposed, was the severe boundary that separated portraiture from genre painting. The most famous of all Hals's paintings, *The Laughing Cavalier*, is, in fact, neither. And no wonder, for the raucous guffaw, with its noisome reek of herring and onions, was the sign of low-lifes, both the people and the pictures.

The van der Laen marriage portrait is something else again, on one level an omnium gatherum of all the stock marital pieties that could have been pulled straight from a domestic-morality manual such as Jacob Cats's *Houwelyck*. Beatrix leans against her solid spouse in a gesture of trusting subordination to his considerable substance. At her feet, inevitably, trails ivy, the symbol of fidelity, while behind the couple a vine, the emblem of fruitful devotion, twines itself around a sturdy trunk. The partners were famously loaded: a prosperous Russian trade merchant married to a local heiress. But what would otherwise be an egregious display of conspicuous fortune is carefully offset by sartorial signals of their old-fashioned homeliness. The sharp clothes may flash with Hals's silky light, but they are sober Christian black and Beatrix sports the kind of aggressively unfashionable millstone ruff which, by the 1630s, was more likely to be found encircling the neck of a matron. And if raw money is modified by old piety, it's also polished by culture, hence the display of their poetic pretensions, embodied by the garden, the kind of place extolled in the gently Arcadian love poetry of P. C. Hooft, complete with Italianate pavilions, classical statuary and fountains.

But Hals has moved the picture well beyond an anthology of allusions. The scene is bright with human as well as botanical nature; the smiles seem spontaneous rather than assumed. In an exquisite touch of intimacy, Hals has the fine silk of her hair escaping her under-cap, the *ondermuts* that was seldom thought proper for portraits, but whose delicate pink seems to rhyme with her rosy complexion. His ability to convey this move to warm informality was technical as well as conceptual. Inspired perhaps by Rubens (for the Flemish presence was strong in Haarlem), Hals's handling of paint was itself looser than anything that had yet appeared in Dutch art, the darting hand suggesting the energetic innocence of impulse.

Of course, the balance between bravura and decorum was always delicate. Hals's portrait of the twenty-something plutobrat Willem Coymans obliges the patrician by incorporating his coat of arms – the black cattle that made him an urban *kooi-man* (cow-boy). But by describing the translucent fallen collar and the gold-embroidered coat through a web of dashing, hectic strokes, Hals manages to give Coymans the look of unbothered insouciance, making his improbable expression of thoughtful self-regard a tad more credible.

We're constantly being cautioned by the anachronism cops not to read backwards and trawl through Dutch art for the ancestry of modern bourgeois informality. And if it's countervailing images of Calvinist sobriety you want, you'll find enough dutiful sobersides in the show. (Casteleyn and de Bancken turn up again in startling profile as Calvinist clones.) But the curators have been right, for the most part, to go for the graceful flash, in the work, for instance, of the satiny Cornelisz Verspronck, which briefly lit up the Low Countries and lingered to haunt the archivists of European memory – Proust, Claudel, Zbigniew Herbert – as the sorry old continent staggered from butchery to banality. Their observation that the seventeenth-century Dutch painters, stereotyped by Hollandophobes like Ruskin as incapable of rising above the prosaically material, illuminated the poetry of daily life turns out to be right. For a generation or two, the Dutch did move art on, and through it ennobled quotidian humanity, investing two genres in particular – landscape and portraiture – with the force of natural truth. That happened because the kind of patrons – the Church and the court – that were least interested in nature fell away as serious players in the Dutch art market. Instead, there were just punters, you and me, tens of thousands of us, who, if we were, say, in whalebone or the rye trade, could afford a few guilders on a Van Goyen riverscape, or a bit more on an image of ourselves, a *contrefeitsel* – us edited into grandeur, or piety or marital devotion or cultured finesse, but us all the same.

Which is not to say that the painters on show at the National Gallery – even Rembrandt – were free to do their thing any way they saw fit. Some had been to Italy, and even those who hadn't (like Rembrandt) were acutely conscious of the idealising strictures of classicism. At each end of the spectrum there were those unbothered by the conflict – pure Italianisers or pure parochialists – but the strongest were somewhere in between and struggled not just with the conflicting demands of imaginative idealism and natural truth, but with a similarly exacting conflict between the obligations of social form and the lure of vitality. In some of the most powerful portraits, dynamism – the implication of movement – has the upper hand, even when the subject is actually standing quite still. So Andries de Graaf, the potentate of Amsterdam money and politics, in Rembrandt's slick version of him in 1639, gets the full *gentiluomo* treatment, leaned against a truncated classical column, legs elegantly contrapposto, his trim frame exuding silkily understated nonchalance. But the billowing swathe of his right sleeve seems to take

on a rhetorical life of its own, as if blown by the Dutch breezes, imply-
ing the dynamic citizen-hero that Rembrandt presumed de Graaf
wished to personify. He may have presumed wrongly, as de Graaf was
one of those who expressed his unhappiness with the master's efforts.

The trade-off between grandeur and energy, monumentalism and
the life-force, became even more problematic when artists were commissioned (at a lucrative rate per head) to paint group portraits. Adding to
the challenge was the requirement, understood as built into the contract
(and famously ignored by Rembrandt in *The Night Watch*), to produce
acceptable individual likenesses at the same time as communicating the
collective ethos of the company. This is still a tough call for corporate
photographers (whether of company retreats or the school cricket team),
who do exactly what the most mechanical of the Dutch portraitists did
in the late sixteenth and early seventeenth centuries: line them up along
the picture plane till they run out of heads, or else stack them up in
terraced rows. To make the job still more complicated, group portraitists
had to register niceties of rank within the companies, so that at a militia banquet no one would confuse the captain with his lieutenants.
Unsurprisingly, the results were inhumanly wooden, an additive
arrangement that managed, in the memorable phrase of Rembrandt's
student van Hoogstraten, to make the sitters look as if they could all be
decapitated with one sweep of the sword.

There was one further non-negotiable requirement made of group
portraits. In addition to documenting the internal coherence of the
company, they also had to engage with those who stood before the paintings, blessing their good fortune that the fate of Amsterdam or Haarlem
was in such capable, confidently civic, inexhaustibly virtuous hands. The
great Austrian art historian Alois Riegl, in the work he wrote on Dutch
group portraiture in 1902, believed this two-way stretch to represent a
breakthrough in the genre, reconciling as it did the internal, but locked-
off, coherence of Italian art with the outwardly directed exuberant show
of the Netherlands. For the first time, so Riegl believed, the connection
between subject and beholder had been brought together in compositions that invited cross-frame attentiveness. That might be true, but it
was also a genre of inspired social fraud, for this bond between Them
and Us came into its own precisely at the moment when the regents of
the Dutch towns were becoming a caste of unaccountable oligarchs. Ah,
the whoppers that faux-naturalism commits.

The pictorial strain of doing all these things simultaneously, having multiple figures participate in a credible scene – chatting, drinking, charitably condescending to orphans or the aged, anatomising – at the same time that they bond with us, was a severe formal test of the available talent. The unavoidability of tables in banqueting pieces meant that figures who would otherwise be showing us their backs have to turn round or lean at forty-five degrees, a move not all group portraitists could convincingly bring off. In merely workmanlike hands the paintings either coagulate in a congested scrum or else fall apart. Hals and Rembrandt were not the only virtuosi who could pictorially multitask. Nicolas Pickenoy and Thomas de Keyser, both represented in the National Gallery show, were dependable workhorses in the genre, but their efforts to make the ensembles come credibly alive are tentative and always play second fiddle to their obligations to deliver likeness and rank. Even Hals, the supreme virtuoso of space and figure-juggling, could buckle under the strain. *The Meagre Company*, the Amsterdam militia piece in the show, is by two hands: Pieter Codde's as well as Hals's, because of a two-year row with the militia officers over whether Hals would finish it in Amsterdam or have it sent back to Haarlem where he was nursing, so he said, a bad leg. (They believed he was stalling for more money.) Exasperated, the company of crossbowmen turned to the local talent, Codde, who may have been in the militia himself. But Codde proved not much more dependable, spending a night in jail in irons along with the maid with whom he was conducting an affair. The double-painting breaks in two, precisely at its gallant centre figure. To the left is Hals's assured flash and dash; to the right, Codde's painfully laboured attempts at spontaneity. No wonder Codde never went near full-length figures again.

The two Rembrandt group portraits – *The Anatomy Lesson of Dr Nicolaes Tulp* of 1632 and *The Staalmeesters: Syndics of the Clothmakers' Guild* from three decades later (1662) – bookend his Amsterdam career and are both stupendous masterpieces that would alone be worth the price of admission. Throwing caution to the winds, Rembrandt bet on making collective dramas that embodied the ethos of the group, while not compromising either on likeness or the connection made from the painting to beholder. But the balance between attention within and attention beyond the frame could not be more different. In the Tulp, all eyes within the arrowhead arrangement of intense concentration are locked on to the professor-anatomist, who dissects the flexor muscles while demonstrating their action with his own free left hand. A single figure at the top of the pyramid, a pentimento revealing that originally he was hatted, looks at us while pointing to the criminal corpse in a concessionary gesture to memento mori. We anatomists are good, but let's not get above ourselves; we all end up like that. But Rembrandt, at least conceptually, has smuggled himself into the scene with the implication that the painterly dexterity needed to bring off the painted anatomy lesson was analogous to the demonstration itself.

The same covert self-insertion happens even more ingeniously in *The Staalmeesters*. It was long assumed that the drama of the scene, with one of the quality-control men rising to his feet, must have been in response to someone entering the chamber of their deliberations and, so Riegl thought, saying something that provoked a response. A cooler generation of critics thought this was so much fantastic projection and insisted this was 'just five gentlemen in black sitting for their portraits'. But four years ago, in a stunning insight, Benjamin Binstock argued that since Rembrandt's initial study drawings for a composition (which he later abandoned for the present arrangement) were made on account-book paper, it was very likely that those drawings were made in the very book we see depicted on their table, thus making artist and sitters true partners in the composition. The two figures, one of whom gestures at a page the other holds, are thus debating the making of art – this work of art.

This subtle visual essay in the collaboration between painter and patrons would have been just the thing to tempt Rembrandt as an exercise in vindication, since he was doubtless still smarting from his greatest fiasco four years before, when his painting of Claudius Civilis and the oath of the Batavians had been rejected by the regents of the town hall, leading him to mutilate the masterpiece. The connection between the two, Binstock further argued, is not just their similarity as groups around a table, but the fact that *The Staalmeesters* was painted on the rough herringbone canvas intended for a replacement for the repudiated Batavians. It gets even better. If the syndics are paying attention to the drawings in the book and then to someone in the room, that someone must surely be Rembrandt himself, so that the syndics are actively glancing from book to painter, taking in the changes he has made to the very scene that we now see. This is a gesture of co-option beyond anything Riegl could have imagined. The master has put himself in our shoes, and vice versa, in a quality-control drama of composition. The syndics are still checking the cloth, but it is in fact the weave of a canvas.

The secret of *The Staalmeesters* can stand for the peculiar genius of Dutch art at this moment in its history; one that wore its prodigious ingenuity lightly. What seems to be the most straightforward visual culture turns out to be a Chinese puzzle; an endless enquiry into the observation and representation of seen things and people. The Dutch were obsessed with nature all right, but very often, and with a confounding depth, that turns out to be the nature of picturing itself.

Rubens

Guardian, 22 October 2005

The thing about entitling your show *Master in the Making* is that it assumes a public already sold on just what it was that got made. But that couldn't be less true in the case of Rubens. In any given museum on any given Sunday, the empty gallery is invariably 'Flemish, 17th Century', where gatherings of massively upholstered nudes shift their dimpled weight opposite a collision of horses and carnivores, while by the door an obscure and pallid saint embraces his martyrdom with rolled-up eyes. Punters enter, take a quick gander, assume the proper expression of the glazed, the cowed, the awed and the baffled, and then accelerate towards the door marked 'Rembrandt'.

Which is a shame, since there are peculiar exhilarations to be found in Rubens that are reproduced nowhere else in baroque art: the strenuous manipulation of sensation, even profound emotion, through purely pictorial muscle; incomparable draughtsmanship; eye-popping colour. Not for Rubens the darkling palette and the stripped-down casting of Caravaggio (though he took much else from the master whose scandalously naturalistic *Death of the Virgin* he tried to buy for the Duke of Mantua), nor the introspective psycho-probes of Rembrandt. Rubens is all about meaty animal energy and high-voltage design, the play of what one seventeenth-century biographer called his *furia del pennello* – the fury of the brush.

But Rubens's surging line was never simply a virtuoso flourish. It was always put at the service of the controlled orchestration of bodies in motion. And as a colourist, no one since Titian and Giorgione came close. Whether he was confecting the most delicate flesh tones or throwing screaming vermilion at the canvas, it was with an eye to modelling forms rather than just filling them, thus making the ancient and tedious battle between *disegno* and *colore* moot.

Put all these gifts together and you get what contemporaries came to recognise as an incomparable marvel – the 'god of painting', as one of those recommending him for an Antwerp altarpiece in 1609 wrote. When he is operating at the height of his powers – as in the Courtauld oil sketch for the *Descent from the Cross*, or the adorably nipple-guzzling *Roman Charity* from the Hermitage – Rubens knocks the stuffing out of you, altering your breathing pattern.

So will this show at the National Gallery be that kind of conversion experience? If it turns out that way – and anyone who loves Rubens and wants to make the enthusiasm infectious must dearly hope so – it will be a triumph of art over concept. For the exhibition is very high-minded: it is so relentlessly bent on tracking each and every influence that went into the evolving artist's manner (though it omits some of those that meant most to him in his earliest days, such as the woodcuts of Holbein and Tobias Stimmer) that at times it seems in danger of disappearing up its own erudition. There are great and good things to be learned here about Rubens's compositional technique, but the over-whelming emphasis on process has tilted the choice of works towards those that can be unpacked as a cluster of compositional drawings, sketches and alternative versions. So we get two versions of *Susanna and the Elders*, neither sensational, rather than Rubens's self-portrait with his first wife, Isabella Brant – a hymn to conjugal fertility – which certainly is.

There's something airless about a show conceived and executed from a place so deeply internal to the academy of connoisseurs that you can practically smell the Chardonnay. In short supply (for the most part) is what, far more than this bit of Raphael or that bit of Michelangelo, actually made Rubens Rubens: what the painter would have called *wellust* and we – because English doesn't have a name for it (goodness, I wonder why?) – would call *joie de vivre*, a hungry instinct for the flesh.

I suppose you have to admire the unfashionable courage of an exhibition so single-mindedly cool to history or biography. I'm among the ranks of those who think the pendulum has swung a little too far away from formal analysis and towards historical context in recent years, so that the pure visual charge of art has sometimes been suffo-cated beneath data-bloated compendia of prices and patrons. No danger here, though, of stooping to vulgar context. No danger of letting the visitor know, for instance, that Rubens grew up in the most bloody theatre of religious war in Europe; that his father – a Protestant convert! – was imprisoned and nearly executed for an affair with the Princess of Orange; that his most important Antwerp teacher, Otto van Veen, criss-crossed confessional lines between Calvinist Leiden and militantly Counter-Reformation Antwerp, or that the painter's early life was a succession of personal, as well as painterly, dramas. Granted that the early *Battles of the Amazons* aren't despatches from the front; granted that they owe much to Leonardo's *Battle of Anghiari*. But isn't it interesting, nonetheless, to wonder whether the bristling cavalry that appears incongruously behind the classical figures don't owe something to Rubens's response to contemporary history?

This isn't just a quibble about wall captions. It's hard to think of a painterly career more tightly entwined with the great events of his time, as well as with the classical pedigree of his craft. And many of those events go straight to the heart of his 'making'. Rubens, after all, first became an artist in Antwerp – a city in which the legitimacy or illegitimacy of sacred image-making had driven men to violence. Nine years before Rubens was born, Calvinist iconoclasts had smashed statues, ripped paintings from the walls of the cathedral. There was a Catholic restoration, but before Rubens was apprenticed there had been another return of Protestant whitewash before it was finally and permanently restored to the Catholic Counter-Reformation. So the intense fervour of Rubens's religious painting is not just art, but spiritual weaponry. And his early career is as much a journey through a war zone as a prolonged exercise in the absorption of classicism.

In fact, the formative period in Italy from 1600 to 1608 is problematic in ways more fascinating than a genealogy of influences can possibly suggest. Like all aspiring artists in Rome, Rubens devoted himself to studying the sculptured riches of antiquity and duly drew the usual suspects: the *Farnese Hercules*, the *Laocoön*, the *Apollo Belvedere*. But the curators are right to insist on his brilliantly expressive amendments, all designed with a view to animating the sculpture. According to his eighteenth-century admirer Roger de Piles, Rubens warned against 'the effect of stone'. He undoubtedly agreed with his brother Philip who wrote to him: 'Away with that apathy which turns men not into human beings but rather into iron, into stone, a stone harder than the Niobic stone of mythology which overflowed with tears.' Rubens's work, then, became an articulate dialogue between classicism and naturalism.

It was also a decisive intervention in the stale dispute between what northern and southern painting were supposed to be. Most famously, Michelangelo, in a conversation with Francesco da Olanda, had let it be known that Flemish artists were tremendously good at painting trees and grass and peasants, the implication being that they were mere skilled illusionists rather than true artists possessed by the divinity of an idea. More than any other Flemish artist before him, Rubens would decisively overthrow the stereotype, establishing himself as a supreme history painter. Without ever apologising for his own gift for earthy naturalism (the sublime landscapist is already evident in detail from early works), he cast himself as a palette-toting humanist philosopher: the *pictor doctus*, the learned painter.

It's a pity, then, that the person most influential in this vocational reinvention − his brother Philip − is largely missing from the exhibition, notwithstanding the fact there are two group portraits that bring the brothers together, one of which happens to be a knockout masterpiece. For Rubens − unlike the archetypal caricature of the isolated melancholic genius (Michelangelo, Caravaggio, Salvator Rosa) − was the most sociable and fraternal of artists. In Rome he mixed with the likes of Dr Johannes Faber, who treated him for a bout of pleurisy and who was, among other things, a friend of Galileo, and a naturalist who had written works on dragons, serpents and parrots.

Fraternity and friendship for the Rubens brothers was not just a sentiment but a philosophy: a golden chain of connections binding like-minded men to each other, and to their teachers in the recent and remote past. The dazzlingly beautiful and moving *Four Philosophers*, painted in the year of Philip's premature death in 1611 and now in the Pitti Palace, anthologises all the deepest thoughts and emotions that made the young Rubens tick. In a classical niche is a vase of four tulips − two open, two shut − not just the northern bloom par excellence imported to the world of the classical south, but emblems of two living and two dead men. The dead are Philip and his teacher, the neo-stoic philosopher and philologist Justus Lipsius. But the chain stretches further, for behind Lipsius and beside the tulips is a bust then thought to be of Seneca, the stoic who counselled men to bend but not break under the worst that fate and history could bring your way: war, tyranny, plague and untimely death. In the end there would be redemption, so images of Roman antiquity and Roman Christianity (a marbled pillar and a view to the church of St Theodore on the Palatine) are paired, while behind the foreground figures stands the no longer quite so young Pieter Paul Rubens, swathed in black.

If the *Four Philosophers* couldn't make the journey from Florence to London, the irony is all the more acute because Rubens, as the exhibition makes clear, did a great deal of travelling before returning to fame and fortune in Antwerp in 1608. Hired by Gonzaga, the Duke of Mantua, to paint a gallery of 'beautiful women', he managed to get leave to go to Rome where he lived, eventually, with Philip in the northern artists' neighbourhood near the Piazza del Popolo. Every so often he would report back to Mantua, sometimes travelling with the Duke to Genoa. There he painted stunning full-length portraits of Genoese aristocratic women, one of which shines in this exhibition: it is a piece of unapologetic costume glamour, the sumptuously loaded brush creamily caressing its subject. Rubens made studies of the Genoese palazzi and obviously loved the flash opulence of a banking republic in which brassy glitz was made elegant by the trappings of classical grandeur. It was like home, but with pomegranates and parrots rather than cheese and ale.

However, official travel brought trials that would test Rubens's neostoical powers of resilience. Sent by the Duke of Mantua with a gift package for the King of Spain and his favourite, the Duke of Lerma (the usual thing – crystal vases full of rare perfume, horses so glossy and well bred they travelled inside their own carriages, original paintings and copies), Rubens endured the nightmare of unpacking the art to find it half-destroyed by damp. The Mantuan minister, who didn't much care for this wet-behind-the-ears envoy displacing him, suggested that he rush off a landscape or two the way Flemings did. Instead Rubens painted the *Heraclitus and Democritus* included in this show, not just to display his philosophical credentials, but – since one scowls and the other laughs at the twists of fate and follies of men – perhaps also as a wry piece of autobiography. The artist who one day would enjoy his reputation as the prince of painters and the painter of princes already knew how to handle power.

None of this would matter were he not also on his way to becoming a great history painter, which is to say the artist of spellbinding altarpieces. Back in Rome, he was lucky with his timing. The Oratorian order was looking for someone to decorate their church. Annibale Carracci had given up painting, Caravaggio was on the run and Guido Reni was too untested. Rubens had his chance: he took several cracks at it and, when it failed because of the intense reflectiveness of the light, took out his neo-stoic manual of adaptability and did them something on slate instead.

Then he returned to Antwerp, breathing a little freer after the conclusion of a truce with the Dutch. In two years he knocked off two transcendent masterpieces – the *Raising of the Cross* and the *Descent from the Cross* – which, if all other Rubens paintings were to go up in flames, would still ensure his claim on the adulation of posterity. Of course, those altarpieces, which are triptychs in the old Flemish style, can't travel. But the National Gallery exhibition provides a rich insight into the ways in which Rubens worked towards what became the grand spiritual machines of the big altarpieces, by means of preliminary studies, drawings, sketches and the 'pocketbook' in which he encyclopaedically gathered images, organised by subject.

What is so striking about those multiple try-outs is the way in which the improvisatory freedom – the rushing force of the pen and brush – manage to be translated so completely to the large-scale works. Rubens's hand flies, but the works are in the best sense weighty, whether conveying the agonising upward heave of the cross – all sweat and raw sinew – or the burden of the crucified Christ dropping onto the blood-red caped figure of John the Evangelist.

The best passages are classicism fleshed out by naturalism: a barking hound, a winding cloth gripped in the teeth of someone at the head of the cross; brutality and pathos, momentum and stillness held in perfect equipoise. For these moments alone it's worth trekking through the mediocre apprentice pieces, and hacking aside the underbrush of scholarly interventions, to get to those stupendous instants when, in front of his *Massacre of the Innocents* or *The Death of Hippolytus*, your eyes widen, your pulse races and you agree that the master has indeed been made.

Turner and the Drama of History

New Yorker, 24 September 2007

Poor old Turner: one minute the critics were singing his praises, the next they were berating him for being senile or infantile, or both. No great painter suffered as much from excesses of adulation and execration, sometimes for the same painting. *Slavers Throwing Overboard the Dead and Dying – Typhoon Coming On* had, on its appearance at the Royal Academy, in 1840, been mocked by the reviewers as 'the contents of a spittoon', a 'gross outrage to nature', and so on. The critic of *The Times* thought the seven pictures – including *Slavers* – that Turner sent to the Royal Academy that year were such 'detestable absurdities' that 'it is surprising the [selection] committee have suffered their walls to be disgraced with the dotage of his experiments'. John Ruskin, who had been given *Slavers* by his father and had appointed himself Turner's paladin, not only went overboard in praise of his hero, but drowned in the ocean of his own hyperbole. In the first edition of *Modern Painters* (1843), Ruskin, then all of twenty-four, sternly informed the hacks that 'their duty is not to pronounce opinions upon the work of a man who has walked with nature three-score years; but to impress upon the public the respect with which they [the works] are to be received'.

The reasons for both the sanctification and the denunciation were more or less the same: Turner's preference for poetic atmospherics over narrative clarity, his infatuation with the operation of light rather than with the objects it illuminated. His love affair with gauzy obscurity, his resistance to customary definitions of contour and line, his shameless rejoicing in the mucky density of oils or in the wayward leaks and bleeds of watercolours – these were condemned as reprehensible self-indulgence. Sir George Beaumont, collector, patron and, as he supposed, arbiter of British taste, complained noisily of Turner's 'vicious practice' and dismissed his handling of the paint surface as

'comparatively, blots'. The caustic essayist William Hazlitt was especially troubled by Turner's relish of visual ambiguity: the sharp line
melting into the swimming ether. Contrary to Ruskin, Hazlitt thought
it was unseemly for Turner to fancy himself playing God, reprising
the primordial flux of Creation. Someone, Hazlitt commented, had
said that his landscapes 'were pictures of nothing and very like'.

But that is precisely what we *do* like, do we not? Turner's art of conjuring something from nothing, and then (unlike God) having the temerity
to deposit the working trace of that mysterious process on the canvas,
has made him a paragon for modernists. He seems to have understood
picturing as a collaborative process between the artist's hand and the
beholder's eye, in which the former laid down suggestive elements and
the imaginative observer assembled them in his mind to make a coherent subject. Sometimes he would help the process along, sometimes not.
But he was much taken by the indeterminacy of the exercise, by forms
that escaped resolution. The sobriety of the hard edge became, one has
to think, a sign of conceptual banality, a weakness in the mind's eye. For
him the purest form, and one that he repeatedly returned to, was also
the most naturally unstable: the rainbow.

Taken to task by an American buyer for the indistinctness of the
very beautiful 1832 painting *Staffa, Fingal's Cave* – Hebridean cliffs
veiled by streaming rain and sea spray – Turner, through an intermediary, begged the American's pardon, for 'indistinctness is my fault'.
But, as that vice turned – for his modernist apostles – into a virtue,
the script changed, and Turner was apocryphally made over into the
defiant independent who had wanted the American to know that
'indistinctness is my *forte*'.

It's often said that Turner had only two true subjects: the anatomy
of light and what Ruskin nicely called the 'palpitating' vitality of paint
itself. His learned preoccupation with optics, the struggles to analyse
and represent the diffusion of light, fathered a poetry of radiance, and
grandfathers him into the ancestry of Impressionism; his emotively
weighty manipulation of pigment did the same for Expressionism. So
it is the Turners that most affronted the stuffy Victorians, mired as
they were in anecdotal sentimentality and ponderous literalism, with
which we most easily identify: pictures big with prophetic courage,
the inkling of an alternative life for paint. With Turner, so this story
goes, the story doesn't matter; it's the opera of the drenching colours,

the unloosed play of the brush, the gouge of his untrimmed thumb-nail scoring a groove through the sticky pigment — that's his claim to immortality. Why should he give a fig about all those gods and heroes and Scriptures and battles?

Except that he did, obstinately and passionately, as the National Gallery's show in Washington blazingly demonstrates. The procession of phenomenal narrative pictures that constitute its core makes it clear that we do Turner no favours by pinning the tinny little medal of First Modernist on him. Subject matter meant a great deal to him, and if claiming him for the poetry or the physics of light blinds us to the seriousness with which he yearned to be Britain's first great history painter, he would not have thanked us. What, I believe, he wanted us to see was that, as far as the monumental oils were concerned, all his radical formal experimentation — the trowellings and the 'mortary' quality of the paint surface that his critics complained of, the scrap-ings and rubbings and stainings — was at the service of those grand narratives. It's correct to think of light as his subject, but when he was most ambitious, light was a protagonist in an epic narrative of creation and destruction — an Anglo-Zoroastrian burn-out.

Regulus, for example, tells a gruesome tale probably drawn from Oliver Goldsmith's *Roman History*, which Turner had in his library. The tragic hero Marcus Atilius Regulus was a Roman consul-general who, captured by the Carthaginians in the First Punic War, was released on parole and sent home to persuade his countrymen to sue for peace. Instead, Regulus urged the Senate to fight on, but, being an honourable gent, returned to Carthage to face the music. To punish him for violating their trust, his captors cut off his eyelids and stood him in the noon sun to go blind. Then they locked him in a barrel with the nails pointing inwards to finish the job.

Turner originally painted the picture in 1828 in Rome, where he took a lot of abuse for histories in which you couldn't make head nor tail of the action. Stung by the criticism, Turner shelved the paint-ing until, nine years later, he sent it to the winter show of the British Institution, in Pall Mall. There, according to contemporary witnesses, he confounded his peers by coating the picture with lumps of flake-white: 'He had two or three biggish hog [bristle] tools to work with and with these he was driving the white into all the hollows, and every part of the surface. This was the only work he did, and it was the finishing stroke.' At the end of the attack, the sun, a fellow Academician reported, was a protruding disc of pigment like a 'boss on a shield'. Even though the white has yellowed somewhat, we can still see this intervention as an enactment of what happened to Regulus: the scalding of the retina, the light that switches off vision – white-out. Viewers complained that Regulus was nowhere to be found, but although there is a characteristically perverse miniature figure that might conceivably answer to the tragic hero, it's more likely that Turner simply virtualised him into the murderous glare. That heavy-handed business with the white pigment wasn't just a proto-Expressionist performance, but a calculated fit between manner and matter.

For Turner, light was not just the enabler of vision. Especially in his histories, he conceived of it as a dramatic actor: the vehicle of emotive as well as optical illumination; the agency of romantic disorientation or, in its absence, the demon of eclipse. And all these states of vision were personal and local, the spectacles of his own story. For Turner, the ultimate subject was always the history of Britain, and he felt that subject in his marrow. Yes, he travelled, relentlessly. Yes, there was Venice and Mount Cenis, and the Loire and the Alps, the Rhine and the Rhône and the Seine. But he always came home; at heart he was a self-conscious British patriot and, more than that, a Londoner, born and bred a five-minute walk from the Thames.

He was born on St George's Day, 23 April, celebrated as the birthday of both Shakespeare and the Prince of Wales. It was the spring of 1775, the week of the 'shot heard round the world' at Lexington Green. So he came to maturity when Britain, shaken by the American debacle, turned to territorial memory for a romantically reinvented bond of nationhood. Geography was history and history was destiny. The young Turner, tramping the countryside in the 1790s, often sketched or painted in watercolours Gothic ruins or vaults where balladeers imagined ancient canticles being moaned in the moonbeams, mossy limestone crypts housing the sleep of ancestors: Ewenny Priory, Tintern Abbey, Stonehenge. The Napoleonic Wars triggered a burst of antiquarianism; greaves and helmets long rusted shut were extracted from dung-floored barns, given a lick of grease and polish, and reassembled to stand guard in the manorial hall.

Commercially astute, Turner knew that there was a ready market for this fabulous junk, but, in any case, he loved it himself. When, in 1802, it was time for a submission that would mark his acceptance as a full member of the Royal Academy, he offered a bardic romance: Dolbadern Castle, in Wales, the prison of the Welsh prince Owain ap Gruffydd, who had been locked up by his brother Llywelyn. The ruin was just a plain circular tower squatting on a modest hillock, but Turner gave it the full Romantic treatment, upping the altitude, lowering the point of view, backlighting the tower and setting it on a plinth of rock, crowned with scudding clouds. As in *Regulus*, the tragic hero of Dolbadern became virtualised, personified this time in craggy stone, not blinding light. Turner was interested not in the deeds of the heroes, but, rather, in the ways in which their memory might be visually transmitted to posterity. It was as though mere flesh and blood, however handsomely booted and spurred, weren't quite sufficient, and neither was the art that purported to celebrate them – better to embody them in rocks and ruins.

His approach to war, too, was radically unheroic. The norm for battle pieces was to memorialise the genius of command and the gallantry of the ranks. Turner had tried this, in 1800, with an innocuous version of the battle of Seringapatam, in southern India, where serried lines of scarlet coats advance on the distant citadel of the Sultan of Mysore. But what he really liked, in common with much of the British public, was a good disaster. Around 1805, a series of calamities – the Plagues of Egypt, the destruction of Sodom, shipwrecks, the panic-stricken and the prostrate – begin to populate his large dark, thunderstruck canvases. In all these gloomy efforts, the human figures are limp, almost invertebrate, their faces summarised in a few caricatural strokes and their bodies weirdly attenuated, as if in a new Mannerism. Turner was not, as sometimes charged, an incompetent figure painter. He had spent years in academic drawing and in his early career had produced conventionally modelled studies. But when it came to the big oils he chose to stylise them, as if in self-conscious repudiation of the classical tradition. (And here it does seem legitimate to see that rejection inaugurating something that would end up with Matisse's *La Danse* or *Les Demoiselles d'Avignon*.) For Turner, the distortions were the agents of narrative: the representation of the figure as victim, the disarticulated plaything of history's mischief.

In the case of the spectacular action painting *The Battle of Trafal-*

gar, Turner did his homework, going to Sheerness to see the hulk of Nelson's flagship, HMS *Victory*, and carefully sketching its splintered beams. But he threw the research away to compose, in 1806, an astounding enactment of the chaos of war at sea, using a viewpoint high up in the mizzenmast shrouds, where, although ostensibly on the British man-of-war, the beholder can as easily imagine himself in the roost of the French sharpshooter who kills Nelson. The entanglement of the ships of the line, like so many lumbering dinosaurs locked in belligerent slaughter, is described through an inchoate massing of sails, each impossible to connect to any vessel in particular. It's a maritime traffic jam, a smoke-choked pile-up with nowhere to go, no visible stretch of *sea*! And, in case people weren't already confused, Turner made matters worse by collapsing two discrete consecutive episodes into one: the French surrender, indicated by the tricolour laid on the deck of Nelson's flagship, and the canonical climax of Trafalgar, Nelson dying, stretched out amid the huddle of his grieving officers. *Victory*'s victory becomes pyrrhic, the tragedy embittering the triumph.

The Duke of Wellington fared no better than Nelson. In 1817, Turner, after visiting the site of the bloody victory over Napoleon, at Waterloo, chose instead to paint the harrowing aftermath: a nocturnal carpet of corpses lit by the sulphurous glare of a rocket, with grieving wives and sweethearts, some of them carrying infants, searching desperately through the human debris. It is a return to the distraught Niobes of the Greeks, the wailing woman as personification of calamity.

Tragic poundings — fires that cleansed, extinctions that were the prelude to rebirths — became the great theme of Turner's mature epics. It was as though the life cycle of the man born on Shakespeare's birthday were an emblem of England's own fate: history written on the body. Turner was tormented by asthmatic wheezes and joint pains, for which he took the narcotic herb thorn apple (consumed daily through the goop that accumulated in the bowl of his pipe). As middle age advanced, he felt a steady drumbeat of decease, the winnowing of those closest to him. In 1825, his patron and first great collector, the Yorkshireman Walter Fawkes, radical in politics and hospitable in character, died in debt; then, in 1829, Old Dad, whom the son had shamelessly exploited as factotum and workhorse, but who had also been his bosom friend; then the heavily landed connoisseur and collector (of women as well as of pictures) George Wyndham, the Third Earl of Egremont, who, after Fawkes's death, had made Turner his house artist, giving him lodging and studio space. In return, he painted, rather ambiguously, a series of glimmering rectangular views of house and park and some of the Earl's business enterprises – such as the Chichester Canal and the Brighton Chain Pier – designed to be set in the panelled walls of the dining room. Two of those paintings Turner elongated, the fish-eye vision emptying the frame and lending the space a sombre fatefulness. The canal is aligned ninety degrees to the picture plane, and, on it, a little man hunched in a coat, a battered hat on his head, sits in a rowboat fishing – one of Turner's favourite pursuits – as a black-sailed brig moves ominously towards us, an allegorical self-portrait smuggled into the commission. A note of elegy seems to hang over Turner's work for Egremont. After going to the Earl's funeral, in 1837, he painted one of the house's great rooms in wild disarray, as if the aristocratic world that the Earl embodied had been attacked by an invasion of light.

Such alterations exercised the most strenuous minds of early Victorian Britain. Many of them, like the architect A. W. N. Pugin and Thomas Carlyle, eulogised what they imagined to be a lost, devotional, architecturally Perpendicular, Christian Albion and waxed wrathful about the materialist hell of the Age of Machinery, with its philistine utilitarianism and worship of what Ruskin, the sherry merchant's son, called, contemptuously, 'the goddess of Getting-On'. In an implausible overreading of *The Goddess of Discord Choosing the Apple of Contention in the Garden of the Hesperides*, Ruskin recruited Turner as an anti-capitalist, but the truth is that his mills were usually neither dark nor satanic. His sketch of the town of Dudley, made around 1830, when the possibility of an English revolution hung in the air along with bituminous fumes, gives obvious prominence to the emblems of an older world – church and castle barely holding their own amid the chimneys. Consuming fires, Turner seems to have thought, were just the medium through which the country had to pass to come to a new national life.

When the Houses of Parliament caught fire, on the night of 16 October 1834, Turner, along with a throng of fellow Londoners, rushed to see the spectacular inferno. Hiring a boat, he bobbed back and forth, riding the tide, at Westminster Bridge. There had been no foul play, but, since a Parliamentary Reform Act had been passed just two years before, amid loudly voiced fears that, unless it was legislated, the kingdom might, like France in 1830, go down in bloody revolution, the relationship between rulers and ruled was in perilous play. A dominating feature of the two *Burning of the Houses of Lords and Commons* paintings that resulted – one now in Cleveland and one in Philadelphia – is the crowds jamming the embankment and Westminster Bridge, watching, fixedly, the cremation of 'Old Corruption'.

This is another authentic first – the painting of the People. Turner was putting on canvas Burke's definition of representative government as a contract between the past and the present. The past is embodied, as if in a Gothic allegory, in the spectacle of the purifying inferno. In the Philadelphia painting, Turner has augmented this feeling of a political altarpiece by turning Westminster Bridge into a structure that seems cut from alabaster rather than limestone, and appears to liquefy into the flame-tinted water at its far end. But the two pictures also look forward to the great issue of the nineteenth century: the test of popular legitimacy. In the Cleveland painting (the two are united in the National Gallery show), Turner broadens the river so that he can give prominence to the rapt masses in the foreground, dramatising their distance from the burning palace of Westminster. One figure, enigmatically, holds up a sign that reads, simply, 'NO'. This does not make Turner some sort of socialist. It is still Britain, and auspicious unrevolutionary stars are twinkling above the Thames. But the poetics of power did absorb him. And although we often think of Turner as the lyricist of the empty landscape, the truth is that the other Turner, the denizen of the London alleys and pubs, was truly Hogarth's heir, with an unerring instinct for the crowd as social animal.

Every so often, that public-minded, historically fretful Turner thought that Britain should confront ugly truths. The doomed *Slavers* was conceived in just such a proselytising spirit and timed for 1840, the year an abolitionist congress was to be convened in London. But Turner's ambition for a history painting that would achieve, through the medium of marine catastrophe, a moral reckoning had been rehearsed around 1835.

He was, once again, playing with fire, and although that 1835 picture is in a radically incomplete state, it's the skeleton of a masterpiece. Flecked with gobs of phosphorescent cinders raining down from the sky into a storm-churned sea, the huge composition was traditionally given the title *Fire at Sea*. For years, it was underrated and underread as a rough sketch. It is in the National Gallery show, where visitors will find it described as *Disaster at Sea*, which is right, but not right enough. Fifteen years ago the scholar Cecilia Powell recognised that the work depicted an actual calamity, or, rather, a crime: the sinking of the *Amphitrite*, in September 1833. Powell made one simple, vital connection that hadn't been noticed before: the frantic figures wrapped about the broken mast and fallen spars of the rapidly sinking wreck are all women and small children. The *Amphitrite* was a convict ship transporting female prisoners and their infants to the penal settlement in New South Wales. Driven off course by a storm in the Channel, it ran aground near Boulogne and began to break up. It was close enough for appalled French witnesses to offer assistance, but the captain, evidently a stickler for the rulebook, declined, on the ground that he had no authority to land his charges anywhere but their Antipodean prison. He battened down the hatches to prevent just such an escape. In desperation, the women broke through, but to no avail. Though one Frenchman actually swam out to the ship with a line, all of the more than 100 women and children drowned. Three crew survived.

The atrocity was widely reported in the press. Ballads were written and sung about it. Turner could not possibly have missed it, and he responded with a painting of timeless tragic power: the *Guernica* of nineteenth-century British art. The bodies are a curling ribbon of writhing, pathetic, naked *women*, arms flung out to the babes who slip from them into the sea for which – in the transparent film of water washing over a spar – the painter deployed all the prodigious gifts of the illusionism he was thought to have abandoned for poetically pretentious freedom. Turner's bodies are already bobbing flotsam. They are helpless, ugly, manic, and they tear us apart. Our mere witness seems to implicate us in the enormity of the cruelty, the proper effect of all great histories from Caravaggio to Picasso. The pity of the thing is relentless, because of the phenomenal coherence of Turner's draughtsmanship, the violence of the storm and the desperation of the victims – who should be flying away, centrifugally, but instead are sucked into the whorl of the merciless elements.

We'll never know why Turner never finished or exhibited the painting. Perhaps he did finish it and this is it. At any rate, the *Amphitrite* was among the 300 or so oils left in his studio when he died, in 1851, and so it was included in his bequest to the nation. Turner was the first painter in the history of art to give his work to the public, rather than to a church or a patron – and this, too, speaks to the intensity of his devotion to the cultural life of the British people. Ruskin was at least right about that.

In the century and a half since Turner was buried, in St Paul's Cathedral, the British have loved him with a grateful ardour that has nothing to do with his place in the genealogy of modernism and everything to do with the poetic visualisation of their history. The year before last, BBC Radio 4 asked listeners to vote for the greatest painting – from anywhere in the world, any time. The hot candidate was, unsurprisingly, Constable's *Hay Wain*, that carthorse idyll by a plashy stream that seems to preserve the English countryside, in all its cowparsley, humming-bee, *Wind in the Willows* summery splendour for ever and ever, amen. But the winner was Turner's *The Fighting Temeraire Tugged to Her Last Berth to Be Broken Up* (1838), a painting not about the embalming of the British past, but about its unsentimental coupling with the future.

Although the sky over the Thames is saturated with a nectarine sunset that seems to mourn the passing of the timber veteran of Trafalgar, reduced to a pallid phantom (Turner, as always, taking liberties), its masts and furled sails are restored as it is tugged to Beatson's breakers' yard, at Rotherhithe. Thackeray, who adored the painting, assumed that Turner had cast the tugboat as the gnomic villain of the piece, dragging the valetudinarian to its last indignity. But Turner – especially in his own last years – was not at all hostile to the incoming empire of technology. Quite the opposite: he believed that the speeding train or the chugging paddle steamer could be turned into a visual lyric that married time with motion. For that matter, since the two vessels are sailing upstream, and thus westwards, the vermilion sky behind them, in the east, may actually be a sun*rise*, a fanfare for the future, not a dirge for the past. That's the wonderful thing about being British: you can never really tell which is which.

James Ensor at MoMA

Financial Times, 3 July 2009

Oh BELGIUM, man! was Zaphod Beeblebrox's oath of choice when his two heads were pushed right to the edge. But if *The Hitchhiker's Guide to the Galaxy* meant the curse to suggest rain-soaked tedium relieved by stabs of edgy peculiarity, it got Belgium wrong, the tedium bit anyway. This is the country that gave us Bosch and Magritte and, right in between, the feverish thing that was James Ensor. By turns lurid, lyrical, mysterious, sophomorically satirical, intimate, raucous, cerebral, macabre, tender, narcissistic, suicidal, iconoclastic, reverent, supersaturated and washed out — and that's just in the first fifteen years of a half-century career — Ensor is the figure no conscientious chronicler of the birth pangs of modernism can afford to overlook, but also the one whom no one has any idea what to do with.

So good for New York's Museum of Modern Art (MoMA) for giving him the first major show in a very long time, even though the curatorial effort to plug him into the genealogy of modern art turns out to be a futile enterprise. He's catnip for the ism-hunter, since he could do the lot. So the wall-captions and the catalogue assiduously nail this and that picture to the ism *du jour* — Impressionism, Expressionism, realism, surrealism, slathery tachism and pretentious symbolism. But his sensibility was as twitchy as a bat, swooping out of the air and vacuuming up whatever took his fancy on any particular Tuesday.

His whole career, at least the interesting two decades of it, was one long carnival guffaw at the higher seriousness of modernism. You can almost hear the kitschily raffish self-portrait — Rubens on absinthe, crowned by a Quentin Crisp snapbrim trilby, primroses bursting from the hatband — squeal with giggles from the wall at the solemnity of the installation. *Oh Belgium, man!*

And not just Belgium, but Ostend: the place you went to for marine calm when Brussels was just too much fun. Which is what Ensor did after a short stint at the École des Beaux-Arts, where he rehearsed a lifetime's habit of getting on everyone's nerves.

King Leopold's Brussels, grown fat on a deadly combination of voracious African imperialism, Liegeois coal and local waffles, was a pincushion for the avant-garde. Its luminaries — the group who called themselves 'Les Vingt' and their critic-patriarch Emile Verhaeren — were alert to anything, within and without their borders, that would shred the overstuffed upholstery of bourgeois academicism. It was Verhaeren who wrote the first gushing review of Van Gogh and who wanted Ensor to exhibit with Les Vingt. He became one of their number, but was never a team player. So in 1880, when antsy modernists were hungering for a spell in the South Seas or the boulevards of Paris, Ensor returned to his native town of Ostend, from which he would seldom budge for the seven decades of the rest of his life.

Which is not to say that Ostend was a dull backwater of a middling province of a Lilliputian kingdom. It boasted a small-time bohemia, oompah and pickled herring on the promenades, chalky Pierrots and madcap Punchinellos; it had beer and bathing huts and curio shops, one of which was owned by Madame Ensor, James's doughty Flemish mother. His father, not so doughty, was an Englishman of means who no longer had them, and had wanted to plant a theatrical sense of himself between the salt marshes and the slate-coloured sea. In their artist son, the two parental tempers — morose and exuberant — bounced off each other, with mood-swinging results.

The twenty-year-old James moved into the loft above the novelty shop and plundered its inventory, especially its grinning or wailing masks, to brilliantly histrionic effect. It wasn't an especially profound or original insight, the Ensorian perception that the grimacing carnival mask might express the Real Persona while the flesh-and-blood face was merely the mask of social convenience, but only Goya and Daumier had made the masquerade such a penetrating genre of psychological portraiture.

Did the obsession with masks actually produce compelling art? The answers in the MoMA show will surprise anyone who thinks they know the mischievous Monsieur Ensor well. *The Scandalised Masks* (1883) is a throwback to the seventeenth-century genre painting of Adriaen Brouwer (for all his antic iconoclasm, Ensor was a great archivist of the Netherlandish tradition), with the startling difference that instead of two *boers* in a tavern, a half-doped snout-nose looks up to see a clogged and bonneted woman, sinister in dark glasses, coming through a door, clasping a wind instrument. Her gesture, also drawn from low-life painting, is unsubtle, the invitation more ominously castrating than seductive.

Much dalliance with intimiste Impressionism follows, with Ensor freckling his light through the tufty woollen gloom of Ostend parlours. But one stunningly weird picture, called, as if to provoke the burghers, *Lady in Distress* (1882), promises something unsavoury: a Sickert of the dank seaside. She's not so much In Distress as completely out of it: eyes half-closed, body sunk into the feather-bedding as if awaiting a shroud. One window is draped with a sallow fabric; at another, the curtain is pulled back, its swag hooked to the wall. But the light coming through the exposed pane is painted with a clotted flake-white impasto, while the backlight behind the closed drape is suggested by the thinnest of paint stains, scraped back with palette knife and brush handle. Light is dark and dark is light. Welcome to Ensor's *univers pervers*.

Occasionally Ensor takes it easy, and the results are breathtaking. The enormous *Rooftops of Ostend* (1884) is Turner meets Jacob van Ruisdael, yet somehow translated into an idiom that was all Ensor's own. The sky, cerulean and pink, creamy and dove-grey, covers seven-eighths of the canvas, and is passionately worked with the palette knife and broad brush, while the crowded roofs below, in their contrapuntal dance of planes, anticipate Cubist townscapes.

But Ensor didn't give a hoot for where he was supposed to stand in the face-off between tradition and modernity. Another revelation of the show is the enormous, monumental charcoal drawings, with their multiple quotations from Ensor's art-god, Rembrandt. Ostensibly scenes from the New Testament, they are set by the artist in a Belgian carnival, complete with high-hatted bandsmen. And if the loss of the Son of God amid the seething throng seems a modern caprice, Ensor knew very well that it looked back to swarming pictures by Bosch and Bruegel, in which the indifferent brutality of the crowd engulfs the redemptive presence of the Saviour.

Ensor himself never really felt redeemed, and after a while the jokes in which genre figures, and his own self-portraits, are replaced by skeletons wear even thinner than the rattle of bones. His mind was too frantic, its demonic energy never crystallising around a painterly language in which form and content marry without acts of self-conscious main-force. He means to jangle, but in the end the cacophony enervates rather than illuminates.

Every so often, though, there are treats when he seems to reach back to the boy who must have watched the waves roll in to the beach: a little version of the Battle of Waterloo, with numberless toy-soldier riders hurled against each other, and, at the other extreme, a cartoon-ish beach scene, complete with smiley-faced Mr Sun, an array of bathing huts, the dip and bounce of beach bums, two men snogging in the foreground – the whole 'ooh missus' malarkey of the thing a little cartwheel of pictorial joy. And you think, this may not be vanguard art, but it has the quick of life in it.

Rembrandt's Ghost

New Yorker, 26 March 2007

In April 1973, the month that Picasso died, he was asked to choose an image to be used as a poster for a show of recent work at the Palace of the Popes, in Avignon. He picked *The Young Painter*, an oil sketch he'd done a year earlier, at the age of ninety – a vision of his dewy beginnings, not his bitter end. The look is naive and apparently artless, but the hand that draws it is heavy with memories, not just of a Barcelona boyhood, but of the archive of painting. The apple-cheeked youth recalls another young painter at the outset of his career, the twenty-three-year-old Rembrandt, picturing himself and his calling around 1629, in a panel not much bigger than this page. The faces are unmistakably similar: gingerbread-clownish beneath a wide-brimmed hat; snub nose; eyes stylised as ogling black holes, as if drawn by a child. The captured moment, in both images, is solemn; the young men pause before their work, brushes in hand, as if locked in a creative trance. A raking light, the illumination of an idea, strikes their faces. 'I don't paint what I see,' Picasso was given to saying. 'I paint what I know.' Rembrandt, his picture tells us, felt the same way: the mind instructing the hand.

It was an unlikely pairing – the cerebral modernist who had made a point of expelling sentiment from painting going wistful over the master whose every brush mark was loaded with emotion. But the fixation was real. The shelves in Picasso's studio at Mougins, in the South of France, were packed with Rembrandtiana, including all six volumes of Otto Benesch's edition of the drawings. And though Picasso could not have seen Rembrandt's little panel at first hand (it was in Boston), he must have plucked that archetypal image of setting forth from one of his books. Radical remaker of art though he was, Picasso always balanced his iconoclastic instincts with a compulsive historicism. In 1936, he had agreed to become absentee director of the Prado, while Madrid was under fascist siege. Constantly measuring himself for admission to the pantheon, Picasso evidently felt that taking down the masters also meant taking them on, and in his time he had mixed it up with, among others, Grünewald, Poussin, Cranach, Velázquez, Goya and El Greco. At the end, though, it was Rembrandt of whom, according to his friend and biographer Pierre Cabanne, he spoke 'ceaselessly'. The haunted self-portraits of those final years, all stubble and cavernous eye sockets, were surely prompted by the series of pitilessly truthful mirror images that Rembrandt executed in his last decade: a dispassionate scrutiny of time's ruin recorded in heavy jowls and pouches. Occasionally, as in the self-portrait as St Paul (in the Rijksmuseum), Rembrandt arched his eyebrows in an expression of quizzical self-recognition, the chastened sinner who might yet imagine redemption. Picasso's face-making, on the other hand, is showy with self-contempt: so many glaring skulls.

Rembrandt first appeared in Picasso's visual imagination in the 1930s, as Janie Cohen points out in her essay 'Picasso's Dialogue with Rembrandt's Art', in the volume *Etched on the Memory*, at a time when the Spanish artist was making an ambitious 'suite' of 100 prints for the dealer Ambroise Vollard. Two qualities in Rembrandt's print-making had sparked a sense of comradeship across the centuries. First, there was the experimental freedom that Rembrandt allowed himself – sketching ideas on the etching plate and then reworking them, adding other designs, sometimes related and sometimes not – so that the overall image developed organically. A 'trial' etching might have a face, a tree and a single eye (his eye) on the same plate, and Picasso imagined this multiplicity of visions as an antecedent for his collage play with discontinuous fragments of objects. But Picasso also identified with Rembrandt's complicated relationship with his models, making them objects, indistinguishably, of aesthetic curiosity and erotic possession.

Picasso's riffs on Rembrandt are all about lusty looking; in his version of Rembrandt's *Jupiter and Antiope*, he casts himself as the horned *Faun Unveiling a Sleeping Woman*, one hand lifting a bedsheet, the other reaching for a voluptuous breast. Rembrandt's original is in fact a bolder and weirder exercise in erotic inspection, the god in faun form leaning over the woman's gently exposed nakedness with an expression of disconcerting benevolence. His gaze, emphasised by a touch of deep-scored drypoint at the eyes, is concentrated entirely on the darkly cross-hatched groin, whose details Rembrandt (after Titian, the greatest soft-porn tease in art) has made tantalisingly invisible. But it's Rembrandt who takes most pains to wipe any hint of the ornamental from his nude. Antiope's chubby chin is lifted, her mouth slightly opened as if in a snore, snouty nostrils upturned, an arm wrapped about her head exposing tufts of armpit hair. Picasso, too much the fastidious classicist to linger on armpits, merely summarises the sleeper's face, in the manner of his countless nude paintings of his mistress Marie-Thérèse Walther.

These two obsessions – experimental print-making and the gaze of disingenuous desire – came together at one serendipitous moment. In 1934, while Picasso was preparing a plate with multiple profiles of Marie-Thérèse, the etching ground cracked. According to his friend and dealer Daniel-Henri Kahnweiler, Picasso improvised around the accident precisely the way Rembrandt was thought to have done in his free-form 'sketchpad' plates, some of which anthologised different images of his wife, Saskia. 'I said to myself: it's ruined,' Picasso noted. 'I'm going to do any old thing on it. I began to scribble. It became Rembrandt.' The doodle did turn into Rembrandt's face, though in all likelihood it wasn't quite the pure accident that Picasso made it out to be. Because his plate of the Marie-Thérèses recalls the Saskias, he was probably, at some level, thinking of Rembrandt before he'd even begun. But, once Rembrandt was summoned, he and Picasso became one and the same. Rembrandt's face on that etching grafts him in the prime of his smiling self-congratulation – complete with curly whiskers and feathered beret – onto the puffier, double-chinned visage of Picasso's own middle age.

Looking at these 'Rembrandt' prints a few years later, Picasso drily commented to his mistress Françoise Gilot that 'every painter takes himself for Rembrandt'. He was right. No artist in the Western canon, not Raphael, not Michelangelo, not even Goya, has been so compulsively co-opted as heroic alter ego as Rembrandt. Painters like Turner, Delacroix and Van Gogh, who self-consciously saw themselves as Rembrandt's apostles, believed that he, more than any other artist, had modelled forms with light and colour rather than with line. The luminous shimmer of paint, not the hard-edged purity of classical sculpture, was their lodestar, and no one, they thought, had liberated its radiance quite like Rembrandt.

There was, to be sure, a good deal of romantic projection involved in seeing Rembrandt as the patriarch of painterly integrity. The poignant trajectory of his biography, from precocious swagger to humiliation, satisfied a sentimental craving for punished temerity. And, while many of the early stories were fanciful (for example, his self-taught simplicity, when in fact he attended both Latin School and, briefly, Leiden University), the documented facts played directly into a narrative of heroic, if not reckless, innovation: the miller's son, mugging in the mirror to get the passions right for his history paintings, and plucked from obscurity by the Prince of Orange's talent scout; the dizzy ascent to fame and riches in money-drunk 1630s Amsterdam, the supermarket of the world; the free-spending owner of prime real estate, dressing himself and his wife in morally dubious poses; a painter who pushed conventions, especially in portraiture and group portraiture; the crash into insolvency and the death of Saskia, of children, of Hendrickje, the companion of his later years; the man, in his sixties, staring again into the mirror, the mugging gone and only humble self-recognition left.

But for every romantic who saw in this career an original free spirit, the inventor of *l'art pour l'homme*, there were severe classicists who condemned his naturalism as self-indulgence. They despised his juvenile relish for the seamier side of the human condition: urinating beggars and babies, cellulite-heavy nudes; copulating lovers in a bed, a fornicating monk in a cornfield. They detested the way he rubbed their noses in a gleeful mixture of the sacred and the profane. Was it really necessary to have a dog defecate in front of the Good Samaritan? It was precisely this contempt for academic propriety – and for the sacred hierarchy of the genres, with its disdain for importing the rawness of daily life into the refined matter of history paintings – which made Rembrandt a hero to the romantics.

The default mode of modern writing about art is to despise any notion of singularity as so much overheated genius-fetishism. So the idea that Rembrandt was the original democrat of subject matter – a maverick who flouted convention to follow the bidding of his muse, and who did push the boundaries of what painting (or, for that matter, print-making) could do well beyond any contemporary conventions –

is dismissed as sentimental anachronism. Perhaps that accounts for the fact that, during the quatercentenary commemorations of his birth, last year, so little attention was paid to what might be called 'the Rembrandt afterglow'. In this coolly empirical view, wary of perpetuating platitudes — such as his supposed indifference to the 'rules' of art, his rough way with some patrons, the self-consciously dramatic manipulation of his paint — the historical Rembrandt was attentive to his patrons and gregarious rather than misanthropic, and abided by the rules of art far more than he sought to violate them. But Gary Schwartz's superb new *The Rembrandt Book* makes plain the disputes between Rembrandt and his patrons over the displeasing difference between what they thought they had commissioned and the delivered work. So it may well be the case that Rembrandt the sociable conformist is more mythical than Rembrandt the 'heretic' (as one of his classicist critics puts it). It has never been in doubt that he wilfully offended classical principles of decorum. Fifty years ago, Seymour Slive's *Rembrandt and His Critics* analysed the strong responses to Rembrandt in the name of upholding the norms of classical decorum. Classicism's first principle decreed that only the representation of ideal forms could give art universal authority, while Rembrandt, these critics asserted, believed the opposite: that only a shockingly unedited version of natural truth could serve art's highest purpose.

This makes Picasso's attraction to Rembrandt even odder, for the Spanish artist was far more of a classicist than a Romantic. Picasso's work of the 1920s and '30s is populated by drawn and painted meditations on the endurance of classicism, and no one performed exercises in the economy of classical line with more elegant finesse. But Picasso was a classicist with a difference: an artist capable of recalling the elements of ideal form precisely in order to puncture its pretensions. Plaster busts sit in his studio across from nudes with mischievously scrambled body parts. A classical head with both eyes seen frontally but situated on a profile isn't really a classical head. The world in which he wandered was Dionysian, prowled by satyrs and Minotaurs — the ominous bestiary that modernist idealism never managed to expel. Picasso recognised in Rembrandt an ancestor of his own dangerous visual intelligence, which could move freely between the aesthetic convenience of the nude and the messier, sexier reality of the naked model: etched images of half-dressed women warming themselves by the stove. Nothing like that stripping truth would happen again until Manet and Degas.

Picasso and Matisse thought there was what they called a 'chain' that connected their understanding of modernism with certain older masters – Velázquez and Goya as well as Rembrandt – who had begun the work of having art ask awkward questions about its own conventions: in this case, the comfortable piety of the nude. That makes Rembrandt's half-naked women (except in the modesty of their undress) the true conceptual ancestors of Picasso's *Demoiselles d'Avignon*, 250 years later. So the inspirational Rembrandt might be at least as important as the historical Rembrandt.

If art's highest purpose was to make visible what Sir Joshua Reynolds called 'invariable' ideas of beauty, Rembrandt was compromised by his earthiness. If art's fulfilment came from the harmonious deployment of light and shade, Rembrandt would be found wanting for the jarring extravagance of his chiaroscuro and his contempt for subtle modulations of tone. If self-effacing absorption within the purity of art's realm was what you were after, Rembrandt's shameless appeal to the beholder, his addiction to the human theatre (often starring himself), the aggressive marks of his own heavy hand were repellently self-indulgent. Reynolds, who was both an admirer and a collector (and who painted a portrait of himself as a young man in an obviously Rembrandtian manner), nonetheless found *The Night Watch* – that explosive, centrifugal discharge of civic energy, at once brilliantly controlled and feverishly liberated – a dismaying, incoherent chaos. He also thought it 'extraordinary that Rembrandt should have taken so much pains' on the *Susanna* in the Mauritshuis in The Hague, 'and have made at last so very ugly and ill-favoured a figure'.

But Reynolds was prepared to forgive Rembrandt his excesses and his wanton disregard for proper finish, because, like many eighteenth-century writers, he considered him a master colourist. When the Romantics acclaimed Rembrandt as an unsurpassed dramatist of light and colour, they turned on its head the assertion that his naturalism belonged to a lesser order of vision than classical idealism. Their message was: Do not confuse common subjects with prosaic painting; Rembrandt proves the opposite – that the divine lives within the husk of mortal things. The critic William Hazlitt, for whom Rembrandt was indisputably 'a man of genius', described him in 1817 as 'the least

commonplace in his grossness of all men' and 'the least fastidious of
the imitators of nature', for 'he took any object, he cared not what,
how mean soever in form, colour and expression, and from the light
and shade which he threw upon it, it came out gorgeous from his
hands'. Truth to nature, which for Hazlitt was 'the soul of art', was,
therefore, the gateway to poetic vision, not the plodding transcription
of matter.

Turner was even more emphatic. Rembrandt, he said in an 1811 lecture
to the students at the Royal Academy, threw over common subjects a 'veil
of matchless colour' so that 'the Eye dwells so completely enthrall'd [that
it] thinks it a sacrilege to pierce the mystic shell of colour in search of
form'. In other words, forget about traditional drawing and composition. It was as a painter who modelled with light that Rembrandt had
done what the critics had declared impossible – revealing, without the
clutter of symbolism, the inner mysteries of outward things, including
the human form and face. He was the perfect painter precisely because
he conveyed both surface and interior, flesh and spirit, body and mind.
While Rembrandt's earliest biographers had supposed him to be the illiterate friend of beggars and boors (and Saskia, the burgomaster's daughter,
a simple peasant girl), the nineteenth-century writers thought him a
profound thinker, *Denker und Dichter*.

They had a point. Rembrandt was, in essence, a conceptual artist,
who manifested his ideas not through classical emulation and high
finish, but through a sketchy roughness that preserved the lightning
strike of what Delacroix called the *première pensée*. It was that direct
hit of the imagining mind that distinguished true art, registering the
flux of life, its contingent, temporal quality, the buddings and shed-
dings that gave human existence its majestic poignancy. Paradoxically,
slick finish lied about nature and humanity. A broken surface, made
with slashes and stabs and unconcerned to cover every corner of the
canvas, better caught the emotive reality of lived life, an unpredictable
affair, sometimes reticently withdrawn, sometimes so exuberantly full
that it could never be contained within the hard-edged line. That was
why not just Van Gogh – a besotted idolater of Rembrandt – but a
whole succession of practitioners of the expressively loaded brush,
from Chaim Soutine to Frank Auerbach, have looked back to
Rembrandt as having struck the first great blow to rid art of the callow
equation between optical appearance and lived experience.

It was those high-minded connoisseurs the brothers Goncourt who, in 1861, spelled out the relationship between Rembrandt's athletic treatment of the paint surface and the expression of human vitality: 'Never has the human form, living and breathing and beating in the light, been conveyed by the brush as by his.' In Rembrandt's work, 'flesh is painted, heads are drawn and modelled as if they emerged physically from the canvas, through a kind of tattoo of colours, a melted mosaic, a moving swarm of dabs which seems like . . . the palpitation of skin in sunlight'.

The transference of that vitality effect from the geometric reproduction of illusory space according to the rules of Renaissance perspective to the vibrating paint surface itself was the beginning of modernism. And though the broken plumes of Titian's late brushwork and the dashes and blotches of Velázquez's painting were also unprecedented departures from high finish, Rembrandt's modernist devotees were right to hail him as their patriarch, however innocent he may have been of willed novelty. If Picasso recruited Velázquez and Manet to the modernist ancestry, how could he not see Rembrandt as the great inaugurator? All art, to some extent, attempts to stand against the transient nature of human experience by supplying an alternative vitality. But often the laborious attempt at 'lifelikeness' risks ending up duplicating deadness. Rembrandt went the opposite way, achieving unprecedented liveliness by marking his portraits with the spoiling work of time, vitality achieved through the candid acceptance of mortality. That way, the moderns correctly saw, he commanded a peerless ability to register fleshly human presence.

For instance, Rembrandt knew the ostensible truth of local colour to be less important than getting its changing tones as it passed through variations of light and shade; that way, colour itself became organic. Compositions like *The Night Watch*, he gambled, would come alive not through an accumulation of posed portraits, but through their atmospheric integration into an irregularly lit drama. The nineteenth-century painter Eugène Fromentin could not have been more mistaken when he wrote, 'The country, the place, the moment, the subject, the men, the objects have disappeared in the stormy phantasmagoria of his palette.' It was precisely because, in defiance of any precedent, Rembrandt whipped up that storm that the Amsterdam harquebusiers march from *The Night Watch* towards us, from their time to ours, with undiminished élan.

In the 1960s, after a thirty-year absence, Rembrandt came calling again, as Cohen points out, entering Picasso's increasingly morbid meditations on his own place in the pantheon. Picasso had undergone surgery for (depending on your sources) either his prostate or his bowel, but, in any case, a procedure that he thought had made him impotent. It's a commonplace that the artist who liked to masquerade as bull or Minotaur equated sexual and creative potency. (Indeed, one of the Vollard prints depicts a blind Minotaur in exactly the same attitude as the blind Tobit groping across a room in Rembrandt's etching.) If Picasso had made a variation of Rembrandt's *Bathsheba* (in the Louvre) back in the 1930s, he might have incorporated himself into the painter's-eye view, which is also King David's as he spies on the perfect nude's ablutions, watching her read his summons to the royal presence and bed. But in his post-op satirical mood Picasso gave Bathsheba the features of his wife, Jacqueline, while making himself, grotesquely, the grinning maidservant washing her mistress's feet in preparation for the royal rape.

Depicting himself as a dwarfish voyeur unmanned by the proximity of imperious nudes, Picasso had even greater need of his fantasy Rembrandt, the artist enacting his virility with his brush. Rembrandt's startling portrait of himself as the Prodigal Son, unsubtly hoisting aloft a long, cylindrical goblet of wine, while Saskia, in the guise of a plump tavern whore, perches on his lap, became in Picasso's etched version a piece of ornamental pornography. His Saskia wears high heels, tart's lipstick and a lurid grin, and, thanks to the Cubist convention of simultaneous front and rear depiction, can flash all her graphically detailed pudenda.

Picasso had become the emasculated onlooker in a perversely imagined Rembrandtian theatre of the senses; others would have to do his strutting and rutting for him. First, improbably, was the central figure in *The Night Watch*, the well-named, for Picasso's purposes, Captain Frans Banning Cocq. Sometimes Picasso would project a slide of the painting on his studio wall, and from the uproar of that scene Captain Banning Cocq would stride into his drawings, paintings and prints as the Musketeer, gripping his officer's cane, especially when confronted by a mighty nude. In one strangely beautiful aquatint, the Musketeer marches, hand on cane, not across an Amsterdam bridge, but towards another stockinged woman offering herself, thighs splayed, from within a curtained bed.

Picasso's recruitment of Rembrandt as the sponsor for his own immortalisation culminated, three years before his death, in a sacrilegious borrowing from Rembrandt's most theatrical etching, *Ecce Homo*, Pilate's display of Christ before the people. In the Rembrandt etching, the Saviour is brought out as if for a curtain call, hands bound, on a high stage; spectators look out from lead-paned windows, an ill-assorted crowd (in the first five states of the etching) jostling below. Picasso borrowed the proscenium stage show, but replaced the mocked Jesus with himself, turbaned, but pathetically reduced in stature: the impotent potentate. Gathered around him, onstage, in the stalls, peering down from the gods, is the teeming cast of characters who have populated his life and work: nudes on and off horses; incarnations of himself as diapered baby-Pablo; Pierrot-Pablo; and, in imitation of the Musketeer, spear-bearing Pablo. In place of the jeering crowd calling for the crucifixion of Jesus there is, predictably, his seraglio, etched in as many styles as he had had lovers and wives.

Self-mockery (just about) saves this 'Theatre of Picasso', as he called it, from egomania. Picasso probably knew of Rembrandt's disturbing final self-portrait, in which he posed as the Greek artist Zeuxis dying of a fit of bilious cackles as he laughed at the old woman whose portrait he was painting. Among the spectators smiling down at Picasso's final act are the bulb-nosed faces of the Rembrandt-Picasso the painter fantasised he had become.

Rembrandt had the life force in his hands, right to the end. That's why Picasso adamantly refused to think of him – or his other mentor-masters – as belonging to 'the past'. 'To me there is no past or future in art,' he said in the early 1920s. 'The art of the great painters who lived in other times is not an art of the past; perhaps it is more alive today than it ever was.' Timelessness is not always an empty cliché; sometimes, as the ninety-year-old Picasso knew when he reached towards Rembrandt as a tonic against extinction, it is full of sustaining truth.

Anselm Kiefer (1)

Guardian, 20 January 2007

How do you like your contemporary art? A quick hit of juicy mischief, a larky take on mortality, binful of bluebottles, pocketful of glitter, everything you never wanted to know and more about the artist's entrails? Right then, give Anselm Kiefer a very wide berth – because, as the show at White Cube, London, will confirm, he doesn't do droll, he does the big embarrassing stuff, the stuff that matters: the epic slaughters of the world, the incineration of the planet, apocalypse then, apocalypse often; the fragile endurance of the sacred amid the cauterised ruins of the earth.

But lately, the undertaker of history has turned gardener. From deep beneath the loam of memory heaped over the canvas, Kiefer's vast, rutted wastelands have germinated brilliant resurrections: pastel blooms, spikes of verdure sprouting irrepressibly through the skin of a hard-baked earth-rind; or peachy-pink poppies trembling atop spindly black stalks that climb gawkily from bituminous slag. So, notwithstanding the *massacre du jour* served up with the cornflakes in our daily newsprint, for Kiefer in his current redemptive temper, hope really does spring eternal.

He must be the most un-hip artist ever shown by White Cube, the very Sanhedrin of cool; barely a contemporary painter-sculptor at all, if the range framing the contemporary goes from coyly self-effacing minimalism to gaudy showboating. What's more, Kiefer does earth-space, not cyberspace. No Luddite, he nonetheless has let it be known that what he dislikes most about computers is the indiscriminate quality of their memory, a universe of data held simultaneously, accessible at the click of a mouse, permanently available and impervious to either natural attrition or poetic distortion. Since nothing may be digitally forgotten, nothing may be truly recalled.

Much of Kiefer's art represents a resistance to this inhuman virtualisation of memory; its lazy democracy of significance, its translation into weightless impressions. The opposing pole from that disposability is to make history obstinately material, laid down in dense, sedimentary deposits that demand patient, rugged excavation. Kiefer's work burrows away at time, and what it exposes also makes visible the painful toil of the dig, skinned knuckles, barked shins and all.

For a German born amid the slaughterhouses of 1945, booting up could never be glibly electronic. Kiefer became famous in the 1970s and '80s for his frontal engagements with the totems of German history: blood-spattered trails befouling the deep Teutonic woods (his name means fir tree) from which the national culture had been proverbially rough-hewn; torch-lit timbered pantheons within which heroes and anti-heroes lay provisionally interred.

By the lights of the transatlantic avant-garde, Kiefer did absolutely everything wrong. The choices were clear. Art either had to be hard-edged in its irreducibly angular minimalism, like Donald Judd's stacked boxes, which drew their ominous power from being nothing other than what they were; or else it had to be ecstatically collapsed into the raw and rowdy universe of signs: op'n'pop, flags and soup tins, one long cackle at art's valetudinarian pretence to hold the moral high ground. To grab our attention amid the modern clamour, art needed to drop the churchiness (especially abstract churchiness), and get out from under all those centuries of pompous sententiousness and obscure storytelling. All painting could be was flat-out play (with the emphasis on flat).

Wrestling with his Teutonic demons – and keeping close company with the likes of Grünewald, Altdorfer and Caspar David Friedrich – Kiefer could scarcely comprehend, much less identify with, the case for painterly amnesia, nor with the posturing for lightness and shallowness (he has never been much of a tease). Stubbornly, his art was always hewed to spatial depth and moral weight, so his landscapes take anti-flatness about as far as it can possibly go, opening immense vistas behind the picture, carved furrows on the surface stretching away to remote distance.

He does not do this innocently, of course. The practice of perspective, invented to imagine a bucolic world where pastoral fancies were enacted in a neverland of happy radiance, is recycled in Kiefer's landscapes to exterminate the fantasy. Kiefer's skies are often black, streaked with the phosphoric licks of a descending firestorm, and what vanishes at the vanishing point are the balmy consolations of rusticity. Bye-bye *Hay Wain*, hello the Somme.

Kiefer also needs immensity in order to frame the ancestral epics of life and death which for him remain art's proper quarry, and which sometimes extend beyond that far horizon into the infinite metaphysical space of the beckoning cosmos, where they interrupt the emptiness with mapped constellations. Events — scriptural, mythic, poetic, historic — are transfigured into written words on the painting, because, for Kiefer, words sanctify the events and figures to which they refer, rather than demystify them.

His seriousness about words, as weighty as the lead from which he forges his books, also puts him at odds with the ironic mode of quotation that has long defined modern art. Instead of mimicking the industrially reproduced comic signage of the mass market, Kiefer marks his pictures with the spidery inscriptions of his own hand, the moving finger quoting, inter alia: Isaiah, Paul Celan, Aeschylus. Wordiness for Kiefer is painterliness. The library and the gallery, the book and the frame inseparable, even interchangeable, in his monumental archive of human memory. Not since Picasso's *Guernica* have pictures demanded so urgently that we studiously reflect and recollect in their presence.

Which may make Kiefer's new work sound like homework (to be severely marked by the forbidding Herr Professor über-Bombast). Nah, thanks all the same, you're thinking, would rather do a day with Damien and Trace. But advance preparation in the *Iliad*, the Kabbalah, not to mention higher scriptural exegesis, is really not the price of admission. For visual drama that (I guarantee) will haunt your dreams, there's no one alive to beat Anselm Kiefer. This is because, along with being a philosopher-poet, he also happens to be a craftsman of phenomenal power and versatility.

For some time, he has been experimenting with work that crosses the boundaries separating not just art and literature, but painting and sculpture. Sometimes (as in the breathtaking *Merkaba*), a *Gesamtkunstwerk* (total artwork) brings together free-standing sculptural elements in stone or lead in continuum with a vertical painted surface, the one acting as a terrestrial transport to the celestial apparition of the other. Some of the paintings on display at White Cube sustain this working method by setting a clump of thorn bushes before an ashy-grey winterscape that speaks (much less ponderously than this makes it sound) of chill death and resurrection. But other paintings – especially in the triptych of confounding masterpieces that, alas, will be travelling to the Gallery of New South Wales in Sydney – have incorporated into the grittily loaded texture of the canvas itself a seething bed of organic (and occasionally inorganic) matter, so that the surface becomes akin to a yeasty humus; alive with golden flecks of straw and hay, twigs, whole branches which poke through the impasto. Another denial of the modernist dogma that authentic paint should never dare to present as anything other than itself.

Kiefer's paint is forthrightly the crusty medium of generation – the baked clay that develops the cracks and fissures from which vegetable life burgeons forth. Even when the paint is, in fact, just that, it is made to clot and coagulate, puddle and pond, or rise in frozen crests as if it were the volcanic material of primordial genesis.

Kiefer's painting, then, is not a representation of some feature of creation so much as a re-enactment of it. And if this sounds a mite up itself, well indeed it is, and none the worse for it. Even if you care not a toss for the esoterica, the richness of classical allusion (such as the catastrophic landscape of the fall of Troy, scarred with explosions of carbon and cobalt, and transmitted via a telephonic connection from Greek peak to peak in mimicry of Agamemnon's beacon signals to faithless Clytemnestra), you can still happily envelop yourself in the blanket of colour and line that fills every centimetre of Kiefer's pictures.

Dazzling, nostalgically psychedelic shots of colour. Beneath the verse from Isaiah that speaks of heavenly mercy, '*Rorate coeli desuper et nubes pluant*' (Drop down ye dew and let the clouds rain upon the just), Kiefer has planted a field of blazing, flamingo-tinted poppies. But the mercy is not unqualified; the flowers are marshalled along perspectival lines all the way to a horizon that is built from raised skeins of greenish-black paint, the corrupted hues of chemical pollution. (Evidently we're not in Monet's picnic country of *Les coquelicots*.) Kiefer's poppies with their black faces can be read interchangeably as columns of warriors or the floral memorials of their fiery entombment. And the petals of the middle distance suggest the flares of combat as much as a field of flowers.

The most startlingly florid of the pictures travels from a paradise garden at its base, with the caked terracotta blossoming in arabesques of brilliant violet, pink and vermilion splashes that coil through the more furrowed landscape. Above it are more verses from Isaiah that open the Palm Sunday liturgy: '*Aperiat terra et germinat Salvatorem*' (Let the earth open and bring forth a Saviour). But Kiefer being Kiefer, there needs be trouble in paradise, so that along the serpentine line of beauty lurks the form of a skeletal snake, its vertebrae constructed from a string of terracotta beads suspended on spinal wire poking from the picture surface. Good and evil, vitality and mortality, thus literally hang sinuously in the balance, it being deliberately unclear whether the serpent is safely fossilised within the sprouting clay, or has shed its casing the better to writhe into freshly devilish incarnation.

This dialogue between martyrdom and resurrection continues into the deeply stirring Palm Sunday installation: eighteen glazed cabinets that house vertically mounted branches of vegetation (mangroves, sunflower pods and dracaenae as well as palms themselves). Stacked atop each other, the cabinets seem not so much vitrines from some botanical museum as the opened pages of a herbiary, Kiefer the tree-man knowingly playing with the conceit of a super-folio, interleaved with sacred revelations. The branches are coated with a thin skin of plaster or white paint so that, at first sight, they seem bleached of life, sapless and forlornly skeletal. But the newly (if tentatively) optimistic Kiefer wants us to register Palm Sunday as a true triumph; the entry to Jerusalem inaugurating the events that lead not just to the Passion but to the Resurrection. Kiefer also knows that, in both pagan and early Christian iconography, the palm with its sword-like branches was known as an immortal tree, which never actually perished but constantly regenerated, a new sheath of fronds budding from the site of a fallen limb. The very earliest representations of the cross in the Coptic Church thus took the form of the living palm. Kiefer has also contrived to display another palm as if it were the feathers of some avian or even angelic wing; a doubly miraculous apparition which, as outsize quill, writes its own revelatory gospel behind the veiling glass.

Like the dirty fields of death sewn with floral brilliance, Kiefer's phantom tree limbs enact a parable of the intertwined fate of nature and humanity. For the erect branches lie or stand against flesh-coloured beds of sand, which in their gracefully voluptuous swirls are unmistakably feminine and invitingly sexual. In one of the most beautiful of the cases, *Hosanna*, the vegetable matter is arranged as a luxuriant pubic tangle; the *prima mater* from which life itself issues. Kiefer has managed somehow (perhaps by treating the case as a kind of bath) to run streams of graphite across the sand and then wash them out to form delicate rills that suggest the ferns and lichens of the first green life to appear on the living planet. Gustave Courbet's lavishly devotional hymn to the pudenda, *The Origin of the World*, is by contrast all frisky slickness. Instead of the erotic quiver, Kiefer gives us a heart-stopping moment, as we suddenly read those marks as simultaneously biological and cosmological, micro and macro; a vision of deltaic capillaries, the pulsing veins and branches of an estuary as seen from an orbiting camera, or up close, the fronds waving gently through a transparent wash of nourishing water.

This is as good, I think, as art ever gets: mystery and matter delivered in a rush of poetic illumination. That Kiefer's work happens to engage with almost everything that weighs upon us in our tortured age – the fate of the earth, the closeness of calamity, the desperate possibility of regeneration amid the charred and blasted ruins – and that it does so without the hobnailed tread of pedestrian polemics, is just one of the many marvels for which we have to thank, yet again, this most indefatigable of modern magi.

In Mesopotamia: Anselm Kiefer (2)

Catalogue essay for the Anselm Kiefer exhibition
Karfunkelfee and the Fertile Crescent, White Cube,
October–November 2009

Anselm Kiefer is talking about bricks. They were, he says, the first toys he remembers playing with: putting something together, one thing above the other, fashioning walls, a place of shelter. He had pulled the bricks from the debris and rubble to which his home town had been reduced by wartime bombing. As it happens, I remember something of the sort myself: my father walking me through the blackened ruins of the East End and the City of London, policemen yelling at me as I kicked balls around bomb sites. Around Stepney, houses still had whole walls torn away, the ruins looking down on patches of weedy grass and bent railings twined with convolvulus. There were piles of bricks everywhere, shattered and sooty as if refired in the kiln of the Blitz. German planes had done this to my city; our planes had done that to Kiefer's. I remember, in the short-trouser years of the early 1950s, compulsively playing with children's brick sets. The best of them boasted actual miniaturised bricks and real cement mortar that I mixed in the kitchen sink with a tiny trowel. Later came the famous Bayko brick sets, grooved Bakelite rectangles that you slid down metal rods to make small houses, or, if time and ambition allowed, mansions, factories, cathedrals. That's what kids did in the years after the war. We ran around the dim streets shouting, kicking stuff in and out of the gutters, and then we went home to build things.

One of Kiefer's perennial obsessions is how history, the Nietzschean demon of havoc, chews up habitat. The maker of art is also the tumbler of edifices. The motif stalks through Kiefer's early master-pieces of the 1970s, like the scarred and begrimed emptiness of the *Märkischer Sand* (1980), stretching to the vanishing point, so that perspective itself becomes the enabler of terror and lament. But other homelands romanticised by picturing are equally grist to the massacre mill: the woodland depth of the *Teutoburger Wald* (1978–80), for instance, where the Roman legions of Varus were annihilated by the Germanic tribes. In all these meditations on hubris, on the scarifying incisions and abrasions that power scores into the earth, houses of shelter and domination – towers, lodges, ziggurats – suffer some sort of stress fracture, from within or without. Constructed from the raw materials over which they loom – sand, clay, stone – they totter, shatter and crumble, returning to the elements from which they were constituted. Bricks that arose from mud fall back to the slather whence they came. Form loosens into unform; unform implies form.

For Kiefer, built structures – including the densely textured deposits of his own works – are always contingent and provisional, and subject to the erosion of time and the caprice of the elements, including human elements. Famous for his challenges to curatorial preciousness – in fact, to the presumption that art must be about permanence – he installs sculptures and sometimes *paintings* outdoors (in the courtyard of his Paris studio, for example) to see what the weather might do to them. (A set of his San Loretto paintings are there right now.) Air, light, wind and rain are co-opted as collaborators in this resistance to finish. Sometimes you see Kiefer's mixed-media pieces locked down in gallery space, like so many tethered King Kongs or blinded Samsons, hulking, shaking their chains, with the pent-up feel of something that wants to break out from polite enclosure. Much of Kiefer's work – like the *Shevirat Ha-Kelim* (the Breaking of the Pots) – has this uncontainable spill; a self-destabilisation, a falling off from the two-dimensional mooring of the wall into our own space.

History's dislodgements, and the subsequent reoccupations of nature, are ancient subjects for Western art – as for scripture and literature – always burdened with tragic foreknowledge. The half-built helical shell of Pieter Bruegel the Elder's *Tower of Babel* (1563) would, for any Renaissance beholder, have implied its own destruction. In Giambattista Piranesi's Roman *veduti*, the overgrown ruin, choked with creepers and bristling with moss and weed, is the subject, not the original architecture. J. M. W. Turner's *Dido Building Carthage* (1815) unsubtly foregrounds the vegetation into which the vanquished empire will decay. It was after visiting Roman ruins in Campania, at Baia and Pozzuoli, that in 1832 Thomas Cole was able to paint his moralising cycle on *The Course of Empire* for the kind of patron acutely conscious of the contingent nature of architectural pomp: the Manhattan merchant Luman Reed.

But Kiefer is acutely aware that nothing beats the twentieth and twenty-first centuries for spectacles of construction and demolition: Albert Speer and *Slaughterhouse Five*, the Kuala Lumpur Tower and 9/11; colossalism matched by incineration. But into his funeral pyres and sulphurous fields of annihilation lately has crept a note of redemptive brightness; germinations poking through the ash; blooms of sharp colour – flamingo, coral, carnation – blossoming through the sedimented strata. Destruction rains down on those big canvases, but from the cake-cracks, pits and chasms nature burgeons. And, as always in Kiefer's work, the modern loops round the aeons to be met by the primordial and mythic. Half-buried, half-exposed within the scarified fields of slaughter, trilobitic forms of early creation lurk. Lately, or so it seems to me, Kiefer's cosmology has taken an ecological turn, inflected with planetary pathos. Inside the vitrines of *Palmsonntag* (2006), Kiefer set branches of palms and other ancient trees, opened like leaves in a book and covered in a ghostly skin of plaster: the botanical lifecycle of seed and bud trapped in a pallid carapace. The beds on which these botanical phantoms arc were drifts of sand, laved in muddy water, allowed to pond and cake, resembling satellite images of deforested silted estuaries – places where human culture began and where its end might be heralded by ecological self-strangulation.

This drawing together of beginnings and endings – these sites that exist simultaneously as cradle and graveyard – continues to haunt Kiefer, caught at a moment in his own time-span when vitality and mortality are nudging up against each other more than our generation likes to admit. While he has been brooding on Mesopotamian origins and endgames, Kiefer has also been producing a series of exceptionally beautiful compositions, triptychs and diptychs enclosed in glass vitrines that revisit one of his earliest and most compulsive themes: the depths of the German woodland. This, too, has been, immemorially, a site of origination and termination. Through the 1970s, Kiefer, whose blankly scorched book was titled *The Cauterisation of the District of Buchen* (1975), returned again and again to an historical memory from which mythic tribal difference sprang: the annihilation of the Roman legions of Varus in the Teutoburger Wald by Germanic warriors. Names and portraits, rendered as if in wood-cut (and sometimes actually so), of the genealogy of this myth of beginnings – from the hero Arminius to romantic poets like Stefan George – snaked through the forest depth, and over a path spattered with blood or dirtied snow. The treatment of pictorial depth itself was a beckoning to memory, and without any consolatory implication that by taking that path some sort of healing transcendence might be achieved. Whatever Kiefer's histories are about, they certainly aren't about cheaply bought closure.

Kiefer's new work retraces some of those apparently inescapable obsessions without merely reiterating them. The form in which the woodland space is housed has changed from the implication – through the line of perspective – of interminable depth, to the box-vitrine: visible but untouchable. The tall glazed cabinets suggest the display cabinets of nineteenth-century natural historians, but, set side by side with no intervening space, also the opened pages or, as we might say, folios of a book. Memory has become, literally, boxed in; the relatively shallow space further obstructed by masses of leafless thornbush climbing the frame, interposed between the beholder and the wood-land depth. Snagged or impaled on this memory briar are doll-scale dresses and costumes, while giant cuspids – the teeth that tear, punc-ture and rend – lurk in the undergrowth. At the base of the snarled growth, memory unspools, the serpent in the garden taking the form of a length of film on which photographic images are printed on lead, Kiefer's favourite medium for embodying things that, heavy as they are, imply slippage and shape-shifting: the ultimately unfixable imprint of time.

The allusion is, of course, to another kind of literary folk memory: the fairy-tales collected and published in 1812 by the Brothers Grimm as *Kinder- und Haus-Märchen* – especially Hansel and Gretel, aban-doned by their mother to feral beasts and the infantiphage witch. (In one particularly haunting composition, Kiefer suspends a floating costume with an empty hood – half monastic habit, half rustic dress – over the wood-space; a presence equally readable as guardian spirit or demonic ghost.) The *ur*-habitat becomes a place of imperilled inno-cence; grisly outcomes postponed or executed. But it is also the primal dwelling place turned into an unsafe shelter. Kiefer figures the tree trunks with broad, slashing, pitchy-black strokes, sometimes leaning towards each other to form an arboreal pointed arch. Knowingly encyclopaedic, these 'organic' proto-architectural leanings recover an entire literature on the origins of Gothic architecture, which its eighteenth-century archivists insisted followed the spontaneous intertwinings and sylvan tunnels of the deep woods and were somehow thus normatively closer to the natural world than to the classical masonry imposed upon it. But there was as Joseph Rykwert and others have reminded us – also an extensive literature on 'primitive classicism' going all the way back to Vitruvius, claiming that its elementary forms – columns, entablature and pediment – themselves originated in rustically modified tree forms: the open-air sacred grove turned into the built temple. Republican Rome apparently preserved such a crude timber temple to remind itself amidst the pomp of its masonry of the rude origins of its virtue and power.

The fate of early dwelling places, the construction and deconstruction of the abodes of culture, seems to preoccupy Kiefer, especially when he shifts his own places of residence and work. The first time I saw his desert-pyramid forms was at the Gagosian show in downtown Manhattan in 1998; the monumental fruit of work done at Barjac in the South of France where, after a period of desolate self-mortification (as in the 1991 painting *Zwanzig Jahre Einsamkeit*), his creative drive had begun to show a phenomenal power surge. The Gagosian exhibition *Dein und mein Alter und das Alter der Welt* (Your and My Age and the Age of the World) was named after a line from Ingeborg Bachmann's poem 'Das Spiel ist aus' (1954). It enacted a monumental link between the Austrian poetess who had also been responsible for introducing German readers to the work of her lover and doomed hero, Paul Celan, whose own *Todesfuge*, written in 1945, had had an incalculable effect on Kiefer's interpretation of German fate and the Holocaust. But in the form of an immense stepped pyramid, half-lost in the swirl of sand that adhered to its abraded surface, Kiefer was also knowingly engaging with the first love poem that Celan had sent to the twenty-two-year-old Bachmann in 1948, *In Aegypten* (In Egypt), in which the old erotic-thanatic intricacies of the ashen-haired Shulamith and the golden-tressed Margareta reappeared: *Du sollst die Fremd neben am schönsten schmücken / Du sollst sie schmücken mit dem Schmerz um Ruth, um Mirjiam und Noëmie.* (Bejewel the stranger who sits beside you most beautifully / Bejewel her with pain for Ruth, for Miriam and for Naomi.) The drifts of scouring sand covering the half-built, half-unbuilt pyramid put in play the tension between solidity and instability, dwelling and rootlessness. In another poem from *Ober Gerauchschlos* (Above Soundlessness), Celan had conjured up the *Sandvolk* ('Sand people', and sometimes also 'Urn people') dwelling in an ultimately barren place beneath an unsparing sky, their lives watered by the tears of their eyes, the ground beneath their feet shifting grains.

Kiefer tells me that not one of the overwhelming paintings shown at Gagosian sold, and that, as he remembers it, the reception, even from critics who had admired his work, like Peter Schjeldahl, was largely hostile. In retrospect this seems astounding, though not surprising. The immense, half-eroded structures, which appeared simultaneously to arise from and collapse back into barren waste, constituted a one-room epic with which the usual opening-night rituals – Manhattan black kit, glasses of white wine – seemed an uncomfortable fit. The troubled-travels of Celan and Bachmann in and out of Egypt – one lover dying by water, the other by fire – could not have seemed further away, for all their inscriptions on Kiefer's great paintings.

It was a test, I suppose, of whether heavy-load maximalism could register at a time when impish minimalism was king of the contemporary art world. The union of art and history had been decreed uncool. Conceptualism sprouted even – or especially – when the concepts were themselves jejune. Desert Storm was a memory; 9/11 and another Iraq campaign were not even bellicose prophecy. One of the paintings from the 1998 exhibition, *Für Ingeborg Bachmann. Der Sand aus den Urnen* (For Ingeborg Bachmann: The Sand from the Urns), is being shown again at White Cube, where it is, however, surrounded with the brickwork paintings that make up *The Fertile Crescent* series. Seeing the stacks of Kiefer's bricks again, laid down in the sand, reminded me that on that earlier opening night in Manhattan I had thought, for some reason, of another hod-load of bricks: Carl Andre's *Equivalent VIII* (1966), bought for the Tate Gallery in 1972. The bewildered or furiously obtuse response to Andre's neatly continuous bed of 120 bricks laid on the floor forced its defenders into an explanation of serial minimalism, but it's fair to say that the high concept of art from which all trace of art-ness, as well as the shaping hand of the artist, had been expunged proved a hard sell to the narrative-hungry British public.

Kiefer, on the other hand, has consistently been the most un-modular of contemporary artists; the least likely to be satisfied with an extruded grid as a sufficient expression of immanent form; the least likely to withdraw the shaping hand of the artist from his work as if it were a contaminant. On the contrary, Kiefer's gestural brushwork is aggressively artisanal, Rembrandtesque, bereft of hard-edged rectangularities, loaded not just with the dense matter of painterly construction, but an unapologetically personal relationship with the histories therein embedded. So Kiefer's bricks are *made* in their clayey, puddly muddiness as he works. Differential drying rates echo the process by which loose clay or mud hardens and cakes, the density of the pigment forming tessellated deposits and stacks. Anything less modular could hardly be conceived of. The work both in its elements and as a whole is organic and shifting like memory itself. Bizarrely, some of it makes me think of John Ruskin's beautiful, if operatic, approach to geology in which solid rock exposes the volcanic tumult responsible for its prehistoric creation. Only Ruskin could describe slaty crystalline as 'quivering', but he would, I think, have understood and enjoyed the charge of mineral energy that Kiefer brings to his brickwork. In this sense, the fertility of Mesopotamia, the slow-motion kinesis of its estuaries, carries through to the edifices that were raised on its river banks. And as if in acknowledgement of this organic relationship with the landscape that produced the hanging gardens of Babylon or the ziggurats of Ur, Kiefer's tesserae are alive with mineral animation. Even when whole fields of them are laid down on an extensive landscape (as in fact they do dry in simple Indian brickworks), the bed, in *Ninife* (2009) for example, heaves, buckles, writhes as if the bricks and topography on which they rest undulate in erotic connection. That would indeed be the Mesopotamian way.

Kiefer's fascination with the ambiguities of construction and deconstruction lead him to treat his brickworks synecdochically; they are fragments that imply the whole. Rising stacks appear as the initial elements of an eventual pyramid; while the walls of the building behind them represent a structure that is both maker and made. Its arched openings and high walls suggest a simple brick factory akin to those which Kiefer himself saw and photographed in south India. But they also imply the grandiose imperial towers and citadels of Chaldea, Assyria and Babylon, which rose from the mudflats only to fall, each in their turn, at the hands of successor empires. The flaring, rusted, hard-fired passages in the ground of some of these paintings, or the half-ruined, ragged-edged turrets, complete the cycle of historical births and deaths in which Kiefer discovers the history of our own times as well as the archaeology of antiquity. Where writing and cultivation and law and architecture began is also where war and annihilation achieved epic consummations. In *Die Siebte Posaupe* (2009) and in the largest painting from *The Fertile Crescent* series, unmistakably fortress-like buildings shed their brick skins as if sloughing off their Babylonian power, to be reduced once more to rubble.

If this seems unsurprising in a German artist, it's not just because of a life that began its memories amidst smouldering rubble and destruction, with *Trümmerfrauen* (rubble women), sweeping amidst the debris for the bricks that might yet make an *Anfang* (beginning) out of a Ground Zero. It's also because it was German archaeology that transformed the study of the ancient Near East. 'Fertile crescent' was a phrase coined at the turn of the twentieth century by the first – and prodigious – American Egyptologist, James Henry Breasted. But the Midwestern Breasted had studied archaeology in Berlin, and his scholarly, impassioned location of the origins of 'Western' culture in the great river societies stretching from the Nile to the Euphrates was an overwhelmingly German enterprise. It was German Assyriologists like Robert Koldewey who first mapped out a credible chronology for the succession of Mesopotamian civilisations, and who also understood that the primary building element from which their mighty and fallen monuments had been made was, indeed, unfired mud brick. When he excavated cuneiform-inscribed brick vestigial walls, Koldewey believed he had discovered the Hanging Gardens of Babylon. His site was all wrong, for the Greek historian Diodorus Siculus clearly locates the gardens beside the Euphrates itself, but in most other respects Koldewey and his German colleagues got it right. The great brick walls – probably of a storehouse – were erected sometime in the reign of Nebuchadnezzar II, towards the end of the sixth century BC: the same period in which the First Temple in Jerusalem was destroyed.

More modern Assyriology has confirmed, though, that unfired

brick structures go right back to the identifiable origins of building itself; perhaps as early as the *fourteenth* century BC, according to the historian of Mesopotamian building materials, Peter Moorey. This kind of information, linking the earliest conceivable structures of shelter, power and ceremony with an unchanged technology that can still be seen today in parts of India, needless to say delights and inspires Kiefer, confirming, as it seems, the ribbon of time within which epics of construction and deconstruction – work arising from floodplain mud and returning to it – unfold along a continuous arc.

That the most recent adventure of military havoc took place in 2003 amidst utter indifference to the conservation of memory will only have reinforced Kiefer's instinct about the conjunction of disaster across the aeons.

From time to time – especially in New York – complaints are voiced about contemporary art's failure to produce some sort of adequate response to the world-shattering moment of 9/11. But it seems naive to expect an equivalent to Goya's *Third of May 1808* (1814), or Picasso's *Guernica* (1937). The risk of banal illustration and moral incommensurability with the magnitude of the massacre is great enough to persuade artists to stay their hand. But anyone in search of a resonant meditation on the instability of built grandeur, on the chronicles of heady calamitous risings and tumblings that constitute the narrative of humanity from Ur to Manhattan, would do well to look hard at Kiefer's *The Fertile Crescent*. As usual, he is incapable of making trivia.

John Virtue: The Epic of Paint

Catalogue essay for *John Virtue: London Paintings*, National Gallery, March–April 2005

There's something missing from John Virtue's skylines: the London Eye. And that's not just because he dislikes the featherlight airiness of the wheel, so at odds with his bituminous, Dante-like vision of a beaten-up, endlessly remade city of men scarred by the damage of history. Virtue's London is more battlefield than playground; his angle of vision the angel's hover rather than the child's expectation of ascent. But his aversion also stems from what the Eye represents: bubble-glazed, sound-sealed enclosure, an encapsulated rotation to postcard epiphany; sites turned into sights and those sights visually itemised rather than bodily encountered. Up it inexorably goes, carrying the happy hamsters, far, far above the grunts and grinds of the town, far, far above London. What Virtue most hates about it – I'm guessing – is its name: the presumption of vision. What his paintings do is take on the hamster wheel; insist that Virtue's vision is the real London eye. Instead of detachment there is smashmouth contact; instead of mechanically engineered, user-friendly serenity, there is the whip-saw excitement of the city; its rain-sodden, dirt-caked, foul-tempered, beery-eyed, jack-hammered, traffic-jammed nervy exhilaration. Instead of a tourist fantasy, there is a place.

These paintings are punk epics: gritty; brazen with tough truth. You don't so much look at them as collide with them; pictures which smack you into vision. This is what all strong painting is supposed to do: deliver a visceral jolt, half-pleasure-hit; half-inexplicable illumination. It's what Rubens, Rembrandt, Turner, Francis Bacon, on top form, all manage. We gasp 'knock-out' and we mean it pugilistically; that we've taken a body blow. But instead of reeling groggily under the impact, we seem to have been given, Saul-Paul-like, a brand-new set of senses. We look at the world differently, we register experience differently, and we wonder how the hell this has been done, with something so economical as canvas streaked with paint; in Virtue's case *black and white* paint? And the answer is not to credit Virtue's paint with resolving itself into something we recognise as previously seen (even if that something is Nelson's Column), but rather to realise that those painted forms are themselves the material of new vision.

Virtue's work is a stunning reminder of what truly powerful painting can yet achieve. The obituary of painting has been written so many times that declaring it premature has itself become a tedious piety. But the dirge drones on: the woebegone longing for the titans of yesteryear, for the Pollocks and de Koonings and Rothkos, under whose auspices paint, liberated from representation, did its own thing, was declared the Life Force. When the usual British suspects (Freud, Hockney, Hodgkin, Auerbach) are wheeled on for refutation of the Death of Paint, and the words 'vigorous' or 'constantly inventive' get uttered, it's with a note of gratuitous appreciation that the club of patriarchs can still turn it on, notwithstanding (it's implied) their veteran years and settled ways. There are, for sure, paint-handlers of prodigious power and originality around among the upstart young'uns – Jenny Saville; Cecily Brown; Elizabeth Peyton; and in a very different key, Rebecca Salter (notice the gender?), but it's also true that painting still seems to feel a need to make a case for itself against exhaustion. That it so often makes that case by ironising its relationship with photography – by fabricating images of such hyper-reality that their synthetic quality simultaneously owns up to the artifice of picturing while implicating photography in the duplicity – is just another symptom of painting's fragile confidence. Gerhard Richter, for instance, works in two minds and two moods: the one a defiant, slathering ooze of viscous abstraction; the other a more nervous and self-conscious dialectic with past masters (Vermeer and Van Eyck) and with today's bad news. Anselm Kiefer, on the other hand, in his most recent metaphysical venturing, has increasingly needed free-standing sculpture and sculptural effect on his canvases, if only in the cause of liquidating the formal boundaries between vision and touch.

'Pure' two-dimensional painting, at its most defensive, seems to have been boxed into a shrinking space between, on the one hand, video art and photography (against which a century ago it could unapologetically define itself) and, on the other hand, sculpture. If the nineteenth- and twentieth-century avant-garde was dominated by painting, with sculpture in an auxiliary relationship, specialising in monumental rhetorical statements whether Rodin or Henry Moore, Giacometti or Zadkine, the hierarchy in our own time seems to have been completely reversed. Whereas painting was once the medium through which the separation between the signs of the world and the work of art could be overthrown, it's usually sculpture these days which makes the most aggressively subversive moves. The fact that the definition of sculpture (Richard Serra's torques, but also Sarah Lucas's car wrecks constructed from unsmoked cigarettes) refuses nailing down only adds more kick to its anarchic exuberance. Once the solid citizen in the studio, sculpture is now the wicked imp of invention. In Britain, its compulsive leitmotif is eros and thanatos, sex and death, but with death the runaway favourite, possibly because the practitioners of the morbid joke are far enough away from its reality to be able to imagine it as a real hoot. The favoured tempers in which these endlessly reiterated obsessions are rehearsed are elegy (Rachel Whiteread) and irony (Damien Hirst).

Irony-connoisseurs are going to have slim pickings amidst the heroically rugged work of John Virtue. For his paintings have been made as if much of contemporary art, or rather the *fashion* of contemporary installation art, had never happened, or at best are a facile distraction from more solidly enduring things. Good for him. Irony is poison to his passion, for his work draws not on death, but life; in the case of the epic paintings he has made while looking at London, the life of a bruised city, caught in the warp of time. But the *élan vital* of Virtue's work also owes its strength to another celebration: of the life of paint itself. Which is why, when you look at a John Virtue, be it one of his 'landscapes' or his London pictures, you see more than the Exe Estuary or St Paul's Cathedral. You see John Virtue himself, in the act of painting, the work a permanent present participle of storming creativity. The modish word to describe such action is 'marks', but that implies discrete traces of remote activity. In Virtue's case, the more you look, the more you see the paint in a state of turbulent self-animation: dripping and drizzling, stabbing and dabbing, like a feverish sorcerer's apprentice. To say that Virtue and his work are unstoppable is to say many things, all of them apposite. But the most important tribute that can be paid to him is to acknowledge that in an art culture comatose from ironic overkill he has asked the straight question – what can paint actually do? And then he has set about supplying an unrepentant, triumphal answer.

Though Virtue's work is fashioned without any thought of the critics in his head, its implications are, in fact, momentous for the debate about the direction of painting in the digital age. The rap against Abstract Expressionism was always about its solipsism; the heady conviction that painting was no more than the manipulation of the materials which constituted it. It was at the point when freedom from figuration – the adrenaline rush of egotistical all-over energy – turned into pseudo-spiritual loftiness, especially with colour-field stainers like Morris Louis and Barnett Newman, that those who yearned for modern painting to embody visual experience of something other than itself began to complain of aesthetic asphyxiation. The take-it-or-leave-it upyoursishness of high abstraction, its priestly *noli me tangere* distance from social experience and from the indiscriminately raucous universe of signs, its warning notices posted against what it imagined to be the mindless crud of pop culture (movies, advertising, the whole gamut of capitalist gimcrackery) began to seem monastically barren. Against that visual scholasticism on rushed the storming postmodernist carnival: Johns's flags and beer cans; Rauschenberg's shrieking collages; Rosenquist's wall-length Cadillacs and mustard-loaded hot dogs; Lichtenstein's comic strip *WHAAM!* 'The world,' as Leo Steinberg nicely, but demurely, put it, 'was let back in again.' How sad, then (and in retrospect, Warhol and his factory of stoned cuteness was a culprit in this), that work made as a breakout from narcissism should somehow reinforce it, posing archly, relentlessly, mercilessly, the dullest question in the world: 'Is it art?' Surely, and I say this imploringly, we no longer give a toss?

Certainly, John Virtue has more important things to care about, perhaps the most important of all being his move to make the dichotomy between modern painting and modern picturing moot. The party line for Abstract Expressionists (or at least their scribes and seers) could be summed up in a nutshell: the more painting, the less picturing there has to be; the *integrity* of painting depending, unconditionally, on the repudiation of picturing. By picturing I mean not just the attachment to description (for evidently that is not John Virtue's thing), but the evocation through the brush of something *about* a seen place, person *or* object. The seen something might not be the apparent surface characteristics of the place, person or object, so that the 'seeing' might be within the mind's eye, rather than a retinal report. So that we might well say that what John Virtue depicts is not London at all, but an idea of London, a sense of London (though not, I think, an *impression* of London). To acknowledge that much is not, for a moment, to compromise the 'reality' of how his eye, his hand and his paint coordinate, but on the contrary to insist that the reality they together make, the reality of a *painting* of London, is, in fact, the only reality worth having, at any rate in the National Gallery.

What John Virtue has made possible is a reunion of painting and picturing, no longer in a relationship of mutual depletion, but something like the opposite — mutual sustenance. No one standing in front of one of his big canvases could think that the force with which they deliver his vision could possibly be communicated in any other way: not digitally, not photographically, certainly not sculpturally. Nor, once seen, can that vision be subtracted from the sense of what London is or, for that matter, what painting is. In our visually over-surfeited but still mysteriously undernourished age, this is not bad to be going on with.

So what is it exactly that Virtue pictures? Well, nature, culture, history — that is, the history of his own craft as well as of the world — and the interlacing of them all in our visual imagination. Even on the evidence of the Exe Estuary paintings, he has never been a pastoralist. Cud-chewing serenity is not exactly the stuff of those roaring black and whites even when, ostensibly, they begin with solitary reflection. In 1958 Frank O'Hara did an interview with one of Virtue's heroes, Franz Kline, in which Kline also confessed himself to be incorrigibly in the stir of things, the artist telling O'Hara, 'Hell, half the world wants to be like Thoreau worrying about the noise of traffic on the way to Boston, the other half use up their lives being part of that noise. I like the second half, right?' Even when he has drawn by the side of a flowing stream or on a gantry swaying above the Thames, I think Virtue, too, is most moved by the buzz of the world; whether gnats humming in the tall grass, the gaseous tremble on the filmy pond or the pullulation of the urban hive. Instinctively, he draws no distinction between history and natural history. So too, like Kline again (and, for those who rejoice at having spotted Virtue's 'source' in Kline's instinctual black-and-white visual operas, one need only quote Brahms congratulating those who detected a touch of Beethoven in the finale of his fourth symphony – 'any fool can see that'), 'I don't feel mine is the most modern, contemporary, beyond the pale kind of painting. But then I don't have that fuck the past attitude. I have very strong feelings about individual paintings and painters past and present.' Which, in Kline's case included, on the positive side, Rembrandt, Bonnard and Toulouse-Lautrec, and in Virtue's, Rembrandt, Turner, Claude Lorrain and Goya.

A catty little debate about Kline turns on the degree to which he is to be thought of as a purely abstract painter or rather as one among many in whose work traces of figuration deliberately lurk; especially since titles like *Crow Dancer* might be read as a tease to identify primitive forms within the heavy onslaught of brushstrokes. But to participate in the quarrel is to miss the point about Kline since the force of his work is precisely to problematise the notion of 'pure' abstraction, and to translate seen (or felt) experience into an independent realm of painted gestures. *Meryon* (1960–1) may have started with the clock tower in Paris, mediated through a nineteenth-century engraver, but Kline's armature completes its Gothic ruin and resolves it into something elementally different.

Equally fruitless would be an argument about whether Kline, or for that matter, John Virtue, are painters of instinct or calculation, since the answer to both is yes. Much of the energy of Virtue's work does come directly from its improvisatory technique; so that the brushstroke seems always to have been freshly and urgently laid. Virtue is a draftsman through and through, yet the sweeping grandeur of his designs is less a matter of carefully calibrated delineation (the passages in his work I like the least are those where he makes linear architectural summaries, however freely rendered), but rather of his involuntary obedience to the accumulated patterning of a lifetime's working practice. His technique is painterly liberty guided by self-education. This makes him that rarest of birds in the studio, the wholly free disciplinarian.

In this complicated negotiation between chance and calculation, it so happens that Virtue has a revolutionary predecessor, the extraordinary eighteenth-century painter, Eton drawing master and print-maker, Alexander Cozens. In his moments of deepest perplexity (and there were many moments in his protean career when he was unperplexed and produced work of great banality), Cozens was exercised by the dissipation of the energy of the *idea* of a work, in the long process of its meticulous execution. This he thought a particular problem with landscapes, where a free sketch from nature would inevitably lose vitality as it was worked up in the studio, often at far remove in time and place from the drawn image, and, according to classical desiderata, guaranteed to drain away its spontaneity. (The phenomenally rich record of Virtue's sketchbooks documents not only the force of fleeting circumstances on his subject matter – light, wind, position – but also his determination to sustain that immediacy in the vastly amplified forms of the paintings.) Through serendipity (for him, the only blessed path), Alexander Cozens happened on a technique he thought might arrest this fatal stagnation of energy and which he called, in a publication, *A New Method of Assisting the Invention in Drawing Original Compositions of Landscape.* Observing the accidental patterning made by a soiled piece of paper, and recalling Leonardo da Vinci's musings on the associative suggestiveness of streaked stones, Cozens took this arbitrary staining as a cognitive tease from which to work up a fully imagined design. In the *New Method*, the stains became Cozens's 'Blots', which provoked from his critics derision and the accusation that he was simply a charlatan.

Cozens was surely responding to Lockean theory about the initially unmediated force of sensory impression, as well as to the lure of the unfettered imagination, so dear to his friend the Gothick plutocrat William Beckford. But this did not make Cozens an entirely impulsive dabbler. His own description of the blots navigates carefully between intuition and calculation: 'All the shapes are rude and unmeaning as they are formed with the swiftest hand. But at the same time there appears a general disposition of these masses producing one comprehensive form, which may be conceived and purposely intended before the blot is begun. This general form will exhibit some kind of subject and this is all that should be done designedly.'

Cozens goes on to justify his *New Method* by claiming it helps stamp the *idea* of a subject (he means this, I think, Platonically, as the original abstract concept of a subject) and is even bolder (or more romantic) by writing that the preservation of that living Idea is itself 'conformable to nature'. By this he does not mean there is a direct match between the concept of a representation and the objective facts of physical form, but rather something like the very opposite: that we are all prisoners (Plato and Locke again) of our machinery of cognition, and *that* is the proper form which the artist should seek to imprint on paper or canvas.

This may sound like an overly philosophical view of the modus operandi of so meaty a painter as John Virtue; yet it's surely not far from the mark. What Virtue gives us is not a visual document of London (in the manner, say, of Wenceslaus Hollar) built from the accumulation of reported details, each in fastidiously gauged and scaled relationship to each other, so much as an overwhelming *embodiment* of London; closer to an East End pub knees-up — the trundle of an old bus grinding its way through the night streets; the peculiar whiff of fresh rain on rubbish-filled streets; the jeering roar of a stand at White Hart Lane (or Highbury); the brimstone glare of a line of Doner KebabChicken-FishnChippy takeaways — than to a Prospect by Canaletto. Virtue's St Paul's is not Wren's architectural 'gem', it's the pre-bleached, grimily defiant mascot of cockneydom: black, hulking, a bit thuggish. And just as he turns the bleached dome black, he equally stunningly turns the dirty old river white. But (as with Kline again) Virtue's blacks and whites aren't polarised absolutes: they drip and smear each other with gleeful impurity; much of the white flecked with a kind of metropolitan ashiness that gives the paint guts and substance; much of the black, streaky and loose, like road tar that refuses to set. His is, in fact, a smoky London, even if painted long after the epoch of the great pea-soup fogs. His vade-mecum is Dickens, not Mayor Livingstone (though an earlier unreconstructed Ken would love these pictures).

Virtue has often sung his ode to pollution; the artist's friend. Whether to embrace or reject the begrimed air, the half-choked light has historically sorted out the men from the boys in London painters. Whistler loved it, of course, though he gussied it up as a dove-grey penumbra hanging moodily over Chelsea Reach. Claude Monet was in two minds about it, cursing it from his room in the Savoy in 1899 for blotting out the fugitive sun. Yet by far the strongest of his paintings — completed in a studio a long, long way from the Thames — were the greeny-grey early-morning images of crowds tramping and omnibussing their way to work over hostile bridges, unblessed by even a hint of watery sunshine. The beatific tangerine sunsets which Monet inflicted on other paintings in the series, on the other hand, glimmer over the Houses of Parliament with a risible absurdity that could only be forgivable as the product of some mildly narcotic stupor.

Likewise, it's a symptom of their meretriciousness – their tyrannical prettiness, their utter failure to connect with anything that ever made London London – that almost all of the paintings produced between 1747 and 1750 by Giovanni Antonio Canaletto feature radiantly cerulean skies. It may just have been that Canaletto was lucky enough to work during days – we have them, to be sure – of empyrean blue hanging over the Thames, but his obligation to sunny optimism extended beyond mere pictorial ingratiation. Canaletto was working for aristocratic patrons like the Duke of Richmond, heavily invested in the building of Hanoverian London, and whose education on the Grand Tour led them to reconceive the port city as the heir to Venice, Amsterdam or even Rome. Hence the earlier import of Italians to do London views – Antonio Joli and Marco and Sebastiano Ricci, for example – since their brief was to confect a fantasy metropolis in which classical memory united with commercial energy. Church façades bask in toasty Latin sunlight, the terraces of grand houses backing on to the Thames are populated only by ladies and gents of The Quality, and the river itself is barely disturbed by the occasional barge. Westminster Bridge, then under construction as a pet enterprise of the Duke of Richmond, was presented by Canaletto as a framing device, the Thames seen through one of its spectacular arches, both brand-new and somehow mysteriously venerable in the manner of a Piranesi *veduta*. The truth, however, was that the bridge was hated by a good section of London artisans and tradesmen, particularly the watermen who saw in it their impending redundancy. As visual paradigms of the New London, then, Canaletto's display pieces were (unlike Hogarth's prints or John Virtue's paintings) emphatically not for the 'middling sort' of people, much less the plebs. This aristocratic preference for poetic fancy over social truth reached a *reductio ad absurdum* with Canaletto's follower, William Marlow, painting in 1795 a *capriccio* in which St Paul's has been transplanted to a faithfully rendered depiction of the Grand Canal in Venice.

We tend to think of Turner (another of Virtue's heroes), or at least Turner the Brentford boy and happy waterman, as the antidote to all this Italianate picturesque contrivance. But of course Turner was as drunk on visions of Italy, and Venice in particular, as any of the *piccoli canaletti*, and was quite capable of turning out editions of the Thames which washed the scummy old stream in a bath of sublimity. And he was never above pleasing patrons, either. The direct ancestor of his 1826 *Mortlake Terrace*, now in the Frick Collection, painted for the nouveau-riche William Moffatt, with its peachy light and strolling gentlefolk is, indeed, Canaletto, and beyond him, the Dutch city painters of the seventeenth century. Related concoctions like Turner's 1819 *Richmond Hill on the Prince of Wales's Birthday*, or the 1825 watercolour of him sketching the serpentine curve of the river and the city about it from the summit of Greenwich Park, are best understood (and forgiven) as patriotic-civic allegories; omnia gathera of the memories, sentiments and loyalties called forth by the London prospect; but this time more in the nature of an implied historical pageant, insular and cocky rather than hybridised and Italianate. And, here, too, the debt is more to the Dutch celebrations of the *genius loci* – Esaias van de Velde's wonderful *View of Zierikzee*, and of course Vermeer's Delft – than to a mechanical reiteration of Roman glories, both departed and resurrected.

At least Turner was struggling to marry up authentic Cockney Pride, an experience of place, with a reimagined painterly aesthetic, rather than simply make the city a creature of swoon-inducing beautification; something which the punky smut of London will always, thank God, resist. It was not the American-ness of Whistler which led him to treat the river as aesthetic trance, but perhaps his permanent and increasingly desperate yearning to be in Paris, yet condemned to languish amidst the likes of William Frith and Augustus Egg as The American in London. The only way to survive was to flaunt it, and this Whistler did by becoming a painterly revolutionary in spite of himself, effectively annihilating his subject for a mood-effect. The rockets fall in gorgeous nocturnal obscurity somewhere, who cares, in the vicinity of Cremorne Gardens. The Gardens were a London pleasure haunt and a particular bête noire of John Ruskin as, of course, was Whistler himself and this painting in particular, for which the word effrontery seemed to the self-appointed guardian of visual truth to have been coined. But to make a Cremornian painting, to present art as epicurean delectability, a luscious dish for the senses, was precisely Whistler's point, one which, again, Paris might have taken as a compliment, but which London found somehow (it couldn't say *exactly* how) indecent.

A great gap opened up in modernism, then, between London as

the site of aesthetic cosmetic and London as the site of raw document; in the nineteenth century between the butterfly effects of Whistler and the reports from the underworld of Gustave Doré; in the twentieth between the visual histrionics of Oscar Kokoschka and in the 1950s the startling photographic streetscapes of the mind-blowingly gifted Nigel Henderson. Leon Kossoff and Frank Auerbach did wonders in regrounding vernacular visions of the city in the worked density of paint, but even they were not quite ready to take on the totemic sights and memories of the war-ravaged city in the way Virtue, born two years after the doodlebugs had done their worst, could. (In fact, the spirit of painterly liberty in the 1950s had its own strong reasons to go nowhere near anything that could be thought of as paying lip service to a Festival of Britain-like cavalcade.)

But that fastidiousness sealed off modernist painting of the city from the broader public whose need was, and may always be, celebratory, not darkly suspicious, or furtively pathological in the Sickert way. And it's the muscular innocence of John Virtue's picturing (along with the bravura of his paint-handling); his instinctive relish of the ant-heap swirl of London; his shockingly brave determination to make work which the untrained eye can immediately engage with, which has helped him achieve something no other painter of or in London has ever managed, a truly populist expressionism. That an entire ensemble of his huge, as well as his merely impressively large, paintings should be hung together in the National Gallery as if in the Hall of Honour in the palace of some prince of Baroque, so that they are experienced as a cumulatively intoxicating rush of spectacle, only makes their deeply democratic quality the more miraculous.

But then Virtue has not been holed up like Monet in the Savoy Hotel, nor taking the morning air like Canaletto with the Duke of Richmond these past few years. Instead, he has been swinging from a gantry, or perched precariously on the roof of Somerset House, London's mean drizzle on his head; its cinders flying in his face; taking the measure of the city very like his cynosure Turner, in his non-Mortlake moments, right between the eyes. The fine frenzy that pushes Virtue along is wonderfully documented in his sketchbooks, but the challenge for him has always been somehow to transform those immediate responses in the studio into something that both registers and transcends its subject matter. In this most difficult of painterly goals he has, I believe, triumphantly succeeded, allowing us to read the great white daub at the heart of so many of his paintings as intrinsically related to its figural source in the Thames. At such moments of recognition, the pulse of the Londoners among us, especially, will race a little faster. But the reason to be most grateful for these epic masterworks is precisely for their resistance to visual cliché, even to cockney sentimentality; for their faithfulness to a London eye that actually sees beyond London. So we must also read the white daub as a white daub; the most thrillingly satisfying white daub conceivable, ditto the great racing black strokes; the gale-force whirl of the brush. Back and forth we go, then, through the picturing and the painting; the two in perfect step, doing the Lambeth Walk, oi! It comes as no surprise, then, to learn that that just happens to be where John Virtue lives.

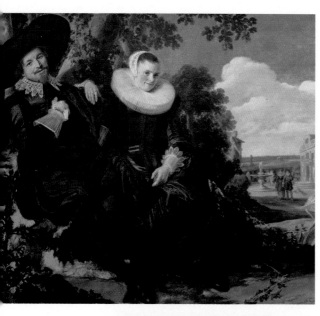

Frans Hals,
*The Marriage
Portrait of Isaac
Massa and
Beatrix van der
Laen, c.* 1622.
Rijksmuseum,
Amsterdam.

Peter Paul Rubens,
The Four Philosophers,
*c.*1608. Palazzo Pitti,
Palatine Gallery,
Florence.

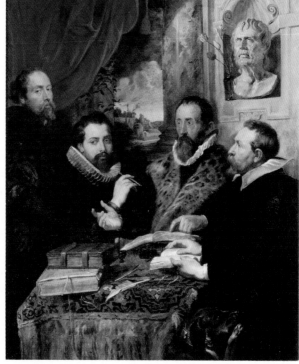

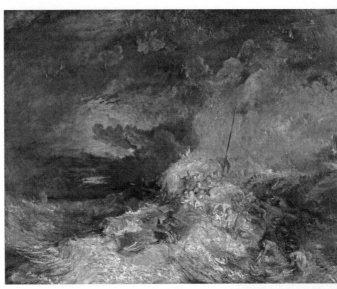

J.M.W. Turner, *A Disaster at Sea,*
'The Wreck of the Amphitrite', *c.* 1835.
Tate Gallery, London.

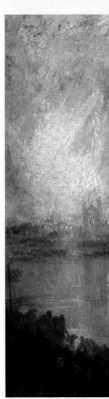

J.M.W. Turner, *The Burning of the
Houses of Lords and Commons*, 1835.
John Howard McFadden Collection,
Philadelphia Museum of Art, Philadelphia.

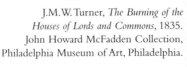

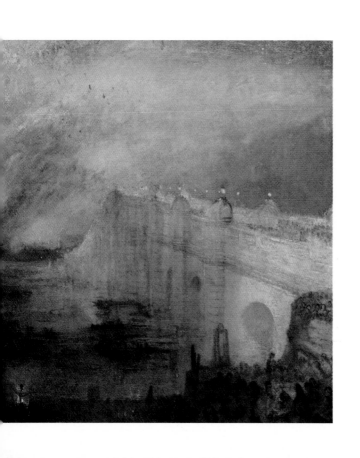

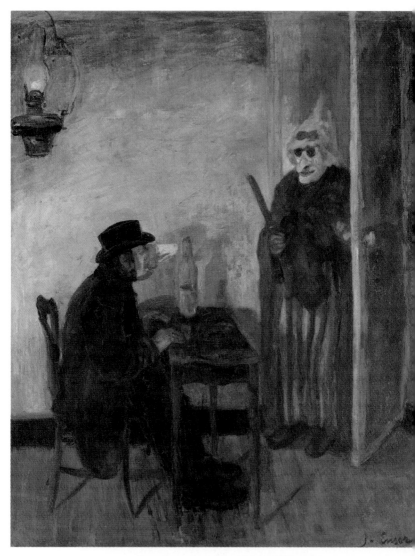

James Ensor, *Scandalized Masks*, 1883.
Royal Museums of Fine Arts of Belgium, Brussels.

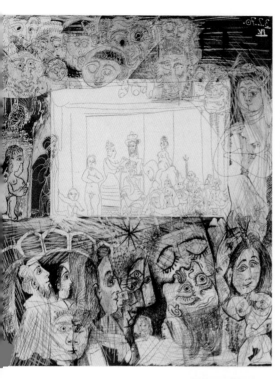

Pablo Picasso,
'Ecce Homo', After Rembrandt
from Suite 156, 1970.
Tate Gallery, London.

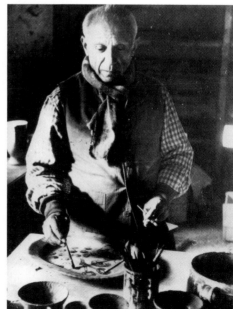

Picasso At Work, c. 1970.

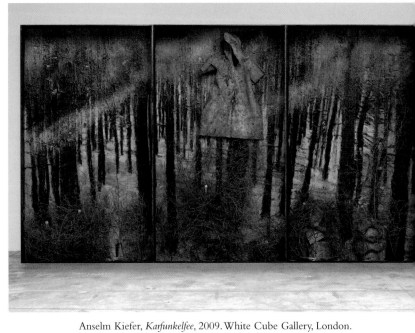

Anselm Kiefer, *Karfunkelfee*, 2009. White Cube Gallery, London.

Anselm Kiefer, *Shevirath Ha Kelim*, 2009. White Cube Gallery, London.

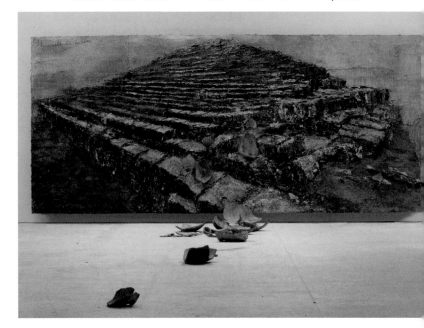

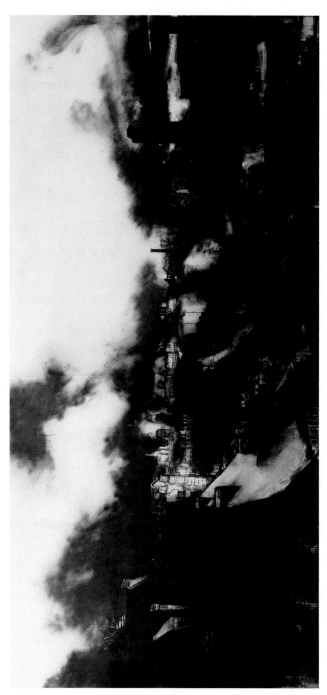

John Virtue, *Landscape No. 711*, 2003–4. Marlborough Fine Art, London.

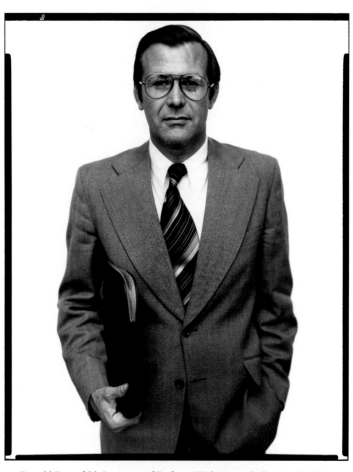

Donald Rumsfeld, Secretary of Defense, Washington, D.C., May 7, 1976.
From *The Family*, a portfolio of 69 portraits. Photograph by Richard Avedon.

Avedon: Power

Guardian, 27 September 2008

Was there ever such a pretty wart? There it sits beside the noble nose, the solitary imperfection in Richard Avedon's impossibly beautiful portrait head of Barack Obama, taken in 2004 when Obama was the wunderkind of the struggling Democrats. You look at the clever, artless, eager child preserved in the star orator, civic gravity and American ardour overlaid on the same face, the open collar an advertisement of moral transparency, and two equally wistful thoughts come to mind. How long ago *that* seems; and how sad it is that the greatest of America's portraitists in any medium isn't around right now to fulfil his project of shooting 'Democracy' in action. But Avedon died, aged eighty-one, in mid-shoot, not long after photographing Obama. He was excited about the work (there was not much about life that didn't excite him); and he talked about 'Democracy' capturing politics as it played out in the lives of regular Americans, rather than a gallery of Players. But on the evidence of some of the pictures, he became drawn to an emblematic freak show; a polemic of the peculiar, easy pickings for an artist with Avedon's sardonic eye. So, predictably, we have the Republican Conventioneer costumed as Lincoln, but emitting the icy glare of an executioner; or the bovine high-school blonde who seems constituted entirely from dairy matter, the satin spikes of her diadem crumpling on her brow, a lazy eye turning her impersonation of the Statue of Liberty into farce. Only in the portrait of 'Specialist John H. Copeland', photographed at Fort Hood, does monstrosity get complicated by pathos. The image of the young soldier separates at the neck. Below is the American empire; the line-backer frame in camouflage fatigues, impossibly bulked up and weighed down by flak jacket; massive gun; a mesh kitbag; above the collar-line, a fresh-faced kid in a buzz cut, doing his best to perfect a roadblock glower, but triggering only an urge to make him a quick cup of cocoa.

Avedon never made any pretence to objectivity; the notion of the dispassionate lens he wrote off as delusion. His work, he frankly confessed, was at least as much about him as his subjects: a vast collective self-portrait of the compulsions he projected on to America's faces and figures. In person Avedon was a merrily humane optimist, warm-blooded and gregarious; to know him was to love him. But he was no sentimentalist and there was a Daumier streak in him: coolly contemptuous of the political masquerade even while he was enthralled by its performances. Like Daumier, he thought that lies and cruelty settled like a crust on the physiognomy: passive cosmetic surgery gone wrong. All he had to do was to supply a lit exposure of the particular features in which moral intelligence or its absence had been inscribed.

As hip as he mostly was, Avedon was, at root, an old-style Jewish moralist whose texts were written in freckles and furrows, pits and pocks. Sometimes those marks and blemishes, which stood out so sharply against the indeterminate white sheet against which his faces posed, were lit as poetic expressions of the persona. So the much mottled but kindly moon-face of John Glenn, astronaut turned Ohio Senator, becomes itself a benign planetary surface. Avedon took delight in tweaking – or annihilating – the expected icon. Ronald Reagan, whose beaming smile warmed millions with its avuncular easiness, he trapped in lower-facial corrugation, as if the firming of power had been withdrawn in retirement along with the presidential motorcade. 'Looking good,' Nancy is said to have murmured as Reagan stood on the chalk lines he had asked Avedon to supply, looking anything but. The gaze off yonder Avedon may have wanted to suggest rueful reflection, but our retrospective knowledge of Reagan's mental fade into Alzheimer's gives the image an altogether different charge. Confronted by his famously affable beam turned into a mask of porky smugness as if fattened at the trough of self-satisfaction, Karl Rove got all steamed up, accusing Avedon of setting him up to look 'stupid'; the arch-amBusher ambushed.

To which, I think, Avedon would have replied with his most roguishly winning grin that all his portraits were collaborations; and that nothing about the meeting of photographer and subject was calculated in advance: not the clothes, not the hair, not the body language. People came as they were. But the truth is a little more complicated than that profession of guilelessness. Avedon did in fact have certain *idées fixes* about the essential whomever; and then, through some astonishing act of photographic magic against that white paper, could make clothes, expression, collude in imprinting the essential them. Accompanied merely by the innocent act of sticking his left hand in his pocket, the trademark glasses a smidgin off kilter, Henry Kissinger's expression assumes the defensiveness of no-penetration concrete berms erected around an American embassy. For all we know, there may have been moments when Kissinger (who can be voluble) let his guard down and surrendered to the Avedon charm offensive. But the caught image is of someone guarding state secrets deep in his trousers. Equally, it's hard not to let what we now know of Donald Rumsfeld's years of catastrophic military bungling cloud our take on Avedon's young myrmidon of the Ford administration. But the insignia of the Organisation Man, whose openings are strictly limited – the slightly superior amusement registered in the narrowing eyes, the dangerous haircut and the barely unzipped attaché case – are already there. Could it be my imagination, or are Rumsfeld's swept-wing lapels converging at the one-buttoned jacket, a cunningly coded sartorial blueprint of the Stealth bomber to come? . . . Nah . . .

Avedon's was a literary and dramatic sensibility more than an aesthetic. Every face, every body came with a potential narrative to tease out. Sometimes, in his own mind, sitters were twinned in some deep and weighty history even when they faced the camera alone. The Carter-Ford election was fought all over again in his studio; Carter, at ease in his loosely fitting Christian simplicity, Ford (slightly unfairly) made to scowl as if a different and nicer man were struggling to break through the stony carapace. Deeper still is the duet of Adlai Stevenson and Dwight Eisenhower, a chapter to itself, in Avedon's visualisation, of post-war American history. The curriculum vitae tells us that Stevenson, the last heavyweight intellectual in Democratic politics before the Arkansas Kid, was twice loser; Ike the winner; which immediately sets up expectations of Avedonian role reversal. And so it seems. Stevenson, photographed when he was Kennedy's ambassador to the United Nations, at the acme of his rhetorical force (especially deployed against the Castro-Khrushchev missiles), looks to his right, but his face is alive with confident wit; the unembarrassed pleasure of a life vindicated. The old boy is blessed with the benison of Camelot. By contrast the post-presidential Ike seems flaky pastry: the eyes unfocused. Stevenson's glance is sideways and down, a man on top of his form; Ike's is distant and upwards, lost in meditation. But it was, in fact, Eisenhower who in his old age had the more important things to say: his farewell presidential address the famous warning against the coming of the self-perpetuating 'military-industrial complex', the beast that would consume American liberty. So Avedon bestows on him the dreamy saintliness of some ancient buddha already mourning his vindication.

The studio was Avedon's theatre, with sitters encouraged to perform and the maestro as the genial director. The only time I went there myself for a group photo of *New Yorker* writers paying homage to their departing editor, the atmosphere was festive, beckoning drinks on a side-table. Avedon orchestrated the afternoon unwinding, encouraging us into showtime exuberance (in our case not a challenge). When the right moment came, he stood beside, not behind, the large-format camera, never taking his eyes off us, a party to the party, and caught the family jubilation just so. It was, I think, his Shakespearean sense of life as play that made him Olympian and intimate at the same time. His strongest pictures tease out the inner, optimised image we all carry around within ourselves, hoping that it might have some relationship to the way others see us: strong, wise, finely featured. But then Avedon puts that naively glamorised version in a dialogue with what he sees himself; the result being, in the subjects with which he had most sympathy, a marvellous dialogue between inner and outward countenance: the anima and its vital casing.

The effect, when successful, is to evoke presence more distinctively than any other photographer who has ever turned their hand to portraiture; more powerfully than Matthew Brady, Julia Margaret Cameron, August Sander or Alfred Stieglitz. For like Rembrandt, Avedon caught the shorthand signature of an entire life and the pose became a print of individual spirit. There *is* Senator Daniel Patrick Moynihan, his face lit with Erasmian amusement at the incorrigible human comedy, the dunderheaded obtuseness of political clods incapable of seeing the finesse of politics as he did, or of taking on the obligation to thought that came with the acquisition of power. Well, well, he would say, nursing his shot glass, marvelling at the mess of it all, bow tie askew, arms akimbo, the Irish-American lilt on the edge of a chuckle, would you believe it? And you look at Avedon's picture, the Senator to the life, and yes, you do.

Cooking and Eating

Cool as Ice

Vogue, August 2007

Summer 1956. Anthony Eden is dreaming dangerous Egyptian dreams which, in the following autumn, will send what little remains of the British Empire right up the creek (aka the Suez Canal). But we don't know about that and, if we did, we wouldn't care. It's the last day of school. We've seen off the eleven-plus, and out there in pebbledash London, beyond the gritty little playground of our primary school, beyond the black spiked railings hung with tendrils of bindweed, there's a siren chiming. Bing-bong, bingety bongety bong. Mr Whippy is calling and we, short-trousered, snake-belted, grimy-kneed, snot-nosed, want what he's got. We want a Ninety-Nine; God, how we want it: that shaggy-bark chocolate stick plunged into a mound of air-pumped chalky glop, which would be called vanilla were it not to defame the dark bean. But then we weren't too organic, not in 1956. So we charge out through the rusting green gates and break into our version of 'La donna è mobile':

> My name's Anton-i-o
> I sell ice cream-i-o
> Down your back-alley-o
> Tuppence a lick-i-o.

The delirium of ice cream is inseparable from juvenile glee; the uninhibited indulgence of the mouth. To get your tongue round a dollop is to become instantaneously childlike again, whatever your age; to cop a mouthful of lusciousness that magically marries opposites: fruit and dairy, the tart and the voluptuous; a shot of excitement meets a scoop of all's well. Yes, yes, doctor, we know the taking of the cone-heaped mound in our greedy gobs makes us blissed-out babies again, tripping down mammary lane: slurp, lick, suck, even, on occasions, drool and slobber. But it's more complicated than milky regression.

Mouthfeel – that's the trade term for the *sine qua non* of a satisfying product. Boardrooms of serious persons in suits will sit around – with tiny plastic spoons? – sliding the stuff in, rolling their tongues around it. Their brows will furrow and their lips purse as they assess texture, smoothness, density, whether the paste is too granular or too unctuous. They will pronounce judgement on the brightness or dullness of flavour; on whether the product has legs. But that's not what James Joyce would have wanted from mouthfeel, is it?

Imagine Molly Bloom doing strawberry flavour: 'A plop in the mouth, and down it goes and more I want more and the stink of the earthy summer and oh there yes there is the silkymilkysmooth mouthfeel and I feel the ice and my heat melts it and then yes I smell the torn berries and my tongue searches for the seeds which arent there . . .' Or, you know, something along those lines.

Not quite your mouthfeel? Come on, you know there's nothing like ice cream to give you that shot of guilty pleasure. Though I am partial to a tart sorbet – rhubarb, mango and the perfect lemon – you need the fatty voluptuousness of ice cream to make you really happy on a drizzly Monday in June. It shoves sense (and thoughts of diet) aside. You don't eat ice cream, you gorge on it. Open wide and dream – perhaps of the perfect, but as-yet-unrealised flavour? Mine would be made from the two most mysteriously succulent Edenic fruits I've ever eaten, both in the Dominican Republic: the milky-fleshed *caimito* – a flood of scented flavour, ethereally light; and its opposite, *nispero* – the unappealingly leathery brown skin concealing a bronze-coloured, honey-tasting flesh.

Where you are and with whom you're eating has much to do with the pleasure quotient. After a sudden storm off the coast of southern Brazil, our day-trip sailboat put in to a bay where the water was churned turquoise. The rain hammered down on the pink sand, but there was a small hut with an overhanging palm roof and under the shelter someone offered us coconut ice cream from the boat. It seemed like Dido's dessert.

When I was growing up in Golders Green there was no question which brand of ice cream was for nice Jewish boys and girls. Joe Lyons's Dairy Maid had been founded by Isidore and Montague Gluckstein of Whitechapel in partnership with Barnett Salmon and old Joe himself. Joe's ices were then British and Jewish, just like us! So we loyally but unenthusiastically sucked on our Orange Maid: the drink on a stick which parents kept on telling you was good for you, and the livid pink-and-white Mivvi, with its secretions of crimson goop – the Shirley Temple of the ice-cream world. The opposition – Wall's – could not have been more deeply *goyische*, since they also made pork sausages and pallid pies packed with gristly-grey mystery mince. The assumption at home was that, somehow, something of the piggy-wiggy must have crept into their Neapolitan Bricks. Which of course made the temptation to dally with the forbidden food irresistible. Heston Blumenthal may think he's the pioneer of bacon ice cream, but for us it was already there in the fabulously sinister form of a Wall's Tutti-Frutti.

The strenuous modern urge to come up with flavours that will make ice cream sexy seems redundant when all that is really needed for the stuff to tickle our fancy is intensity. Getting that intensity suspended in a smooth paste of frozen cream is enough of a feat without wasting time on sensationalism. The past masters of ice-cream making knew all about the lure of the savoury. Frederick Nutt's *Complete Confectioner of 1789* offered thirty-two flavours, including barberry, brown bread, damson and Parmesan cheese, which turns out to be nothing more than a frozen soufflé and lacks the conviction of his 'grape' flavour (actually made with elder, the *grappe de sureau*). If it's serious shock-ice you're hunting, you need to hop on a plane to Otaru Unga in Hokkaido, Japan, where apparently you can sample their chicken-wing, horse-flesh, sea-urchin, squid-ink, crab and (less dauntingly) pickled-plum and cherry-blossom flavours. Beside those exercises in kamikaze infusions, our home-grown Purbeck's Chilli Red seems hopelessly sedate, its speckling of hot flakes neutralised by the ocean of fatty Dorset cream. A few of the modern curiosities do actually work, especially in New York: Il Laboratorio del Gelato's Toasted Sesame Seed is wonderful because the custard seems to have been infused, not just scattered with seedy mix-ins. Larry's in Washington DC has a halvah ice cream which isn't at all bad. And another idea whose time you might think ought never to have come is Mario Batali's Olive Oil, but it's actually rather seductive, the little beads of oil hanging glossily on the salty cream like green sweat.

What is it about frozen desserts that tempts makers into these adventures in the gratuitous, instead of concentrating their ingenuity on nailing, say, the perfect pistachio?

A classic instance of something that should have been killed on the drawing board is the work of a team of marketing geniuses who must have thought it would be really cool to stick their perfectly good fruit sorbets in plastic tubes, thereby realising what may be the single worst packaging idea in food history. The result is called Ice Pulp. You can either shove the thing directly in your mouth, as if you suddenly remembered you'd forgotten to brush your teeth, or else you can squeeze a fat worm of blood-orange or mango sorbet on to — what exactly — a spoon, a fruit, a friend?

Would the Emperor Nero have gone for Ice Pulp? In the more fanciful ice-cream histories he is credited with being the original Mr Whippy, despatching teams of moaning slaves to the Apennine peaks to fetch back straw-wrapped wagonloads of ice, which would then be flavoured at his table with honey, pulped fruit, or possibly the remains of critics rash enough to under-praise his poetry. It was the sheer labour-intensive, conspicuously wasteful grandeur of the whole enterprise, the improbability of conserving ice in hot climates, that made it a royal project in the first place. An early recipe survives from the reign of the Mughal Emperor Akhbar, and though the predictable tales of Marco Polo bringing the taste for frozen sherbets back from Mongol China are apocryphal, it seems likely that Renaissance Europe got the iced-fruit habit from the Arab-Moorish presences in Sicily and Spain.

But there was — and is — nothing very complicated about the technology for making this most paradoxical of delights. Believe me, if I can do it — with just a little cylinder that sits in the freezer overnight while the infused custard or fruit syrup is chilling, and which then takes a mere twenty to thirty minutes of electric paddling to turn itself into ice cream or sorbet — all of you can, too. A relative newcomer to the genre, I've whipped up some not-half-bad ice creams — ginger and honey, green tea, fig and brandy, and the 'scalded apricots' of Elizabeth Raffald's 1769 recipe. My only advice: don't skimp on the egg yolks — Thomas Jefferson prescribed six for his vanilla — and never use low-fat milk. Sorbets are even more of a pushover. And if you can't serve them in the cups and glasses made of ice that feature in the Victorian cookbooks, put a few assorted scoops of rhubarb, lemon and blood-orange in a tall wine glass and you'll put a smile on the faces of kids of all ages sitting at your table.

In America, once the great ice king of Boston, Frederick Tudor, had discovered that pine sawdust was the perfect preservative for mass-packed ice and began to sell it commercially, and once sugar had gone from a luxury to an everyday commodity, a whole culture grew up around the rituals of home-made ice cream. The weekly batch involved the whole family, romping kids to stooped grans, taking turns with the churning paddle as the harvest of peaches, picked from the tree, formed itself into a fragrant mouthful of perpetual summer. The fact that the churning required attention even when others were off at church only made the treat more wickedly irresistible; homely and sinful at the same time: a Tom Sawyer picket-fence moment, bathed in shoo-fly innocence.

The American hunger for ice cream has always been an ache for a prelapsarian way of life that never was. Successive brandings have spoken to whichever paradise seems to have been most poignantly left behind. Great Depression? Right, invent the Good Humor (choc) Bar. In the Sixties, Reuben Mattus created the fake Scandiwegian brand of Häagen-Dazs, with its meaninglessly hovering umlaut, to comfort a country still crying over its murdered president. Home-style ice-cream makers have always looked for hills to nestle in, rather than be Nestléd, so Ben and Jerry resettled amidst the Green Mountains of Vermont in the late Seventies. The high-minded folksy earnestness in which the Ben & Jerry's brand wrapped itself was an obituary for the acid age: the iconography of the tubs with their self-righteous screeds and vaguely R. Crumb graphics servicing the fantasy that the thrusting yuppie was, at least as he gobbled Cherry Garcia, in Woodstock for ever.

On Main Street, the soda fountain had been a ra-ra American institution, a defining fixture of the town since before the Civil War; a souser-free anti-bar where milky wholesomeness took the peril out of bobby-soxers' scarlet lipsticks. The places themselves shimmered with splendour, boasting ornate gilt-frame mirrors and towering chrome fountains. The post-war, post-welfare-state version in Britain was the milk bar. Its antiseptically tiled walls – intended, I guess, to be redolent of the dairy – were closer to a scrubbed-down NHS ward. The juke'n'jive espresso bar soon meant that its days were numbered. But before we got to drainpipe trousers, we sat there in the mournful brightness with our boatloads of banana splits, on which reposed snail-like deposits of ersatz cream. Choc ices, in the back row of the cinema between snogfests, were our best friends, since one could carry on biting, affecting cool indifference, as a free hand set off on its voyage of exploration.

The days of toxically lurid lollies like the unsubtly rocket-shaped, horizontally banded (lime, lemon, strawberry) Zoom, the Jelly Terror, Mr Merlin's Magic Purple Potion, Lord Toffingham (with its tongue-beckoning toffee drip) and the unforgettable Lolly Gobble Choc Bomb are long gone. In place of the thrillingly irradiated industrial-waste aesthetic we have the return of the bucolic: flavours that take you back to Ambridge and the village fete. In place of Mrs Thatcher (who worked as a chemist for Lyons), we have thatched-cottage memories; our own version of sempiternal Albion where the bumblebees hum and Ratty sculls the stream. So September Organics (based near Hereford, and thus at one with the cows) offers a Blackberry and Apple Crumble flavour, and its Brown Bread (another standard recipe of the eighteenth-century books) is about the first I've tasted that actually brings off that elusive combo of yeasty-crumby-creamy. But it's possible to be led too far up the hedgerow. Cinnamon, as my co-tasting friend Cassata pointed out, is a volatile spice and needs to be almost dangerously fresh to infuse into the waiting custard. Often, as with pistachio nuts, the temptation is to compensate for fugitive flavour by aggressive roasting which releases a coarsely augmented version of the flavour. Over-sweetening is another trap into which otherwise perfectly good ice creams fall, but then I'm someone who would much rather sample Dentist's Mouthwash Sorbet than be forced to consume a tub of Butterscotch-Anything.

My very first experience of what real ice cream might actually taste like was in the late Fifties in Glasgow, where an Italian community ruled the vans. Marine Ices on Haverstock Hill in north London is one of the last outposts of that unapologetically fruit-creamy world. But first-hand experience of the *gelaterie* of Florence, Lucca, Orvieto, Rome and Naples has developed in me the craving for something as close as possible to the vivid, unclouded flavours that sit in the stainless-steel basins of Pasqualetti, Perché No and Badiano. Oddono's of Bute Street in Kensington does a pretty decent approximation, even if we are expected to congratulate them on their vanilla hailing from Madagascar, their pistachios from Sicily. The most successful crossovers are marriages between English memories and Italian tradition. But there's still nothing in the shops to compare with the brilliant Ciao Bella brand available in and around New York, nor with the even more spectacular stuff coming out of Jon Snyder's Il Laboratorio del Gelato on the Lower East Side. Were their Prune-Armagnac, their Fresh Mint, their Vanilla Saffron and their Strawberry, which tastes more of strawberries than most strawberries do, not so palate-blowingly fabulous, you couldn't forgive the pretentiousness of their brand name. But they are. Nothing I've ever tasted in Britain comes close, with one sensational exception: an Elderflower Crush Sorbet made by the terrific Jude's somewhere around Winchester. Most of their product – chocolate, mango – is good, but the elderflower number, which dances its way down your greedy gullet and which still has you begging for more, is about as close to perfection as modern *gelato* will ever get.

Is it possible to get a bit too worked up about ice cream? In the dawn of the Häagen-Dazs epoch (which did promise flavours that were 'orgasmic'), Gael Greene, the food critic of *New York Magazine*, claimed that it was 'not excessive to rank the ice-cream revolution with the sexual revolution, the women's movement and peace for our time'. 'Great ice cream,' she wrote, as if declaiming the Gettysburg Address, 'is sacred, brave, an eternal verity.' Jeez, Gael, it ain't *that* good, but okay, it's pretty damned close.

Ice-cream recipes

Blood-orange and rosewater sorbet
Makes 6–10 portions

150g caster sugar
750ml freshly squeezed blood-orange juice
100ml orange juice
100ml lemon juice
2 tbsp orange zest
1 tbsp rosewater (or to taste)

Put the sugar and 100ml of water in a small saucepan on a high heat. Bring to the boil and stir until the sugar dissolves.

Turn the heat down and stir for about three minutes until the syrup thickens. Transfer the syrup into a bowl, add the juices, zest and then rosewater and stir well. Allow the mixture to cool and set in the fridge for at least four hours, or overnight.

Pour the fruit syrup into an ice-cream maker and follow the manufacturer's instructions.

Note: the rosewater will make this a fairly soft-spooning sorbet.

Carrot, apricot, cardamom and saffron kulfi
Makes 6–10 portions

500g carrots, peeled and cut into small chunks
200g sugar
250g good-quality (Turkish) dried or fresh, stoned apricots
150ml whole milk
150ml evaporated milk
½ tsp saffron threads, crushed
20 cardamom pods
50g pistachio nuts

Put the carrots in a small saucepan and add just enough water to cover them. Add 100g of sugar, bring to the boil and then turn the heat to low and cook slowly for twenty minutes, uncovered, stirring occasionally. Add the apricots and cook on a very low heat for another twenty-five minutes, adding a little water if necessary. Purée the carrot-apricot mixture in a blender, check for sweetness and put to one side.

Boil or microwave the whole milk on a high heat for fifteen minutes. Use a spatula to stir and scrape down the sides to mix any 'skin' into the milk. Repeat this for three more fifteen-minute batches. Add the evaporated milk and remaining sugar to the mixture and cook for a further ten minutes. If a rubbery skin has formed, this time remove it.

Crush the saffron using a pestle and mortar and add to the milk mixture. Leave to cool for twenty minutes.

Pound the cardamom pods in the mortar to release the black seeds, discard the skins, then crush the seeds well. Put the pistachio nuts into the mortar and crush coarsely. Add the nuts and seeds to the milk. Stir the carrot-apricot purée into the saffron-cardamom thickened milk, then transfer the lot into a bowl and leave to chill in the fridge for at least four hours, or overnight.

Pour into an ice-cream maker and follow the manufacturer's instructions.

Serve this in chilled glasses, with sliced fresh mangoes and papayas, sprinkled with a little freshly squeezed lime juice.

Cinnamon and honey ice cream
Makes 6–10 portions

1½ cinnamon sticks, broken in half
250ml full-fat milk
650ml cream
2 tbsp powdered cinnamon
3 tbsp clear honey
6 egg yolks
50g caster sugar

Put the cinnamon sticks in a small frying pan on a medium-low heat and dry-roast until they release their fragrance. Be careful not to burn the sticks. Then put the milk, half the cream and the sticks into a medium, heavy-based saucepan and whisk in the powdered cinnamon. Bring almost (but not completely) to the boil, stirring constantly. Reduce the heat, add the honey and stir for a further five minutes so that the cinnamon can infuse. Take off the heat. Leave to stand for five minutes, then remove the cinnamon sticks.

In a bowl, whisk the egg yolks with the sugar until the mixture is pale yellow.

Whisk 50ml of the hot milk mixture into the egg and sugar; then add the rest. Return to the pan and stir over a low heat for seven to ten minutes until the custard coats the back of a spoon. Take off the heat and leave to cool thoroughly.

Taste for fragrance. If it's a little underwhelming, this is the moment you can, if you like, add some super-high-quality powdered cinnamon. It will fleck the ice cream, but what's wrong with that?

Whip the remainder of the cream in soft peaks and fold into the mixture. Chill for at least five hours in the refrigerator or, better still, overnight.

Turn the mixture into an ice-cream maker and follow the manufacturer's instructions.

Serve with brandy snaps.

Note: cinnamon loses its strength very easily, and for this recipe to work the spice needs to infuse the custard. So if, when you open the jar or bruise the end of a stick you don't get a fierce shot of fragrance, buy some fresh.

Sauce of Controversy

Guardian, 26 November 2008

What is the single, best word to describe the pleasure of a great bolognese sauce? Rich. And right now, in lean economic times and at the start of a long, cold winter, we will be wanting some of that richness, won't we? Which must be why sales of 'mince' are up 16 per cent. It's an easy, irresistible, almost childish pleasure: the ground meat dissolved into a dark blood-red sauce until they are one and the same; no hacking, slicing or cutting needed; a slurpy goodness; the oily bolognese hanging on to the slippery pasta; guaranteed joy in a world that's just ruled it out.

In 1973, the National Theatre put on a production of the Neapolitan playwright Eduardo de Filippo's *Saturday, Sunday, Monday*, in which a family falls apart along with the meat sauce. A character played by Laurence Olivier was at the centre of it all, but the real star was the *ragù*: actually cooked onstage, filling the theatre with the narcotic aroma of sizzling onion, garlic, tomatoes and meat. The acting was terrific, but who cared? Audiences applauded and rushed out to the nearest trattoria – only to be disappointed by a garish, thin, red concoction.

You don't want that, but what do you want; or rather whose *ragù* or meat sauce? It's a subject that can start fights among partisans. I've borrowed this and that from hostile parties and over many years of experiment developed a version that brings you a bowlful of Italian splendour in icy times.

First, and most essentially, you need time. Bolognese sauce isn't fast food. If you're assuming you can get home late, fry up some minced beef, bung a can of tomato purée on it, let it sit for ten minutes and cook the spag, you might as well go to the sub-standard local Italian after all. Think of the real bolognese as a party of shy ingredients who need careful introducing to each other if they're going to get happily intimate. You will need forty minutes to an hour to get everything going and at least another hour for the sauce to develop its gorgeousness. If you have a whole afternoon, better still, or if you can cook a big batch and leave it to combine and develop (preferably not in the fridge) overnight, so much the better.

Other than time, here's what you must have: three different kinds of meat: veal, beef and, in some form or other (minced loin, or sausage or pancetta), a bit of a pig. Some classic recipes insist on hamminess as in pancetta, but it depends on whether you want that cured quality or not. It's certainly not as essential as the mashed chicken livers which, in a true bolognese sauce (such as Elizabeth David's on page 323), are really obligatory: they give the dark substance and pungency you're after. If you have liver-haters in the house, don't tell them; they won't notice.

The procedure – which also calls for the cook to drink something happy-making, say a Morellino de Scansano – is always the same. Sauté your *odori*: onion, garlic, parsley, finely chopped carrot (quite a lot of that), celery (ditto). Then remove them to a bowl while you're browning the meats; drain some (not all) of the fat; return the meat; add chopped peeled tomatoes and a tablespoon of purée; salt, pepper, oregano, a smidgin of thyme, ditto basil. Sauté the chicken livers separately until just the brown side of pink, mash them up and add to the pot. Then add beef or chicken stock. Bring to a simmer.

Now the second Big Decision faces you – the wine: red or white? Both are actually fine, but they make for a different style of sauce. The red can be aggressive, which works if you are on a two-day bolognese, as it will have time to be fully absorbed by the other ingredients; but, if you're going to be eating it the same evening, use white and let it just help the meat melt.

About half an hour before serving, grate a little Parmesan cheese into the sauce and let it blend – irrespective of whether you're going to sprinkle more on the final dish.

Last trick – don't drown the spag in the sauce. The oily grains should hang on the pasta rather than smother it.

And cook enough to freeze a load. You will be grateful on those long, dark winter nights. Or mornings. I've had it for breakfast and, believe me, it will change your whole day. Sometimes I've even spooned it down cold. So sue me.

Or try one of these classics:

> *Marcella Hazan's version*
> Serves 4–6
>
> 1 tbsp vegetable oil
> 4 tbsp butter
> ½ cup chopped onion
> ⅔ cup chopped celery
> ⅔ cup chopped carrot
> ¾ lb ground beef chuck
> salt
> fresh ground black pepper
> 1 cup whole milk
> whole nutmeg
> cup dry white wine
> 1½ cups canned Italian plum tomatoes, torn into pieces, with juice
> 1¼–1½ lb pasta (preferably spaghetti), cooked and drained
> freshly grated Parmigiano-Reggiano cheese at the table

Put the oil, three tablespoons of butter and the chopped onion in a heavy 3.3-litre (6-pint) pot and turn the heat to medium. Cook and stir the onion until it has become translucent, then add the chopped celery and carrot. Cook for about two minutes, stirring the vegetables to coat well.

Add the ground beef, a large pinch of salt and a few grindings of pepper. Crumble the meat with a fork, stir well and cook until the beef has lost its raw, red colour.

Add the milk and let simmer gently, stirring frequently, until it has bubbled away completely. Add a tiny grating, about an eighth of a teaspoon, of fresh nutmeg and stir.

Add the wine and let it simmer until it has evaporated. Add the tomatoes and stir thoroughly to coat all the ingredients well. When the tomatoes begin to bubble, turn the heat down so that the sauce cooks at the laziest of simmers, with just an intermittent bubble breaking through the surface. Cook, uncovered, for three hours or more, stirring from time to time. While the sauce is cooking, you are likely to find that it will begin to dry out and the fat will separate from the meat. To keep it from sticking, add half a cup of water as necessary.

At the end of cooking, however, the water should be completely evaporated and the fat should separate from the sauce. Taste and correct for salt.

Add the remaining tablespoon of butter to the hot pasta and toss with the sauce. Serve with freshly grated Parmesan on the side.

> *Elizabeth David's version*
> Serves 6
>
> 85g uncooked bacon or ham (both fat and lean)
> butter
> 1 onion
> 1 carrot
> 1 small piece of celery
> 225g lean minced beef
> 115g chicken livers
> 3 tsp concentrated tomato purée
> 1 glass white wine
> salt and pepper
> nutmeg
> 2 wine glasses meat stock or water
> ½ a tsp nutmeg, freshly grated if possible

Cut the bacon or ham into very small pieces and brown them gently in a small saucepan in about 15g of butter. Add the onion, the carrot and the celery, all finely chopped. When they have browned, put in the raw minced beef, and then turn it over and over so that it all browns evenly. Add the chopped chicken livers, and after two or three minutes the tomato purée, and then the white wine. Season with salt (taking into account the relative saltiness of the ham or bacon), pepper and a scraping of nutmeg, and add the meat stock or water.

Cover the pan and simmer the sauce very gently for thirty to forty minutes. Some cooks in Bologna add a cupful of cream or milk to the sauce, which makes it smoother. I add a light sprinkle of nutmeg. Another traditional variation is the addition of the ovarine or unlaid eggs which are found inside the hen, especially in the spring when the hens are laying. They are added at the same time as the chicken livers and form small golden globules when the sauce is finished.

When the *ragù* is to be served with spaghetti or tagliatelle, mix it with the hot pasta in a heated dish so that the pasta is thoroughly impregnated with the sauce, and add a generous piece of butter before serving. Hand the grated cheese round separately.

Cheese Soufflé

Guardian, 2 March 2009

In 1958, when I was thirteen years old, the days of the midweek seemed to melt aimlessly into each other. Saturday night couldn't come fast enough: winkle-pickers, drainpipe trousers, hanging around Golders Green bus station eyeing the birds and doing a bit of back-combing. But I didn't need a diary to tell me how far away the weekend was. The evening aromas coming from the kitchen as I struggled with my Latin verbs would check off the days.

Wednesday brought a pungent sheepy smell emanating from the greyish lamb and barley soup my mother optimistically called Taste of the Garden of Eden. Expel me, please. Haddock in the air? That would be Thursday. Eaten cold, two days later, for breakfast, it wasn't all that bad. When the fried flakes started to glow with a slight morning iridescence, the thing turned edible. The faintest whiff of roasting garlic? That would be what my sister and I uncharitably dubbed Friday Night Memorial Chicken; a venerable object smeared on the breasts with a dab of Marmite meant to cheer the bird up as it emerged defeated from the oven. Rattling inside the little cavity was that one solitary clove of garlic: the exotic knobble that my mother conceded as a romantic touch amid the iron regimen of her unvarying weekly routine.

So when I learned to cook in the 1960s, the discovery of food was always about experiment: an aversion to routine of any kind. There were certain trusty books at hand; my guides and mentors – Elizabeth David's *French Provincial Cooking* and *Italian Food*, and Simonne Beck, Louise Bertholle and Julia Child's *Mastering the Art of French Cooking*. And I quickly learned that there were some things I did better than others – bouillabaisse, *soupe au pistou*, *stufato di manzo* (Italian beef stew) – but I shunned anything resembling a familiar repertoire: a bistro edition of my mother's kitchen. So I would recklessly take chances with dinner parties on dishes I had never tried before. Sometimes they worked; sometimes they didn't.

Zwiebel, an Alsatian onion tart from Elizabeth David, had exactly the buttery-golden texture and voluptuous ooze running to the walls of the pastry shell, but a beef Wellington served up to impress historians was a glutinous ruin. Undaunted, the riskier the combo of pastry and whatever it was, the more I was up for it. It took a few disasters with a classic Russian salmon *koulibiak*, but on the third try at a summer dinner party in my neo-brutalist Cambridge don's rooms, I pulled it off, passed the vodka and watched as conversation stopped and guests forked their way to quiet joy.

Years later, with small children running round my American kitchen, cooking was still ordained as adventure. Living in New England, the family was going to eat seafood – and I didn't mean fish fingers. In late February, the very first tiny, intensely sweet shrimp of the season would be driven down from Camden, Maine, by a ruddy-faced fisherman who would park his van on a suburban hill, pack a huge plastic tub of them for a few dollars, and we would gorge through the weekend, sucking the meat from the delicate shells. Then there was lobster, the scariest imaginable food for children, which we educationally set before them. We cracked a claw open for my four-year-old daughter, who was leaning towards the glistening oily white flesh when a cry of horror came from my smaller son sitting in his high chair. 'No, Chloë! Don't put it in your mouth,' he wailed, staring in horror at the lurid marine cockroach. She did.

But, even as I turned into an unstoppably crazed gazeteer of world cuisine – Maghrebi *maqluba* (upside-down aubergine and rice casserole), Burmese *beya kwaw* (split-pea fritters) that fell apart in the pan – I knew it was unfair to recruit my kids as fellow gastro-explorers in the name of principled eclecticism. Small children are nature's little conservatives. They are warmed by fulfilled expectations. They have favourites in the kitchen – and why deny them? So I developed some dishes that could satisfy my longing for complicated exercises in flavour fusions, but still be food that the children loved: a lemony-chickpea chicken stew first encountered in Claudia Roden's Middle Eastern books, and the much-requested *raan*, a Kashmiri roast lamb dish in which the joint is marinaded in three separate coats: a garlic-and-roast-spice rub; a paste of saffron, crushed pistachio and almonds blended with yoghurt; and finally, a sumptuous drizzle of honey. After two (or preferably three) days tight-wrapped in film in the fridge, out it comes and slow-roasts (or rather disintegrates beneath its nutty-spicy-sweet golden mantle of flavours) and you have something that's both main course and pudding all at once.

Raan was all very well for the weekend (marinade Friday night; eat on Sunday), but the more hectic family life became, the more I needed a range of dishes that would make them happy as they smelled the cooking when they came in from lacrosse or science lab on a bleak muddy evening in February, or while they got stuck into homework. They had to be dishes that wouldn't take an age to prepare (though dinner was usually around eight, two hours after most American kids had eaten, allowing their friends to stop round for a second supper). And it had to be a meal I wanted to shop for, after a day's teaching or writing.

Getting to know the shopkeepers makes a difference, turns a transaction into a gossip with friends. At the Korean greengrocer I want to know when the New Jersey asparagus might show up in May, but also how Monica is doing off in Montana with her one-year-old. At the butcher's in Chappaqua, they'll find me a rabbit for a pasta sauce, but I worry how Tony manages after losing his wife in a battle with cancer. At Harold's place they'll be smoking sturgeon and whitefish and complaining it's been too long since they saw me, while across the street at Mount Kisco Seafood I'll talk cricket with Pauly from India, but baseball with Brian and Joe even though they're Yankees fans and I'm a diehard Red Sox loyalist. We switch to Pink Floyd or politics and they tell me the Copper River salmon from Alaska is in — and only for a precious two weeks. So I'll take a long beautiful fillet and power-roast it in the oven with a light crust of fine-chopped fresh herbs.

The trick is to set the roasting pan, liberally greased with butter (olive oil, if you must) and a layer of herbs, in a fierce oven, say 225°C, until the green stuff is on the turn of crisping. Then you set the fish on top, skin-side up, for just four minutes for a piece about 1.5cm thick, until the skin peels off with just the touch of a knife. Turn, season and cover the now exposed side of the fillet with more herbs (parsley, coriander, thyme, even tarragon — just not rosemary) and roast for another four. The fish cooks perfectly, buttery and golden-crispy on the outside, perfectly juicy inside. Kids of all ages, even fish-haters, love it.

So the herby salmon became an item in the repertoire I swore I would never have. But actually family cooks need these staples; together they make a kitchen portrait of their table life together. And with any luck, as they grow up and leave home and start their own kitchens, the children will take those food memories with them. There is an Italian meatloaf – *polpettone* – that I made a lot, which, before he became a vegetarian, my son liked so much that he wrote his college application essay about father–son bonding in the hunt for the perfect meatloaf recipe, ending with the triumph of the *polpettone rustica*. It's a homely, lovely thing; a coarse blend of veal and beef, into which you knead some chopped-up stale white bread, soaked in milk, a few grams of finely grated Parmesan, a beaten egg and that's about it. But then instead of packing it into a loaf tin, you make a freeform Swiss roll or big sausage of it, roll it in flour and carefully set it in a casserole of foaming butter or oil together with a couple of sprigs of thyme, a bay leaf and a sage leaf. You let the roll bubble and brown a little, add a glass of white wine or (better for some reason) dry vermouth and then put it in a 180°C oven with the lid off. After thirty minutes take the pot out, and carefully turn it over with spatulas (wooden are best, as non-flexible) and let it cook another thirty to forty minutes. Serve with some sauté potatoes and a *salsa verde* and you can guarantee supper bliss.

There are other indispensable items in the Schama repertoire: a wonderful simple dish of flattened chicken fillets dredged in paprika and cayenne cornmeal, fried and set on a bed of rocket that has been doused in chopped summer tomatoes, their juice marrying with some good olive oil and a little sherry vinegar, the whole thing crispy and sloppy, hot and fresh, all at the same time. Then there are sword-fish steaks marinaded in an Asian blend of soy, mirin, grated ginger, garlic and chopped spring onions, and barbecued for seven minutes a side.

But what the kids moaned for, craved, especially in dark winter months, was the simplest of all: a cheese soufflé. Simple? Yes, it could hardly be simpler, and also virtually infallible as long as you have a dependable oven. The prep takes perhaps twenty minutes; the cooking, filling the kitchen with luscious, toasty-cheesy aroma, another twenty-five to thirty minutes, during which time you can make a salad or a pan of spinach to cut against the voluptuous ooziness of the soufflé. So the whole thing takes maybe forty-five minutes – a doddle for hard-pressed cooks in midweek. And though soufflé cooking scares people off – what if it fails to rise? (it never does) – the only art you have to learn is the difference between mixing and folding the cheese-yolk mixture into the beaten whites.

Once you've tried it, you'll know there's nothing to it and, unless you're a cholesterol timebomb, it will be at the heart of your very own family repertoire too.

> *Cheese soufflé*
> Serves 4
>
> 6 eggs, separated into 4 yolks and 6 whites
> 2 tbsp butter plus tsp for greasing soufflé dish
> 1½ tbsp plain flour, plus dusting for the soufflé dish
> 200ml milk
> 170g grated Gruyère
> 2 tbsp Dijon mustard
> 1 tsp salt
> 50g finely grated Parmesan
>
> For accompaniment
> Either watercress salad with walnuts and a drizzle of balsamic
> dressing, or shredded cavolo nero crisped in the oven for 10
> minutes with 3 tbsp olive oil

Pre-heat the oven to 190°C. Butter a large (1.8l) ovenproof soufflé dish and dust with flour.

Separate the eggs: whites into a large bowl, yolks into small one.

On a medium-high heat, melt the butter in a large saucepan; add the flour and blend with either a wooden fork or a small whisk, stirring all the time for two minutes, so that the mix doesn't form lumps. It should make an elastic goop.

Add the milk and continue to stir or whisk for about four minutes until the mixture forms a dense creamy mass – the béchamel.

Add the grated Gruyère and stir until smooth. Remove from the heat. When tepid, whisk in the egg yolks, mustard and salt.

Beat the whites preferably by hand with a balloon whisk, but an electric beater works just fine, until they form soft and floppy peaks.

Using a flexible plastic or rubber spatula, fold the cheese-mustard mix into the whites (or vice versa, it really doesn't matter). What does matter is that you fold, not beat or aggresively stir. Folding just means diving the spatula to the bottom of the bowl, lovingly bringing it up and over again to blend the mix. It's always much better to undermix than lose air by thrashing it into submission.

When the mixture is nicely married, pour into the buttered, flour-dusted soufflé dish. It should fill all but 1cm below the lip. With a knife, cut a circle in the top of the mix – to create a crown – and sprinkle over the finely grated Parmesan.

Set the soufflé dish in the oven and turn the heat down immediately to 175°C.

While the soufflé is cooking, assemble a simple salad – watercress or rocket with a light dressing, a little acid to cut against the creaminess of the soufflé.

Bake for twenty-five minutes before peeping. Test doneness with a skewer. It won't collapse. If the skewer comes away cleanly and, depending on whether you want an oozy, flowing centre or a drier soufflé, stop right there or cook for another four minutes. Serve with the watercress salad or a dish of crispy cavolo nero or spinach.

Simmer of Love

Vogue, February 2008

Whoever would have thought that a writer as bony as Virginia Woolf would be the one to extol the majesty of beef stew in all its gloppy glory? In *To the Lighthouse*, Woolf transforms a dinner party, wretched with unspoken strong feeling, into a moment of tender communion. What accomplishes this miracle? A Swiss maid sets down on the table a big brown pot of *boeuf en daube*. Suddenly, everything and everyone is enveloped in the welcoming fug of meaty steam. Aromas of bay and wine hang benevolently over these tediously self-absorbed types. Flinty minds liquefy. The ladle ladles, they all tuck in, human sympathy descends on the refined company. They begin to resemble actual human beings. The beleaguered hostess, Mrs Ramsay, is so swoony at her 'triumph', through which egotism has melted into the 'confusion of savoury yellow and brown meats' lying in the casserole, that she commits a white lie, claiming the dish is 'a French recipe of my grandmother's' when in fact it is (needless to say) the creation of her cook, Mildred.

And, for a moment, you, too, reader, are held in a contented drool. Unless, that is, you are a cook — which, you then suddenly realise, Mrs Woolf could not possibly have been herself. *Boeuf en daube? Yellow* meats? *What* 'yellow' meats? A chicken foot lurking in there along with the beef and onions, is there? And then the credibility of the scene falls apart just like a lengthily braised joint, except less appetisingly. For now you also recall that, a few pages previously, Mrs Ramsay had been agitated that her diners would not assemble on time because, she worries, where a *boeuf en daube* is concerned, 'everything depended upon being served up to the precise moment they were ready. The beef, the bay leaf and the wine — all must be done to a turn. To keep it waiting was out of the question.' But this description, from the most fastidiously observant English novelist of the twentieth century, is exactly what a *daube* is *not*.

Stews are the most forgiving dishes. Under their tight-shut lid they can be allowed to simmer away for hours on end, provided they don't dry out – which they won't if you buy cuts with enough fat to lubricate the slowly dissolving tissue, and so long as you poke your nose in the pot from time to time to check for dwindling juice. Stews seem to possess an organic vitality independent of the cook. Left alone overnight, even in the fridge, benevolent unions and fusions happen, so that the longer they go on, the better they get. Eating a stew on the day it's cooked is okay. Eating it the day after is an improvement, and spooning down a bowlful for breakfast two days later is a wholly different experience from cornflakes. It's this steady gathering of richness, the accumulating intensification of flavour that, over the centuries, made stews a rare sustenance amidst the emaciated life of the rural poor, for they could be simmered in an iron cauldron over a slow fire, or set in a bed of cinders waiting to be devoured after a long day of herding or harvesting. They are the dish *par excellence* of cultures without timepieces.

Early French cookbook writers like Menon, who equated social stability with the culinary traditions of the *terroir*, praised the *marmite perpetuelle* – the perpetual poultry-pot, never allowed to be emptied or taken from the heat, so that the broth left from the long poaching of one bird would then welcome the arrival of the next, which in turn would contribute its own golden oozings, on and on for ever in a great unbroken chain of nourishment. When the *marmite perpetuelle* seemed to have vanished from rural cuisine at the close of the nineteenth century, its elegists thought the end of true cooking was nigh.

How odd is it that being 'in a stew' is a description of sweaty anxiety when, in fact, the food is a balm for the fretful: a slow, voluptuous yielding, long bundles of fibre softening in a gently bubbling bath of oily wine or, in the Flemish *carbonnade*, yeasty beer. We think of stews as wintry comforts but they are sure-fire proof against dirty weather, hot or cold. The most satisfying *daube* I remember making was in the summer of 1972 when an ugly Mediterranean storm-system stalled over the Côte d'Azur, where I was holidaying with a girlfriend in a walk-up rental in Cagnes-not-really-sur-Mer. The place wasn't much to talk about, but the tiny kitchen boasted a mighty *marmite*. After an overnight marinade of the beef in local olive oil (no cold-pressed extra-virgins known in 1972, not to us anyway), barnyard-smelling red Minervois wine, a tablespoon of vinegar and a fist of herbs and garlic, we rendered some cubed bacon in the morning, softened some carrots in the fat so they took on a vivid glaze, and let the usual mess of sliced onions and garlic go gently translucent. I had brought along with me the bible of all novice cooks, Elizabeth David's *French Provincial Cooking*, and it was her *daube provençale* that we made, throwing in a greasy slab of salt pork, some sprigs of thyme and parsley and oregano, bay leaves from the tree outside the old limestone house, a handful or two of black olives, a few bashed peppercorns and some curls of orange zest. The storm growled overhead in an inky sky, wooden doors in the hilltop village banged, and stray cats screeched in the lightning. Wishing the stew a happy simmer, we went to bed, the scent of Provençal thyme welling through the rooms. Every so often we'd get up to slurp the mysteriously harmonising concoction from a big old spoon or throw some rough cognac on the surface, setting light to it for cheerfulness's sake, hoping not to incinerate the rental. It was meat and drink, breakfast, lunch and supper, that sumptuous *daube*. We wiped bowls with hunks of stale baguette or ate it on beds of slippery noodles, beads of oil glimmering on the pale ribbons as the feast saw off the bullyboy thunder. The festive, recklessly amorous Elizabeth, we thought, would have approved.

So if there's joy promised in the consumption of a richly cooked stew, why don't we see more of them on the menus of ambitious contemporary restaurants? Partly, I suppose it's because their messiness doesn't sit well in a plating culture that wants you to ooh and aah at the exquisiteness of presentation; a thin tile of (please God, no) sea bass, skin side up, its silvery surface demurely crisped at the edges, perched just so on a plinth of spinach while teeny-weeny broad beans do a dainty little dance around the perimeter of the dish. Cute. Stewing meat of whatever kind is never cute; it's the slob on the plate, leaking incontinently towards the beckoning mash. But gastro-aesthetes are wrong to write off stews as simple stuff. Done right, they are complex compositions, but they are, certainly, earthy: redolent of the farmyard and not for the dainty. In Oklahoma some years ago, I was treated to a bowl of burgoo. Even if the squirrel was, as I suspected, yard-kill, who cared when it luxuriated in a brick-colour smoky sauce of chipotle chillies, plum tomatoes, garlic and beer? A true *civet* — whether classically of hare or any other four-legged critter — is defined by two additions to the pot: the onions or chives from which the dish gets its name, and the blood of the animal stirred in before final reheating. Among American cowboys, as my friend Blanquette reminded me, sonofabitch stew, made from brains, tripe, hooves, innards, tongue and 'mountain oysters' (balls, to you) – in fact, anything that doesn't get to be hamburger – is still prime rodeo fare.

There's also the sense among contemporary chefs that *boeuf bourguignon* and its kindred stews are old hat; along with the paprika-lurid goulashes and *coqs au plonk* that featured heavily in the Paris *bistros* of the Fifties, like Chez Allard and Louis XIV on the place des Victoires, and which gave Anglo bohemians groaning from limp veg and leathery beef the impression they had arrived in a real-food world. In the Sixties those dishes, served with halfway decent bread, became the staple of the first London 'bistros' I could afford, like the Chanterelle in Chelsea, places where (unlike today) you went to be *un*seen, except by your romantic prospect. Never mind the flouncy waiters in their blood-red shirts, a plateful of *coq au vin* seemed a declaration of class war on the aristo fare at toffish places like the Mirabelle, with their anaemic sole sitting in a puddle of béchamel. We smoked Gitanes hung on our nether lip, Belmondo-style, across from turquoise-eyeshadowed dates dragging artichoke leaves through their incisors.

Or, courtesy of Elizabeth David, Jane Grigson and, later and more dauntingly, Mesdames Bertholle, Becks and Child's *Mastering the Art of French Cooking*, we would whip up our own versions of *boeuf bourguignon* on a solitary, erratically sputtering gas ring in a college staircase kitchen, much to the horror of the Cambridge cleaning ladies, who smelled nasty habits along with the nasty garlic.

And it was a bonus that those of us who were historians were, we thought, cooking (in the most legitimate way) our research, as well as vice versa. High politics turned us off as much as *haute cuisine*. Instead, we marinated ourselves in Fernand Braudel's history of the food migrations of the centuries; the Europeanisation of exotic foods like sugar or spices like pepper and cloves. The revolutions we really rated as world-changing were the appearance of the American potato and tomato, not the storming of the Bastille. Redcliffe Salaman's epic history of the tuber was a must-read (it still is). Before long our cookbooks were also our texts of history and ethnography: Alan Davidson's stupendous works of encyclopaedic scholarship; Elizabeth Ayrton's *The Cookery of England*, which introduced us to cooks like Gervase Markham in the seventeenth century, Elizabeth Raffald and the punchy Hannah Glasse in the eighteenth. In the British Museum Reading

Room I'd play truant from teaching undergraduates Abelard or Eisenhower and dally instead with Robert May's *The Accomplisht Cook* (1660) or Varenne's *Cuisinier Français* (1651). And gradually I became aware of the epic battle between Spit and Pot. Spit People were aristocratic roasters; birds and beast, trussed and turned; Pot People were the plebs: lengthy braisers.

There was never any doubt I was a Pot Person. The closest my mother – who grew up in the Jewish East End, and whose idea of lamb stew was something worryingly thin and grey – ever got to rhapsodising about food was when she described taking the iron pot of *cholent* (the stew of meat and vegetables – which, if done right, had raw eggs in their shells buried within) to a communal baker's oven before the onset of the Sabbath on Friday night. Nothing, she said, was quite like taking the lid off the *cholent* pot by the time the family got back from synagogue the next day. '*Taam gan eden*,' she would murmur dreamily – 'The taste of the Garden of Eden.'

Stews are the inclusive food, uniting multitudes – your family, your friends, your tribe – around the same capacious, endlessly nourishing pot. When the Grand Constable of the Dauphiné, during a time of religious war at the end of the sixteenth century, wanted to win friends and allies, he'd bring his *grande marmite* to town and put on a spread for 500. A surviving recipe written in his hand calls for, among other ingredients, 160 pigs' trotters (a good source of gelatine thickening), 100kg of beef, 40 bottles of red wine, 24 of white, 32 chickens and 25kg of mushrooms. But this was small potatoes compared to the great *sancocho* of Caracas, in which, earlier this year, in a mass demonstration of Chavezian state philanthropy (or megalomania), a single pot containing 5,000kg of meat and 7,000kg of vegetables, including yucca, okra and plantains, bought the loyalty of at least 17,000 satisfied Venezuelans.

Stews are bringers of contentment to a discontented world. I don't know of any other kind of food, except perhaps freshly baked bread and cakes, guaranteed to fill a kitchen with such a sense of abundance. They violate all the cool modern conventions, for they demand fat and time and copious carbs – mashed potatoes or parsnips, pasta or bread – to soak up the juicy mess. You'll have skimmed much of the killer grease half an hour or so before serving, so there's no obligation to cleanse the palate with anything sharply green. Don't even think about spinach, though the collapse of a summer salad on an oily plate is one of the table's great acts of surrender. Forget about anything leaner or meaner (like green beans): that's like inviting Lent to the carnival. And as the winter nights close in and the craving for those unctuous, oozing, life-sustaining stews becomes irresistible, do yourselves a favour: make a large pot at the weekend and it will last all week, nourishing your very own Perpetual Pot of Pleasure.

Stew recipes

Boeuf en daube provençale
(Remembered and adapted from Elizabeth David)
Time: 3 hours 30 minutes (plus marinating time)
Serves 6

1½kg stewing beef, cut into 2½cm cubes

For the marinade:
2 tbsp olive oil
2 medium carrots, coarsely sliced
1 stick celery, finely chopped
2 cloves garlic, finely chopped
3 medium shallots, finely chopped
1 tbsp rosemary, chopped
1 tbsp thyme, leaves stripped from sprigs
1 tbsp flat parsley, finely chopped
12 peppercorns, cracked
a pinch of salt
1 bottle robust red wine – Gigondas or Cahors

For the stew:
plain flour for dusting
1 tbsp olive oil
200g streaky bacon or pancetta, diced
2 garlic cloves, smashed but not chopped
2 bay leaves
1 tbsp fresh thyme
4 good-quality anchovies, minced (optional)
zest of ½ medium orange
50g good-quality black olives

125g mushrooms

75ml cognac

fresh parsley, finely chopped, for garnish

Prepare the marinade one or two days in advance of serving the *daube*: heat the olive oil in a frying pan and sauté the carrots, celery, garlic, shallots and herbs on a medium-low heat for about three minutes, until the herbs release their aroma.

Put the beef in a bowl, combine with the marinade, season with the pepper and salt and add the wine. Cover and leave overnight. If steeping longer, turn the meat in the marinade every few hours.

When you are ready to cook the *daube*, use a slotted spoon to remove the beef from the marinade, pat dry on paper towels and dust with flour.

Pre-heat the oven to 125°C, gas mark ½.

On a medium heat, heat the oil and fry the bacon or pancetta in a casserole until it begins to crisp. Remove the bacon from the pot and set aside. Turn up the heat and brown the beef in batches.

Return the bacon to the dish, add the beef and marinade, and then the garlic, bay leaves, thyme, anchovies (if used) and zest. Put on the lid, place in the oven and cook for at least three hours, until the meat falls apart.

About thirty minutes before serving, add the olives and mushrooms, and continue to cook. Warm the cognac in a ladle, pour over the stew and set it alight.

Garnish with parsley and serve from the pot with bread or flat noodles – the traditional Provençal way.

Chickpea-lemon chicken stew with couscous

Time: 1 hour 30 minutes (plus soaking time)

Serves 4

425g chickpeas (prepare as below, but if you are short of time, use tinned and drain and rinse well)

1 small onion, peeled

2 garlic cloves, peeled

For the stew:

4 tbsp light olive or safflower oil

2 large onions, thinly sliced
4 cardamom pods, cracked
2 tsp turmeric
1 tsp cumin seeds
3 garlic cloves, crushed
1 tsp ground cumin
½ tsp cayenne
½ tsp ground ginger
1 tsp coriander seeds, coarsely crushed
1 organic chicken, cut into 8 pieces
the juice of 3 lemons (if possible unwaxed)
250ml chicken stock
1 lemon (preserved if possible), cut into pieces
15 green olives, pitted
salt and freshly ground pepper, to taste
fresh parsley or coriander for garnish

Prepare the chickpeas before cooking the stew: place them in a colander and rinse well. Then put them in a bowl of cold water at room temperature and soak overnight. Transfer to a saucepan over a medium heat, add the whole onion and garlic cloves, bring to the boil, then remove from the heat and leave to soak for two to three hours, until almost tender.

Heat two tablespoons of the olive oil in a tagine or casserole dish on a low heat and sauté the onions, cardamom pods, turmeric and cumin seeds for ten minutes, until the onions are soft but not brown.

Add the garlic, ground cumin, cayenne, ground ginger and coriander seeds, turn the heat up to medium and fry for a further three minutes.

Remove the spiced-onion mix and set aside in a bowl. Add the remaining two tablespoons of oil to the casserole and brown the chicken pieces on a medium heat for about ten minutes, until golden. Season with a little salt and pepper, then add the lemon juice and chicken stock to the pot so that the chicken pieces are fully covered.

Put a lid on the pot and simmer on a medium heat for thirty minutes.

Drain the chickpeas. Add to the stew with the lemon chunks and olives. Simmer for a further thirty minutes, until the meat is beginning to fall off the bone and the liquid has become a thick sauce.

Serve the stew in bowls, spooned onto a pile of couscous, and garnish with finely chopped fresh parsley or coriander.

My Mother's Kitchen

Observer Food Magazine, 11 October 2009

It was when my mother minced the tip of her forefinger into the *klops*
that I realised her cooking owed more to enthusiasm than finesse. No,
I'm wrong. It was when she decided not to bother to *search* for the little
piece of alien flesh amidst the beef, but carried on kneading the meat
with the onions, that I got a sense of her priorities, at the top of which
was Just Getting It Over With. I was nine. The kitchen intrigued me
for it seemed some sort of battlefield in which my mother laid about
various ingredients until they surrendered and accepted their fate in
a long, hot oven. She would never have used the term *batterie de cuisine*,
but she took pride in the more fearsome of its implements, in particular the heavy-duty steel hand mincer, which, after it had been polished
to military brilliance, was attached to the kitchen table. All kinds of
food went down its helical screw-mouth: translucent cod and haddock
fillets on Thursdays for the *gefilte* fish; unusual extra chicken breasts
for fried balls served up sometimes on Sundays, and the mid-week
jumbo meatballs, the legendary *klops* of her strenuous attack. Into the
screw were also fed lashings of onion and, if she was in a mood to
lighten the fish or chicken, a beaten egg or two. I don't remember her
crying out in pain when she pulled her slightly chewed-up finger out
of the mincer, though there was a hearty Yiddish curse or two sent in
its direction. Like Basil Fawlty scolding his Austin, she had Warned
It Before and now it would just have to take the consequences. Into
the sink went her finger; on to the slightly drippy wound went an
Elastoplast and on she went with the *klops*. At nine I could (on select
occasions) be a sanctimonious little perisher and knew that I could put
a stop to the inexorable grinding by asking her whether the ground
fingertip was, in fact, kosher, and if not, would it write off the whole
dish – one of my father's favourites? I also knew that she would brush
the objection aside with one of her more devilish laughs and that

would be the end of it, other than swearing me to silence as Father and my older sister tucked into the *klops*.

Later, when she worked as the Field-Marshal of Kosher Meals on Wheels in the Jewish East End, getting up before dawn to travel across London to see all the housebound got their lunches, and relished every minute of it, I realised that it was not the food that was my mother's foe so much as the domestic kitchen itself. A bundle of animal energy in a pretty little package, she just was not cut out for the middle-class housewife role in which she had got somehow stuck, and all the displaced, ferocious energy, and slightly manic, often comical, action drama just needed a bigger stage to operate on. As far as I could tell, Trudie had always been this way. As a little girl, Chaya Gittel – the name she went by in Whitechapel and Stepney – had the startling looks that made people want to chin-chuck her or (for her), worse, pinch her cushiony cheeks: black curls and cobalt-blue eyes; a killer combo. But when she was made to dress up, and the curls were trained into ringlets, people found out in a hurry she was more spitfire than angel. Her father, my grandfather Mark, the only one of a gang of Lithuanian-Jewish brothers who stopped in Stepney rather than moving north to Liverpool to catch the New York ship, was a butcher. So when Chaya, over furious protest, was forced to dress up in silks and satins imported at great expense from my grandmother's Vienna relatives for Special Occasions, my mother's way to make a tomboy statement was to take the butcher's shears and slash it to ribbons. The thrashing she got made her repent not one bit. She set her jaw firmly and swore she would do it again.

Perhaps it was the butcher-shop childhood that did it, but my mother grew up seldom relishing food; and certainly holding herself apart from the fatty wallowing in the joys of the Jewish table, which she looked on, often, with undisguised contempt – even, or especially, when she was forced to cook it. Food and its relentless preparation was somehow a chore, an enemy of life. During the war she worked for de Havilland aircraft, Girl Friday to test pilots, one of whom used to take her for spins in his roadster, a bottle of Scotch handy in the glove box. She got to like un-Jewish things: Thames Valley pubs and good hard Cheddar with the odd dark vein running to the rind. My mother thought the test pilot an ace and always laughed at the memory of his fine madness. He ended in a ball of flame, but that only made the story perfect as far as she was concerned.

In her girlhood Chaya befriended a turkey whose lame strut — a ritual impurity — had saved it from the slaughterer's knife. She called it 'Loomie' — the Lame One — and taught it to limp up and down the stairs. Girl and bird bonded with terrible intensity and spent much time in each other's company. Then, inevitably one day, Loomie disappeared, sold by my grandfather to a gentile colleague for a destiny with Christmas. My mother threw one of her majestic tantrums, barricaded herself in her birdless room, emerging only to grab her younger brother and attempt to run away south, dragging her teary-eyed little sibling all the way past London Bridge on the road she hoped ended in Brighton, before being picked up by an amazed but kindly copper. All her life she stayed wary of butchers, and had the Insider's Knowledge to make their lives miserable should she suspect they were overcharging for poor cuts and stringy quality. Burly men in stained aprons from Stamford Hill to Temple Fortune would hide behind the *Wieners* or hurry to the cold room when they saw Trudie barrel through the glass door. I sometimes thought the curse of the Lame Turkey hung over her entire treatment of poultry, especially the terminally overcooked Friday-night chicken, whose ghastly pallor was enlivened by a coating of Marmite so that it emerged from the oven looking like a society matron who had been mistreated at a tanning salon. Within its cavity rattled a lonely duet of garlic cloves, an exotic concession to my father's savoury cravings.

My father belonged to a different Jewish food tradition — Rumanian with a dash of Sefardi ancestry — so that rice, dried fruit, and stuffed vine leaves (with the more Ashkenazi sweet-and-sour cabbage substituting in my mother's version) were dishes that made him happy and, above all other things, I think, aubergines; still not easy to find in the 1950s. My mother eked out the joy of the aubergine, sometimes making a purée laced with more garlic than she usually found acceptable, and stuffing them with minced beef (without, so far as I know, the addition of human parts) in which the spices of my father's mother's kitchen — cinnamon and allspice — played a dangerous, appetising part.

When she felt she was not Under Obligation, Trudie could turn out some good simple things. Her pride and joy, a thick, glutinous lamb-and-barley soup she called 'Ta'am Gan Eden' — the Taste of the Garden of Eden — never quite lived up to its billing as far as I was concerned; the muttony pungency of kosher lamb somehow obliterating the stewed vegetables. But she made wonderful egg noodles to go with the chicken soup that preceded the *Poulet à la Marmite*; and I would help her slice the egg-rolls into quarter-inch strings and lay them out on greaseproof paper. Every so often I would steal one of the yellow ribbons, popping it in my mouth before the high-speed hand of my mother slapped it away. Then there were the fried fish balls: Sefardi Jews' gift to Britain (for everywhere else in the Jewish world, *gefilte* fish is poached). Whatever the precise mix of egg, matzo meal, onion and spices that went into the devouring mincer, my mother got it right, and the smell and sound of the discs, going tawny brown in their bath of hot oil, was when I wanted to be in the kitchen. As far as I was concerned, she never made enough, for though they were fried on a Thursday, I would gobble one down for breakfast the next morning and by Saturday, somehow (though my mother complained about their lengthy residence in the fridge), they had taken on some mysteriously enriched flavour that was, for me, heaven to the palate. In synagogue that morning, my hair slicked up into a pompadour hardened with a secret recipe of Brylcreem and Uhu glue, deep in discussion about the fortunes of Spurs and the fabulous Valentine twins up in the gallery whom we ogled from below, I knew that I smelled faintly of haddock beneath the Old Spice. But you know what, dear foodies, I didn't give a damn.

Mouthing Off

Oxford Food Symposium, September 2009

There's not much I won't or can't eat. I've eaten crocodile in Holland; barbied kangaroo at Uluru and mountain oysters in Cody, Wyoming. But tongue, even though Fergus Henderson in his recipe for 'Ox Tongue and Bread' lyricises about its slices as 'like little angel's wings', has always tested my gag reflex. (Come to think of it, I'm not sure I'd want little angel's wings in my mouth either.) Lambs' tongues are a particular problem – like pigs' tongues, so I'm told – because, being pretty much the same size as our own, a confusing subject and object of mastication, one stands a fair chance of biting the former rather than the latter. Given that tongues are dense with cell receptors (fifty to a hundred for each so-called bud), the experience – as you all know – can be acutely painful and bloody. But there's another telling aspect to my lingophobia, which is all to do with the separate, but (I want to argue) connected functions of the tongue, that, in my case, precludes the possibility of consumption. Biting one's tongue is an act expressing pre-emptive remorse in the mouth, where the tongue is in fact the processing agency of pleasure. And more significantly for those of us in the word business, the fear of tongue-biting seems to me an anxiety about muting the organ of articulation without which our experience of food seems (whether this is right or wrong is the subject of these remarks) incomplete. So it's the threat of damaging or mutilating the multi-tasking organ which is both the instrument of utterance and consumption that is at the root (not to pun) of my tongue-anxiety, I suppose. Do any of us here really want to eat our own words?

La langue, is of course a gastro-structuralist's dream, especially when allied to the palate; though in its connection between language and eating, one that seems not to have occurred to Saussure himself. He may or may not have read Brillat-Savarin's *Physiologie du Goût*, but he never seems to have reflected on the fact that, assuming *la langue* (as he coined it) is the prior wiring that makes *la parole* – individual utterance events – possible, it is actually the elemental experience of taste, registered on the tongue's cell receptors, which gives rise in the infant to sound-communication; and that, further evolved, is the defining characteristic of what distinguishes humans from dumb beasts. We are, as has often been noted, the language animal. But it's probably only in this symposium that two of the tongue's three purposes – taste and speech – can be thought of as functionally connected; one kind of experience informing and structuring the other.

Almost all of the nerve endings in a newborn are centralised in tongue and mouth, so that the former acts as an astonishingly precocious processor of information coming from the maternal breast and its milk. The hunger instinct and what to do about it is activated there, but babies also use their tongues expressively to register difference of mood and wants. In this sense, from our very earliest days, 'utterance', however basic, and consumption are tongued. The infant sucks, generates a sound, but in turn that sound, learned by the baby as a signal to prompt parental attention, will cue up a feed. It is, you might say, a perfect feedback loop and the most elementary bonding between using the tongue to consume and the tongue to communicate. Scientific studies have shown – and the experience of many parents will have borne it out – that during that first year of life a baby is surprisingly omnivorous, using the tongue and palate to explore, in addition to breast milk, an extraordinary range of sensations across the four taste categories of sour, sweet, salty and bitter (and perhaps, who knows, even including umami). Our own daughter at this very early stage liked nothing better, we discovered – in contravention to all the received wisdoms about the baby-food purées – than blue cheese (Stilton in particular), lemons, olives and (on, I hasten to say, the rare occasions when she got a chance to sample it) caviar. Likewise, much early language originates in response to flavour. Our daughter's first identifiable word, both descriptive and commanding, was 'apple' (or rather 'a-boo'). It seems to be only beyond the first year or fifteen months that the dislike for some strong food flavours sets in and a much more conservative separation between likes and dislikes, much of it almost certainly socially learned from siblings and beyond, modifies the initial lingual adventurousness.

So does all this biological and behavioural information make the case from which we can begin our proceedings here, that if our defining characteristic is indeed as language animal, the lingo compulsion does actually get under way with mother's milk; that as soon as we eat, we feel the need to make some noise about it, a sound that will end up as verbalisation and, eventually, writing. It's certainly the case – as I'll want to argue in a little while – that we do seem culturally and socially wired for this connection, and that while beasts roar with hunger or grunt with satisfaction, our own feeding process demands something more complex. It's been a standard form of commentary by relatively sophisticated travellers, observing those whom they think of as relatively unsophisticated natives, to make a point of commenting on the savagery of eating in speed and silence, akin, they usually say, to animals. That at least was the view of the many travellers to the United States in the nineteenth century, especially the French and the English who, like Colonel Basil Hall, Fanny Trollope and Dickens, never passed up an opportunity to comment on the velocity and utter silence with which Americans, especially on the frontier, in river boats – but also in large taverns and hostelries – ate. In 1827 in Memphis, Tennessee, Mrs Trollope observed her fellow diners at a hotel eating 'in perfect silence and with such astonishing rapidity that their dinner was over literally before ours began . . .'; (when) 'they ceased to eat they darted from the room in the same moody silence which they had preserved since they entered the room . . .' As for their successors, 'the only sounds were those produced by knives and forks with much chorus of coughing'. In subsequent commentaries of this kind words like 'animal' or 'scarcely human' were applied to this habitual scene. From the beginning, as seen by foreigners, America was the habitat of social regression: the land of silent as well as fast food.

In contrast, the instinct to register relish through description and discussion – to make a commentary on what was being eaten part of the digestive process – has been established as a protocol of civility. As soon as there are texts, there are food compulsions, not least of course in the Bible, which can fairly be characterised as food-obsessed, whether in the morphology of taboos, complicated distinctions in Leviticus and Deuteronomy between clean and unclean, but also of course in prophetic poetics. At almost every critical turning point of scriptural teleology, outcomes presumably fated by that mercurial crosspatch Jehovah turn on food choices: the fruit that evicted men and women from the paradise garden; the fratricide of the horticulturalist against the pastoralist (an argument over which form of oblation was satisfactory to the deity); the mess of pottage that disrupted the family hierarchy and delivered priority to Jacob; Samson's honey, the Baptist's *wild* honey and locusts; the Singer of the Song's pomegranate fixation, as we might reasonably call it – and on and on. The point is not just that, in the infancy of culture, food allusions and narratives merely occur, but that they are heavy signifiers of outcomes. Much, as Margaret Visser would say, 'depends on dinner'.

So if we accept that in culture, rather than nature, there can be no eating, and perhaps no cooking, without talking and writing, the manner of utterance in speech and on the page bears a heavy load of signficance, whether in rhetorical spectacle (like television); the language manners of menus (the subject of another contribution to the symposium and a subject that obviously repays close semiotic reading); or the growth of the vocalising habit in waiting staff which in the United States, perhaps to reverse that earlier reputation for taciturnity, has become a kind of social preaching often done by not-very-good performers. A chosen diction, an affect of language – and this is usually very self-conscious – carries with it a code of values about the nature of the food and its preparation. The A-line decorum with which the heavily frocked Fanny Cradock presented her cooking lessons on television in the 1950s made it plain that they were meant for the women who aspired to be epitomes of bourgeois propriety. (Though for some of us, this programmed role-playing was strangely, perhaps wonderfully, subverted by Fanny's androgynously deep voice, especially when she put the whiskered Johnny in an apron.) At something like the opposite pole, a half-century later, Gordon Ramsay's 'F Word' compressing – let's say it, shall we, and strip it of its coyness – sex and alimentation, fucking and feeding, not to mention the insertion of fuck into almost every moment of embattled cooking, is a possibly over-strenuous way of proclaiming (whether we agree or not) that earthiness is a signifier of social authenticity, a combative liberation from the culinary preciousness of haute cuisine. Since Ramsay's game is, the implication goes, unquestionably well hung, his is cooking for, by and with the People.

Other choices of diction and tone summon up other messages.

Fergus Henderson, in *Nose to Tail Eating*, tells us 'How to Eat Radishes at Their Peak'. 'Pile your intact radishes onto a plate and have beside them a bowl of coarse sea salt and the good butter.' Now no one is in any danger of confusing a recipe written like this – in fact the choice of recipe itself – with anything written by the Eff-Chef or Jamie Oliver. But there's something about that insistent definite article – '*the*' good butter. What 'the good butter' does sound like, *very* like, is John Evelyn's treatise on salad, the *Acetaria*, published in 1699, or in fact any cookbook from post-Baconian (no pun intended again) England of the seventeenth and pre-Romantic eighteenth century – Gervase Markham or Hannah Glasse. 'Take a faire carp and scour him well,' etc. Together with Henderson's aphorisms passed off as dispassionate culinary science and zoology: 'Woodcock defecate before they fly, so they can be roasted with the guts in, which heightens the flavour.' (I bet it does.) The message not so deeply coded is that Henderson's cooking is benevolently archival and is all about a return to the imagined English pastoral of Parson Woodforde or Squire Western, in which nature, slaughter and cooking, blood and guts, snout and tripe, were assumed elements in the native kitchen and table. There are moments in Henderson's asides as well as instructions that don't quite add up – as in the requirement for Jellied Rabbit: 'Use tame or particularly beautiful wild rabbits for this' – as if we would ever be in a position to reject wild rabbits that weren't *particularly* beautiful; but it doesn't matter because the nativist visceralism of his food regime is so romantically distinctive and strong. The backward historicist journey, away from fusion, faddism and fashion, is meant, I think, as consolatory therapy for contaminated urbanism. 'Even just writing this recipe down,' he says of his Fish Pie, as if presenting himself as someone who, notwithstanding blood and guts, is prone to attacks of urban neuralgia, 'its soothing qualities have quite' (notice that Wildean '*quite*') 'restored me from the fragile state in which I was.' We don't really need the confessional tone to make the pie; but we register it as a delineator of authorial personality: the poetic romantic butcher-cook seeking to reattach English cooking to its pre-industrial roots.

It won't take much prompting, for any number of these gastro-dialectics to come to mind, so many of which were expressed in self-conscious choices of linguistics. It wasn't just what Marinetti had to say when he spat in the eye of *la cucina di nonna*, but the way that he said it. But you can't beat the pioneers of 'fooding' – Alexandre Cammas and Emmanuel Rubin – for exploiting the implications of language to communicate their version of an eating and cooking revolution.

Le style est l'homme même . . . the very neologism of 'fooding' is of course not accidental. Using *franglais* not just casually, but as the masthead of a manifesto, is a gesture comparable to Marinetti's choice of diction but perhaps even more aggressive, since it confronts not just the classicism of haute cuisine and its *langue*, but even more particularly of course the romance of *terroir*, over the past decades something of an obsession on both sides of the English Channel. In this sense 'fooding', the *mot*, attacks the presumptions of two sorts of assumed superiority: the hierarchy of the old school and the fables of provincial authenticity; the mysteries of the earth that are said to be the antidote to die-stamp globalisation (though *dico* does actually praise *terroir* and the slow-food movement). Cultural nationalism in France has such a high stake in its food regimes that of course, as Cammas and Rubin well know, to overturn it in favour of a kind of promiscuous cosmopolitanism is to reach for the most transgressive strategy imaginable, in thinking of not just gastronomy's but France's place amidst the cultures of the world and in particular those of the Anglo-Saxon world; the sense that France is somehow holding out the promise of regional richness against the debased thinness of globalisation.

Fooding practices – the shameless embrace of the snack, the brief, intensely concentrated hit of food before moving on to somewhere and something else, preferably from an absolutely different food culture – intentionally violate much of the holy writ of *gastronomie*: concentration, slowness, uniformity, coherence, meditative pleasure and even, or rather especially, the hierarchy of courses beginning with savoury appetiser or hors d'oeuvre and ending with sweet dessert. (That deconstruction also operates, of course, in the programme of Ferran Adrià and his followers in the United States, like Grant Achatz.) But what strikes me about *fooding* now is how much the lingo effect is crucial to their subversion. In 2004, Cammas and Rubin published *Fooding, le Dico*. Classically French in wanting to create a lexicography of a moment and a manner, it violated for a start the definition of what a dictionary *was*, at least by relatively modern standards, following the spectacularly brilliant '*Dictionnaire égoïste de la littérature française*' of Charles Dantzig in being '*dictionnaire totalement subjectif*'; though it's the kind of subjectivity that in a way recalls pre-*Encyclopédie* Voltaire.

In the *dico* you'll find potted biographies of the new heroes, Adrià, Moreno Cedroni and Victor Arganzonis – '*Che Guevara du barbecue*' – along with shout-outs to those who, like Anthony Bourdain, have at some point violated the protocols. But there are also entries on 'crumble'; Duralex glass; 'jerk chicken' (*à consommer sans modération sur fond de steel bands déchaîné, au célèbre carnaval londonien de Notting Hill*); and '*sardines à l'huile*' (*les sardines en boîte ont perdu leur image trash cabanon pour devenir une nourriture éminemment bobo, symbole du retour aux plaisirs simples*).

The overthrow of '*gastronomie*' for 'fooding' is the most dramatic instance, I suppose, of normative proclamation in the remaking of food culture, but all these examples are instances where language-acts are not just incidental to, but inseparable from, the constitution of food universes. It may be that right now we are suffering from lexical gourmandism; have become too logorrhoeic for our own good, whether it's the almost unimaginable proliferation of food journalism and cookbooks; the multiplication of television food programmes (I plead guilty as an accomplice to some of this); the appalling habit (marked in the United States) of training waiting staff to deliver lengthy disquisitions and sermons on their specials – often, and inaccurately, with the personal pronoun attached (as in 'my seabass today comes with wild rice and a stuffing of celery root and rutabaga'); or even a verbalised *explication de texte* on how to construe the menu and its philosophy (this happens in Tom Colicchio's Craft and, I'm sorry to say, in one of my favourite places in the world, Dan Barber's Blue Hill at Stone Barns, where the tableside lecture reaches almost the point of theology). Then there is the menu itself – a work, all too often, of faux-literature minus any obligation to obey the basic rules of syntax. In exasperation I've made it my own rule of thumb – and I recommend it to you – never to order any item described with more than one verb. And the redundancies I've never been able to get, but which get lodged in the repertoire – 'pan-fried' for instance. Where else are they going to fry it – in a bucket?

Could it even be – and I hesitate to mention this at the food symposia

– that, as Michael Pollan has recently suggested and I've long thought, we have got to the point of diminishing returns, of an inverse relationship between the second-hand consumption of words about eating to the first-hand experience of cooking it, or even reflectively eating it? A kind of ersatz gastronomy has arisen (the so-called 'gourmet' kitchen) in which cooking and eating experienced in restaurants and in journalism are . . . about celebrity chefs – but never taking the culture home. This may be because too many restaurant critics aren't themselves cooks.

The sheer ubiquity and quantity of food-wording has also lowered the bar of quality ('Best Food Writing' anthology, most of the writing was feebly anecdotal) to the point of almost complete depleted exhaustion. So that there are, in effect, two food-word cultures operating side by side; one empty and ephemeral, the language itself casually or reflexively set down, and then a surviving remnant of a different genre – that presumably we are all here to honour – which sees the experience of food as a way of illuminating the nature of human behaviour, habit, mindset; to set out what exactly it is that humans do, not only when they feed, but when they register their feeding on the speaking tongue and the writing mind. What in the end *is* that language reaching for that I argued earlier was somehow behaviourally, if not actually biologically, wired to cooking and eating – and, for that matter, farming and butchering, or hunting and gathering? The answer surely is fixing through a kind of verbal re-enactment; which means it's an act of translation from one sort of experience to the other, in the sure knowledge that much – perhaps the essence – will indeed be lost in translation, as it is indeed lost in comparable verbal exercises when we try to speak or write about music or sex, but without any diminution of the compulsion to try. At its most egregious is the negotiation made in wine description in which complex perfumes are rendered as what they are not and could never have been, but the approximation of which makes a kind of olfactory shorthand – thus 'cedar', 'blackberries', 'leather', and many more nonsensically summoned aromas.

That's a mere matter of convenience, the more improbable the sensory allusion – Roquefort, gunpowder – the more prodigious the reputation of the nose in question. But real seekers after translation are trying, however futilely, something different, for at some level we are all enticed by the possibility that encoded within the fix established by even inadequate re-enactment is the promise of perfect repetition (which also seldom happens in music or sex). And sometimes, what gets lost in *actual* translation has its own unmistakable richness.

Take this wonderful item, for instance, supplied from Z. Guinaudeau's *Fez*, in the recipe for Mchoui kindly given to me by my friend, the brilliant cook and cookbook writer, Alice Sherwood:

Choose a young sheep, fat but not too big. *Bsmillah*. Plunge the knife into the carotid and let the blood spout out to the last drop. Wash the gash in the throat seven times. Make a hole with the point of the knife just above the knee joint of one of the back legs between flesh and skin. Put a stick through this hole and turning it round, start to loosen the skin. Through this opening blow till the air gets to the forelegs and makes them stick up. The sheep will then swell and stiffen as though it had been a long time in water . . . Quickly while an assistant stops up the hole cut the skin between the legs and skin the sheep like a rabbit. Be careful not to cut the trotters or the head and respect the horns . . . Hang up the hide to clean; put aside the liver and heart and hang them up. Give the tripe to the women who will scrape, rinse and put it to dry.

Or the wonderful and related Choua:

Divide the head in two having first cut with scissors and singed the wool which still remains stuck on the skin. With a chopping knife dig out the horns. Tap and shake this pitiful mask to oust any worms that may still remain in the mouth and nose of the animal. Take out the brains, clean them with ashes then plenty of water . . . The part much appreciated is the eye. You insert a finger delicately in the socket; a quick turn of the nail and the orb will fall out, extricate it and eat, well seasoned with salt and cumin.

Now what these passages do, it seems to me, is to succeed through the sheer clumsiness, you might say the sheer *failure*, of translation. Put another way, the translation of the experience survives or is owed to the mistranslation of the idiom. The original language – which is richly rhetorical, Muslim, tribally poetic – preserves the social totality of the experience; the union of butchery and cookery – without the inevitable flattening, the cultural dilution that happens when a cross-idiom translation goes more smoothly; the rough original. What we have here is the whole picture untouched; the crawling worms in the nose.

This rich description of what it is we do when we plant, harvest, slaughter, butcher, knead, bake, roast and consume ought not, of course, to be left to the inadvertent payload of inadequate translation. The strongest food writers aim exactly for that wraparound translation effect. It's seldom that they are restaurant critics or recipe collectors and publishers. The philosopher Michael Oakshott was much given to saying that while you could reduce cooking to a recipe, you couldn't do the same with politics. Many of us, as my friend Adam Gopnik pointed out, would reverse that truism: it's cooking which defies reduction to recipe; politics, alas, is reduced all too easily.

So how to convey that socially inflected rich description without always sounding like an anthropology seminar? The very best writers – those in a class of their own – have embedded their cookery – and their recipes – in remembered experience; part memoir, part re-enactment. And when I say embedded, in Elizabeth David's case, at least in the most prodigious of all her books, *French Provincial Cooking*, this is literally true – in the layout of her best books, ingredients and cooking procedures are – deliberately, I'm quite sure – made to disappear inside the text of the essay in social recollection or the gastronomical archive. David had a famously liberating, free-and-easy attitude towards recipes as strict instructions, asking the British to try stripping down a dish to its essentials, a 'primitive' version, or to experiment with flavour augmentations if the simplified version lacked savour. To *get* at a recipe, say, for an *anchoïade*, you have to go by way of M. Caramelo at La Réserve in Beaulieu . . . 'expensive, solid, elegant in an old-fashioned way . . . the anchoïade here was outstandingly good and I remember, in spite of the immense portions served, ordering, much to the amusement of the head waiter, a second helping. When I returned to the restaurant a few days later he was ready with my double portion of anchoïade even before I had even asked for it.' Or to get to the wonderful passages on daubes you have to go via Pierre Huguenin, *Les meilleurs recettes de ma pauvre Mère* . . . 'During the holidays at Gemeaux . . . when we arrived at my grandmother's dark kitchen on Sunday after Vespers it was lit by a ray of sunshine in which the dust and the flies were dancing and there was a sound like a little bubbling spring. It was a daube which since midday had been murmuring gently on the stove, giving out sweet smells which brought tears to your eyes . . .' The effect of David's heaped remembrances is to turn any individual dish into a kind of archive of social experience and its record – so that companion figures show up through her pages – Pomiane and the ubiquitous Curnonsky; Abdre Croze, an obscure mayor of Saint-Rémy for the bouillabaisse; a gathered company through time. And it was this Proustian act of poetic fusion, along with the invitations – which (unlike Julia Child) often lived up to the cult of simplicity (invoking Escoffier) that Elizabeth David constantly advertised – which first really got me and some of my generation cooking in the 1960s. What we felt truly translated in her paragraphs was remembered sensuality.

Which cues up and leaves the best for last, I suppose, the greatest food writer who has ever lived, or at least written in English: Mary Frances Kennedy Fisher, whom even the supercool authors of '*le dico*' revere for the sublimity of her prose. In MFK, Elizabeth David's tendency to embed the recipe within memory, archive and ethnography became even more completely dissolved. You don't, I think, really go to her for the recipes – I'm not sure I have ever actually cooked one. What you do go to her for is the exactly rendered experience of human hunger, passion, devouring; and for an as yet absolutely matchless, poetic talent (and I use this term carefully, because it seems to me that Mary K did actually have that enviable talent for conjuring sharp and sensuously registered precision out of thin air that is the poet's forte). Here, for instance, from a justly famous (or it had better be), tiny essay, called cleverly 'Borderland', which finds her in Strasbourg with Al Fisher in February, in a freezing, 'cramped dirty apartment across from the sad zoo, half full of animals and birds frozen too stiff even to make smells'. Now there is a recipe – of a sort – buried in this essay, but MFK sets up the bleakness of the place she's in (at a polar extreme, you'll note, from Elizabeth David who never wrote about cold, grim places), in order to introduce her 'dish', if we should call it that: 'tangerine sections warmed on the radiator'. 'My pleasure in them is subtle and voluptuous and quite inexplicable. I can only describe how they are prepared.'

Now listen to the way this 'recipe' is communicated: a kind of literary seduction, a thing done with mind and eye and tongue, absolutely

self-conscious – again in the poetic vein – the seductive effect of alliteration, with all kinds of details that have not a lot to do with the
tangerine treatment, but everything to do with the material presence
of the woman herself who is fingering them:

> In the morning, in the soft sultry chamber, sit in the window peeling
> tangerines, three or four. Peel them gently, do not bruise them as you watch
> soldiers pass, and past the corner and over the canal towards the watched
> Rhine. Separate each plump little pregnant crescent. If you find the Kiss,
> the secret section, save it for Al.
>
> Listen to the chambermaid thumping up the pillows and murmur
> encouragement to her thick Alsatian tales of 'l'intérieur'. While she
> mutters of seduction and bicyclists who ride more than wheels, tear
> delicately from the soft pile of sections each velvet string. You know
> those white pulpy strings that hold tangerines into their skins? Tear
> them off. Be careful.

You are then supposed to lay out a newspaper on the hot radiator
and lay the sections on them so that they plump up in the heat. They
perfume the room. Night comes on and 'the soldiers stump back from
the Rhine'.

> The sections of tangerines are gone and I cannot tell you why they are so
> magical. Perhaps it is that little shell, thin as one layer of enamel on a
> Chinese bowl that crackles so tinnily, so ultimately under your teeth. Or
> the rush of cold pulp just after it. Or the perfume. I cannot tell.
>
> There must be someone, though, who knows what I mean. Proba-
> bly everyone does because of his own secret eatings.

Here, next to nothing is lost in translation and, because of the
perfect word-play, the shell crackling under one's teeth like Chinese
enamel followed by its opposite, the rush of cold pulp, we are, for a
moment, in MFK's body, indeed in her mouth. Which is as good a place
as anywhere to end.

Remembering

Omaha Beach

Financial Times, 13 June 2009

For the integrity of democracy, this was the worst of weeks and the best of weeks. Fresh-cut flowers laid on the graves of D-Day heroes were barely beginning to wither when the misbegotten whelp of Mosleyism got its first seats in the European parliament. In London, Gordon Brown was shedding ministers like leaves from a tree attacked by death-watch beetle. I was in Dublin beside the oily Liffey for the Writers' Festival. There, I quickly discovered, the Irish were confronting their own demons, every bit as corrosive to public faith in their governing institutions as the expenses scandals in Britain.

To mangle Tolstoy, while every economic boom is the same, every economic bust implodes in its own peculiar way, throwing up gobs of squalor in its wake. In Britain we have long told ourselves that, while we may be a bit frayed at the edges, by God we know how to run a parliamentary democracy. But now the culture that gave us Gladstone versus Disraeli has sunk into the taxpayer-funded dredged moat where bottom-feeders lurk in terror of the exposing hook and line.

In Ireland the capacity of the moral bog to swallow public trust may be even more profound. The official report, published last month, on the maltreatment of children in Ireland's 'Industrial Schools' was all anyone wanted to talk about in Dublin. From 1940 through the 1980s, tens of thousands of children were victims of physical and sexual abuse at the hands of lay staff and teachers in institutions run by Christian congregations. In its dry understatement, the report is one of the most horrifying documents of systematic social cruelty to be published since the war. Children despatched there by the Irish courts as 'unruly' were treated as feral beasts, beaten with instruments designed to inflict maximum pain.

The betrayal of public trust amounted to a shocking collusion between Church and state to look the other way. Lay perpetrators would be reported to the Gardai, but seldom prosecuted, and members of religious orders known to have committed atrocities on their wards were dealt with within the Church. But now all the sweaty procrastination has been swept away in a great tempest of public fury, not least because Irish taxpayers are going to have to foot the €1.3 bn (£1.12 bn) bill for reparations to traumatised victims. This is the collateral damage of great social and economic implosions. When one kind of public credit – the assumption that investment trusts are not frauds; that commercial banks can actually cover their obligations to depositors; or that the people's representatives aren't slurping at the public trough – comes apart, the entire social contract can unravel at dizzying speed.

Which was a good reason to go to Normandy for the sixty-fifth anniversary of D-Day and register the unequivocal good of which democracies are equally capable along with habitual acts of infamy. Historical commemorations are always tricky things, never more so than in the case of great battles. Those who fought them often tell us who didn't how hard it is to convey the reality in narratives, be those reports a day or a half-century later. And so we euphemise. Military history maps with their arcing arrows trap the unbearable reality of dismembered boys within a code of antiseptic graphic conventions. Those little shaded boxes shadow-box with the truth.

Added to this is the muffling effect of ceremonious decorum. But in this particular case, expectations that our new American Pericles would soar above funerary platitude ran the opposite risk of turning the occasion into yet another exercise in Obamania. Posters in the window of the local tourist office featuring Potus in cool threads and proclaiming – apparently the idea of the mayor of the city – 'YES WE C(AEN)' only added to the foreboding.

The biggest invasion was by re-enactors. On the evening of 5 June, the front at Grandcamp-Maisy, between Pointe du Hoc and Omaha Beach, had D-Day-vintage Jeeps in tan paint parked opposite the sea wall. Inside the Brasserie du Guesclin, Frenchmen and young women impeccably uniformed for 1944 tucked into their *foie de lotte marine* and *turbot grillé*. From GI uniforms there came, disconcertingly, voices that hailed from Bremen or München-Gladbach. It's a well-meant gesture against oblivion, but somehow deaf to the music of time. Most of the re-enactors – in their late twenties and thirties – are too old, their trousers too sharply creased, too fabulously *buff* to impersonate the skinny kids of D-Day, in the grip of animal instincts of self-preservation. When it comes to the bidding of memory, less is more.

Later that evening, I stretched out on a wooden *chaise* in a Norman manor-house garden, fleshy roses blooming on the limestone walls, and let the emptiness carry me back to the tens of thousands packed in the transport ships sixty-five years ago — trapped, panicky and seasick — on the bobbing tide while Eisenhower decided it was go; to silk parachute gear dropped over the heads of tow-haired quarterbacks from Milwaukee. As the first stars came out, a wind soughed through the Normandy oaks and then, suddenly, the fading horizon eerily flared and the stillness was struck by the dull boom of fireworks from distant Utah Beach. But the dogs of the Calvados didn't know the noise was innocent thunder, and yipped and yowled as their forebears did all those Junes ago.

Weather was a famous obsession of the D-Day planners, forcing Ike to postpone the landings by a day. But the meteorological gods were kind to the veterans, many in wheelchairs, some magnificently spry and upright, crowding into the American Cemetery at Colleville-sur-Mer. So the sun shone on the affable curls of Tom Hanks; the band struck up 'Moonlight Serenade'. The 'Battle Hymn of the Republic' followed, rendered with such mournful beauty that our hearts were already in our mouths. Anticipation hung in the air along with Potus's chopper which, heralded by rotor wind, spinning eddies of new-mown grass over the heads of the crowd, finally descended.

Speech Idol then got under way with Nicolas Sarkozy delivering a blinder, full of unembarrassed poetic passion; summoning up images of twenty-year-olds on their ships caught in silence; silence hanging as well over the German machine-gun nests that awaited them. Was this *Sarko*, invoking the tears of parents bidding their sons farewell? Was this the gigolo of the Elysée forcing us to see bodies rolling in the soaking sand? *Evidemment.* The peroration was even more aston-ishing coming from a successor of Charles de Gaulle, as Sarkozy laid a rhetorical bouquet of heartfelt gratitude on the graves of the dead and the heads of the living.

So truth, in the tragic genre, had against the odds already been spoken, and was only briefly forced to take a back seat to gung-ho plat-itude when the Canadian Prime Minister Stephen Harper quoted a soldier whom, he claimed, couldn't wait to get to Omaha Beach. Gordon Brown rallied with a moving vision of the liberating armada, but then scuttled it with large invitations to honour their memory by Making the World a Better Place. Exit Thucydides, enter Hallmark Cards.

As usual it fell to the Historian-in-Chief to get to the heart of the matter: asking why D-Day still meant so much to us. It was, he said, the sheer improbability of success. However appalling the cock-ups of that day, this could not be true when the immensity of the American and British industrial smash-machine was brought to bear against the overstretched Reich. But Obama's second answer nailed it: that, for all the imperfections and flaws of the Allies, the absolute moral clarity that bound together the men of 6 June, the obligation to resist and uproot a regime that had been fed on the appetite for 'subjugation and extermination', radiated a redemptive glory over the human condition. *Mirabile dictu*, decency is possible. And such historical outcomes, said the Historian, summoning his own inner Tolstoy, do not happen according to any grand historical design. They are merely the aggregated acts of countless individual human agents who for one moment were lit by the simplicity of moral purpose.

So, when you are all losing your cornflakes on the unedifying news of the day, just hold that imperishable event close, honour the wrinkles that were once just twenty-year-olds trying to make it to the end of the beach and, while they were at it, made the world a better place.

Gothic Language: Carlyle, Ruskin and the Morality of Exuberance

London Library Lecture, 12 July 2008

When Ralph Waldo Emerson was giving a course of lectures in London in 1831, Carlyle did his new friend the honour of going to hear him and, of course, chaffed him for being so cowardly as to read from a prepared text instead of facing the terror and exhilaration of impromptu – Carlyle's own preferred style. No terror, no life force. So, I thought, in honour of one of the Presidents of the Library I should do the same and then I thought, well, no, the occasion is quite terrifying enough already, and besides *that* kind of life force may not be what the patrons of the London Library need on an evening in July, or at any rate such a lecture, even though it might take unanticipated and thrilling twists and perhaps even on occasion rise to a Carlyean level of romantic vehemence but go on and on rather like this Carlyleo-Ruskinian sentence and feel in the end quite as long as *The French Revolution*. So apologies in advance for this quasi-reading.

This is probably the only audience in London to whom the question 'why does no one read Ruskin and Carlyle any more?' would be a gross impertinence. But then we know that London Library readers aren't exactly the common clay, so just to confirm my suspicions about everyone else I went round the corner to Waterstone's and asked if they happened to have anything, anything at all by Carlyle? 'FIRST NAME' was the response of the kindly person at Information as she tapped the computer. And there was every single title with a big fat Zero by their side indicating not on shelves, not in inventory, no orders placed; no demand. Ruskin fared only slightly better with a travellers' edition of *Stones of Venice* and that was it.

Though Kenneth Clark, sixty years ago, made a valiant effort to prescribe 'Ruskin for the Modern Day', no one paid it much heed and the green volumes of *Modern Painters*, never mind *Fors Clavigera* and *Munera Pulveris* go on gathering title dust. There are I suppose plenty of reasons NOT to read Carlyle. In particular, it probably doesn't help that his biggest fan in the 20th century was Hitler. And Carlyle was an equal opportunities hater, detested Jews as much as Negroes . . . (he called them something different) – so it was rather delicious when I discovered that Hotel Carlyle in New York (itself a wondrous oxymoron when you think about it) was named in honour of the great man by its builder Moses Ginsberg. Ruskin is a byword for sniggering about sex; and preciousness. But when I nonetheless assign both of them to students at Columbia what they gag on right away is the language. In a course on what I loosely call Earth Writing, I assigned them the page on Slaty Crystalline in volume 4 and they probably hadn't expected to read this:

And behold as we look farther into it, it is all touched and troubled like waves by a summer breeze, rippled far more delicately than seas or lakes are rippled; THEY only undulate along their surfaces, – this rock trembles through its every fibre like the chords of an Eolian harp – like the stillest air of spring with the echoes of a child's voice. Into the heart of all those great mountains, through every tossing of their boundless crests, and deep beneath all their unfathomable defiles, flows that strange quivering of their substance.

Or how about Carlyle in the introduction to *Cromwell*, attacking Drysasdust antiquarianism:

Dreariest continent of shot rubbish the eye ever saw, confusion piled on confusion to your utmost horizon's edge, obscure, in lurid twilight as of the shadow of death, trackless, without index, without fingerpost or mark of any human foregoer – where your human footstep, if you are still human, echoes bodeful through the gaunt solitude peopled only by somnambulant Pedants, Dilettants and doleful creatures, by Phantasms, errors, inconceivabilities, by Nightmares, Norroys, griffins, wyverns and chimeras dire . . .

' "What the hell is *that?*" ' is pretty much the usual response: 'Prose run mad' as Thackeray put it – and he was a friend; embarrassing poetry? Yes in both cases perhaps. For it was precisely this determination to make the distinction between the poetry and prose moot, to create what some of you might still think of as a Frankenstein of a genre – poetic non-fiction; but at any rate a style of prose writing that concerns itself with some of the defining characteristics of verse: an attention to cadence, to the sonorities of words, sentences leaping from the matrix of syntax to do their own thing in aid of what Carlyle praised in Ruskin as 'melody of utterance' and in another moment as 'poetic indignation'. What bound them together as a 'minority of two' (Carlyle's characterisation in 1865) was their impatience with empty grammatical decorum. Such writing – very often the writing of their critics – amounted they thought to a kind of literary embalming, a film laid over the raw vitality of history, or painting. Both Ruskin (the young Ruskin at any rate) and Carlyle struggled for years with what we might call a problem of translation: how to catch and fix that subject matter without rendering it inert. Doing justice to the original meant, they romantically thought, more than simply total immersion in its lived reality but as much as a muscular re-enactment – of the French or Puritan Revolutions; or the construction of a painting by Tintoretto or Turner, or even, when Ruskin fancied himself privy to the design of God (which was much of the time), entering into the mystery of his terrestrial creation and producing something as oxymoronic as lyric geology. The issue for both of them was not so much that writing about history and art was second-hand; almost all non-fiction would share that quality; but that revelling in the second-handedness was prized by the guardians of the trade as a model of the report well-written, the work well done. To be distant was, in that view, elegant, trustworthy, sound; when to be close, they believed, was to be true. Their passion was engaged in the redefinition of clarity: to replace the reliability of distance with the unreliable but more faithful experience of proximity. The clarity of distance proceeded from the superiority of hindsight. But Carlyle in particular yearned to make the reader humble in the face of ultimately inscrutable providence and thus recover through rude force, the uncertain outcomes of history and art, to set the reader down again on the edge of undetermined possibility. And this, for Carlyle and Ruskin, was always more than an aesthetic challenge. To make readers exult, tremble, panic once more, whether in the workshop of Tintoretto or the National Convention, was to rescue them from the besetting sin of intellectual complacency; history as the unfolding of inevitability. It was also to remake the historian's vocation as resistance to disappearance; 'the etiolation of human features into mouldy blank', as Carlyle put it of the seventeenth century.

To put it another way; the writing rules of the Johnsonian eighteenth century had been above all committed to transparency and harmony. The brute chaos of the world mastered as knowledge. That knowledge was cool in its dispassion. What Ruskin and Carlyle wanted to generate was a different kind of knowledge; one that proceeded from warm-bloodedness; one that proceeded from total absorption in its subject to the point of letting go of the usual mechanics of perception. What was commonly taken to be vision, comprehension, they believed was – a word they both liked – 'owlish'; a form of blindness, for it did no more than measure surfaces. It was not so much sight as surveying. Though they revered the masters who had ventured afresh with language – Wordsworth and Coleridge above all, and with some reservations Hazlitt – they still felt that none of the conventions was capable of pulling the reader into uncomfortable, attentive, proximity; the abolition of body space between past and present, subject and object. On the other hand, if some sort of diction could be fashioned that attacked the automatic quality of reading, the reader might be provoked into a kind of creative partnership with the writer, become sparring partners in a battle for the recovery in language of lived experience. Only that way, Carlyle believed, could what the Dryasdusts had doomed to be the 'grand unintelligibility of the Seventeenth Century' become audible once more. And the writing that did this work might itself be read as confrontationally heroic; its scars and scrapes, nicks and cuts, all unapologetically registering the force of the travail needed to make it. In some sense, the rugged endeavour of that work itself was meant to become a moral exemplum for readers. For both of the seers, noble handwork was the only salvation to a culture otherwise in thrall to the die-stamp of the machine, the aim of which was uniformity.

Carlyle is always wanting, as a preliminary tactic, to obliterate the mediocre; scorch through its defensive primness. So it's not surprising, then, that fire is the natural element of what he imagines to be a resurrection of the lost Gothic-native vigour of old English prose. When you read *The French Revolution* you smell smoke. Images of fire – bituminous, carboniferous – lick through its pages. Sometimes its very words seem printed in hot soot; the world consumed by the revolution, as Carlyle writes, is 'black ashes'. Mirabeau is a *'fiery fuliginous mass which could not be choked or smothered but would fill all France with smoke. And now it has got air, it will burn its whole smoke substance, its whole smoke-atmosphere too, and fill all France with flames'*. Paris doesnt just fall to the revolution in July

1789, it burns: '*Let conflagration rage; of whatsoever is combustible! Guard rooms are burnt, Invalids mess rooms . . . straw is burnt three cartloads of it hauled thither, go up in white smoke; almost to the choking of Patriotism itself; so that Elie with singed eyebrows had to drag back one cart . . .* ' An entire chapter is – for no reason the subsequent narrative clarifies – called 'Flame-Pictures' . Revolutionary events do not just happen, they ignite, and in a great climactic passage just before the onset of the Terror (though admittedly the book has more climaxes than it does pages) France itself becomes a '*kindled Fireship*'. The Girondins and the Jacobins ? '*Here lay the bitumen stratum, there the brimstone one; so ran the vein of gunpowder of nitre, terebinth and foul grease.*'

You might say it was a Romantic commonplace, this playing with fire, when speaking and writing of epic events, though you won't find it in Wordsworth's version of the French Revolution nor in Romantic history before Carlyle because he single-handedly invents the genre. Critics habitually (and sometimes without quite sensing what they're doing) characterise Carlyle's style as pyrotechnic; the simultaneous blazing forth of vehement heat and blinding light springs from what we might call his Presbyterian Zoroastrianism; the sense that fire is the element of destruction and rebirth. Remember that he learned German in the first instance to read geology and it seems likely to me that in the great debate over the origins of the world, and in particular its mountains, Carlyle is certain to have been a vulcanist rather than a neptunist. He loved it when metaphors turned material, so naturally he was among the massive crowd (which included Ruskin's hero Turner) watching the Houses of Parliament burn down the evening and night of 16 October 1834. It was about a month after Carlyle had begun work on *The French Revolution* and on that particular day he'd been working (reluctantly) with the Dr Dryasdusts in the British Museum, returning home to Cheyne Row with his usual 'museum headache'. Looking from his back windows he noticed the angry red glow, opened them, inhaled the acrid smoke and hurried off as fast as he could to join the crowds on the Embankments. Though he heard some of the spectators complain that 'it didnt make a good *fire*', it was certainly hot enough for Carlyle's – as for Turner's – imagination to see the incineration as a cleansing of the fetid sty of corruption, from which phoenix-like some purer form of British constitution would surely arise. That the destruction of the house of Old Corruption had been caused by the burning of tally sticks, the record as Carlyle saw it of accumulated iniquity, only made it all the better. It seems likely, then, that he transferred the 'flame-picture' he had directly witnessed to the conflagration of the French monarchy.

But even had Parliament not burned, *The French Revolution*, would have been a work of spontaneous literary combustion, because of course, *it did*. Behind all of Carlyle's obsession with flames lay the trauma of his own manuscript being literally consumed by them. On the evening of 6 March 1835, John Stuart Mill, friend and kindly, if often baffled, review editor, paid an unannounced late visit to Cheyne Row, along with his beloved Harriet Taylor, and stood distraught on the doorstep barely able to get any words out (even more unusual for Mill than Carlyle). This was entirely understandable, since what he had to say was that the only manuscript of Volume One of *The French Revolution* (up to the Flight from Varennes) had been accidentally destroyed by a maidservant at his – or it wasn't clear – Mrs Taylor's house. The servant had apparently thought it was fire-kindling. Now it says a lot for Carlyle's genuine affection for Mill that he didn't immediately think there was something fishy about this account – unfinished though the manuscript was, it was still mighty big, and how much paper do you need, after all, to start a fire in a middle-class London parlour? Jane Welsh Carlyle had her suspicions that Harriet Taylor might have had a hand in this and that Mill was gallantly taking responsibility for her disaster, but they were rejected out of hand as unworthy and unlikely by her husband. Carlyle even unconvincingly claimed that it had actually been a relief to hear Mill's news, as he had initially thought he had come to announce that he had run off with Mrs Taylor.

But a night of great anguish followed in which Carlyle felt 'something cutting or hard grasp me around the heart'. In the morning he resolved to persevere and – shortly after – to accept Mill's anguished offer of money to sustain him through the unexpected additional time that he would need to complete the work. Again one has the impression that Carlyle, more feeling than he sometimes let on, did this at least as much out of a wish to be tender to Mill's burden of guilt as of a need to pay his bills (though that need was certainly always exigent). He proceeded to write the first section of Volume Two and then, the hard part, go back to the beginning and start over with Volume One. Like any of us faced with such a Sisyphean task, he suffered terrible ordeals of doubt; idealising what had been lost for ever to the flames as the irrecoverable original, hundreds of pages of *mots justes*, beside which the remembered version he was now actually writing was a pallid simulacrum, the impostor of necessity. He would write feverishly but then become blocked by panic; during one period lasting many weeks, capable only of reading low romances on the couch, 'the trashiest heap of novels available'. In late spring he consigned the rewrite to a drawer, calling it 'a mass of unformed rubbish'. With the summer of 1835 came a renewed burst of energy to replace what he always described to his brother Jack (who, possibly unfeelingly, gave Carlyle a vivid description of the eruption of Pompeii) as his 'poor burnt manuscript'. By the end of August he'd finished, went to see his family in Scotland, watched the flame-tail of Halley's comet and sent the manuscript to Mill (who'd kept his distance from Cheyne Row for some time) to read.

Mill would indeed read it and praise the 'prose-poem' to the skies both to Carlyle and in print when he reviewed its publication in 1837. How much this was an act of reparation or the truthful candid judgement of friend and editor, neither of them would ever be able to judge. But for both of them the saga of destruction in the flame, and rebirth as Word-Phoenix, had a very particular significance. While we will never know what the first manuscript of Volume One was like, it seems unlikely that the book as written was some sort of pale ghost of its original, for it spoke with unrepentant literary aggression against the conventions, even Romantic conventions, of the day: the weird sublimity, the drug-rush hyperbole, the manifold transgressions against grammar, syntax, word order, the confrontational lapel-grabbing relationship with the reader ('O beloved brother blockhead'); the ecstatic ejaculations and fulminations; the wild and wandering digressions, all of which had already made Carlyle unsellably notorious or at the very least an acquired taste. How about this for the procession of the Estates General:

> Yes in that silent marching mass there lies Futurity enough. No symbolic Ark like the old Hebrews do these men bear: yet with them too is a Covenant; they too preside over a new Era in the History of Men. The whole Future is over there, and Destiny dim-brooding over it, in the hearts and unshaped thoughts of these men, it lies illegible, inevitable. Singular to think they have it in them, yet not they, not mortal, only the Eye above can read it – as it shall unfold itself in fire and thunder, in siege and field artillery, in the rustling of battle banners, the tramp of hosts, in the glow of burning cities, in the shriek of strangled nations!

Steady ON, you might yourselves be saying, and it was Mill who, after reading *Sartor Resartus*, which it's safe to say was almost certainly not his cup of tea, and after trying to edit Carlyle's long essays on Cagliostro and the Diamond Necklace, tried to do so himself in ways more likely to appeal to the author than the literary Lord Jeffrey's advice that he should simply 'try and write like a gentleman'. Here is a typical passage from 'Cagliostro':

> Meanwhile gleams of muddy light will occasionally visit all mortals, every living creature (according to Milton, the very Devil) has some more or less faint resemblance of a Conscience; must make inwardly certain auricular confessions, absolutions, professions of faith – were it only that he does not yet quite loathe and so proceed to hang himself. What such a Porcus as Cagliostro might specially feel and think and be were difficult in any case to say, much more when contradiction and mystification designed and unavoidable so involve the matter . . .

Mill in response: 'About that Cagliostro and that Teufelsdreck, by the way, it has frequently occurred to me of late to ask of myself, and also of you, whether that mode of writing between sacrcasm or irony and earnest be really deserving of so much honour as you give it by making use of it so frequently. The same doubt has occasionally occurred to me respecting much of your phraseology, which fails to bring home your meaning to the comprehension of most readers so well as would perhaps be done by commoner and more familiar phrases . . . the style would often tell better on the reader if what is said in abrupt exclamatory interjectional manner were said in the ordinary grammatical mode of nominative and verb'. 'No surgeon can touch the sore places in a softer hand than you do', Carlyle wrote back to Mill, and continued poignantly that 'I daily reflect on this with great sorrow, but it is not a quarrel of my seeking. I mean that the common English mode of writing has to do with what I call the hearsay of things and the great business for me in which I alone feel any comfort is recording the *presence*, bodily concrete coloured presence, of things for which the Nominative and verb as I find it here and Now refuses to stand me in stead.'

What Carlyle was aiming at, he made clear to Mill, was to write prose poetry; because the matter of *history* was too profound, too cosmically disorderly to be confined to the utilitarian neatness habitual to those whom Carlyle derisively called the 'cause and effect' people. The 'right history of the French Revolution', Carlyle wrote to Mill in 1833, would be 'the grand poem of our times', and the 'man who could write the Truth of that were worth all other writers and singers'. Mill warned Carlyle that if he persisted he would face a rough ride, for 'the prejudices of our utilitarians are at least as strong against some of your writings as those of any other person whatever'. But Carlyle protested that this was the only way he knew and the only way he wished to impart, and enact, history. He knew he would offend every convention of literary decency but in the spirit of the Gothic Romantics he revered, like Schiller, Jean Paul Richter and Schlegel, unruly violent energy registered the upheavals that shaped historical outcomes. He told himself that 'if the things come out from the right place, I say to myself it will go to the right place. It is a simple plan this but a desperate one.'

In the end Mill accepted Carlyle's reinvention of historical voice to the extent of using, in his enthusiastic review of *The French Revolution*, precisely the term – 'epic prose poem' – that had made him scratch his head in the first place. But other guardians of the way history – and prose writing more generally – ought to be written, like John Sterling (usually a friend), remained decidedly unentranced, objecting to the 'headlong capriciousness . . . the lawless oddity and strange heterogeneous combination of allusion'. Carlyle's style was 'positively barbarous' and among his neologisms, Stirling, editor of *The Atheneum*, in particular, hated 'environment', 'complected' and 'visualise' as the affectations of a wilful obscurantist. Carlyle wrote back that 'if one has thoughts not hitherto uttered in English books, I see nothing for it but that you must use words not found there, you must *make* words.' Stirling, like many other critics, thought it was Carlyle's immersion in German literature that produced the interminable sentences, the prodigious superabundance of expression which gives harshness and strangeness; the '. . . jerking and spasmodic violence; the painful subjective excitement'.

Those thoughts, demanding heightened forms of utterance, began as Carlyle in his twenties began to dip into history himself: the usual suspects, Hume, Voltaire, Gibbon and Smollett's *Complete History of England*. Gibbon's style he found intermittently entertaining, but in the end the self-conscious orotundity, the ironic polish, seemed to him more to do with a kind of self-admiring verbal strut than a true effort to embody the matter at hand. And it mattered a great deal, I think, that the young Carlyle was reading the canon of 'philosophical history' – in Edinburgh and then beginning to write in Craigenputtoch, for those were two quite different Scotlands. It was exactly Enlightenment Scotland, with its eirenic cultural climate; its commitment to universal truths unproblematically discoverable through rational inquiry, which were somehow a thin medium with which to represent the drive of much history. Unless, that is, the whole point of history was, as the rationalists and empiricists claimed, 'philosophy teaching by experience'. But that was to make history no more than a demonstration of propositions arrived at a priori in the logic chamber. The choice of prose for such exercises would certainly be classically Johnsonian: grave or witty, balanced, restrained, never exclamatory.

But Carlyle belonged to an entirely different Scotland – that of the Presbyterian Calvinism of the south-west border country, and, to him, the most natural diction was Scripture and the first true history the Bible of the Authorised Version. Scripture, with all its thunderings, exordia, calls to judgement, and prophetic passion, which he felt had a more archaic and therefore more instinctively direct connection to that which it narrated than the decorously Augustan forms in which most contemporary historical writing seemed lengthily marinaded. Then Carlyle read Homer, and his convictions about the polite artificiality of most eighteenth-century history only strengthened. In part this was because he believed that the recounting of history was an instinctive, ubiquitous and even involuntary human act. 'A talent for history may be said to be born with us, as our chief inheritance. In a certain sense all men are historians. Is not every memory written quite full with Annals where joy and mourning, conquest and loss, manifoldly alternate . . . ?' There is no recounting of an hour, a day, a year, Carlyle thought, which does not take the form of historical narration, be the subject paltry or grand. 'Our very speech is curiously historical. Most men, you may observe, speak only to narrate, not in imparting what they have thought, which is indeed often a very small matter, but in exhibiting what they have undergone and seen, which is a quite unlimited one. Cut us off from narrative, how would the stream of conversation, even among the wisest, languish into detached handfuls . . . Thus, as we do nothing but enact History, we say little but recite it.' Since our lives are constructed in such narrations of a verbal, improvised, and undecorous kind, so should the history of public deeds and great matters preserve that spark of naturally untutored report.

Conventionally decorous prose was, Carlyle believed, the opposite from the broken-faceted literary vitalism he was groping his way towards; being just the serviceable prose of cerebral self-confirmation. It would be writers who abandoned themselves more freely to the flux of history, and to the dense plenitude of the human past – its ungovernable commotions – and who somehow battled their way to a style that registered that inchoate turbulence, who would more easily bring together the magic moment and the rolling of the aeons. In 1830, two years after Thomas de Quincey had pronounced the art of rhetoric in English prose writing dead, Carlyle published the first of two essays on history, setting out what might be expected of it. Above all, he attacked the self-referentiality of most historical language; its mistaken supposition that submitting the partiular to some pre-determined notion of the general was tantamount to the assignment of significance:

> Alas, do our chains and chainlets of causes and effects which we so assiduously track through certain hand-breadths, years, square miles, when the whole is a broad deep immensity, each atom 'chained' and complected with all. Truly, if it is Philosophy teaching by experience, the writer fitted to compose it is hitherto an unknown man . . . better it were that mere earthly histories should lower such pretensions more suitable for Omniscience than human science . . . and aiming only at some picture of things acted, which picture itself will at best be a poor approximation . . .

In the disingenuous guise of a turn towards methodological modesty, the satisfaction of merely painting 'a picture of things acted', Carlyle was in fact, of course, proposing a titanic ambition: to reinvent history entirely. For if the first job was dense picturing, the Enlightenment loftiness would have to go. When you read Gibbon you heard him and only him. To be sure you certainly heard Thomas Carlyle in his work, but when he got to work using every tool in the repertoire of sensuous memory – music, smell, colour, texture – you heard everyone else too, and the din was transporting.

> See Camille Desmoulins, from the Café de Foy, rushing out, sibylline in face; his hair streaming, in each hand a pistol! He springs to a table; the Police satellites are eyeing him; alive they shall not take him, not they alive him alive. This time he speaks without stammering: Friends, shall we die like hunted hares? Like sheep hounded into their pinfold; bleating for mercy, where there is no mercy, but only a whetted knife? The hour is come; the supreme hour of Frenchman and Man; when Oppressors are to try conclusions with Oppressed; and the word is, swift Death, or Deliverance forever. Let such hour be well-come! Us, meseems, one cry only befits: To Arms!

Let universal Paris, universal France, as with the throat of the whirlwind, sound only: To Arms! To Arms! yell responsive the innumerable voices: like one great voice, as of a Demon yelling from the air: for all faces wax fire-eyed, all hearts burn into madness. In such, or fitter words does Camille evoke the Elemental Powers in this great moment . . . – Friends, continues Camille, some rallying sign! Cockades, green ones – the colour of Hope! As with the flight of locusts, these green tree-leaves; green ribands from the neighbouring shops, all green things are snatched and made cockades of. Camille descends from his table, stifled with embraces, wetted with tears: has a bit of green riband handed him, sticks it in his hat.

Now, aside from Carlyle's cosmic interpellations, which come fast and furious, this long passage does everything he promises in his new history: it propels the reader abruptly into the immediate physical presence of the event. It heightens the effect by conscious use of poetic devices – the aspirate alliteration of the 'hunted hare' (spondees were a speciality, though not here); the inversions and repetitions that convey precisely the breathless, deathless self-dramatisation of the revolutionary protagonists' 'Alive they shall not take him, not they alive, him alive' – we by the way have to supply the commas that make voiced sense of that; but which also re-enact Desmoulins's imperfect conversion from stammerer into orator; the melodramatic sententiousness: 'swift death or deliverance forever' (absolutely authentic to the moment, then, and the place – remember, the Palais Royal where all this is unfolding is a site of theatres and burlesques as well as speech making); Carlyle's unmatched feel for expressive etymology, his cunning in its deconstruction so that he italicises the *well* in 'well-come', preserving and reinforcing the precise semantic load of 'bienvenu'. And, then, not least there is the organic vitalism, by metaphorical indirection; a spectacular vision, at once close up and panoramic, of the city swarm, a huge sudden pullulation, the snatch of leaves to use as cockades, an unstoppable mass of voracious creatures taking to the air, 'the flight of locusts'. (And one could go on ad infinitum within this single passage, and on almost every page, with close readings that would reveal a richness of utterance and complexity of poetic strategy that make comparisons with his idols, Milton and Dante, not entirely ridiculous.)

What Carlyle has done here – and in all his historical writing – is to replace what he takes to be the falsely contrived persona of the dispassionately Olympian narrator with the impassioned oracular poet-bard, a modern

Herodotus or Livy- a persona unembarrassed to become part of the action himself; a protean companion in written speech who, by turn, may dissolve himself into the protagonist (in this case Desmoulins), only to re-emerge as either choric stage-director – 'So hangs it, dubious, fateful in the sultry days of July', or 'On, then, all Frenchmen that have hearts in your bodies! Roar with all your throats of cartilage and metal, ye Sons of Liberty' – or (this about the September massacres and the uneasy relationship between atrocity and the words that must inadequately convey their report) as judicial interlocutor: 'That a shriek of inarticulate horror rose over this thing, not only from French Aristocrats and Moderates, but from all Europe, and has prolonged itself to the present day, was most natural and right. The thing lay done, irrevocable; a thing to be counted besides some other things, which lie very black in our Earth's Annals, yet which will not erase therefrom . . . Well may mankind shriek, inarticulately anathematising as they can. There are actions of such emphasis that no shrieking can be too emphatic for them. Shriek ye; acted have they.'

Carlyle described *The French Revolution* as a revolution of a *book* in itself, which, having heard a lot of it now, you might for better or worse agree, depending on how you feel about revolutions; a book, he said, thinking of the incendiary ordeal he had to go through to write it, 'born out of blackness and sorrow'. Its stuttering diction, its whirling, convulsive shakes and spasms, were meant to trample on the literary complacencies, but also of course to present the writer in some sort of mysterious deep kinship with his subject. The historian posturing as hero did not preclude moments of selective self-effacement. Much of this alternation between egotism and self-annihilation Carlyle took from his German Romantics. His early biography of Schiller, published in 1825, was, at the same time, a genuine effort to sketch a portrait of Promethean loneliness, but also mapping the journey that writing ought to take, from examining the surface of the world into its more invisible wellsprings. *Sartor Resartus* was his retort to what he called 'the gospel according to Richard Arkwright' – or, in 'Signs of the Times', the mechanical age. Vocation was to isolate the cladding of the external world, 'the flowery earth-rind', but then to peel it away to expose the elements that truly mattered; the infinite rolling ocean of existence, within which the external world was a mere islet. In this manner, it was what the French Revolution revealed when it tore away the politeness of the world, what Carlyle called 'the age of Imposture', that was both horrifying and exalting, but which, above all, was real.

That journey from exterior surfaces and commonplace responses, towards something more impalpable, bonded Carlyle not just to the German romantics but to American transcendentalists like Emerson, with whom Carlyle became an improbably close friend and correspondent. More than once in response to Emerson's adoring blandishments Carlyle seriously considered making a journey, like so many of his literary contemporaries, to the United States, only to pull back when he suspected himself of doing it for precisely the base mercenary reasons he deplored in everyone else. And, besides, despite the good Transcendentalist of Concord, Mass., Carlyle in the end suspected America to be supremely the land of low appetites and money-grubbing, only a bit more successful at those enterprises than the British. What he failed to see – and this is partly bcause in his formative years American writing meant, mostly, Washington Irving, and for him (for all of us), worse, Fenimore Cooper, whom he wrote off as a Leatherstocking Walter Scott – was the histrionic strangeness of that country's literature; the entitlement that Hawthorne, Melville (*Moby-Dick* and *The French revolution* could have been written by the same hand I sometimes think) and the ejaculatory Walt Whitman gave themselves to cut absolutely free from British presumptions about what strong writing was. Whether or not Carlyle ever read them (and there's no evidence that he did), their own oracular, broken, encyclopedically heterogeneous manner; their gift for re-making or ignoring syntax; their embedding poetic meter in the heart of prose, certainly owed something to the way they read him.

The most eloquent tribute of this unlikely kinship, the sense that Carlyle had freed them from deference to English politeness, came from Henry David Thoreau, who actually read the *Complete Works* to that date while living in his sylvan hermitage on Walden Pond between 1845 and 1847.

Emerson had given him the books and had told Thoreau how badly received many of them had been, *Sartor Resartus* above all. Thoreau wrote that he knew very well the kind of 'aged and critical eye' that could not make head or tail of Carlyle's style, which to them 'seems to abound only in obstinate mannerisms, germanisms and whimsical ravings of all kinds . . . we hardly know an old man to whom these volumes are not hopelessly sealed.' But Thoreau took Carlyle's language as natural as the rough New England countryside to which he compared it. (It was, he implied, the only thing worthwhile to have come out of England since Wordsworth and Coleridge). 'The language they say is foolishness and a stumbling block to them, but to many a clear-headed boy they are plainest English and dispatched with such hasty relish as bread and milk' . . . 'Not one obscure line or half line did he ever write. His meaning lies plain as the daylight, and he who runs may read; indeed, only he who runs and *can* read can keep up with the meaning'. What Thoreau found deeply moving, so *American*, in Carlyle was his populist enlargement of the literary voice; to cover a whole world of sound – 'He can reduce to writing most things – gestures, winks, nods, significant looks, patois, brogue, accent, pantomime, and how much that had passed for silence before does he represent by written words. The countryman who puzzled the city lawyer, requiring him to write among other things his call to horses, would hardly have puzzled him; he would have found a word for it, all right and classical, that would have started the team for him.'

What Thoreau appreciated about Carlyle was his ability to liberate language from its gentility; and make its ideas seem 'but freshly living, even the body of it not having passed through the ordeal of death . . . the smallest particles and pronouns all alive within it'. But also, of course, Carlyle's heroic Gothic rudeness; the humour 'vigorous and titanic', the challenging, not to say confrontational, relationship with the reader, 'O beloved blockhead brother of mine'. And possibly, more than anything else, the sense that Carlyle's writing was never ever mechanical, stamped and pressed from any sort of die; that it reached back into the humus-damp earth and had the sappy vigour of a young tree.

Thoreau's perception of what Carlyle wanted to do with the language, but also to literary culture in the Anglophone world, was accurate. In 1838, the year after *The French Revolution* appeared, Carlyle published a long essay on Scott, ostensibly a review of John Gibson Lockhart's seven-volume biography and vindication of his father-in-law. It was a mostly merciless put down of Lockhart (whose book on Burns he had praised), whose pointless copiousness provoked Carlyle to comment, 'There is a great discovery still to be made in Literature, that of paying literary men by the quantity they do not write' (in which case, of course, Carlyle would have been worse off than he was). Then the damning verdict, defining faint praise: 'he has accomplished the work he schemed for himself in a creditable workmanlike manner. It is true his notion of what the work was, does not seem to have been very elevated. To picture-forth the life of Scott, according to any rules of art or composition so that a reader . . . might say to himself "There is Scott, there is the physiognomy and meaning of Scott's appearance and transit on this earth, such was he by nature, so did the world act on him, so he on the world" . . . this was by no manner of means Mr Lockhart's plan.' But then Carlyle went on to skewer poor dead Scott as an exemplum of what a serious writer and serious writing should not be. Scott, in effect, was irredeemably prosaic, led by ambitions that were entirely worldly, content to live on the surface. 'His power of representing things . . . his poetic power, like his moral power, was a genius in extenso, and we may say not intenso. In action, speculation, broad as he was, he rose nowhere high, productive without measure as to quantity, in quality he for the most part transcended but a little way the region of commonplace. It has been said "no man has written as many volumes with so few sentences that can be quoted." Winged words were not his vocation'. What could be said on Scott's behalf was that he knew what he was, was free of cant, and had a 'sunny current of true humour and humanity, a joyful sympathy . . . the truth is, our best definition of Scott were perhaps that if he was no great man then something much pleasanter to be, a robust, thoroughly healthy and withal very prosperous and victorious man'.

He was, Carlyle implies, a perfect fit for the age, but the age of veneer which called out for attack-writing to strip it away. Better by far to separate oneself from its anodyne pseudo-accomplishments, aim for something else entirely, something rugged, shambling, unco-ordinated, and do so in a tongue that would shake the reader awake into new vision; to have writing, just so much paper and printer's ink, nonetheless force the reader into the urgent immediacy of his or her own fate.

The way, then, that Carlyle *talked* to Britain was to summon the past to upbraid the present for its vain, shallow, sense of time; to attack the vainglorious quality of its self-admiration which he diagnosed as moral indolence; a failure of the shared imagination.

If Carlyle's verbosity has, I fear, proved infectious, to the point of making the no less verbose Ruskin disappear, I want, at any rate, to finish with him. It's the right way round, I think, to take Carlyle first because, without him, there is no question that Ruskin would not have come to his own unembarrassed poetic diction; would not have waged war on the desiccated conventions of art writing, thank you Sir Joshua Reynolds (Hazlitt always honorably excepted, although Ruskin didn't), just as Carlyle waged war on the empty nostrums of history. They shared much of the bigger enterprise, the preaching of the salvation of handwork over machine manufacture; the mistrust of classicism; the sanctification of profuse ornament as embodying the connection of man and nature, a connection threatened by the tyranny of mensuration; a sense that the ultimate enterprise was to make the sheer plenitude of human existence (as well as the transcendence of landscape) the expression of God's benevolence (or, in Carlyle's case, his stern sovereignty).

But instead of making himself the embodiment of arduous creativity, constantly playing to the gallery, Ruskin in *Modern Painters* of course displaced all that Promethean recklessness, obstinacy and suffering onto the slightly surprised shoulders of his god Turner. There is, you'll doubtless be happy to hear, no time to talk about this in any detail – many have before me – Robert Hewison, Wolfgang Kemp, and others. But what sometimes seems to me to get taken for granted is the performative quality of Ruskin's writing in *Modern Painters*. He's after the same thing as Carlyle's *French Revolution*; namely, unparalleled immediacy; the sense of Being There, but the 'There' is not just, or sometimes not at all, a reproduction of Turner's making of the work so much as Ruskin's personal unmediated encounter with it. But that's an encounter at a level of almost madness-inducing intensity and total immersion, to the point at which Ruskin – how consciously we'll never know, since, unlike Carlyle, he seldom if ever feels he must answer for his style – writes exactly as he supposes Turner must paint; with a kind of gorgeously incontinent abandon. When he wrote about Turner's *Land's End* in the last book of Volume One of *Modern Painters*, he deluded himself into thinking that what he was doing was analytical description, dense ekphrasis, if you like. But what he was actually doing was word painting, word singing in Carlyle's sense, in which the rhythmic music of the paragraph is everything. If it's a poem, it's a tone poem – Ruskin the impassioned conductor controlling the orchestra of alliteration, assonance, allusion, sudden metaphor, the words and the water they describe rolling over each other. It's hard to remember when you hear this that he is just describing a picture – and in some senses of course he isn't; or rather, the picture is of the storm-tossed author's nerve endings:

> . . . the Land's End, the entire order of the surges where every one of them, divided and entangled among promontories as it rolls in and beaten back part by part from walls of rock on this side and that side, recoils like the defeated division of a great army, throwing all behind it into disorder,

breaking up the succeeding waves into vertical ridges which, in their turn, yet more totally shattered upon the shore, retire in more hopeless confusion, until the whole surface of the sea becomes one dizzy whirl of rushing, writhing, tortured, undirected rage, bounding and crashing and coiling in an anarchy of enormous power, subdivided into myriads of waves of which every one is not, be it remembered, a separate surge but part and portion of a vast one, actuated by internal power, and giving in every direction the mighty undulation of impetuous line which glides over the rocks and writhes in the wind, overwhelming the one and piercing the other with the form, fury and swiftness of a sheet of lambent fire . . .

STOP! STOP! you cry, and, dear, patient, fellow London Library Readers, I actually have.

A History of Britain: A Response

American Historical Review, June 2009

If I confess to some astonishment at writing this response, it is only because I am even more astonished – and moved – that the *American Historical Review* judged a fifteen-part television series worthy of sustained critical consideration in the pages of an *AHR* Forum. I would be churlish not to preface my comments by first thanking all three commentators for the intellectual generosity with which they approached their subject, and for the marked absence of condescension towards a project which, had they tackled it themselves, they would, I believe, have discovered to be every bit as exacting as any more conventionally scholarly project.

It is eleven years since I started work on *A History of Britain*, nine years since the first film shoot in Orkney, and six years since the last episodes were broadcast on terrestrial channels in Britain and the United States. (Although, gratifyingly, the series has had a continuing life on cable broadcasts and on DVDs, both as an educational tool and as popular entertainment.) So looking back on the enterprise from this distance is, for me at any rate, something of an exercise in cultural history itself. But it is also an opportunity to reflect on the part that the television documentary plays in diffusing historical knowledge; provoking debate and enriching the common culture with a sensibility informed by the past could not be more timely. For the scholarly community is surely at a crossroads in considering the forms by which history is communicated within and beyond the academy. The digital moment is no less pregnant with consequences for the survival of the interpreted past than was the transition from oral to written word in antiquity, and from written to print culture in the Renaissance. Whether we like it or not (and I have my own load of mixed feelings), we are unquestionably at the beginning of the end of the long life of the paper-and-print history book. The exigencies of economic austerity are likely to only hasten a process that is already under way. Print books will of course survive their eventual demise in the marketplace of knowledge, and monographs custom-printed from digital sources will doubtless endure as physical objects, perhaps even on library shelves. But in shorter order than the profession has yet taken in, most history will be consumed, especially beyond the academy, in digital forms: on interactive websites; as uploadable films; from electronic museum sites, archives and libraries – a prospect towards which most university scholars seem (at best) cool, and to which we are taking precious few steps to acclimatise future generations of historians.

While I was working on *A History of Britain*, moved by the possibility of passing on some insight to students about the ways in which scholarly history might be popularised for much broader audiences without compromising its integrity, I was rash enough to propose an optional graduate seminar called 'History beyond the Academy'. I thought I might actually offer instruction on script-writing, on developing treatments and budgets for a variety of hypothetical projects: radio documentaries, digital textbooks, interactive public exhibitions, children's books, films. Further, I imagined that along with disciplined practical instruction about these skills, such a class would debate the long and complicated history of the relationship between scholarly and popular writing. I have always tried to preach what I have practised: that the two lives of a historian, within and without the academy, are mutually sustaining, each necessary for the other to flourish, and that without their interdependence we are doomed to an intellectual half-life, cut off from the nourishment of, and responsibility to tend the curiosity of, the non-academic world. The proposal was greeted in some quarters with polite dismay as an act of pedagogical subversion. 'Do you want to create second-class citizens among the students?' was one rhetorical question put to me by way of dissuasion. (For the record, I persisted and, some years later, though only *once,* taught the course as planned.)

It was from this conviction that our calling not only invites us but requires us to reach beyond the academy that I undertook, with great trepidation – and exhilaration – *A History of Britain*. Although it is sometimes referred to as 'The BBC History of Britain', my cautionary resort to the indefinite article was of course not casual. Whatever the outcome of the series, my role as narrator and interpreter presupposed the provisional, candidly subjective character of the project. I have never pretended otherwise. In fact, it was, I confess, a slight impatience with the assumption (in, for example, Ken Burns's documentaries) that a multiplicity of voices somehow guarantees balance or authentically interpretative pluralism that provoked me, perhaps perversely, to raise the hermeneutic stakes by offering one historian's vision. As all the commentators have pointed out, there were many inherent dangers in the approach, not least narrative arrogance. But I deliberately set out to challenge what seemed to me the unexamined assumptions of pseudo-balance presupposed by the choir of talking heads approach.

It doesn't require much knowledge about film-making to realise that the impression of openness given by replacing a single voice with a quartet or more is, in fact, just that. Unless one of those voices supplies the script (at which point pluralism ceases), the director selects those whom he or she chooses to be heard. What is said, how much of a voiced comment is heard, and where it gets cut into the body of the film is invariably an auxiliary of the directorially written script, and its effect is conditioned by its relation to the visual archive. In these documentaries the single director is the historian, whatever the captions may say. And the edit is the final draft. The scripts for *A History of Britain*, on the other hand, were entirely mine. There was no 'vast team of researchers', just a single junior colleague per film, usually the assistant producer, who also had to deal with locations, fixers and the usual production multi-tasking that makes documentaries possible. So, for better or worse, almost all of the research work that went into those scripts was my own. The determination of locations was likewise a collegial process, with discussions about how this or that site might work with evidence and storyline. If not on a shoot, I was part of the editing process by which the 'pieces to camera' were integrated with archival evidence, attending screenings of the cut through its many stages or making edit suggestions long-distance. I worked with the composer John Harle and directors on the score, and in some cases on the dub itself. For critics who think I had already arrogated too much authority to my narration, I suppose this hands-on integration into the production compounds the sin. But faced with the choice between, on the one hand, a role that restricted me to on-camera opinions, with the creative history really being made by directors and editors, and, on the other hand, the possibility of more total immersion, I had no doubt which approach would be more satisfying and, for the audience, more honest.

A History of Britain was never purely monovocal. But instead of cutting to colleagues, the films were thickly seeded with contemporary voices, from Orderic Vitalis to George Orwell, sometimes deliberately offering competing versions of the same event. And when dispute was material to the historical matter – for example, in Oliver Cromwell's treatment of Irish prisoners of war and civilians – I did my best to present both sides of the argument, without, however, disingenuously abdicating my role as arbitrator of evidence, the same persona that we all habitually adopt in our writing. What I did not want was for the films to turn into seminars, for those are two incommensurately distinct forms of communication. (For that matter, just how genuinely open the professorially led seminar ever is to a democratic plurality of opinion is quite a question, as Pierre Bourdieu has reminded us.) But given that my task was to try and create a broad popular audience for the narrative of British history, and to hold it week after week, my choice was to eschew an echo chamber of authorities in favour of a companionship in which the narrator took viewers along with him on a journey of shared illumination. When the opinionated voice provoked, the provocation was, I hope, always candid, stirring debate, counter-argument and dissent, often robustly expressed on the website, which was itself richly supplied with both general and scholarly essays, many of which took healthy exception to my own version.

In this kind of project, story must come first, the handmaid and condition of analytical debate, not the other way about. This is no more than to follow the obvious rule set out by the historians of antiquity, and it corresponds to the most rudimentary phenomenological understanding of the way non-scholars order the experience of time. Re-presenting (with all the knotty issues of evidence retained) is one of the most complex and demanding tasks that historians can set themselves, even though professional scholars, wary of narrative theory, sometimes imagine it to be the amateur version of the discipline. Story is the thread that connects our scholarly work with the listening, reading public, and we break it at our peril. To weave those threads into a rich fabric, the executive producers (Janice Hadlow and Martin

Davidson, both thoughtful historians in their own right) and I believed that a single unapologetically opinionated writing and speaking voice could create and retain a mass audience, the breadth of which was commonly said at that time to be unavailable to television history. Many commentators cite the great example of Kenneth Clark's *Civilisation* as a model, to which I would also add the more inspirational example of Jacob Bronowski's *The Ascent of Man*, and Alistair Cooke's stunning tour de force *America: A Personal History of the United States*. But at the time of the planning of a television history of Britain, that tradition of personal essay had all but died out. This was not entirely the case, since writer-presenters such as Michael Wood remained a model of what could be done in this medium, but it was still largely true that the interpretative single-voice form had been written off as a vestigial remnant of oak-panelled patrician broadcasting. Democratic television, on the other hand, was assumed to be fly-on-the-wall actuality: a day in the police station, the trauma room or the schoolroom in the deadpan style of Fred Wiseman, and often very brilliantly realised for television by directors such as Roger Graeff.

But at the very heart of the kingdom of fly-on-the-wall, there were subversives – Michael Jackson, then controller of BBC2, and Janice Hadlow, then in charge of one of the two history divisions of the BBC – who nourished a suspicion that if you stood the received wisdoms on their head, you might be closer to the truth. Their belief, widely dismissed at the time as quixotic, was that there was a pent-up public demand for a single-voiced, chronologically ordered history on the grand scale, richly informed by social and cultural history but unapologetically *évènementielle*, when the events in question happened to be of the order of magnitude of the Norman Conquest, the dissolution of the monasteries, the Civil War, the Industrial Revolution, the Irish famine, and so on. And not just on television, but in schools around Britain, where history was being rationed to perhaps two hours a week at best, and where the curriculum was set out as a series of disconnected modules known as 'Hitler and the Henries', the non-academic public was being starved of just such a grand narrative.

I never intended the series to be empty of social history, still less of the experience of 'the people', as Miri Rubin and to some extent Linda Levy Peck charge. Nor was it. But television is a work of the eye, and the life of the people necessarily had to be embodied in what could be looked at: dwellings and artefacts – the tiny, profoundly poignant Saxon church at Bradwell; the surviving remnant of a lost Catholic world in the rood-screen paintings at Binham Priory; the shocking photographs of the Indian famines of the late nineteenth century taken by missionaries; and, as Peck kindly mentions, the unspeakably moving tokens left by mothers depositing their infants at the Foundling Hospital. The very first images seen (other than the tidal shore) were of the village of Skara Brae and the hearth and ornaments made in that world remote both spatially and temporally from the Anglocentric world. And if, at the end of the film, the camera moved in on the exquisite 'Alfred Jewel' in the Ashmolean, it was both as a materialisation of royal sovereignty and to convey a sense of the precarious allegiance to that earliest of English courts on the part of those who beheld it. We took viewers into a fifteenth-century manor house, the deserted cottages of Irish famine victims, the fields of Bengali cultivators, the homeless shelters of London in the Slump. Equally, where the voices of people remote from the centre of power were available and integral to the bigger plot, we did our best to make them heard: from the world of the Roman legionaries on the Hadrianic frontier preserved in the Vindolanda tablets, to the anonymous Irish monk who believed he might be the last survivor of the Black Death, to Leveller women and the victims of Peterloo.

So what, exactly, needs defending here? The decision to fill the second episode with the story of the Norman Conquest, or the third with the struggle between Church and state in the reigns of the Angevins? If so, I readily plead guilty as charged. Professor Rubin wanted a much more intensive dose of social history and a good deal less narrative of the powerful, but of course at the heart of many of the formative dramas were insurrections against the mighty – from the Peasants' Revolt to the Puritan revolution to Chartism – that we could hardly have been more conscientious in examining. But it is true that our remit was to put social flesh on the history of power, for contests over power were what ultimately created Britain.

In the end, though, ostensible dichotomies between narrative and analysis, between political and social history, exist more in the methodological imagination than in historical practice. Film-making is the best instructor in the meaninglessness of that divide. Meeting the technical demands of a medium where it is imperative that one assumes no prior knowledge of a subject or period, while refraining from patronising the viewing audience, is itself a serious education in the economy of explanation. In any given programme, there would be self-evidently major issues – Cromwell's treatment of the Irish, Jacobitism, the Sepoy rebellion – all of which, if the historian is doing his work properly, presuppose familiarising the audience with the responsible protagonists, their ideologies and actions – before it is possible to introduce debate. All this takes time, narrative care and a respect for the intrinsic dramaturgy of the medium. Films are not consumed like books and cannot be written like them. (Which is why I wrote three companion volumes, precisely to expand the scope of what I was able to compass in a bare fifty-eight minutes.) Within the covers of a book, readers may move back and forth as attention and interest prompt. In the television documentary, propulsive visual and spoken energy is critical. In these respects, the medium is actually something of a throwback to pre-professional forms of historical narration, all the way from Herodotus, the crafting of narrative that *performs out* its analysis rather than headlines it. It must use scholarship responsibly without ever subjecting the audience to a sense of their being examined or overburdened with scholarly dispute, yet it must speak to that audience's trust that the narrator has earned his credibility with knowledge.

So there is, in fact, a poetics of television history, which needs to be respected if the form is to accomplish its own particular kind of communication – for millions rather than thousands. Such a poetics presupposes a strictly non-fiction dramaturgy, bound together by a clear and compelling narrative arc, and its making is quite as formidable a challenge as, say, the formal composition of post-Ciceronian oratory. Documentaries never work as a succession of loosely stitched-together sequences about this and that matter, social or political, each given their ration of minutes according to some preconceived hierarchy of significance. The distinction is the difference between even the most skilled lecture and a film able to retain its audience from beginning to end (a tougher assignment on television than in the cinema, given the freedom to wander between choices). Profusion risks confusion, and confusion is the harbinger of boredom, which in turn is the cue for a switch to Monday-night football. Peter Stansky remembers the scintillating lectures delivered by A. J. P. Taylor as television performances, but those happened more than forty years ago, in a different cultural universe. Since then, the challenge to deliver knowledge, argument and non-fiction stories through the digital media has become much more formidable, and if historians want to reach an audience beyond the academy (of course it's possible that the vast majority do not), then some attention has to be paid to the particular demands – and rich opportunities – offered by long-form documentary film and video.

One historian's inclusiveness is another's unforgivable omission, of course, but in any event, the pursuit of inclusiveness is the death of plot. To take a specific instance of what Professor Rubin surprisingly dismisses as the 'antics of kings', the foregrounding of the great conflict over law, and the relative authority of Church and Crown which was at the heart of the matter in the Henry II–Becket dispute, needed setting up (as did the history that would culminate in Hastings and Domesday) so that viewers, the vast majority of whom would not have known much about the Angevins, could become familiar with the parties and persons involved. And of course there are occasions when the fate of not just the state but the people hangs on the person of the prince. I own up to believing – as forthrightly stated – that however prepared by religious dissent since the Lollards, in the end the English break from Rome was an act of the redefinition of sovereignty executed by a monarch desperate for a male heir. It seems peculiar to have to defend this view as antiquated. All that matters is whether it is true. That Anne Boleyn also happened to be a learned Protestant is material to this issue, and I tried to say as much. But the notion that that programme paid no attention to the experience of the world beyond the court is an inattentive reading of the film, and I appreciate Professor Peck's alternative view. Equally, of course, the issue of issue for Elizabeth I was one that would affect the entire fate of English religion. What we were doing with 'The Body of the Queen' was, as is often the case in the whole series, 'debate by stealth', in this case applying the questions set out in Ernst Kantorowicz's *The King's Two Bodies* about the distinction between the body natural and the body political (made moot in the Queen's case), as well as much more recent literature on gender and sovereignty, to the fatefully intertwined story of Elizabeth and Mary Stuart. Those who wanted to experience the film as an engagement with the politics of gender, the reproductive biology of sovereignty as it played out across the Anglo-Scottish border, could do so; those who wanted to sit back and drink in an astounding dynastic drama could do that, too. I don't see any need to apologise for our attention to the second kind of demand. Both kinds of audience were entitled to their respective needs, and we tried our level best to satisfy them without compromising scholarship or debate.

All this took hard work. I confess to being a little surprised that in her account of the meetings with BBC producers during an earlier version of the project, Professor Rubin rather airily divided up the labour into what she imagined historians would, or rather would not, do, and what 'the production team' would tackle, the more strenuous labour, she implies, being undertaken by the latter. But for this historian, at any rate, both the magnitude of the challenge and the satisfaction of creation rested in that division of labour being made moot, in the historian doing his best to master the exacting craft of television film. This means, at the bare minimum, relearning script-writing as an entirely different exercise from book-writing, one that not only has to be constantly responsive to what the viewer is looking at, but has to be conceived, from the outset, as a series of visual sequences, each one itself a succession of shots, understanding, in fact, the syntax of the cut. (I am personally allergic to the meaningless dissolve except in instances where it dramatises the memory link between past and present. In one of the episodes in my most recent series, *The American Future: A History*, for example, we mixed through from a shot of a stony creek on the Gettysburg battlefield to a Civil War photograph of the same site with a dead soldier lying in the gulley.)

I don't altogether disagree with Peter Stansky's objections to the clumsiness of poorly enacted reconstructions. Done badly, they can induce cringe-making alienation from the historical moment rather than realise the ambition of bringing the viewer close to it. But sometimes a kind of film synecdoche or emblematics can work powerfully on the viewing imagination, especially when both approaches have a connection with the documentary and cultural report. So, for example, a shot of a single bonnet bowling along a field in the aftermath of Peterloo worked, I believe, quite well in summoning the ghosts of the massacre, since contemporary reports commented on the clothes of the victims left behind in the panic. Instead of a wide shot of the Cabinet War Rooms (very much a museum of a moment), we used shots of apparently incidental details – a row of coat hooks, an ashtray – to convey the whole.

And when rooted in a strong sense of the iconology of the period, emblematics can visualise a historical scene far more expressively than either a shot of a document or a low-budget piece of acting. To convey the fury of Henry II at the defiance of Becket, for example, we used close-up shots of a hawk's beak opening and shutting (to the rhythm of unseen proffered mice), an image entirely in keeping with the spirit of royal bestiaries and the falconry of which the King was fond. We used the same kind of technique with a white peacock's display to suggest the significance of charisma for the Elizabethan court, making the kind of connections between plumage, virginal whiteness, the elaborate ruffs of court dress and the grandiose paintings that captured them, all in a single shot. And sometimes less is simply more. To convey the plight of the fugitive Mary Stuart from Scotland, we took up position at exactly the right place, near Workington on the Cumbrian side of the Solway Firth, where the Derwent flows into the sea. But there was no boat and no fake Queen of Scots. All the camera did was to track slowly along the shore, shooting the slow lap of the waves while the commentary evoked the documented record of her sorry condition. The eyes of the viewer saw tidal water, but their mind's eye saw the Queen.

I can't emphasise enough that these aren't 'tricks' designed to bewitch the viewer into historical romance. The royal hunt, the reality of exile and the relationship between power and display are all serious historical matters on which matters of sovereignty turned. The same sort of attentiveness inspired the idea of illustrating, albeit briefly, the effects of the Black Death with emptiness and absence, unattended farm implements, or the Popish Plot with the playing cards that were circulating at the time. In many instances, the careful building of the visual and narrative structure of a film turned on the realisation of a unifying conceit. The last programme in the series had somehow to give a sense of the fate of the British Empire from the turn of the twentieth century to the Second World War, a feat of economy that would have been impossible had we tracked conscientiously through from the Liberal governments of Edwardian Britain to the Labour victory of 1945 and everything in between. Instead I decided to concentrate on what two utterly different figures made of the destiny of Britain in the age of economic disaster and totalitarian aggression: Churchill and Orwell, to begin with Churchill's death and to end with Orwell's. But as the fifteenth programme in a long, sustained narrative also had to serve as coda, the director, Clare Beavan, and I decided that the style would give the feeling of Mass Observation documentary, black and white even when it was actually not. And the mood would be an engagement with elegy, a deep strain in British writing, prose and verse, and the binding conceit would be the lament for, or resistance to, ruin.

Sometimes serendipity is the best ally. I had been filming a sequence (in the end dropped from the edit) for the late-eighteenth-century episode at the Royal Naval Dockyards at Chatham. Between shots of masts and spars, during the inevitable waits for the location to be lit, I wandered into a warehouse-cum-dry-dock that was, in fact, half-breakers' yard, half-repository of rubbish, inhabited mostly by pigeons and piled high with the debris of centuries: cannonballs; a motor launch broken in two; a 1940s vintage limousine covered with feathers and bird droppings; bits of submarine. Seen from a high platform above, it was a wonderland of imperial redundancy. And it gave us both a sequence near the beginning of 'The Two Winstons' and our poetic motif. Off we went, the director and I, hunting for abandoned and boarded-up country houses and, most challengingly, an airfield of the right Second World War vintage that had not been converted for more modern use. After a very long search, we found one in Norfolk, complete with original control tower and broken windows, Tannoy speakers, and long grass growing in the cracks opened in the runways. Eureka! For the defiant Churchill speeches of 1940 at the time of the Battle of Britain, we needed neither the much-viewed archive footage of the Prime Minister nor photo stills of the 'Few' by the side of their Spitfires, much less a Winston impersonator in a dubious homburg. All we needed were yawning-wide shots of that airfield, open and desolate to the flat country, and the superlative *vox humana* of Churchill sounding over the East Anglian wind. What we were fighting against, of course, was familiarity. Running the film archive would simply have made that problem worse, because it would have subconsciously cued up the imminence of the eventual victorious outcome. What Clare Beavan and I wanted to restore was a sense of the terrifying loneliness of the British at that moment. Ghostly emptiness was the way to do that, with not so much as the faintest sound of cranking aircraft engines to cut the admixture of bravery and fear. Behind the sequence, of course, was the usual serious historical issue: the yen by Halifax and others to find a way to settle with the Axis without compromising the empire. Pulling the viewer into a mood that had nothing of the bulldog breed about it would, we hoped, restore contingency to the history.

Now, I recognise that this account may seem a long way from what most of the readers of the *American Historical Review* recognise as the work of the historian. Our first duties are to nourish our academic community and our research, to ensure that future generations of historical scholars are sustained and encouraged and that new paths of research and debate are opened. Courses have to be taught, dissertations examined, articles and books written, appointments made. In making the fifteen episodes of *A History of Britain* for the BBC, I had to ask for exceptional generosity of leave from my kind colleagues at Columbia University, although between the three spells of shoots, I returned to campus as working professor. But the main obstacle to broadening our conception of what it means to be a historian in the digital age is, I think, force of habit, the axiomatically self-reproducing nature of the profession – the sense that, somehow, popular and scholarly history are mutually depleting. I can only say that everything I did and everything I learned while making these films led me to believe that the very opposite is true: that the two arms of our métier are mutually strengthening, and that without an abiding sense that we can work to make the past live for the public, we will doom ourselves to an intellectual graveyard: that of the connoisseurship of the dead.

The Monte Lupo Story

Review of *Faith, Reason and the Plague in 17th-Century Tuscany* by Professor Carlo M. Cipolla, *London Review of Books*, 18 September 1980

Professor Cipolla's new book, *Faith, Reason and the Plague*, puts one in mind of a Florentine *espresso*: minuscule in size; briefly stimulating in effect; and extortionate in price. At £7.50 for eighty-five pages of text, his readers will be shelling out eight pence a page, a tariff which, I couldn't help but calculate, would have put my own first book in the shops for around £65 a copy. Not for nothing, then, is he renowned as the most economical of economic historians, specialising in small books on big subjects — literacy, population, technology and the like. Many of these have brilliantly succeeded in dealing with complex historical problems within the space of a nutshell. In this case, however, the shell is altogether more imposing than the nut.

The book comes expansively inflated with puffery in two styles: the High (or Reverential) Puff and the Low (or Fastidious) Puff. The High Puff asks us to believe that the book 'is of immense historical importance' as 'it presents a picture of the real life of ordinary people who constituted the overwhelming majority of the population of pre-industrial Europe . . . on whose shoulders the high civilisations of the Renaissance, the Baroque and the Enlightenment were built'. In other words, without taking into account the plague victims of a Tuscan hill village in 1630–1 or, by extension, anything that ever happened to anyone at any time between 1400 and 1800 — our contemplation of Michelangelo, Bernini and Voltaire is callow and impoverished. The Low Puff refers more tactfully to 'spare' prose and 'deft' strokes, evoking the warbling of the piccolo rather than the swell of the *vox humana*.

I should in fairness add that for your £7.50 you get three appendices (one transcribed from an earlier work); a bibliography of fifteen items, thoughtfully printed in very large type and stretching over two pages; lists of contents and figures taking a page apiece; and a good deal of white surface area, all contributing to take the page-count into three figures. Professor Cipolla helps this along by interpolating between his more strictly historical observations strangely delphic utterances of the sort one usually associates with Christmas crackers: 'loneliness is the price a man has to pay when in a position of power'; or, in more cybernetic vein: 'there are people who because of their biomass, physical dignity or psychic energy easily assert their authority on others'. Apart from ruminations on biomass deficiency, there are the obligatory frequency diagrams designed to translate the perfectly obvious into the statistically awesome, and illustrations which are verbally recapitulated in the text. But all the cladding and padding and wadding and stuffing can't conceal that this is a very short book about a very small town over a very brief period in time. To be blunt, it is a footnote cranked up into a Cecil B. de Mille production.

Given the extreme simplicity of the episode recounted, even eighty-five pages seem a bit luxurious. Far from Professor Cipolla telescoping its details, he has elongated them into a historical shaggy-dog story with a correspondingly inconclusive pay-off. Its outlines can be summarised semaphorically in the manner of those invaluable contents lists in nineteenth-century history books. Plague hits Tuscan village of 500 souls in 1630; Florentine health magistracy puts formidable Dominican in charge of quarantine; opposition from truculent inhabitants who resent their already rudimentary subsistence further confined by irksome restrictions on movement; resurgence of petty crime; mortality recedes with winter cold; monk departs; plague revives early 1631; mayor fails to enforce regulations, dies in harness; monk recalled as attempts to ban religious procession meet with angry resistance from local priest and populace; procession goes ahead; quarantine stockade at one of the city gates vandalised at night; outraged roving commissioner summons insomniac busybody who claims to have witnessed the misdeed, but (it being night) fails to identify culprits; witness rather than vandals thrown in jail until story believed; culprits undiscovered, plague recedes again; monk departs again; commission concluded inconclusively; end of story.

Professor Cipolla fleshes out these bare bones with some striking characterisation, but much of it is of the kind sneered at by historians when they encounter it in historical novels. When unsupported by anything except the most circumstantial evidence, there is invariably a resort to the emphatic and the imperative: 'While he rode at an early hour towards the castello, he must have been thinking about those Monte Lupans'; 'he must have been inquisitive by nature'; 'like so many talkative people . . . Pandolfo must have felt pleasantly self-important'. Similarly, when the action threatens to flag, Cipolla stokes it up again by imaginative use of dramatic hyperbole, generally of the Mills and Boon variety: 'He had not slept at all during the night and now in less than twenty-four hours he had experienced the whole gamut of emotions ranging from excited curiosity to the heights of euphoria down to the depths of terror.' Since this refers not to attendance at a witches' sabbath or an auto-da-fé, but to the busybody's nocturnal snooping, followed by his informing and subsequent cross-examination, the reader might be pardoned for thinking Professor Cipolla's threshold of excitement rather lower than average. At the very end of the tale the ghost of the immortal Edgar Lustgarten walks again (scripted by *Monty Python*): 'Who broke down the stockade at Monte Lupo? Was Pandolfo lying when he swore he had not recognised the evil-doers? And what role was played by the carpenter? These are questions that must remain unanswered.'

If the devotee of history-as-thrills is not likely to find much in this book to set his spine tingling, can the scholar learn anything fresh? Given the immense literature on plague and its social impact (to which Professor Cipolla has made distinguished contributions, but on which the massive volumes of Jean Biraben might be thought to have said the last word), it is hard to see that the Monte Lupo story is much more than a minor, if picturesque, addition to our knowledge. It comes as no surprise to discover an individual cleric like the Dominican Father Dragoni transcending the disputes of Church and state over the stringency and propriety of prophylactic regulations, and enforcing the wishes of the latter rather than the former. Humanist or even monastic clergy throughout plague-stricken Europe often gave their Christian pastoral duties a higher priority than they gave to traditional rites, usages and customs. One important aspect of the Counter-Reformation Church was precisely this kind of *attack* on popular ceremony. Nor is it startling to find no positive correlation between religious processions and plague mortality. Ever since Creighton's classic history it has been supposed that by far the most common (albeit not exclusive) agents of transmission were, not other people, but the fleas of *Rattus rattus*.

Carping aside, the most depressing aspect of this offering is what it implies about the pigmification of historical scale. The time has long since passed when historians dealt exclusively with the grand scenarios of power; the life and death of empires and nation states; their wars and revolutions, diplomacy and business. It was a salutary corrective to turn instead to the history of the unsung masses, and from the most recalcitrant and ostensibly ephemeral sources, ingenious and gifted historians such as Richard Cobb, Olwen Hufton and E. P. Thompson have produced masterpieces of historical reconstruction in which the lives of the obscure and the downtrodden are given the front of the stage. There was, and is, a serious purpose in viewing elite culture and its politics from the perspective of the common individual struggling to survive. But this is not the same thing as assuming that *all* historical events have an equivalent call on the historian's attention, or that any scrap of evidence, however inconsequential, which is capable of being written up with a modicum of imagination and literary competence demands rescue from oblivion. On the contrary, much of it could do with being sent straight back there. The indiscriminate celebration of the humdrum threatens to dissolve history into a random aggregate of disconnected episodes, ancedotally related. And the result of such a process is not merely the substitution of a mosaic comprised of myriad, imperfectly fitting chips of the past for a possibly over-coherent picture of Great Events, but an invitation to study the individual fragments as though they each were miniaturised versions of the whole. This 'microcosmic' view – the absolute opposite of Febvre's and Braudel's equally unattainable '*histoire totale*' – is, in effect, a neo-pointilliste heresy of immense positivist vulgarity. Its premise must be that history is comprised of discrete actions and events, each as worthy of study as the next, since each contains within it some element of the universal. At the most banal level – Tolstoy's preference for the cosmic significance of the ear of ripening wheat over the cosmic significance of Napoleon – this is necessarily true. But to conclude, for example, that a study of the distribution of Bolshevik posters in Plotsk is quite as important as a study of the Petrograd Soviet is tantamount to a declaration of war on causal explanation: a relapse into egregious relativism.

It is time, perhaps, to reinstate the significance of significance. Or is it too quaint to insist that the historian's work involves explanation and argument, and that this necessarily entails an evaluation of evidence? And that only when such evaluation, comparison, selection, is undertaken can evidence be brought to bear on a predefined problem or a preconceived hypothesis? Has there been such a loss of nerve among historians that they now swallow uncritically the social anthropologist's dictum that to describe is to explain? For 'thick description' can mean thin understanding, if what is being thickly described has lost its anchorage in the larger measures of time and space.

The signs of a creeping *Montaillou* syndrome are ominous. The local, the anecdotal, the parochial, the gossipy and the intimate threaten to tyrannise historical fashion quite as thoroughly as the public, the national and the political once did. As the demand for 'readable' history becomes a hunt for the scraps and shards, the rags and bones of evidence, from which a good yarn might be knocked together, the historian is in danger of becoming a kind of beachcomber among the casually washed-up detritus of the past. If this goes further we shall revert to what we were before Thucydides had grander ideas: bards, tellers of tales, ministering to a culture terrified by the fragility of the contemporary, and seeking in chronicle an inverted form of augury. Or, less apocalyptically, we may end up as minor entertainers in light prose. Should that happen, the High Puffer's boast that if 'more history books were written like this they would drive novels off the market' will be put to the test. And on the evidence of this kind of tittle-tattle, it will be history, rather than the novel, which will meet with a rude comeuppance.

No Walnuts, No Enlightenment

Review of *The Business of Enlightenment* by Robert
Darnton, *London Review of Books*, 20 December 1979

No walnuts, no Enlightenment, it seems. For, as Robert Darnton tells
us in his epic chronicle of the Life and Times of the quarto edition
of the *Encyclopédie*, it was nuts and resin from the Midi together with
Paris turpentine and linseed oil which made the ink (six monstrous
250-livre barrels) which primed the type which printed the thirty-
six million sheets which comprised the quarto which lowered the price
which Spread the Word which overthrew superstition which disarmed
the Old Regime and inaugurated the rationalist millennium. Or was
it?

Historians have long been given to attributing the French Revolution and all its unholy works to the corrosive influence of the
Philosophes. The counter-revolutionary Abbé Barruel saw the revolution as a conspiracy hatched by malevolent acolytes of Voltaire:
freethinkers and freemasons bent on subverting the authority of
Christian monarchy. Less histrionically, Alexis de Tocqueville shared
the assumption that the diffusion of Enlightenment scepticism had
unfastened the ties of deference and order underpinning the Old
Regime. It was characteristic of the fecklessness of intellectuals, he
argued, to attack established institutions without much bothering
about what might replace them.

For Marxist historians, this approach was unduly generous to
thinkers and scribblers, investing, as it did, the world of ideas with
an autonomy that was unreal. Since, in their view, the revolution was
a product of inexorably shifting social forces, the Enlightenment
could be no more than an expression of that movement: in Ernest
Labrousse's awesome phrase, '*la prise de conscience bourgeoise*'. The
Philosophes were correspondingly relegated to the role of window-
dressers for the ascendant power of the bourgeoisie. One of the many

satisfying results of Robert Darnton's prodigious research has been to dispose of these hoary pieties once and for all. By painstakingly tracking down virtually all of the 8,000-odd subscribers to the quarto, he has been able to show that a preponderant majority belonged to precisely those sections of the French elite that were the first to suffer from the revolution: rentiers; office-holders; landowners with pretensions to cultivation; 'enlightened' clergy; Parlement lawyers. Many of these were noble; very few of them were engaged in anything that could be described as capitalist enterprise. Commercial travellers in pursuit of subscriptions found meagre pickings in the great centres of trade and industry like Nantes and Lille, where they grumbled of philistinism and avarice. In an ancient centre of administration and law like Besançon, though, the mixture of ennobled professionals and *bien-pensant* noble academicians yielded a bonanza for the purveyors of Enlightenment by mail order.

Both the anti-revolutionary and the Marxist views were, in any case, based on bald assertion rather than evidence. Both tended to extrapolate an ethos from an arbitrarily summarised version of the Great Texts, and then assign it significance or insignificance as their preconceptions dictated. But we are all contextualists now. Instead of ruminating in a documentary void on the social resonance of political philosophy, cultural historians look to political milieu and the currency of polemics, to routes and means of transmission and to the vulgarisation, rather than the refinement, of original texts, for clues to an understanding of their impact. While form seems to be of more interest than the interpretative scrutiny of content, and the printer's bench has replaced the philosopher's cell as the focus of attention, this should not be taken as a reaction of vulgar empiricism against the over-rarefied nature of old-style *Kulturgeschichte*. At its best, and when not mesmerised by the nuts and bolts of ideology – the minute enumeration of column inches and censors' pencil stubs – it is an authentically historical way of examining the process by which words become deeds; ideas animate action; and the heresies of one generation transmogrify into the orthodoxies of the next.

In this work of historiographical reorientation, Professor Darnton's magisterial study stands as a major landmark. The measure of his extraordinary achievement is that, for all the countless volumes that have been written on the Enlightenment, his is the first to have understood it, and to have succeeded in describing it, as a social phenomenon. This he has done, not by pondering the exegetical niceties of manuscripts nor by tracing the distribution of the expensive folio edition, but by going directly instead to its 'stepchild', the mass-market quarto: 'ragged, blotchy and unkempt'. Thus he begins where most intellectual historians lose interest: with Diderot's ill-tempered refusal to have anything to do with a proposed revised version, in 1768. This was not because his editorial genius could not bear the prospect of alterations to the sacred text, but for precisely the opposite reasons. He now regarded the whole *Encyclopédie* as '*un gouffre où ces espèces de chiffoniers jetèrent pêlemêle une infinité de choses mal digérées, bonnes, mauvaises, détestables, vraies, fausses, incertaines et toujours incohérentes*'.

The massive work of revision and correction was deflected into the alternative project of the quarto – making the *Encyclopédie* available at a third of the original price to thousands of subscribers. This change of course represented a deliberate entrepreneurial decision to go for quantity rather than quality, and for fast, fat profits rather than lingering scholarly endeavour. And it was in researching the genesis of this momentous enterprise that Darnton hit on a historical goldmine of staggering richness: the papers of the Swiss publishers and printers, the Société typographique de Neuchâtel. Though the STN were to be muscled out of much of the action that followed by the heavy brigade of French publishing, the intricacy and density of their records enabled Darnton to unravel the entire history of the launching, manufacture and marketing of the quarto.

His narrative follows the speeding *diligences* conveying the ill-assorted syndicate of business partners between Paris, Lyons and Neuchâtel, each group wheeling and dealing to outmanoeuvre the other while fending off lightning raids by press pirates profiting from an age innocent of copyright protection. It moves among the peregrinations of rag-pickers scouring Burgundy for the linen shreds needed to produce the mountains of paper consumed by the book, and records the unpredictable behaviour of master printers, downing tools for an impromptu foray into the local cabaret or disappearing down the road towards the beckoning finger of a rival employer offering better wages. The excruciating scissors-and-paste labours of tame abbés, hired to sort, file and rearrange copy, are documented, as are the perspiring journeys of solitary travelling salesmen, working the provinces for orders, attempting to drum up promotion, and greasing the palms of smugglers crucial for the selling of what was still, at least officially, an illegal book. Frustrated booksellers in Montpellier and Le Havre and Dijon fret and fume as promised deliveries fail to materialise or arrive with blotched paper and disintegrating bindings. But finally, at the end of the chain, the subscribing customer, his thirty-six volumes complete (including three of plates), could count himself, for less than 400 livres, as the advance publicity cunningly promised, among the advance guard of modern civilised man: the owner of a work which more than any other had, 'with giant steps', 'accelerated the progress of reason'.

Professor Darnton has marshalled this immense mass of detail with skill and elegance to cause the minimum of pain and maximum of illumination. Quite apart from the challenging nature of its conclusions, it is a work which brilliantly succeeds in clothing the dry bones of history with living flesh. His resourcefulness is such that, on the basis of a single thumb print smearing a page in Volume 15, he was able to piece together the biography of the peripatetic and slovenly artisan who left it there. Over-inking was a dodge used to lighten the formidable task of pulling the press bar, and it was from the irate correspondence of the STN with their contract printer, complaining about the abuse, that this pocket biography was rescued from oblivion.

In the interminable procession of Lives of the Famous — royal and political — which week after week testify to the bankruptcy of the historical imagination, Robert Darnton's magnificent book stands as an inspirational example. Its time-scale is perfectly calculated for the examination of a complex phenomenon in depth: it is not bogged down in triviality, nor does it get lost in the vast deserts of the *longue durée* demanded by the most severe practitioners of 'total history'. Its prose is as sharp as its perception, and for all the texture of its detail, the book avoids the kind of micro-history now favoured by, for example, Emmanuel Le Roy Ladurie, in which the relating of a single episode, garnished with a gloss of elementary social anthropology, is meant to proclaim self-evident significance. This is simply the imaginative re-creation of a momentous enterprise, set in the framework

of an important historical argument. As such it will become one of
the classics of modern historical literature.

Much of the originality of the book derives from its yoking together
– as the title implies – of cultural and economic history. Its account
of the launching and management of the huge and unwieldy business of the quarto is essential reading for an understanding of
entrepreneurial practice and malpractice in the eighteenth century.
The extensive arsenal of extortion, conversion of funds, counterfeiting, blackmail, bribery and press piracy is offered as a record of
big-time capitalism in its tooth-and-claw phase. A relatively mild form
of everyday dishonesty sanctioned, for example, the use of promotional literature announcing the publication of a new work, together
with prices and prospectuses, without the slightest commitment to
going ahead, should this preliminary sortie fail to elicit an encouraging response. More serious was the naked blackmail practised by
pirates (one with the engaging name of Grabit), who threatened to
publish available material at undercutting rates until bought off by
the harried publisher at an exorbitant price. Much of what is recorded
here suggests the thinness of the line between crime and business,
though Darnton's suggestion that this was in stark contrast to a more
'managed' capitalism in industrialising Britain seems open to debate.

Because of the extraordinary assortment of rogues and fools, villains
and victims assembled in the book, some of its narrative has the
compelling quality of an eighteenth-century morality novel. The
backwoods provincial Swiss, turgid with Calvinist probity, innocent of
deep guile, but with their nostrils quivering at the scent of profit,
plunge headlong into the murky waters of quasi-illegal publishing,
only to swim straight into the grateful jaws of the giant (French) pred-
ators gliding in the lower depths. That they eventually surfaced again
without being swallowed alive, but after being treated to a severe
mauling, was less the result of their own astuteness than of the
predictable and mutual hostility of the two most accomplished and
ravenous sharks: Joseph Duplain and Charles-Joseph Panckoucke.

The two men were not, in fact, interchangeable types. Duplain, the
press baron of Lyons, was the more uncomplicated and gangsterish.
Specialising in rapid turnover and massive profit margins, he never
hesitated to use graft, strong-arm pressure and extortion to secure them.
While tyrannising his subcontractors to produce the goods, he was

quietly creaming off enormous sums by falsifying his inventory of sales. Even he, however, could go too far and expose himself to lethal counter-attack by his long-suffering and suspicious business partners. Having educated themselves in the kind of tactics that were second nature to Duplain – industrial espionage, sabotage, false greetings of amity – the STN together with Panckoucke sprung the trap for their delinquent partner. In one of the most memorable passages in the book Duplain was confronted with irrefutable evidence of his gigantic swindle, and forced into disgorging 200,000 livres to extricate himself from disgrace and ruin. While this was a colossal sum, and while their cut provided the Swiss with some balm for their wounded innocence and shrunken profits, it was nothing like enough to impede Duplain's progress towards his heart's desire: the purchase of royal office, carrying with it a patent of nobility. And it was a paradox, absolutely typical of late eighteenth-century France, that the semi-criminal buccaneering capi-talist should see the goal of all his plots and stratagems as absorption into the class of the landowning aristocracy.

Panckoucke, who had some tart asides to offer on his ex-partner's pretensions to lord it as 'Duplain de St Albine', was an altogether more complex personality. So far from speeding after Duplain down the highway of illicit gain towards noble status, Panckoucke veered off after the quarto away from quantity and back, as he supposed, to qual-ity. In the closing sections of his book, Darnton traces his subsequent career, dominated as it was by the colossal, ruined edifice of the *Ency-clopédie Méthodique*; the ultimate work of compilation, arranged according to rules of subject, not the absurd dictation of the alphabet. The 'ultimate *Encyclopédie*' was intended by Panckoucke to replace the solecisms and anachronisms of which Diderot had complained so bitterly. But the effort needed to tackle this work of revision proved so exhausting that it cast a long and dark shadow over Panckoucke's remaining years, growing ever more monstrous like some intellec-tual Fonthill that threatened to crash down from its precarious foundations and bury its architect amid the debris.

Professor Darnton sees Panckoucke's obsession with the project of the *Encylopédie Méthodique* as an anticipation of the habits of nine-teenth-century robber barons for whom 'speculation had become an end in itself'. It is certainly true that the scale of the gamble, costing Panckoucke nearly two million livres and involving 100,000 articles collected in forty-two quarto or eighty-four octavo volumes, dwarfed anything that the Enlightenment had yet produced or even conceived. But rather than this growing out of Panckoucke's admittedly omnivorous appetite for big-time business, it was the product of his fixation that the tomes of the *Encyclopédie Méthodique* would provide the key with which the mysteries of the modern world would be disclosed. In other words, he had come to believe his own promotional literature – an unpardonable lapse for a publisher. He even appears to have cherished the view that the systematic organisation of knowledge, its classification into great monolithic compartments of the intellect, would make men happy and free. '*L'homme devient autant libre plus il a l'esprit cultivé*,' he opined, following Condorcet rather than Rousseau; and he stuck by this faith as his great project hit the reefs and started to founder.

A mighty debacle was in sight long before the Revolution made it a certainty. Deadlines were broken: the brigades of editors assigned responsibility for the mammoth sections into which the work was divided procrastinated, as subsidised intellectuals are prone to do, and failed to deliver copy. Panckoucke's costs sky-rocketed and his subscribers began to defect as he importuned them for more time, more volumes and more subscriptions.

So far from the French Revolution representing the consummation of Encyclopedism, the opposite turned out to be the case. Although Panckoucke initially greeted it with warmth, he very soon felt its adverse effects. The costs of both manpower and materials shot up, and both were diverted to service the more urgent needs of the revolution: broadsides, pamphlets, patriotic ballads and the like. He had been prudent enough to diversify into journalism, but the kind of ephemeral literary flotsam and jetsam washing around the streets of Paris, and soaking up precious print and paper, was anathema to his sense of the weighty and the durable. More galling still, as soon as he had brought out the immense compilation on legal institutions, the revolution wiped the slate clean of antique usages and arcane precedents, thus rendering it useless as a work of reference.

All this was hard to take, and as the revolution turned militant, Panckoucke's huffing and puffing against scurrilous invective and irresponsible fly-by-night printers became more exasperated. Rejected at the polls, he took to advocating the old system of guilds and licences as a way of restoring orderly regulation. This was not simply a case of sour grapes. For all the ostensible 'liberalism' of the *Encyclopédie* enterprise, it turned out in the end to have been crucially dependent on the institutional peculiarities of the Old Regime. A state in which official censorship coexisted alongside actual permissiveness had been ideally suited to Panckoucke's sort of publications. The formal disapproval of the Parlement courts, the occasional book-burning by the public executioner, promoted his reputation as a purveyor of the avant-garde, while the reality of toleration and even encouragement on the part of Louis XVI's court protected him from serious jeopardy. Like much that was dynamic in this period – Atlantic trade, for example – his publishing operated within the interstices of formal institutions where the spirit of modernity was struggling to free itself from the dead weight of antiquity.

Indeed, both Panckoucke and Duplain had needed the power of the French monarchy as an occasional tactical weapon. When confronted by a Swiss-printed octavo which threatened to undercut the quarto just as they had undercut the folio, they used the full muscle of police power to deny the trespassing pocket edition any entry to the French market.

In a more oblique sense, the entrepreneurs, like the authors of the *Encyclopédie*, had worked, not in irreconcilable antipathy to, but in symbiotic relationship with, the Old Regime. They were grateful for its more self-parodying anomalies as points to score off, and like Voltaire in his denunciations of *mortmain*, actually embellished their abuse for propaganda purposes. Many of the King's ministers had long come to acknowledge the truth of much of what the *Philosophes*, and indeed the physiocrats, urged. But with some exceptions, such as the emancipation of Protestants in 1787, their institutional immobilism precluded their being able to do much about it.

No such tacit generosity coloured the militant stage of the revolution which profited from their inadequacy. Instead of embracing Panckoucke's creed of liberating reason, sanctimonious Jacobinism turned violently and with savage repugnance on the luke-warm morality of the *savant* and the *bel esprit*. Academicians were reviled (not infrequently by renegades among their own number) as parasites who in their lust for royal and noble favour had battened on to the verminous cadaver of the old order. Against their celebration of pure rationality were ordained the transcendent values of social piety, simplicity of manners, stoical virtues and righteous anger.

It was only when the fierce flame of this irascibility burned itself out with the Terror that those who had evaded its punishments, or who had at least temporarily colluded in its indignation, surfaced once more in a guise that would have been familiar to Panckoucke. By this time, he had prudently silenced his tirades, but had abandoned the wreck of the *Encyclopédie Méthodique* to his family before dying in 1798. Had he survived just a few years longer, one suspects he would have been gratified by the ethos of Bonaparte's Consulate. For in place of editorial patronage, the state had taken over the management of classified data and had transformed their practitioners – land survey- ors, engineers, mathematicians and *polytechniciens* – into the freshly exalted caste of professional experts, showering them with the status and the subsidies which they have never relinquished.

If this extraordinary denouement fails to yield a satisfactory answer to the question I posed at the outset – the connection between Enlight- enment and revolution – it may well he because it was, all along, the wrong question to put. If, instead of characterising the revolution as the harbinger of the New Era, one sees it as a convulsion of nostalgic desperation, and its protagonists, not as men with their gaze directed at a scientifically organised or capitalistically managed future, but rather as artisans and landless peasants rebelling *against* the prospect of such a future, then its historical separation from the late eighteenth century and the mid-nineteenth century becomes clearer. And if we formulate a new question – did the Enlightenment and its most ambi- tious creation, the *Encyclopédie*, help bring to birth a modern world in which aggressive capitalism was to be partnered by scientific deter- minism, *notwithstanding* the interruptions of revolutionary upheavals? – then, after reading Robert Darnton's thrilling and luminous volume, we can venture a tentative answer. *Oui, hélas.*

Abolishing the Slave Trade in Britain and America: Sound and Fury or Deafening Silence?

Stanford University Presidential Lecture, 2007

When was it exactly during the bicentennial commemorations of the abolition of the slave trade that I became aware of just how much had changed in Britain? Was it when Ghanaian *memnon* horns, alerting villagers to the imminence of a slave raid, sounded from the choir screen in Westminster Abbey? Or was it a little later when a robed young militant writer harangued the Queen in the nave, the monarch rather grandly allowing the shouting to go on for a full four minutes before the agitator was strong-armed out of the abbey. (Hmm, I thought, just try that one in Washington DC and see what happens.) After the service I asked Kate Davson, the direct descendant of William Wilberforce, who read from a speech to the House of Commons, what she thought. 'Oh,' she said rather sweetly, 'I understand so well. The pain never goes away, does it?' That's the Wilberforces for you: Christian to the end.

Or was it when I – the lapsed Jew – found myself standing in the pulpit of All Saints Church, Fulham, on the invitation of its parish vicar Joe Hawes, who had decided, 194 years after the burial of the abolitionist Granville Sharp, to give the patriarch of the campaign the church funeral he'd been denied by the parish priest of the day? There had, apparently, been no love lost between Sharp and the vicar, the latter suspecting the former of Dissenter views about the liturgy even while professing allegiance to the Church of England. So in July 1813 the church funeral was abruptly cancelled, and Sharp was permitted a summary few words by the graveside in the churchyard. To the vicar's intense vexation, all of abolitionist London – black and white – came anyway. The service this year was an act of reparation for the affront;

the eulogist was the aforesaid Jew, and the congregation about as ethnically mixed as you could imagine – among them, however, being members of the prolific Sharp family, looking (how tenacious these British genes are) exactly like their evangelical forebears. When the ceremonies began with one of Granville's own duets played on his own English horns, preserved – aptly enough – in the Horniman Museum, the centuries just folded in on themselves in a quantum way and we were not so much commemorating as virtually re-enacting. (Rather in the way Collingwood thought all history had, in some sense, to be imaginative re-enactment before it could ever be analytical interpretation.)

But commemoration of the British abolition of the slave trade there most certainly has been – during March of this year, it seemed almost 24/7: a day of 'Resistance and Recollection' at the British Museum (readings to schoolkids as well as grand utterances by the likes of Wole Soyinka); a fine exhibition in Westminster Hall of documents and artefacts, including the travelling box used by Thomas Clarkson on his peregrinations around Britain, shackles, yokes, coffee beans grown by ex-slaves in free Sierra Leone, and the famous *Am I Not a Man and a Brother* Wedgwood medallion reproduced by the abolitionist entrepreneur in tens of thousands; the print of the Liverpool slaver *Brookes*, with its sardine-can-packed African bodies, which we know likewise made its way into thousands of homes around the country; two new museums of slavery – one in Liverpool, another about to open in the Docklands in London; my own book about the fate of the escaped slaves who sided with the British in the revolutionary war turned first into a ninety-minute television film and then into a stage play, which has run in London and is currently touring in the North of England.

Now obviously this saturation coverage isn't to be explained merely as an act of historical piety – and the tone of the proceedings has often been (this has to be a good thing) clamorously self-interrogatory. Issues of reparations and apologies have indeed come up (for what it's worth, if one of my German contemporaries came up to me and said, 'Tremendously sorry about Auschwitz, won't happen again, I promise', and all that, I'd say, 'Well, if it makes you feel better, right, but it doesn't really cut it'). More important, though, the commemorations have been an occasion on which to ask serious questions about national identity and allegiance in Britain; the legacy of empire; and in particular unsentimental questions about being black and British over the last 200 years.

But in all this vocal theatre of memory, in all the waves of sound and fury, one rather remarkable fact has been completely ignored: Thomas Jefferson signed an Act prohibiting the slave trade to the United States, and by American traders, into law three whole weeks before George III gave the British equivalent the formal royal assent. But you can hardly blame the British for overlooking this, since the commemoration has gone entirely missing on this side of the pond. Google it, and you'll find nothing at all, not even the commemorative stamp that I was told was planned – in the age of universal email about the most exiguous form of tribute imaginable. In fact when Charles Rangel, the New York Congressman and one of the leaders of the Black Caucus, proposed a motion of commemoration and congratulation, it was to the British Parliament, not to his own legislature that preceded it! This recalls perhaps the fact that in 1808 congregations of black churches in Philadelphia sang anthems to the British abolition of 1807, hoping that 'Columbia's chains' would follow – not noticing that they already had. When the General Assembly of the United Nations formally marked the anniversary on 26 March, the American delegate, Richard Terrell-Miller, a white career diplomat whose Senate confirmation preceded the anniversary by nine days, actually failed to mention that the United States had done likewise.

This dramatic contrast between contemporary fanfares and alarums on the one side and deafening silence on the other repeats the pattern set 200 years ago. Researching the debates on the subject in the Ninth Congress in late 1806 and early 1807, Matthew Mason noticed just how much the dog failed to bark in the night. President Jefferson, who – schizophrenic as always on matters of race – was heartily glad to see it pass, referred to it very little in his letters and private papers. What was on his mind – and that of Congressmen and most of the American press – was something they thought much more dramatically important: the capture of Aaron Burr and the unravelling of his conspiracy to detach the western territories from the Republic; and the interference with American commerce posed by the mutual commercial wars of the French and British Empires. Attendance in the House of Representatives and Senate when the abolition of the slave trade was discussed was thin, and the debates themselves were almost never over moral fundamentals, but rather skirted the ethics for intensive examination of the pragmatic details of enforcement. Was slave trading to be a felony or a misdemeanour (with very different penalties prescribed as a result)? What was to be the fate of slaves taken from apprehended ships? Were they to be automatically manumitted? Or treated, in effect, as contraband? Would the measure extend the prohibition to coastal inter-state traffic? On all these questions, exactly as you would expect, representatives from the Lower South were militantly intransigent. Government interference with inter-state trade was taken to be an extension of federal power so gross as to be tantamount to a violation of the constitution, and provoking from John Randolph an explicit threat – in 1806 – of secession. If trading in slaves was to be treated – as northern proponents like Senator Stephen Row Bradley from Vermont, and Representative John Smilie of Pennsylvania wanted – as a felony, the implication was that convicted persons might be subjected to the death penalty. No southerner, said Randolph and others, would ever assent to the execution of one of their number for committing a deed which they would never consider a crime. And since, of course, the vast majority of likely illegal trading ventures would take place at southern ports and in southern waters, the outlook for enforcement was not auspicious. Most ominously of all, for the fate of the Bill, southern representatives set their face against any possibility of liberating slaves taken from captured ships, thus releasing large numbers of black freedmen into their own slave societies. (Remember that from the 1790s onwards states in the Lower South – and some areas of the Upper South – had been doing their utmost to rid themselves by expulsion of troublesome populations of free blacks.) To admit more was, southerners like Peter Early of Georgia insisted, to light the fires of insurrection. It would be, he said, 'an evil greater than slavery itself'. The only recourse beleaguered southerners would have, said Early, was 'self-defence – gentlemen will understand me – [we must] either get rid of them or they of us; there is no alternative . . . Not one of them would be left alive in a year.'

It's important to remember that many of the most forthright and articulate assailants of Jefferson's Act – or rather those who wanted to amend it into harmlessness – were actually either Virginians like John Randolph or Virginians by origin like Peter Early, even though he had moved to and spoke for the Lower South. What the debate – such as it was – at the end of 1806 implied was an early fracture within the leadership of the South itself, and not always just along regional lines. Madison was, as usual on this issue, uncomfortably in the middle –

endorsing the Act, provided it did not cause too much 'inconvenience' to his fellow plantation owners like the President, who sustained his moral schizophrenia to the end. Not least, of course, because Jefferson and Madison – not to mention their faithful correspondent in Massachusetts, former President Adams – well knew that the price, first of Confederation, then of making a Union, then of enacting a constitution, had been deferring to the Lower South on both the trade and the institution of slavery itself. Postponing legislation concerning the slave trade for twenty years had been the condition of making the constitution possible (and there were in 1807 those who refused to accept the law as valid, considering that Jefferson had anticipated by a year the end of that moratorium even though the law was not to come into effect until 1808). This had been the Faustian bargain that had made the United States, and (to mix metaphors) the poisoned chalice that the temporising Virginians – Jefferson and Madison – knew very well would be passed along to their posterity.

Jefferson had a peculiarly corrupted and tortured conscience about all this. His original draft of the Declaration of Independence had included a ferocious paragraph attacking the slave trade – 'cruel war against human nature itself, violating its most sacred rights of life and liberty in the persons of a distant people . . . captivating and carrying them to slavery in another hemisphere, or to incur miserable death in their transportations thither'. That paragraph had been duly stricken from the final draft, 'in complaisance to South Carolina and Georgia', but Jefferson had in any case made this one of the colonists' grievances against Britain by blaming the whole trade on the King – 'the warfare of the Christian King of Great Britain'! Responsibility for the glaring inconsistency between the 'self-evident' truth that 'all men are created equal' and the fact of slavery thus was conveniently displaced onto the person of the offending monarch and his culpable ancestors. Nothing to do with us of course – heavens, no! And now the King and his 'courtiers', as Jefferson liked to call them, were compounding the evil by actually conspiring to foment armed insurrection among the slaves by promising them their liberty if they remained loyal to the Crown. Such diabolical Machiavellianism!

Behind this rich exercise in historical disingenuousness lay the nagging anxiety of the Founding Fathers that to face squarely up to the contradiction between the promises of the Declaration and the reality of the slave economy was to bring the Union down before it ever had a chance of consolidation. This was, of course, merely to post- pone what Jefferson and Madison and Adams and many others predicted would be the inevitable conflict, which indeed came to pass a half-century later. It's a matter of deep poignancy, as Pauline Maier saw in her book on the Declaration, that subsequent pragmatists like Stephen Douglas contorted themselves in knots to make the promise of equality something like a utopian principle — a nice idea — never actually to be implemented, or intended for whites only, while for the young Abraham Lincoln, even in his law-practice days in Springfield, it always meant precisely what it said. Not only did Jefferson, as it were, move on to other matters — the Louisiana Purchase — while hoping for the best, but it was during his presidency that an all-time record number of slaves were imported into the United States (many of them on British ships) precisely in anticipation that perhaps the trade would be subject to eventual prohibition?

In some fundamental sense, then, directly broaching the issue in 1806 and 1807 was to toy dangerously with what was perceived as a fragile union. To add sectional bitterness to the divisions that already beset the United States — between Federalists and Republicans over the extent of central power, and to do it at a time when the country was beset with dangers from abroad and at home — was to do damage to an already vulnerable body politic. No wonder Jefferson soft-pedalled it and conceded many of the South's demands. Slaving after January 1808 would not be a felony and would be punished by fines. There was to be no interference with inter-state commerce in humans, and scant provi- sion was made for any sort of naval enforcement of the prohibition. The navy, such as it was, had its hands full keeping American waters free of privateers, or British and French ships taking prizes, without taking further duties on itself. The poisoned chalice was passed quietly on.

Historically, then, the abolition of the slave trade in the United States pointed in every respect to a future of disunion; of national disinte- gration, a reckoning to be paid in blood. And I suppose that's why there's been so little disposition to celebrate or commemorate it in this anniver- sary year. But there's something else at work here in some larger sense about the selectivity of public memory in this country, the tendency, especially at a time of — what shall we call it? — military perplexity, to use history for consolation. I was reminded of this by watching episodes of Ken Burns's egregiously titled PBS documentary series *The War* (as if only the American experience counted): an immense exercise in elegiac self-congratulation. Whatever our troubles, there was at least one war which was fought for indisputably noble motives and which by and large turned out well. The consolatory and redemptive pay-off – history as lullaby – is unmistakable. But this was not what the first authentically critical historian of our tradition – Thucydides – had in mind for us at all. He was, after all, a general who had taken part in the conflict he chronicled and that made him not an elegist, but a gadfly for the complacent. I'm always struck by the passages from the *Peloponnesian Wars* for use in American core curricula – almost always Pericles's funeral oration, hymning the liberty for which Athenian men sacrificed themselves – a speech text which may be the only compromised passage in that history since Thucydides, a rebarbative critic of Herodotus's playing fast and loose with the sources, conceded it was based on the report of someone who might have heard the Dear Leader. The real *telos* of the work, as you know, is quite different, a damning indictment of the Athenian imperial hubris that leads them to Syracuse and catastrophe. The march to self-destruction is the point of the book and it immediately establishes as a birth-text, Western history as an exercise in merciless self-criticism; its temper cautionary, its intelligence sceptical, its pay-off – as often as not – tragic. History is the memory of comeuppance for the next generation; its integrity bound up with its honesty and its abhorrence of patriotic self-ingratiation. Thucydides's history – our history – is no one's cheer-leader.

Which brings me, inevitably, to my own countrymen across the ocean and the place of the moment of abolition in British cultural memory. Now it's true that the British are hardly exempt from the kind of patriotic self-congratulation – history as moral reassurance – that I've implied is an issue in its American popularity. It's equally true, though, that disasters like Dunkirk are as likely to be meat and drink for writers and readers as Trafalgar and D-Day. From Dr Johnson's famous epithet about patriotism being the last refuge of a scoundrel to the ingrained scepticism against hero-worship in British history, it's also true that the cautionary temper has on the whole served British commemoration reasonably well. So although there was certainly an element of back-patting going on in the commemorations of abolition – especially since it led, after a generation, directly to the parliamentary abolition of slavery itself in 1833 (rather than the opposite in the American case), with figures like Thomas Clarkson agitating for and presiding over both – it's also true that this year has been an occasion for looking into the glass of time darkly, in particular for a re-engagement in the debate over the relationship of slavery to economic power.

What's been impressive, I think, though, is the degree to which the moment hasn't just been a reheating of Eric Williams's *Capitalism and Slavery*, the ur-text which a half-century ago attacked abolitionism as a movement of convenience, made possible only when the Atlantic sugar economy was in decline, made irrelevant by the new laissez-faire manufacturing economy. No scholars (to my knowledge) would seriously try and argue that any longer, nor the indisputability of the timing of abolition occurring at the zenith of the slave and sugar economy, rather than during its decline.

It's precisely because the instrumentalist argument from social expediency (once, but no longer, put by David Brion Davis) can't possibly be empirically sustained that the bicentennial has prompted historians – and the common culture more generally – to engage again with abolition as a moral act; one in which it's just conceivable that the protagonists meant what they said, especially when figures like Granville Sharp, the archdeacon's son, and Thomas Clarkson, intended for the ministry (and who took up abolitionism as a kind of Pauline conversion when he learned about the *Zong* from a sermon preached by Dr Peter Peckard in the Cambridge University Church of St Mary's), invoked Christian religion.

The essential reason why, I believe, the commemoration of abolition became so much an event in the national culture in this year of 2007 is because the debate performed very much the same function 200 years ago. Linda Colley, in *Britons*, has written about the role that the agitation against the slave trade played in creating a kind of national politics, and one which included as political actors for the first time hitherto-excluded constituencies like women. That's absolutely right, but I want to push the argument further and, in contrast to the American sense that anti-slave-trade campaigning was a nation-breaker, suggest that in Britain it was a nation-maker; perhaps, along with the romanticism of the past that took place during the wars against the French, *the* single most powerful force in the making, or rather the remaking – the re-formation – of Britain.

And this was, paradoxically, the fruit of defeat. American victory — won at the price of not pushing the contradiction between the Declaration of Independence and the social reality to the point of threatening the union — made a powerful incentive to let that particular sleeping dog lie, for at least twenty years. In Britain, defeat led to bitter soul-searching, in the first instance on the part of critics of the American war like Granville Sharp, Edmund Burke and Charles James Fox. But the sense in which Britain was the new Nineveh or indeed Sodom, punished for its manifold sins — its corruption, its profanity, but above all its inhumanity to fellow men, reduced to chattels and beasts of burden — was a common refrain in the early rhetoric of the abolitionists. Whereas the fate of the United States depended on *not* grasping this particular nettle, the fate of Britain, the castigators of slavery insisted, was conditional on its doing just that.

And in striking contrast to Congress, skirting around the big moral principles of national self-definition in its debates, those in Parliament were almost nothing but. The orations made in the late summer of 1806 — and perhaps precisely because it was under attack from reformers demonising it as nothing more than the unclean temple of 'Old Corruption' — transformed the Houses of Commons and Lords into a rhetorical theatre for the redefinition of the legislature, and by extension the British constitution — King in Parliament, the Law and the Church working together to extirpate the abomination. Fox — who was junior to Lord Grenville in the government, but its senior spokesman in the House of Commons — began his speech with encomia, not just to Wilberforce, but to his most famous political adversaries, William Pitt and Edmund Burke, both of whom were conveniently dead. (Fox was shortly to follow in September of that year, leaving Grenville to steer the legislation through its final readings the following March.) Waxing magnanimous, Fox quoted Burke: 'to deal and traffick not in the labour of men but in men themselves, was to devour the root, instead of enjoying the fruit, of human diligence'. The 1791 speech of Pitt (his bitterest foe in precisely that year of revolution) was: 'the . . . most powerful and convincing eloquence that ever adorned these walls, a speech not of vague and shewy ornament but of solid and irresistible argument founded on a detail of indisputable facts and unquestionable calculations . . .' Fox summoned the ghosts of the past masters of the House in a demonstration of cross-party unity on this one great matter. A succession of extraordinary speeches followed, including two of them – by the one-armed hero of the American war, Banastre Tarleton, and General Isaac Gascoine, both of Liverpool – against the motion. But it was left to the brilliant Solicitor General Samuel Romilly to be the most uncompromising of all about what was at stake, which was nothing less than the integrity of Parliament and the honour of the nation. Romilly upbraided the two Houses for delaying as long as they had, since Wilberforce's original motion was introduced in 1791, exhorting them to come to a more ethically proper conclusion. Like other orators in the House, he dismissed the argument that slavery and the traffic had existed in all cultures and societies since antiquity as being no reason at all why Britain should not step forth (he implied especially in the light of American hypocrisies) to embrace the mantle of moral dignity and end it. (In the Lords, Beilby Porteus, the Bishop of London, one of the staunchest of the abolitionists, made the point that to argue from custom, to argue from *is* to *ought*, might as well justify the Chinese practice of mass exposure of infants to die.) Neither the fate of the Atlantic economy (or of Bristol and Liverpool), Romilly said, nor the possibility that abolition might simply be a gift to the French or the Spanish empires at a time when we were at war with them, could possibly justify perpetuating a *malum in se*, this unconscionable evil. The year 1796 had been set by the House as 'the utmost limit allowed for the existence of that most abominable and disgraceful traffick and yet it still subsists'. (It was the fault of the Lords, he said, that the Act had not gone through earlier.) 'I can very well understand that nations as well as individuals may be guilty of the most immoral acts from their not having the courage to inquire into their nature and consequences.' But in 1789 Parliament *had* so inquired and it was:

> established by a great body of evidence that the African slave trade is carried on by rapine, robbery and murder and by fomenting wars . . . thus are these unhappy beings in order to supply this traffick in human blood torn from their families . . . Now sir after all this has been proved, after it has been ascertained by indisputable evidence that this trade cannot be carried on without the most iniquitous practices, that murder, rapine and robbery are the foundations of it . . . that wars are fomented to support this traffick; that most disgusting cruelties attend it in the passage of this unhappy part of our species from their native home to the place of their

slavery, that they are there subjected to a cruel and perpetual bondage, I
do say that this trade ought not to be suffered to continue for an hour; it
is a stain upon our national reputation and ought to be wiped away.

When it was claimed that merchants would have to be compensated, Romilly replied, 'ought the debts of the people of England to
be paid with the blood of the people of Africa? . . . the people of
England are not to consent that there should be carried on in their
name a system of blood, rapine, robbery and murder . . . because we
must make some compensation to some individuals'.

This was also the nub of Wilberforce's argument – that the issue
spoke to 'the inestimable advantages of a free constitution'. When
others said the timing was poor because of Britain's continuing
involvement in the wars with Napoleon and his allies, Wilberforce
(and this was before Trafalgar, and while Napoleon had established
an invasion camp on the Channel) retorted to the contrary:

> if ever there was a period in which this country, circumstanced as we
> are, had an opportunity of setting a glorious example to all the other
> nations of the earth and of giving a proof of the inestimable advan-
> tages of a free constitution, of an enlightened policy and of all the
> blessings Providence has bestowed upon us, the present is that moment
> and we ought to hail it with joy as giving us an opportunity of shew-
> ing the world that we are not . . . a sordid race looking exclusively to
> our own interest and pursuing it through the oppression of others . . .
> but that we are a nation governed by the rules of justice, which are
> dictated by true wisdom . . . no society any more than any individual
> can be long upheld in prosperity upon any other principle.

The subtext of this flamboyance, and the targets of its righteousness,
were of course the false prophets of liberty – American and French –
who paraded their ostensible devotion to freedom before the world while
countenancing servitude and despotism. (Napoleon encouraged the slave
trade and would formally reintroduce it two years later.)

The motion passed by an overwhelming majority in both Houses, and
the final bill by 289 to 16 – in contrast to the exact 60–60 division in
Congress over the ban on inter-state commerce, a tie broken against the
motion by Speaker Macon from North Carolina. But the alteration of the

position in the British Parliament was of a piece with the evangelical reform movement that was attempting to create a new empire, a Christian empire in fact, established, as Romilly said, on virtue rather than interest, or rather through strenuous attempts to redefine the national and imperial interest so that it squared with evangelical notions of virtue and, perhaps even more important – and certainly as popular – newly romantic notions of English (rather than British) history.

This had always been the driving force of the principal campaigners. Granville Sharp had taken up the cause of abducted blacks in the streets of London – in the 1760s – certainly because he believed the plight of slaves was a violation of Christian ethics (there was a great deal of Talmudic hair-splitting in the debates about whether the Israelites had or had not countenanced bondage), but also because he believed passionately in something at least as sacred, that is the unbroken integrity of the English Common Law by which he held (from an Elizabethan case) 'the air of England was too pure for a slave to breathe' – or that once upon these shores all men and women had the same rights to the King's justice. Hence Sharp's unremitting tournament with Lord Chief Justice Mansfield over the status of escaped slaves that had been recaptured by former masters, with the intention of forcible deportation and sale in the West Indies. Sharp's campaigns in the 1770s – fortified at least by his correspondence with American abolitionists like Anthony Benezet and Benjamin Rush – were a reformer's tour of the British constitution. After the law came the Church, whose indifference to the 'accursed thing' (as he called the slave trade) appalled him. Bishops and archbishops were deluged by memoranda and booklets until they capitulated and were converted. After the prelates of the Church, Sharp wanted to recover what he imagined in his Gothic romance to be the pristine forms of democracy: the 'frankpledge' elections of householders to local offices of 'tithingmen' and 'hundreddors', and so on up the chain of governance to a reformed and morally cleansed national representation.

It wasn't just Sharp, of course, but the saints of the Clapham Sect – Zachary Macaulay, Henry Thornton, Hannah More and Wilberforce himself – who saw the campaign against the slave trade as the first act in a great national purification. After the Act went through on 25 March 1807, it was said that Wilberforce turned to Thornton and said, 'Well, Henry, what shall we abolish now?' – and the answer was the lottery! But attacks were launched not just on electoral corruption, but on all manner of social evils, from prostitution to climbing boys and demon gin. Prompted by Malachy Postlethwayte, erstwhile propagandist for the Royal African Company, turned early critic of the trade, then by Adam Smith and finally by the Quaker merchants and bankers – Samuel Hoare and Joseph Woods – an intensive debate was joined as to what was, and what was not, a moral form of commercial activity. In their campaigns to persuade supporters to refrain from using 'slave-made' products, they made much of the addictive and 'enslaving' quality of tobacco and rum that corrupted the freedom of the consumer as much as it was purchased by the blood of those who had laboured to produce it.

And if all this seems somehow marginal now to the main act – the transformation of Britain into an industrial and military empire – that judgement seems, to me at any rate, the anachronistic projection back from a perspective of social science. What the campaign to remake British national identity turned on was as much bound up with moral judgements as the Protestant Reformation and the seventeenth-century Puritan moment. The evangelical movement was the descendant of both of those earlier reformations, and it was of course the nursery of Victorian self-belief that they had indeed managed to reconcile the demands of power, money and Christian morals. That one might think them deluded in this conviction doesn't in any way diminish the force of its original coherence. The fact, too, that after the Irish union of 1801, Great Britain was an indivisible constitution made the reformers believe that what was enacted in Westminster would hold good for the whole country. The centralisation of the British state worked to optimise reform, just as the confederated nature of the American constitution worked against it.

But there was, of course, one respect in which the British reformers of 1807 were no more certain than their American counterparts: whether the abolition of the *trade* was the harbinger of emancipation, or whether it pre-empted serious consideration of it. In the United States, the horror at freeing blacks from captured slavers was in part a matter of precaution against insurrections, but also because politicians from the Lower South argued it would lead to unrealisable expectations of general emancipation throughout. Both Jefferson and Charles James Fox were at pains to deny any such thing was anticipated, much less taken for granted. Fox went out of his way to treat any such imputation as an anti-abolitionist canard. Even William Wilberforce, notoriously, was at best an extreme gradualist, who believed that prior property rights could not be interfered with, and that there had to be a period of education and apprenticeship before slaves could possibly be trusted with their liberty. Only Granville Sharp – to his dying day – and the Clarkson brothers were immediate emancipationists, and it was the re-publication of Thomas's great history of the abolition of the trade which kick-started, in the 1820s, the campaign for emancipation itself that culminated in the Act of 1833–4.

That campaign, historians are beginning to emphasise, was a trans-atlantic one in many respects. It was in London that the great international Abolitionist Congress was held in 1840, patronised by the Prince Consort and for which Turner painted his notorious and doomed *Slave Ship*. It was in Britain that Harriet Beecher Stowe's *Uncle Tom's Cabin* found its most rapturous and extensive readership. It was in Newcastle upon Tyne that Frederick Douglass found his personal eman-cipators, so that it was logical that the lecture tour, which established him as the great charismatic orator of abolitionism, took place in 1845 in Ireland and Britain. Speaking to rapt assembly rooms in the places where the Clarksons had first agitated for the abolition of the trade in blood – in Manchester and Leeds, Birmingham and London, even in Liverpool – Douglass imagined a British Empire which lived up to its promises and which, since 1838, and especially beneath the ensign of the Royal Navy combing the African coast for slavers, was the true bene-factor of enslaved Americans. He exaggerated enormously the colour-blind character of the British, so overwhelmed was he by being taken into Parliament, to stately homes and cathedrals. (Had he gone visiting, say, Thomas Carlyle, he might have come away with an entirely different and less rosy view.) But in one respect he was right: in the stren-uousness of their determination to make their own moral revolution in Britain, the saints had refused to sweep under the carpet the most repug-nant and morally catastrophic issue of the day. A pity, then, that he couldn't have been in Westminster Abbey to hear the Queen yelled at by her Anglo-African subject, for that would have confirmed for Douglass that, for all their selective sanctimoniousness, the British are, sometimes, capable of taking the truth on the chin.

A League
of Its Own

Red October

Guardian, 29 October 2004

It was the opening of *Catch-22*: love at first sight. Yossarian? Me. The
Chaplain: a grungy hole of a baseball ground called Fenway Park. A
chilly Boston night in April 1982, the Red Sox playing the Oakland
A's, managed by the somewhat recovering drunk, ex-Yankee Billy
Martin. What was I doing there? No idea.

Cricket and football (our football) were my games and would stay
that way, never mind that I was living in Boston. Every month my dad
had taken me to Lords to see Middlesex – the Comptons, Freddie
Titmus, Alan Moss – and I'd happily inhaled the mix of beer tankards
and fresh-cut grass while Arthur Schama went blissfully to sleep as
the county lost yet again to Sussex (Ted Dexter). In winters it was
White Hart Lane – starting early – when Alf Ramsey played for them
in his long baggy black shorts, and then into the glory glory years of
Nicholson, Blanchflower, Mackay and the dashingly undependable
Greaves. So why would I want to waste my time watching glorified
rounders in what looked like a terrible dump, its drab paint a bilious
grey-green and peeling, just like the girders on the elevated freeway?

Because my friend John Clive had nagged and nagged and I had
given in. He was an unlikely Sox fan himself: my colleague in the
Harvard history department; biographer of Macaulay; originally Hans
Kleyff from Jewish Berlin: big, round, soft and exuberant with dark-
brown eyes, and a hoarse chuckle. He loved great historical writing,
Apple Brown Betty (a pudding, not a call girl) and the Red Sox. So
(grudgingly bemused) I went along for the ride, all innocent of the
imminent and irreversible Change in Life, the *coup de foudre*; the date
with fate that was about to hit.

My nose got it before the rest of me did. Walking among the mass
of the Sox Nation converging on the ballpark, up Yawkey Way, the
nose surrendered to the smell of Italian sausage and frying onion

peddled from the street stalls. You eat them sandwiched in hot doughy rolls, with screaming yellow mustard dripping out the end, and we did. Holy shit, there was something in those sausages; something that obviously made people happy, for happy this crowd surely was: kids and grandpas; lots of loud Boston women with insecure dye-jobs and square shoulders encased in warm-up jackets that had seen many years of heartache; dads with six-year-olds riding on their shoulders. A crowd pouring through the gates from tough Irish Southie, patrician Marblehead or, like us, from bosky Lexington.

Inside, Fenway was unpromising: a mass scurrying up and down dark and dirty ramps; programmes hawked, the notorious horse-trough toilets already brimming horribly from hours of Yawkey Way beer. But then, the climb up the steps into ballpark heaven: a blaze of golden light; grass as damply brilliant and as soft as a meadow in County Donegal; men in blue-and-red jackets gently warming up; a thuck-thuck as the baseball hit the mitt; an ancient organ that sighed and groaned and wheezed and sang while welcoming us to the inner sanctum of the cathedral; an even more ancient announcer, the late, great Sherm Feller, who from the depths of his avuncular baritone declared, 'Ladies and gentlemen, boys and girls, welcome to Fenway Park', and from the ladies and gentlemen and boys and girls a soft roar of mass pleasure that rippled round the stands, and my cricket-loving, football-doting self was a hopeless, helpless goner; Middlesex and Spurs were yesterday's passions. This, I thought, as I improbably caught the bag of peanuts chucked at me from fifteen feet by the vendor, was where I had to be. This was home.

The Red Sox won that evening: veterans (as I rapidly learned) charging round the bases, such as 'Yaz' Yastrzemski, a high-octane hulk; taciturn Jim Rice, the slugger leaping at the edge of the outfield to hoist in what seemed sure home runs; Dwight 'Dewey' Evans, natty in his trim moustaches, an elegant stance at the plate, cracking line drives through the emerald grass. So we went home happy, but being the Red Sox Nation, morning-after moodiness replaced the brief euphoria. *Catch-22* – we won, but actually we should have lost – began in earnest. There were anxieties about the veterans. How long could this bunch hack it? Was it Yaz's last hurrah? And indeed I had noticed the air of slightly decrepit gentility – like much of Boston – hanging over the team as they chawed their chewing tobacco.

I had no idea, of course, what I'd got myself into. I was still clue-less about recognising pitches, especially from the bleachers or the box seats way out behind third base; couldn't tell a cut fastball from a slider if they hit me in the face. (It takes time, but believe me, it repays study. Great pitchers can turn the ball in mid-air in ways that spin bowlers have scarcely dreamed of.) Much more ominously, I had no idea of the dreaded history: the feckless sale of Babe Ruth to the Yankees by the owner Harry Frazee, reputedly to finance the Broadway musical *No, No, Nanette*; the ensuing 'Curse of the Bambino'; the failure to win a World Series since the Kaiser hung up his helmet.

I vaguely knew of the Yankees–Sox rivalry, but – since the Bronx Bombers were themselves regularly bombing in the 1980s – who cared? I had no idea whatsoever of the saga of torment; the moments of deluded euphoria (Carleton Fisk hitting the walk-off homer in Game 6 of the 1976 series against Cincinnati) before the crushing putdown (the loss of the same series in Game 7); an epic of sustained pain that by compari-son made the pecking of Prometheus look like a day at the beach.

I would learn in the worst possible way: the notorious 1986 World Series against the New York Mets. In the American League Champi-onship series (semi-finals to you lot) the Sox had come from a strike away from being eliminated by the California Angels, when a pitcher called Donnie Moore served a fat one over the plate to Dave 'Hendu' Henderson, who saw it coming with his name on it, grinned one of his gap-toothed grins and sent it away. Stuck with the stigma of being the 'goat', poor Moore went into a depressive slide and committed suicide. We went into the World Series against the Mets high on confi-dence – we had the brilliant pitching duo of Roger Clemens and Bruce Hurst and some of those unbowed veteran hitters from the early '80s. One strike away from Winning It All in Game 6, a ball notoriously trickled through the open gate of Bill Buckner's bandy legs and the Mets came back from the grave. In Game 7 it was our hearts into which the stake was driven.

Years – decades – of roller-coaster elation and despair followed. In the meantime I had done something unforgivable, saddled my own two kids with this infatuated allegiance; taken them to Fenway, shoved peanuts and sausages into their faces, made them do the 'wave'; embar-rassed them with my roaring abuse of visiting Yanks; taught them (yes, I could do that now) the difference between the cut fastball and the slider; in short, pretty much ruined their blameless lives.

This came home to me in the worst possible way, almost exactly a year ago when I took my son, eighteen, and grown prematurely wise in Soxian pessimism, to Yankee stadium to see the seventh and deciding game of the American League Championship. Around the seventh inning, well up on the Yanks, our ace Pedro Martinez pitching, we dared a cautious smile of anticipation. The Yankee fans were leaving in depressed droves; those that weren't were scowling at us or hiding their faces in their hands. Then Martinez, kept in for an inning too long, suddenly folded, surrendering hits. Amidst pandemonium the game tied, and then a homer by the aptly named Aaron Boone won it for the Evil Empire. My son's face was drained of colour, but he was the grown-up attempting to console his unhinged father. So now you know why I was up at 4 a.m. on Thursday morning watching every last pitch of the game with St Louis online; now you can measure the combination of ecstatic disbelief and narcotic jubilation coursing through my veins as our ace closer, Keith Foulke, made the last out.

A bit OTT? Absolutely not, my world-weary cricketing friends. Anything is possible in 2004: the trains will run on time; balmy breezes will drift over Wales in December; the lion will lie down with the lamb; and, oh yes, a Red Sox fan will, come January, be sworn into office as the forty-fourth President of the United States.

Acknowledgements

No writer can survive much less prosper without the kindly and infinitely patient help of good editors. I have been exceptionally lucky to have had a whole phalanx of these cunning saints who have often been lumbered with pieces that are excessive (in almost every way) and cry out for sharp but sympathetic intervention. They have all managed somehow to trim and nick and cut without the object of their attention feeling much pain. My gratitude to them is one of the few things that is truly beyond words. In particular I want to thank, at the *New Yorker*, Ann Goldstein, David Remnick and Dorothy Wickenden; at the *Guardian*, Lisa Allardice, Ian Katz and Merope Mills; at British *Vogue*, Charlotte Sinclair; at *Harper's Bazaar*, Lucy Yeomans; at the *Financial Times*, Lionel Barber, Jan Dalley, Caroline Daniel and James Mackintosh; at *The New Republic*, Leon Wieseltier; at *The New York Review of Books*, Robert Silvers; and at the *London Review of Books*, Mary-Kay Wilmers.

I should also like to thank my publishers – Will Sulkin at Random House and Dan Halpern at Ecco Books for their generous enthusiasm in seeing scribbles turned to print. Kay Peddle at Random House has been the soul of vigilant kindness.

But the book would never have seen the light of day without the care, patience and commitment of Jennifer Sonntag to whom I owe more than I can say for keeping the over-laden ship that is SS Schama more or less afloat.

contact the relevant primary publishers in each instance. The publishers would be pleased to correct any omissions or errors in any future editions.

Travelling

'Sail Away: Six Days to New York on the Queen Mary 2', *New Yorker,* 31 May 2004

'The Unloved American: Two Centuries of Alienating Europe', *New Yorker,* 10 March 2003

'Amsterdam', an uncut version of the essay in John Julius Norwich, (ed.), *The Great Cities in History,* 2009

'Washington DC', an uncut version of the essay in John Julius Norwich, (ed.), *The Great Cities in History,* 2009

'Brazil', *Financial Times* Diary, 22 November 2008

'Comedy Meets Catastrophe', *Financial Times,* 26 September 2009

Testing Democracy

'9/11', *Guardian,* 14 September 2001

'The Dead and The Guilty: 9/11 A Year On', *Guardian,* 11 September 2002

'The Civil War in the USA', *Guardian,* 5 November 2004

'Katrina and George Bush', *Guardian,* 12 September 2005

'In its severity and fury, this was Obama at his most powerful and moving', *Guardian,* 30 August 2008

'Bye-Bye Dubya', *Guardian* 3 November 2008

'The British Election', *Guardian,* 5 May 2005

'Virtual Annihilation', originally published in Ron Rosenbaum (ed.), *Those Who Forget the Past: A Question of Anti-Semitism,* 2004

Talking And Listening

'TBM and John', originally in *After the Victorians: Private Conscience and Public Duty in Modern Britain,* Peter Mandler and Susan Pedersen (eds.), 1994

'Isaiah Berlin', *The New Republic* 31 January 2005

'J. H. Plumb', introduction to the new edition of *The Death of the Past,* Niall Ferguson (ed.), 2003, reproduced with permission of Palgrave Macmillan

'Rescuing Churchill', *The New York Review of Books,* 28 February 2002

'The Lost Art of Great Speechmaking', *Guardian,* 20 April 2007

'The Fate of Eloquence in the Age of the Osbournes', Phi Beta Kappa
Oration, Harvard University, 3 June 2002
'Barack Obama', *The Independent*, *23* January 2009

Performing

Richard II, note from the Almeida Theatre Production of *Richard II*,
Almedia at Gainsbrough studios, 2002
Henry IV, note for Royal Shakespeare Company production, 2008
'Martin Scorsese: Good Fella', Financial Times, 31 October 2009
'Charlotte Rampling: "A Documentary of Me"', *Harper's Bazaar*,
January 2010
'Clio at the Multiplex', the *New Yorker*, 19 January 1998
'True Confessions of a History Boy', National Theatre programme essay
for Alan Bennett's *The History Boys*, May 2004

Picturing

'The Matter of the Unripe Nectarine: High ground/low ground and
Ruskin's Prejudices', Christ Church Symposium, on the centenary of
Ruskin's death, Oxford, 1 April 2000
'Dutch Courage', *Guardian*, 23 June 2007
'Rubens', *Guardian*, 22 October 2005
'The Patriot: Turner And The Drama Of History', the *New Yorker*, 24
September 2007
'Carnival and Cacophony', *Financial Times*, 4 July 2009
'Rembrandt's Ghost: Picasso Looks Back', the *New Yorker*, 26 March 2007
Anselm Kiefer (1), *Guardian*, 20 January 2007
'In Mesopotamia: Anselm Kiefer (2)', Catalogue essay for the Anselm
Kiefer exhibition *Karfunkelfee and the Fertile Crescent*, White Cube,
Hoxton Square and Mason's Yard, October-November 2009
'John Virtue: The Epic Of Paint', National Gallery catalogue essay, 2007
'Avedon: Power', *Guardian*, 27 September 2008

Cooking And Eating

'Cool as Ice', *Vogue* © The Condé Nast Publications Ltd, August 2007
'Sauce of Controversy', *Guardian*, 26 November 2008
'The Great G2 Recipe Swap: Cheese Soufflé', *Guardian*, 2 March 2009
'Simmer of Love', *Vogue* © The Condé Nast Publications Ltd, winter
2008

'My Mother's Kitchen', *Observer Food Magazine*, 11 October 2009

'Mouthing Off', Oxford Food Symposium, September 2009

Remembering

'Omaha Beach', *Financial Times* Diary, 13 June 2009

'Gothic Language: Carlyle, Ruskin and the Morality of Exuberance', London Library Lecture, 12 July 2008

'*The History Of Britain*: A Response', *American Historical Review*, June 2009

'The Monte Lupo Story', *London Review of Books*, 18 September – 1 October 1980

'No Walnuts, No Enlightenment', *London Review of Books*, 20 December 1979

'Abolishing the Slave Trade in Britain and America – Sound and Fury or Deafening Silence?', Stanford University Presidential Lecture, 2007

In A League of Its Own

'Red October', *Guardian*, 29 October 2004

www.vintage-books.co.uk